The Predicament of Culture

THE PREDICAMENT

Twentieth-Century Ethnography,
Literature, and Art

James Clifford

OF CULTURE ⚲

HARVARD UNIVERSITY PRESS
Cambridge, Massachusetts, and London, England
1988

Library of Congress Cataloging in Publication Data

Clifford, James, 1945–
    The predicament of culture twentieth-century ethnography,
literature, and art / James Clifford.
        p. cm.
        Bibliography: p.
        Includes index.
        ISBN 0–674–69842–8 (alk. paper) ISBN 0–674–69843–6 (pbk. : alk. paper)
        1. Ethnology—History—20th century. 2. Ethnology—Philosophy.
I. Title.
GN308.C55 1988   87–24173
306'.09—dc19   CIP

For my mother
Virginia Iglehart Clifford

ACKNOWLEDGMENTS

The chapters gathered in this book were written between 1979 and 1986. During these years I have enjoyed the encouragement of friends and colleagues in many fields, most of whom I have publicly thanked in earlier versions of some of these chapters. To mention their names again here would result in a long, ultimately impersonal list. I trust that those who have helped me know of my continuing gratitude.

This book emerges from a period of unusual theoretical and political questioning in several disciplines and writing traditions. The provocation, criticism, and guidance I have received from many others working along similar lines are only imperfectly acknowledged in the book's citations.

For help in thinking through the chapters composed specifically for this volume I would like to thank James Boon, Stephen Foster, George Marcus, Mary Pratt, Paul Rabinow, Jed Rasula, Renato Rosaldo, William Sturtevant, and Richard Wasserstrom.

I am grateful for fellowship support during the past seven years from the American Council of Learned Societies, the American Philosophical Association, and the National Endowment for the Humanities Summer Stipend program.

This book was written during my academic affiliation with the History of Consciousness Program at the University of California, Santa Cruz. It reflects something of the ethos and energy of that extraordinary group of scholars and graduate students. I would like to single out for special thanks my colleagues Donna Haraway, Hayden White, and Norman O. Brown.

Lindsay Waters of Harvard University Press offered acute editorial suggestions. Special thanks to Jacob, who shared the word processor, and to my wife, Judith Aissen, for love and for not being infinitely patient.

Santa Cruz, California   J.C.

CONTENTS

ILLUSTRATIONS

The Predicament of Culture

We were once the masters of the earth, but since the gringos arrived we have become veritable pariahs . . . We hope that the day will come when they realize that we are their roots and that we must grow together like a giant tree with its branches and flowers.
                    —FRANCISCO SERVIN, PAI-TAVYTERA, AT
                    THE CONGRESS OF INDIANS, PARAGUAY, 1974

Introduction: The Pure Products Go Crazy

SOMETIME AROUND 1920 in a New Jersey suburb of New York City, a young doctor wrote a poem about a girl he called Elsie. He saw her working in his kitchen or laundry room, helping his wife with the house cleaning or the kids. Something about her brought him up short. She seemed to sum up where everything was going—his family, his fledgling practice, his art, the modern world that surrounded and caught them all in its careening movement.

The poem William Carlos Williams wrote was a rush of associations, beginning with a famous assertion:

The pure products of America
go crazy—

and continuing almost without stopping for breath . . .

mountain folk from Kentucky

or the ribbed north end of
Jersey
with its isolate lakes and

1

valleys, its deaf-mutes, thieves
old names
and promiscuity between

devil-may-care men who have taken
to railroading
out of sheer lust for adventure—

and young slatterns, bathed
in filth
from Monday to Saturday

to be tricked out that night
with gauds
from imaginations which have no

peasant traditions to give them
character
but flutter and flaunt

sheer rags—succumbing without
emotion
save numbed terror

under some hedge of choke-cherry
or viburnum—
which they cannot express—

Unless it be that marriage
perhaps
with a dash of Indian blood

will throw up a girl so desolate
so hemmed round
with disease or murder

that she'll be rescued by an
agent—
reared by the state and

sent out at fifteen to work in
some hard pressed
house in the suburbs—

some doctor's family, some Elsie—
voluptuous water
expressing with broken

brain the truth about us—
her great
ungainly hips and flopping breasts

addressed to cheap
jewelry
and rich young men with fine eyes

when suddenly the angry description veers:

as if the earth under our feet
were
an excrement of some sky

and we degraded prisoners
destined
to hunger until we eat filth

while the imagination strains
after deer
going by fields of goldenrod in

the stifling heat of September
Somehow
it seems to destroy us

It is only in isolate flecks that
something
is given off

No one
to witness
and adjust, no one to drive the car

These lines emerged en route in Williams' dada treatise on the imagination, *Spring & All* (1923). I hope they can serve as a pretext for this
book, a way of starting in with a predicament. Call the predicament ethnographic modernity: ethnographic because Williams finds himself off
center among scattered traditions; modernity since the condition of root-
lessness and mobility he confronts is an increasingly common fate. "El-

sie" stands simultaneously for a local cultural breakdown and a collective future. To Williams her story is inescapably his, everyone's. Looking at the "great/ungainly hips and flopping breasts" he feels things falling apart, everywhere. All the beautiful, primitive places are ruined. A kind of cultural incest, a sense of runaway history pervades, drives the rush of associations.

This feeling of lost authenticity, of "modernity" ruining some essence or source, is not a new one. In *The Country and the City* (1973) Raymond Williams finds it to be a repetitive, pastoral "structure of feeling." Again and again over the millennia change is configured as disorder, pure products go crazy. But the image of Elsie suggests a new turn. By the 1920s a truly global space of cultural connections and dissolutions has become imaginable: local authenticities meet and merge in transient urban and suburban settings—settings that will include the immigrant neighborhoods of New Jersey, multicultural sprawls like Buenos Aires, the townships of Johannesburg. While William Carlos Williams invokes the pure products of America, the "we" careening in his driverless car is clearly something more. The ethnographic modernist searches for the universal in the local, the whole in the part. Williams' famous choice of an American (rather than English) speech, his regionally based poetic and medical practice must not cut him off from the most general human processes. His cosmopolitanism requires a perpetual veering between local attachments and general possibilities.

Elsie disrupts the project, for her very existence raises *historical* uncertainties undermining the modernist doctor-poet's secure position.[1] His response to the disorder she represents is complex and ambivalent. If authentic traditions, the pure products, are everywhere yielding to promiscuity and aimlessness, the option of nostalgia holds no charm. There is no going back, no essence to redeem. Here, and throughout his writing, Williams avoids pastoral, folkloristic appeals of the sort common among other liberals in the twenties—exhorting, preserving, collecting a true rural culture in endangered places like Appalachia. Such authenticities would be at best artificial aesthetic purifications (Whisnant 1983). Nor does Williams settle for two other common ways of confronting the rush

---

1. "Elsie" also displaces a literary tradition. In Western writing servants have always performed the chore of representing "the people"—lower classes and different races. Domesticated outsiders of the bourgeois imagination, they regularly provide fictional epiphanies, recognition scenes, happy endings, utopic and distopic transcendences. A brilliant survey is provided by Bruce Robbins 1986.

of history. He does not evoke Elsie and the idiocy of rural life to celebrate a progressive, technological future. He shares her fate, for there really is "no one to drive the car"—a frightening condition. Nor does Williams resign himself sadly to the loss of local traditions in an entropic modernity—a vision common among prophets of cultural homogenization, lamenters of the ruined tropics. Instead, he claims that "something" is still being "given off"—if only in "isolate flecks."

It is worth dwelling on the discrepancy between this emergent, dispersed "something" and the car in which "we" all ride. Is it possible to resist the poem's momentum, its rushed inevitability? To do so is not so much to offer an adequate reading (of a poetic sequence abstracted from *Spring & All*) as it is to reflect on several readings, on several historical "Elsies." Let this problematic figure with her "dash of Indian blood," her ungainly female form, her inarticulateness stand for groups marginalized or silenced in the bourgeois West: "natives," women, the poor. There is violence, curiosity, pity, and desire in the poet's gaze. Elsie provokes very mixed emotions. Once again a female, possibly colored body serves as a site of attraction, repulsion, symbolic appropriation. Elsie lives only for the eyes of privileged men. An inarticulate muddle of lost origins, she is going nowhere. Williams evokes this with his angry, bleak sympathy— and then turns it all into modern history. Two-thirds of the way through the poem, Elsie's personal story shifts toward the general; her own path through the suburban kitchen vanishes. She, Williams, all of us are caught in modernity's inescapable momentum.

Something similar occurs whenever marginal peoples come into a historical or ethnographic space that has been defined by the Western imagination. "Entering the modern world," their distinct histories quickly vanish. Swept up in a destiny dominated by the capitalist West and by various technologically advanced socialisms, these suddenly "backward" peoples no longer invent local futures. What is different about them remains tied to traditional pasts, inherited structures that either resist or yield to the new but cannot produce it.

This book proposes a different historical vision. It does not see the world as populated by endangered authenticities—pure products always going crazy. Rather, it makes space for specific paths through modernity, a recognition anticipated by Williams' discrepant question: what is "given off" by individual histories like Elsie's? Are the "isolate flecks" dying sparks? New beginnings? Or . . . ? "Compose. (No ideas/but in things) Invent!" This was Williams' slogan (1967:7). In *Spring & All* the

human future is something to be creatively imagined, not simply en-
dured: "new form dealt with as reality itself . . . To enter a new world,
and have there freedom of movement and newness" (1923:70, 71). But
geopolitical questions must now be asked of every inventive poetics of
reality, including that urged by this book: Whose reality? Whose new
world? Where exactly does anyone stand to write "as if the earth under
our feet/were an excrement of some sky/and *we* . . . destined . . ."?

People and things are increasingly out of place. A doctor-poet-
fieldworker, Williams watches and listens to New Jersey's immigrants,
workers, women giving birth, pimply-faced teenagers, mental cases. In
their lives and words, encountered through a privileged participant observation both poetic and scientific, he finds material for his writing. Williams moves freely out into the homes of his patients, keeping a medical-
aesthetic distance (though sometimes with great difficulty, as in the
"beautiful thing" sequences of *Paterson,* book 3). The meeting with Elsie
is somehow different: a troubling outsider turns up *inside* bourgeois domestic space. She cannot be held at a distance.

This invasion by an ambiguous person of questionable origin anticipates developments that would become widely apparent only after the
Second World War. Colonial relations would be pervasively contested.
After 1950 peoples long spoken for by Western ethnographers, administrators, and missionaries began to speak and act more powerfully for
themselves on a global stage. It was increasingly difficult to keep them
in their (traditional) places. Distinct ways of life once destined to merge
into "the modern world" reasserted their difference, in novel ways. We
perceive Elsie differently in light of these developments.

Reading against the poem's momentum, from new positions, we are
able to wonder: What becomes of this girl after her stint in William Carlos Williams' kitchen? Must she symbolize a dead end? What does Elsie
prefigure? As woman: her ungainly body is either a symbol of failure in
a world dominated by the male gaze *or* the image of a powerful, "dis-
orderly" female form, an alternative to sexist definitions of beauty. As
impure product: this mix of backgrounds is either an uprooted lost soul
or a new hybrid person, less domestic than the suburban family home
she passes through. As American Indian: Elsie is either the last all-but-
assimilated remnant of the Tuscaroras who, according to tradition, settled
in the Ramapough hills of Northern New Jersey, *or* she represents a Native American past that is being turned into an unexpected future. (During the last decade a group of Elsie's kin calling themselves the Ramapough Tribe have actively asserted an Indian identity.)[2] Williams'

assimilation of his symbolic servant to a shared destiny seems less definitive now.

"Elsie," read in the late twentieth century, is both more specific and less determined. Her possible futures reflect an unresolved set of challenges to Western visions of modernity—challenges that resonate throughout this book. Elsie is still largely silent here, but her disturbing presences—a plurality of emergent subjects—can be felt.[3] The time is past when privileged authorities could routinely "give voice" (or history) to others without fear of contradiction. "Croce's great dictum that all history is contemporary history does not mean that all history is *our* contemporary history . . ." (Jameson 1981:18) When the prevailing narratives of Western identity are contested, the political issue of history as emergence becomes inescapable. Juliet Mitchell writes in *Women: The Longest Revolution* (1984): "I do not think that we can live as human subjects without in some sense taking on a history; for us, it is mainly the history of being men or women under bourgeois capitalism. In deconstructing that history, we can only construct other histories. What are we in the process of becoming?" (p. 294). We are not all together in Williams' car.

⋏

Only one of Elsie's emergent possibilities, the one connected with her "dash of Indian blood," is explored in this book. During the fall of 1977 in Boston Federal Court the descendants of Wampanoag Indians living in Mashpee, "Cape Cod's Indian Town," were required to prove their identity. To establish a legal right to sue for lost lands these citizens of modern Massachusetts were asked to demonstrate continuous tribal existence since the seventeenth century. Life in Mashpee had changed dramati-

---

2. The Native American ancestry of the isolated and inbred Ramapough mountain people ("old names" . . . from "the ribbed north end of/Jersey") is debatable. Some, like the folklorist David Cohen (1974), deny it altogether, debunking the story of a Tuscarora offshoot. Others believe that this mixed population (formerly called Jackson's Whites, and drawing on black, Dutch, and English roots) probably owes more to Delaware than to Tuscarora Indian blood. Whatever its real historical roots, the tribe as presently constituted is a living impure product.

3. "Natives," women, the poor: this book discusses the ethnographic construction of only the first group. In the dominant ideological systems of the bourgeois West they are interrelated, and a more systematic treatment than mine would bring this out. For some beginnings see Duvignaud 1973; Alloula 1981; Trinh 1987; and Spivak 1987.

cally, however, since the first contacts between English Pilgrims at Plymouth and the Massachusett-speaking peoples of the region. Were the plaintiffs of 1977 the "same" Indians? Were they something more than a collection of individuals with varying degrees of Native American ancestry? If they were different from their neighbors, how was their "tribal" difference manifested? During a long, well-publicized trial scores of Indians and whites testified about life in Mashpee. Professional historians, anthropologists, and sociologists took the stand as expert witnesses. The bitter story of New England Indians was told in minute detail and vehemently debated. In the conflict of interpretations, concepts such as "tribe," "culture," "identity," "assimilation," "ethnicity," "politics," and "community" were themselves on trial. I sat through most of the forty days of argument, listening and taking notes.

It seemed to me that the trial—beyond its immediate political stakes—was a crucial experiment in cross-cultural translation. Modern Indians, who spoke in New England–accented English about the Great Spirit, had to convince a white Boston jury of their authenticity. The translation process was fraught with ambiguities, for all the cultural boundaries at issue seemed to be blurred and shifting. The trial raised far-reaching questions about modes of cultural interpretation, implicit models of wholeness, styles of distancing, stories of historical development.

I began to see such questions as symptoms of a pervasive postcolonial crisis of ethnographic authority. While the crisis has been felt most strongly by formerly hegemonic Western discourses, the questions it raises are of global significance. Who has the authority to speak for a group's identity or authenticity? What are the essential elements and boundaries of a culture? How do self and other clash and converse in the encounters of ethnography, travel, modern interethnic relations? What narratives of development, loss, and innovation can account for the present range of local oppositional movements? During the trial these questions assumed a more than theoretical urgency.

My perspective in the courtroom was an oblique one. I had just finished a Ph.D. thesis in history with a strong interest in the history of the human sciences, particularly cultural anthropology. At the time of the trial I was rewriting my dissertation for publication. The thesis was a biography of Maurice Leenhardt, a missionary and ethnographer in French New Caledonia and an ethnologist in Paris (Clifford 1982a). What could be farther from New England Indians? The connections turned out to be close and provocative.

In Melanesia Leenhardt was deeply involved with tribal groups who had experienced a colonial assault as extreme as that inflicted in Massachusetts. He was preoccupied with practical and theoretical problems of cultural change, syncretism, conversion, and survival. Like many American Indians the militarily defeated Kanaks of New Caledonia had "tribal" institutions forced on them as a restrictive reservation system. Both groups would make strategic accommodations with these external forms of government. Native Americans and Melanesians would survive periods of acute demographic and cultural crisis, as well as periods of change and revival. Over the last hundred years New Caledonia's Kanaks have managed to find powerful, distinctive ways to live as Melanesians in an invasive world. It seemed to me that the Mashpee were struggling toward a similar goal, reviving and inventing ways to live as Indians in the twentieth century.

Undoubtedly what I heard in the New England courtroom influenced my sense of Melanesian identity, something I came to understand not as an archaic survival but as an ongoing process, politically contested and historically unfinished. In my studies of European ethnographic institutions I have cultivated a similar attitude.

人

This book is concerned with Western visions and practices. They are shown, however, responding to forces that challenge the authority and even the future identity of "the West." Modern ethnography appears in several forms, traditional and innovative. As an academic practice it cannot be separated from anthropology. Seen more generally, it is simply diverse ways of thinking and writing about culture from a standpoint of participant observation. In this expanded sense a poet like Williams is an ethnographer. So are many of the people social scientists have called "native informants." Ultimately my topic is a pervasive condition of off-centeredness in a world of distinct meaning systems, a state of being in culture while looking at culture, a form of personal and collective self-fashioning. This predicament—not limited to scholars, writers, artists, or intellectuals—responds to the twentieth century's unprecedented overlay of traditions. A modern "ethnography" of conjunctures, constantly moving *between* cultures, does not, like its Western alter ego "anthropology," aspire to survey the full range of human diversity or development. It is perpetually displaced, both regionally focused and broadly comparative, a form both of dwelling and of travel in a world where the two experiences are less and less distinct.

This book migrates between local and global perspectives, constantly recontextualizing its topic. Part One focuses on strategies of writing and representation, strategies that change historically in response to the general shift from high colonialism around 1900 to postcolonialism and neocolonialism after the 1950s. In these chapters I try to show that ethnographic texts are orchestrations of multivocal exchanges occurring in politically charged situations. The subjectivities produced in these often unequal exchanges—whether of "natives" or of visiting participant-observers—are constructed domains of truth, serious fictions. Once this is recognized, diverse inventive possibilities for postcolonial ethnographic representation emerge, some of which are surveyed in this book. Part Two portrays ethnography in alliance with avant-garde art and cultural criticism, activities with which it shares modernist procedures of collage, juxtaposition, and estrangement. The "exotic" is now nearby. In this section I also probe the limits of Western ethnography through several self-reflexive forms of travel writing, exploring the possibilities of a twentieth-century "poetics of displacement." Part Three turns to the history of collecting, particularly the classification and display of "primitive" art and exotic "cultures." My general aim is to displace any transcendent regime of authenticity, to argue that all authoritative collections, whether made in the name of art or science, are historically contingent and subject to local reappropriation. In the book's final section I explore how non-Western historical experiences—those of "orientals" and "tribal" Native Americans—are hemmed in by concepts of continuous tradition and the unified self. I argue that identity, considered ethnographically, must always be mixed, relational, and inventive.

Self-identity emerges as a complex cultural problem in my treatment of two polyglot refugees, Joseph Conrad and Bronislaw Malinowski, Poles shipwrecked in England and English. Both men produced seminal meditations on the local fictions of collective life, and, with different degrees of irony, both constructed identities based on the acceptance of limited realities and forms of expression. Embracing the serious fiction of "culture," they wrote at a moment when the ethnographic (relativist and plural) idea began to attain its modern currency. Here and elsewhere in the book I try to historicize and see beyond this currency, straining for a concept that can preserve culture's differentiating functions while conceiving of collective identity as a hybrid, often discontinuous inventive process. Culture is a deeply compromised idea I cannot yet do without.

Some of the political dangers of culturalist reductions and essences are explored in my analysis of Edward Said's polemical work *Orientalism* (1978a). What emerges is the inherently discrepant stance of a post-colonial "oppositional" critic, for the construction of simplifying essences and distancing dichotomies is clearly not a monopoly of Western Orientalist experts. Said himself writes in ways that simultaneously assert and subvert his own authority. My analysis suggests that there can be no final smoothing over of the discrepancies in his discourse, since it is increasingly difficult to maintain a cultural and political position "outside" the Occident from which, in security, to attack it. Critiques like Said's are caught in the double ethnographic movement I have been evoking. Locally based and politically engaged, they must resonate globally; while they engage pervasive postcolonial processes, they do so without overview, from a blatantly partial perspective.

Intervening in an interconnected world, one is always, to varying degrees, "inauthentic": caught between cultures, implicated in others. Because discourse in global power systems is elaborated vis-à-vis, a sense of difference or distinctness can never be located solely in the continuity of a culture or tradition. Identity is conjunctural, not essential. Said addresses these issues most affectingly in *After the Last Sky,* a recent evocation of "Palestinian Lives" and of his own position among them (1986a:150): "A part of something is for the foreseeable future going to be better than all of it. Fragments over wholes. Restless nomadic activity over the settlements of held territory. Criticism over resignation. The Palestinian as self-consciousness in a barren plain of investments and consumer appetites. The heroism of anger over the begging bowl, limited independence over the status of clients. Attention, alertness, focus. To do as others do, but somehow to stand apart. To tell your story in pieces, *as it is.*" This work appeared as I was finishing my own book. Thus my discussion of *Orientalism* merely anticipates Said's ongoing search for nonessentialist forms of cultural politics. *After the Last Sky* actively inhabits the discrepancy between a specific condition of Palestinian exile and a more general twentieth-century range of options. It is (and is not only) as a Palestinian that Said movingly accepts "our wanderings," pleading for "the open secular element, and not the symmetry of redemption" (p. 150).

☆

I share this suspicion of "the symmetry of redemption." Questionable acts of purification are involved in any attainment of a promised land, return to "original" sources, or gathering up of a true tradition. Such claims to purity are in any event always subverted by the need to stage authenticity *in opposition to* external, often dominating alternatives. Thus the "Third World" plays itself against the "First World," and vice versa. At a local level, Trobriand Islanders invent *their* culture within and against the contexts of recent colonial history and the new nation of Papua–New Guinea. If authenticity is relational, there can be no essence except as a political, cultural invention, a local tactic.

In this book I question some of the local tactics of Western ethnography, focusing on redemptive modes of textualization and particularly of collecting. Several chapters analyze in some detail the systems of authenticity that have been imposed on creative works of non-Western art and culture. They look at collecting and authenticating practices in contemporary settings: for example the controversy surrounding an exhibition at the Museum of Modern Art in New York City over the relations between "tribal" and "modern" art. How have exotic objects been given value as "art" and "culture" in Western collecting systems? I do not argue, as some critics have, that non-Western objects are properly understood only with reference to their original milieux. Ethnographic contextualizations are as problematic as aesthetic ones, as susceptible to purified, ahistorical treatment.

I trace the modern history of both aesthetic and ethnographic classifications in an earlier setting: avant-garde Paris of the 1920s and 1930s, a radical context I call ethnographic surrealism. Two influential museums, the Musée d'Ethnographie du Trocadéro and its scientific successor, the Musée de l'Homme, symbolize distinct modes of "art and culture collecting." Their juxtaposition forces the question: How are ethnographic worlds and their meaningful artifacts cut up, salvaged, and valued? Here culture appears not as a tradition to be saved but as assembled codes and artifacts always susceptible to critical and creative recombination. Ethnography is an explicit form of cultural critique sharing radical perspectives with dada and surrealism. Instead of acquiescing in the separation of avant-garde experiment from disciplinary science, I reopen the frontier, suggesting that the modern division of art and ethnography into distinct institutions has restricted the former's analytic power and the latter's subversive vocation.

Since 1900 inclusive collections of "Mankind" have become institutionalized in academic disciplines like anthropology and in museums of art or ethnology. A restrictive "art-culture system" has come to control the authenticity, value, and circulation of artifacts and data. Analyzing this system, I propose that any collection implies a temporal vision generating rarity and worth, a metahistory. This history defines which groups or things will be redeemed from a disintegrating human past and which will be defined as the dynamic, or tragic, agents of a common destiny. My analysis works to bring out the local, political contingency of such histories and of the modern collections they justify. Space is cleared, perhaps, for alternatives.

人

This book is a spliced ethnographic object, an incomplete collection. It consists of explorations written and rewritten over a seven-year period. Its own historical moment has been marked by rapid changes in the terms—scientific, aesthetic, and textual—governing cross-cultural representation. Written from within a "West" whose authority to represent unified human history is now widely challenged and whose very spatial identity is increasingly problematic, the explorations gathered here cannot—should not—add up to a seamless vision. Their partiality is apparent. The chapters vary in form and style, reflecting diverse conjunctures and specific occasions of composition. I have not tried to rewrite those already published to produce a consistent veneer. Moreover, I have included texts that actively break up the book's prevailing tone, hoping in this way to manifest the rhetoric of my accounts. I prefer sharply focused pictures, composed in ways that show the frame or lens.

Ethnography, a hybrid activity, thus appears as writing, as collecting, as modernist collage, as imperial power, as subversive critique. Viewed most broadly, perhaps, my topic is a mode of travel, a way of understanding and getting around in a diverse world that, since the sixteenth century, has become cartographically unified. One of the principal functions of ethnography is "orientation" (a term left over from a time when Europe traveled and invented itself with respect to a fantastically unified "East"). But in the twentieth century ethnography reflects new "spatial practices" (De Certeau 1984), new forms of dwelling and circulating.

This century has seen a drastic expansion of mobility, including tourism, migrant labor, immigration, urban sprawl. More and more people "dwell" with the help of mass transit, automobiles, airplanes. In cities on six continents foreign populations have come to stay—mixing in but often in partial, specific fashions. The "exotic" is uncannily close. Conversely, there seem no distant places left on the planet where the presence of "modern" products, media, and power cannot be felt. An older topography and experience of travel is exploded. One no longer leaves home confident of finding something radically new, another time or space. Difference is encountered in the adjoining neighborhood, the familiar turns up at the ends of the earth. This dis-"orientation" is reflected throughout the book. For example twentieth-century academic ethnography does not appear as a practice of interpreting distinct, whole ways of life but instead as a series of specific dialogues, impositions, and inventions. "Cultural" difference is no longer a stable, exotic otherness; self-other relations are matters of power and rhetoric rather than of essence. A whole structure of expectations about authenticity in culture and in art is thrown in doubt.

The new relations of ethnographic displacement were registered with precocious clarity in the writings of Victor Segalen and Michel Leiris. Both would have to unlearn the forms that once organized the experience of travel in a time when "home" and "abroad," "self" and "other," "savage" and "civilized" seemed more clearly opposed. Their writings betray an unease with narratives of escape and return, of initiation and conquest. They do not claim to know a distanced "exotic," to bring back its secrets, to objectively describe its landscapes, customs, languages. Everywhere they go they register complex encounters. In Segalen's words the new traveler expresses "not simply his vision, but through an instantaneous, constant *transfer,* the echo of his presence." China becomes an allegorical mirror. Leiris' fieldwork in a "phantom Africa" throws him back on a relentless self-ethnography—not autobiography but an act of writing his existence in a present of memories, dreams, politics, daily life.

Twentieth-century identities no longer presuppose continuous cultures or traditions. Everywhere individuals and groups improvise local performances from (re)collected pasts, drawing on foreign media, symbols, and languages. This existence among fragments has often been portrayed as a process of ruin and cultural decay, perhaps most eloquently by Claude Lévi-Strauss in *Tristes tropiques* (1955). In Lévi-Strauss's global vision—one widely shared today—authentic human differences are disintegrating, disappearing in an expansive commodity culture to become, at best, collectible "art" or "folklore." The great narrative of entropy and loss in *Tristes tropiques* expresses an inescapable, sad truth. But it is too neat, and it assumes a questionable Eurocentric position at the "end" of a unified human history, gathering up, memorializing the world's local historicities. Alongside this narrative of progressive monoculture a more ambiguous "Caribbean" experience may be glimpsed. In my account Aimé Césaire, a practitioner of "neologistic" cultural politics, represents such a possibility—organic culture reconceived as inventive process or creolized "interculture" (Wagner 1980; Drummond 1981).[4] The roots of tradition are cut and retied, collective symbols appropriated from external influences. For Césaire culture and identity are inventive and mobile. They need not take root in ancestral plots; they live by pollination, by (historical) transplanting.

The "filth" that an expansive West, according to the disillusioned traveler of *Tristes tropiques* (p. 38), has thrown in the face of the world's societies appears as raw material, compost for new orders of difference. It is also filth. Modern cultural contacts need not be romanticized, erasing the violence of empire and continuing forms of neocolonial domination. The Caribbean history from which Césaire derives an inventive and tactical "negritude" is a history of degradation, mimicry, violence, and blocked possibilities. It is also rebellious, syncretic, and creative. This kind of ambiguity keeps the planet's local futures uncertain and open. There is no master narrative that can reconcile the tragic and comic plots of global cultural history.

It is easier to register the loss of traditional orders of difference than to perceive the emergence of new ones. Perhaps this book goes too far in its concern for ethnographic presents-becoming-futures. Its utopian, persistent hope for the reinvention of difference risks downplaying the destructive, homogenizing effects of global economic and cultural centralization. Moreover, its Western assumption that assertions of "tradition" are always responses to the new (that there is no real recurrence in history) may exclude local narratives of cultural continuity and recovery. I do not tell all the possible stories. As an Igbo saying has it, "You do not stand in one place to watch a masquerade."

My primary goal is to open space for cultural futures, for the recog-

---

4. For recent work on the historical-political invention of cultures and traditions see, among others, Comaroff 1985; Guss 1986; Handler 1985; Handler and Linnekin 1984; Hobsbawm and Ranger 1983; Taussig 1980, 1987; Whisnant 1983; and Cantwell 1984. Familiar approaches to "culture-contact," "syncretism," and "acculturation" are pressed farther by the concepts of "interference" and "interreference" (Fischer 1986:219, 232; Baumgarten 1982:154), "transculturation" (Rama 1982; Pratt 1987), and "intercultural intertexts" (Tedlock and Tedlock 1985).

nition of emergence. This requires a critique of deep-seated Western habits of mind and systems of value. I am especially skeptical of an almost automatic reflex—in the service of a unified vision of history—to relegate exotic peoples and objects to the collective past (Fabian 1983). The inclusive orders of modernism and anthropology (the "we" riding in Williams' car, the Mankind of Western social science) are always deployed at the end point or advancing edge of History. Exotic traditions appear as archaic, purer (and more rare) than the diluted inventions of a syncretic present. In this temporal setup a great many twentieth-century creations can only appear as imitations of more "developed" models. The Elsies of the planet are still traveling nowhere their own.

Throughout the world indigenous populations have had to reckon with the forces of "progress" and "national" unification. The results have been both destructive and inventive. Many traditions, languages, cosmologies, and values are lost, some literally murdered; but much has simultaneously been invented and revived in complex, oppositional contexts. If the victims of progress and empire are weak, they are seldom passive. It used to be assumed, for example, that conversion to Christianity in Africa, Melanesia, Latin America, or even colonial Massachusetts would lead to the extinction of indigenous cultures rather than to their transformation. Something more ambiguous and historically complex has occurred, requiring that we perceive *both* the end of certain orders of diversity and the creation or translation of others (Fernandez 1978). More than a few "extinct" peoples have returned to haunt the Western historical imagination.[5] It is difficult, in any event, to equate the future of "Catholicism" in New Guinea with its current prospects in Italy; and Protestant Christianity in New Caledonia is very different from its diverse Nigerian forms. The future is not (only) monoculture.[6]

---

5. The continued tribal life of California Indians is a case in point. Even, most notorious of all, the genocidal "extinction" of the Tasmanians now seems a much less definitive "event." After systematic decimations, with the 1876 death of Truganina, the last "pure" specimen (playing a mythic role similar to that of Ishi in California), the race was scientifically declared dead. But Tasmanians did survive and intermarried with aboriginals, whites, and Maori. In 1978 a committee of inquiry reported between four and five thousand persons eligible to make land claims in Tasmania (Stocking 1987:283).

6. Research specifically on this issue is being conducted by Ulf Hannerz and his colleagues at the University of Stockholm on "the world system of culture." In an early statement Hannerz confronts the widespread assumption that "cultural diversity is waning, and the same single mass culture will soon be

   To reject a single progressive or entropic metanarrative is not to deny the existence of pervasive global processes unevenly at work. The world is increasingly connected, though not unified, economically and cultur-ally. Local particularism offers no escape from these involvements. In-deed, modern ethnographic histories are perhaps condemned to oscillate between two metanarratives: one of homogenization, the other of emer-gence; one of loss, the other of invention. In most specific conjunctures both narratives are relevant, each undermining the other's claim to tell "the whole story," each denying to the other a privileged, Hegelian vi-sion. Everywhere in the world distinctions are being destroyed *and* cre-ated; but the new identities and orders of difference are more reminiscent of Williams' Elsie than of Edward Curtis' idealized "vanishing" American Indians. The histories of emergent differences require other ways of tell-ing: Césaire's impure cultural poetics, Said's dispersed "Palestinian Lives," Mashpee's reinvented tradition—there is no single model. This book surveys several hybrid and subversive forms of cultural representa-tion, forms that prefigure an inventive future. In the last decades of the twentieth century, ethnography begins from the inescapable fact that Westerners are not the only ones going places in the modern world.

   But have not travelers always encountered worldly "natives"? Strange anticipation: the English Pilgrims arrive at Plymouth Rock in The New World only to find Squanto, a Patuxet, just back from Europe.

---

everywhere." He is skeptical: "I do not think it is only my bias as an anthropol-ogist with a vested interest in cultural variation which makes it difficult for me to recognize that the situation for example in Nigeria could be anything like this. The people in my favorite Nigerian town drink Coca Cola, but they drink *buru-kutu* too; and they can watch *Charlie's Angels* as well as Hausa drummers on the television sets which spread rapidly as soon as electricity has arrived. My sense is that the world system, rather than creating massive cultural homogeneity on a global scale, is replacing one diversity with another; and the new diversity is based relatively more on interrelations and less on autonomy" (Hannerz n.d.: 6).

"White Man," Onyeocha, a performer at Igbo
masquerades. Amagu Izzi, southeast Nigeria, 1982.

Part One ⚶ Discourses

Clifford takes as his natives, as well as his informants, . . .
anthropologists . . . We are being observed and inscribed.
—PAUL RABINOW, "REPRESENTATIONS
ARE SOCIAL FACTS"

1. On Ethnographic Authority

T HE 1724 frontispiece of Father Lafitau's *Moeurs des sauvages ameri-quains* portrays the ethnographer as a young woman sitting at a writing table amid artifacts from the New World and from classical Greece and Egypt. The author is accompanied by two cherubs who assist in the task of comparison and by the bearded figure of Time, who points toward a tableau representing the ultimate source of the truths issuing from the writer's pen. The image toward which the young woman lifts her gaze is a bank of clouds where Adam, Eve, and the serpent appear. Above them stand the redeemed man and woman of the Apocalypse, on either side of a radiant triangle bearing the Hebrew script for *Yahweh*.

The frontispiece for Malinowski's *Argonauts of the Western Pacific* is a photograph with the caption "A Ceremonial Act of the Kula." A shell necklace is being offered to a Trobriand chief, who stands at the door of his dwelling. Behind the man presenting the necklace is a row of six bowing youths, one of them sounding a conch. All the figures stand in profile, their attention apparently concentrated on the rite of exchange, a real event of Melanesian life. But on closer inspection one of the bowing Trobrianders may be seen to be looking at the camera.

Lafitau's allegory is the less familiar: his author transcribes rather than originates. Unlike Malinowski's photo, the engraving makes no reference to ethnographic experience—despite Lafitau's five years of research among the Mohawks, research that has earned him a respected place among the fieldworkers of any generation. His account is presented not as the product of firsthand observation but of writing, in a crowded workshop. The frontispiece from *Argonauts,* like all photographs, asserts presence—that of the scene before the lens; it also suggests another presence—that of the ethnographer actively composing this fragment of Trobriand reality. Kula exchange, the subject of Malinowski's book, has been made perfectly visible, centered in the perceptual frame, while a participant's glance redirects our attention to the observational standpoint we share, as readers, with the ethnographer and his camera. The predominant mode of modern fieldwork authority is signaled: "You are there . . . because I was there."

This chapter traces the formation and breakup of ethnographic authority in twentieth-century social anthropology. It is not a complete account, nor is it based on a fully realized theory of ethnographic interpretation and textuality.[1] Such a theory's contours are problematic, since the activity of cross-cultural representation is now more than usually in question. The present predicament is linked to the breakup and redistribution of colonial power in the decades after 1950 and to the echoes of that process in the radical cultural theories of the 1960s and 1970s. After the negritude movement's reversal of the European gaze, after anthropology's *crise de conscience* with respect to its liberal status within the imperial order, and now that the West can no longer present itself as the unique purveyor of anthropological knowledge about others, it has become necessary to imagine a world of generalized ethnography. With expanded communication and intercultural influence, people interpret others, and themselves, in a bewildering diversity of idioms—a global condition of

_____

1. Only English, American, and French examples are discussed. If it is likely that the modes of authority analyzed here are able to be generalized widely, no attempt has been made to extend them to other national traditions. It is assumed also, in the antipositivist tradition of Wilhelm Dilthey, that ethnography is a process of interpretation, not of explanation. Modes of authority based on natural-scientific epistemologies are not discussed. In its focus on participant observation as an intersubjective process at the heart of twentieth-century ethnography, this discussion scants a number of contributing sources of authority: for example the weight of accumulated "archival" knowledge about particular groups, of a cross-cultural comparative perspective, and of statistical survey work.

what Mikhail Bakhtin (1953) called "heteroglossia."² This ambiguous, multivocal world makes it increasingly hard to conceive of human diversity as inscribed in bounded, independent cultures. Difference is an effect of inventive syncretism. In recent years works such as Edward Said's *Orientalism* (1978) and Paulin Hountondji's *Sur la "philosophie" africaine* (1977) have cast radical doubt on the procedures by which alien human groups can be represented without proposing systematic, sharply new methods or epistemologies. These studies suggest that while ethnographic writing cannot entirely escape the reductionist use of dichotomies and essences, it can at least struggle self-consciously to avoid portraying abstract, ahistorical "others." It is more than ever crucial for different peoples to form complex concrete images of one another, as well as of the relationships of knowledge and power that connect them; but no sovereign scientific method or ethical stance can guarantee the truth of such images. They are constituted—the critique of colonial modes of representation has shown at least this much—in specific historical relations of dominance and dialogue.

The experiments in ethnographic writing surveyed in this chapter do not fall into a clear reformist direction or evolution. They are ad hoc inventions and cannot be seen in terms of a systematic analysis of postcolonial representation. They are perhaps best understood as components of that "toolkit" of engaged theory recently recommended by Gilles Deleuze and Michel Foucault: "The notion of theory as a toolkit means (i) The theory to be constructed is not a system but an instrument, a *logic* of the specificity of power relations and the struggles around them; (ii) That this investigation can only be carried out step by step on the basis of reflection (which will necessarily be historical in some of its aspects) on given situations" (Foucault 1980:145; see also 1977:208). We may contribute to a practical reflection on cross-cultural representation by undertaking an inventory of the better, though imperfect, approaches currently at hand. Of these, ethnographic fieldwork remains an unusually

---

2. "Heteroglossia" assumes that "languages do not *exclude* each other, but rather intersect with each other in many different ways (the Ukrainian language, the language of the epic poem, of early Symbolism, of the student, of a particular generation of children, of the run-of-the-mill intellectual, of the Nietzschean, and so on). It might even seem that the very word 'language' loses all meaning in this process—for apparently there is no single plane on which all these 'languages' might be juxtaposed to one another" (291). What is said of languages applies equally to "cultures" and "subcultures." See also Volosinov (Bakhtin?) 1953:291, esp. chaps. 1–3; and Todorov 1981:88–93.

sensitive method. Participant observation obliges its practitioners to experience, at a bodily as well as an intellectual level, the vicissitudes of translation. It requires arduous language learning, some degree of direct involvement and conversation, and often a derangement of personal and cultural expectations. There is, of course, a myth of fieldwork. The actual experience, hedged around with contingencies, rarely lives up to the ideal; but as a means for producing knowledge from an intense, intersubjective engagement, the practice of ethnography retains a certain exemplary status. Moreover, if fieldwork has for a time been identified with a uniquely Western discipline and a totalizing science of "anthropology," these associations are not necessarily permanent. Current styles of cultural description are historically limited and are undergoing important metamorphoses.

The development of ethnographic science cannot ultimately be understood in isolation from more general political-epistemological debates about writing and the representation of otherness. In this discussion, however, I have maintained a focus on professional anthropology, and specifically on ethnography since 1950.[3] The current crisis—or better, dispersion—of ethnographic authority makes it possible to mark off a rough period, bounded by the years 1900 and 1960, during which a new conception of field research established itself as the norm for European and American anthropology. Intensive fieldwork, pursued by university-trained specialists, emerged as a privileged, sanctioned source of data about exotic peoples. It is not a question here of the dominance of a single research method. "Intensive" ethnography has been variously defined. (Compare Griaule 1957 with Malinowski 1922:chap. 1). Moreover, the hegemony of fieldwork was established earlier and more thoroughly in the United States and in England than in France. The early examples of Franz Boas and the Torres Straits expedition were matched only belatedly by the founding of the Institut d'Ethnologie in 1925 and

---

3. I have not attempted to survey new styles of ethnographic writing that may be originating outside the West. As Edward Said, Paulin Hountondji, and others have shown, a considerable work of ideological "clearing," oppositional critical work, remains; and it is to this that non-Western intellectuals have been devoting a great part of their energies. My discussion remains inside, but at the experimental boundaries of, a realist cultural science elaborated in the Occident. Moreover, it does not consider as areas of innovation the "para-ethnographic" genres of oral history, the nonfiction novel, the "new journalism," travel literature, and the documentary film.

the much-publicized Mission Dakar-Djibouti of 1932 (Karady 1982; Jamin 1982a; Stocking 1983). Nevertheless, by the mid-1930s one can fairly speak of a developing international consensus: valid anthropological abstractions were to be based, wherever possible, on intensive cultural descriptions by qualified scholars. By this point the new style had been made popular, institutionalized, and embodied in specific textual practices.

It has recently become possible to identify and take a certain distance from these conventions.[4] If ethnography produces cultural interpretations through intense research experiences, how is unruly experience transformed into an authoritative written account? How, precisely, is a garrulous, overdetermined cross-cultural encounter shot through with power relations and personal cross-purposes circumscribed as an adequate version of a more or less discrete "other world" composed by an individual author?

In analyzing this complex transformation one must bear in mind the fact that ethnography is, from beginning to end, enmeshed in writing. This writing includes, minimally, a translation of experience into textual form. The process is complicated by the action of multiple subjectivities and political constraints beyond the control of the writer. In response to these forces ethnographic writing enacts a specific strategy of authority. This strategy has classically involved an unquestioned claim to appear as the purveyor of truth in the text. A complex cultural experience is enunciated by an individual: *We the Tikopia* by Raymond Firth; *Nous avons mangé la forêt* by Georges Condominas; *Coming of Age in Samoa* by Margaret Mead; *The Nuer* by E. E. Evans-Pritchard.

The discussion that follows first locates this authority historically in the development of a twentieth-century science of participant observation. It then proceeds to a critique of underlying assumptions and a review of emerging textual practices. Alternate strategies of ethnographic authority may be seen in recent experiments by ethnographers who self-consciously reject scenes of cultural representation in the style of Malinowski's frontispiece. Different secular versions of Lafiteau's crowded scriptorial workshop are emerging. In the new paradigms of authority the

---

4. In the present crisis of authority, ethnography has emerged as a subject of historical scrutiny. For new critical approaches see Hartog 1971; Asad 1973; Burridge 1973:chap. 1; Duchet 1971; Boon 1982; De Certeau 1980; Said 1978; Stocking 1983; and Rupp-Eisenreich 1984.

writer is no longer fascinated by transcendent figures—a Hebrew-Christian deity or its twentieth-century replacements, Man and Culture. Nothing remains of the heavenly tableau except the anthropologist's scumbled image in a mirror. The silence of the ethnographic workshop has been broken—by insistent, heteroglot voices, by the scratching of other pens.[5]

⅄

At the close of the nineteenth century nothing guaranteed, a priori, the ethnographer's status as the best interpreter of native life—as opposed to the traveler, and especially the missionary and administrator, some of whom had been in the field far longer and had better research contacts and linguistic skills. The development of the fieldworker's image in America, from Frank Hamilton Cushing (an oddball) to Margaret Mead (a national figure) is significant. During this period a particular form of authority was created—an authority both scientifically validated and based on a unique personal experience. During the 1920s Malinowski played a central role in establishing credit for the fieldworker, and we should recall in this light his attacks on the competence of competitors in the field. For example the colonial magistrate Alex Rentoul, who had the temerity to contradict science's findings concerning Trobriand conceptions of paternity, was excommunicated in the pages of Man for his unprofessional "police court perspective" (see Rentoul 1931a,b; Malinowski 1932). The attack on amateurism in the field was pressed even further by A. R. Radcliffe-Brown, who, as Ian Langham has shown, came to epitomize the scientific professional, discovering rigorous social laws (Langham 1981:chap. 7). What emerged during the first half of the twentieth century with the success of professional fieldwork was a new fusion of general theory and empirical research, of cultural analysis with ethnographic description.

The fieldworker-theorist replaced an older partition between the "man on the spot" (in James Frazer's words) and the sociologist or anthropologist in the metropole. This division of labor varied in different national traditions. In the United States for example Morgan had personal knowledge of at least some of the cultures that were raw material for his

---

5. On the suppression of dialogue in Lafitau's frontispiece and the constitution of a textualized, ahistorical, and visually oriented "anthropology" see Michel de Certeau's detailed analysis (1980).

sociological syntheses; and Boas rather early on made intensive field-work the sine qua non of serious anthropological discourse. In general, however, before Malinowski, Radcliffe-Brown, and Mead had success-fully established the norm of the university-trained scholar testing and deriving theory from firsthand research, a rather different economy of ethnographic knowledge prevailed. For example *The Melanesians* (1891) by R. H. Codrington is a detailed compilation of folklore and custom, drawn from his relatively long term of research as an evangelist and based on intensive collaboration with indigenous translators and infor-mants. The book is not organized around a fieldwork "experience," nor does it advance a unified interpretive hypothesis, functional, historical, or otherwise. It is content with low-level generalizations and the amass-ing of an eclectic range of information. Codrington is acutely aware of the incompleteness of his knowledge, believing that real understanding of native life begins only after a decade or so of experience and study (pp. vi–vii). This understanding of the difficulty of grasping the world of alien peoples—the many years of learning and unlearning needed, the problems of acquiring thorough linguistic competence—tended to dom-inate the work of Codrington's generation. Such assumptions would soon be challenged by the more confident cultural relativism of the Malinow-skian model. The new fieldworkers sharply distinguished themselves from the earlier "men on the spot"—the missionary, the administrator, the trader, and the traveler—whose knowledge of indigenous peoples, they argued, was not informed by the best scientific hypotheses or a suf-ficient neutrality.

Before the emergence of professional ethnography, writers such as J. F. McLennan, John Lubbock, and E. B. Tylor had attempted to control the quality of the reports on which their anthropological syntheses were based. They did this by means of the guidelines of *Notes and Queries* and, in Tylor's case, by cultivating long-term working relations with so-phisticated researchers in the field such as the missionary Lorimer Fison. After 1883, as newly appointed reader in anthropology at Oxford, Tylor worked to encourage the systematic gathering of ethnographic data by qualified professionals. The United States Bureau of Ethnology, already committed to the undertaking, provided a model. Tylor was active in founding a committee on the Northwestern Tribes of Canada. The com-mittee's first agent in the field was the nineteen-year-veteran missionary among the Ojibwa, E. F. Wilson. He was replaced before long by Boas, a physicist in the process of turning to professional ethnography. George

Stocking has persuasively argued that the replacement of Wilson by Boas "marks the beginning of an important phase in the development of British ethnographic method: the collection of data by academically trained natural scientists defining themselves as anthropologists, and involved also in the formulation and evaluation of anthropological theory" (1983:74). With Boas' early survey work and the emergence in the 1890s of other natural-scientist fieldworkers such as A. C. Haddon and Baldwin Spencer, the move toward professional ethnography was under way. The Torres Straits expedition of 1899 may be seen as a culmination of the work of this "intermediate generation," as Stocking calls them. The new style of research was clearly different from that of missionaries and other amateurs in the field, and part of a general trend since Tylor "to draw more closely together the empirical and theoretical components of anthropological inquiry" (1983:72).

The establishment of intensive participant observation as a professional norm, however, would have to await the Malinowskian cohort. The "intermediate generation" of ethnographers did not typically live in a single locale for a year or more, mastering the vernacular and undergoing a personal learning experience comparable to an initiation. They did not speak as cultural insiders but retained the natural scientist's documentary, observational stance. The principal exception before the third decade of the century, Frank Hamilton Cushing, remained an isolated instance. As Curtis Hinsley has suggested, Cushing's long firsthand study of the Zunis, his quasi-absorption into their way of life, "raised problems of verification and accountability . . . A community of scientific anthropology on the model of other sciences required a common language of discourse, channels of regular communication, and at least minimal consensus on judging method" (1983:66). Cushing's intuitive, excessively personal understanding of the Zuni could not confer scientific authority.

Schematically put, before the late nineteenth century the ethnographer and the anthropologist, the describer-translator of custom and the builder of general theories about humanity, were distinct. (A clear sense of the *tension* between ethnography and anthropology is important in correctly perceiving the recent, and perhaps temporary, conflation of the two projects.) Malinowski gives us the image of the new "anthropologist"—squatting by the campfire; looking, listening, and questioning; recording and interpreting Trobriand life. The literary charter of this new authority is the first chapter of *Argonauts*, with its prominently displayed photographs of the ethnographer's tent pitched among Kiriwinian dwellings. The sharpest methodological justification for the new mode is to be found in Radcliffe-Brown's *Andaman Islanders* (1922). The two books were published within a year of each other. And although their authors developed quite different fieldwork styles and visions of cultural science, both early texts provide explicit arguments for the special authority of the ethnographer-anthropologist.

Malinowski, as his notes for the crucial introduction to *Argonauts* show, was greatly concerned with the rhetorical problem of convincing his readers that the facts he was putting before them were objectively acquired, not subjective creations (Stocking 1983:105). Moreover, he was fully aware that "in Ethnography, the distance is often enormous between the brute material of information—as it is presented to the student in his own observations, in native statement, in the kaleidoscope of tribal life—and the final authoritative presentation of the results" (Malinowski 1922:3–4). Stocking has nicely analyzed the various literary artifices of *Argonauts* (its engaging narrative constructs, use of the active voice in the "ethnographic present," illusive dramatizations of the author's participation in scenes of Trobriand life), techniques Malinowski used so that "his own experience of the natives' experience [might] become the reader's experience as well" (Stocking 1983:106; see also Payne 1981, and Chapter 3). The problems of verification and accountability that had relegated Cushing to the professional margin were very much on Malinowski's mind. This anxiety is reflected in the mass of data contained in *Argonauts*, its sixty-six photographic plates, the now rather curious "Chronological List of Kula Events Witnessed by the Writer," the constant alternation between impersonal description of typical behavior and statements on the order of "I witnessed . . ." and "Our party, sailing from the North . . ."

Argonauts is a complex narrative simultaneously of Trobriand life and ethnographic fieldwork. It is archetypical of the generation of ethnographies that successfully established the scientific validity of participant observation. The story of research built into *Argonauts,* into Mead's popular work on Samoa, and into *We the Tikopia* became an implicit narrative underlying all professional reports on exotic worlds. If subsequent ethnographies did not need to include developed fieldwork accounts, it was because such accounts were assumed, once a statement was made on the order of, for example, Godfrey Lienhardt's single sentence at the beginning of *Divinity and Experience* (1961:vii): "This book is based upon two years' work among the Dinka, spread over the period of 1947–1950."

In the 1920s the new fieldworker-theorist brought to completion a powerful new scientific and literary genre, the ethnography, a synthetic cultural description based on participant observation (Thornton 1983). The new style of representation depended on institutional and methodological innovations circumventing the obstacles to rapid knowledge of other cultures that had preoccupied the best representatives of Codrington's generation. These may be briefly summarized.

First, the persona of the fieldworker was validated, both publicly and professionally. In the popular domain, visible figures such as Malinowski, Mead, and Marcel Griaule communicated a vision of ethnography as both scientifically demanding and heroic. The professional ethnographer was trained in the latest analytic techniques and modes of scientific explanation. This conferred an advantage over amateurs in the field: the professional could claim to get to the heart of a culture more quickly, grasping its essential institutions and structures. A prescribed attitude of cultural relativism distinguished the fieldworker from missionaries, administrators, and others whose view of natives was, presumably, less dispassionate, who were preoccupied with the problems of government or conversion. In addition to scientific sophistication and relativist sympathy, a variety of normative standards for the new form of research emerged: the fieldworker was to live in the native village, use the vernacular, stay a sufficient (but seldom specified) length of time, investigate certain classic subjects, and so on.

Second, it was tacitly agreed that the new-style ethnographer, whose sojourn in the field seldom exceeded two years, and more frequently was much shorter, could efficiently "use" native languages without "mastering" them. In a significant article of 1939 Margaret Mead argued that the ethnographer following the Malinowskian prescription to avoid interpreters and to conduct research in the vernacular did not, in fact, need to attain "virtuosity" in native tongues, but could "use" the vernacular to ask questions, maintain rapport, and generally get along in the culture while obtaining good research results in particular areas of concentration. This in effect justified her own practice, which featured relatively short stays and a focus on specific domains such as childhood or "personality," foci that would function as "types" for a cultural synthesis. Her attitude toward language "use" was broadly characteristic of an ethnographic generation that could, for example, credit as authoritative a study called *The Nuer* that was based on only eleven months of very difficult research. Mead's article provoked a sharp response from Robert Lowie (1940), writing from the older Boasian tradition, more philological in its orientation. But his was a rear-guard action; the point had been generally established that valid research could, in practice, be accomplished on the basis of one or two years' familiarity with a foreign vernacular (even though, as Lowie suggested, no one would credit a translation of Proust that was based on an equivalent knowledge of French).

Third, the new ethnography was marked by an increased emphasis on the power of observation. Culture was construed as an ensemble of characteristic behaviors, ceremonies, and gestures susceptible to recording and explanation by a trained onlooker. Mead pressed this point furthest (indeed, her own powers of visual analysis were extraordinary). As a general trend the participant-*observer* emerged as a research norm. Of course successful fieldwork mobilized the fullest possible range of interactions, but a distinct primacy was accorded to the visual: interpretation was tied to description. After Malinowski a general suspicion of "privileged informants" reflected this systematic preference for the (methodical) observations of the ethnographer over the (interested) interpretations of indigenous authorities.

Fourth, certain powerful theoretical abstractions promised to help academic ethnographers "get to the heart" of a culture more rapidly than someone undertaking, for example, a thorough inventory of customs and beliefs. Without spending years getting to know natives, their complex languages and habits, in intimate detail, the researcher could go after selected data that would yield a central armature or structure of the cultural whole. Rivers' "genealogical method," followed by Radcliffe-Brown's model of "social structure," provided this sort of shortcut. One could, it seemed, elicit kin terms without a deep understanding of local vernacular, and the range of necessary contextual knowledge was conveniently limited.

Fifth, since culture, seen as a complex whole, was always too much to master in a short research span, the new ethnographer intended to focus thematically on particular institutions. The aim was not to contribute to a complete inventory or description of custom but rather to get at the whole through one or more of its parts. I have noted the privilege given for a time to social structure. An individual life cycle, a ritual complex like the Kula ring or the Naven ceremony, could also serve, as could categories of behavior like economics, politics, and so on. In the predominantly synecdochic rhetorical stance of the new ethnography, parts were assumed to be microcosms or analogies of wholes. This setting of institutional foregrounds against cultural backgrounds in the portrayal of a coherent world lent itself to realist literary conventions.

Sixth, the wholes thus represented tended to be synchronic, prod-

ucts of short-term research activity. The intensive fieldworker could plausibly sketch the contours of an "ethnographic present"—the cycle of a
year, a ritual series, patterns of typical behavior. To introduce long-term
historical inquiry would have impossibly complicated the task of the
new-style fieldwork. Thus, when Malinowski and Radcliffe-Brown established their critique of the "conjectural history" of the diffusionists, it was
all too easy to exclude diachronic processes as objects of fieldwork, with
consequences that have by now been sufficiently denounced.

$$\curlywedge$$

These innovations served to validate an efficient ethnography based on
scientific participant observation. Their combined effect can be seen in
what may well be the tour de force of the new ethnography, Evans-
Pritchard's study *The Nuer*, published in 1940. Based on eleven months
of research conducted—as the book's remarkable introduction tells us—
in almost impossible conditions, Evans-Pritchard nonetheless was able
to compose a classic. He arrived in Nuerland on the heels of a punitive
military expedition and at the urgent request of the government of the
Anglo-Egyptian Sudan. He was the object of constant and intense suspicion. Only in the final few months could he converse at all effectively
with informants, who, he tells us, were skilled at evading his questions.
In the circumstances his monograph is a kind of miracle.

While advancing limited claims and making no secret of the constraints on his research, Evans-Pritchard manages to present his study as
a demonstration of the effectiveness of theory. He focuses on Nuer political and social "structure," analyzed as an abstract set of relations
between territorial segments, lineages, age sets, and other more fluid
groups. This analytically derived ensemble is portrayed against an "ecological" backdrop composed of migratory patterns, relationships with
cattle, notions of time and space. Evans-Pritchard sharply distinguishes
his method from what he calls "haphazard" (Malinowskian) documentation. *The Nuer* is not an extensive compendium of observations and
vernacular texts in the style of Malinowski's *Argonauts* and *Coral Gardens*. Evans-Pritchard argues rigorously that "facts can only be selected
and arranged in the light of theory." The frank abstraction of a political-
social structure offers the necessary framework. If I am accused of describing facts as exemplifications of my theory, he then goes on to note,
I have been understood (1969:261).

In *The Nuer* Evans-Pritchard makes strong claims for the power of scientific abstraction to focus research and arrange complex data. The book often presents itself as an argument rather than a description, but not consistently: its theoretical argument is surrounded by skillfully observed and narrated evocations and interpretations of Nuer life. These passages function rhetorically as more than simple "exemplification," for they effectively implicate readers in the complex subjectivity of participant observation. This may be seen in a characteristic paragraph, which progresses through a series of discontinuous discursive positions:

> It is difficult to find an English word that adequately describes the so-cial position of *diel* in a tribe. We have called them aristocrats, but do not wish to imply that Nuer regard them as of superior rank, for, as we have emphatically declared, the idea of a man lording it over others is repugnant to them. On the whole—we will qualify the statement later—the *diel* have prestige rather than rank and influence rather than power. If you are a *dil* of the tribe in which you live you are more than a simple tribesman. You are one of the owners of the country, its vil-lage sites, its pastures, its fishing pools and wells. Other people live there by virtue of marriage into your clan, adoption into your lineage, or of some other social tie. You are a leader of the tribe and the spear-name of your clan is invoked when the tribe goes to war. Whenever there is a *dil* in the village, the village clusters around him as a herd of cattle clusters around its bull.   (1969:215)

The first three sentences are presented as an argument about translation, but in passing they attribute to "Nuer" a stable set of attitudes. (I will have more to say later about this style of attribution.) Next, in the four sentences beginning "If you are a *dil* . . . ," the second-person construc-tion brings together reader and native in a textual participation. The final sentence, offered as a direct description of a typical event (which the reader now assimilates from the standpoint of a participant-observer), evokes the scene by means of Nuer cattle metaphors. In the paragraph's eight sentences an argument about translation passes through a fiction of participation to a metaphorical fusion of external and indigenous cultural descriptions. The subjective joining of abstract analysis and concrete ex-perience is accomplished.

Evans-Pritchard would later move away from the theoretical position of *The Nuer*, rejecting its advocacy of "social structure" as a privileged framework. Indeed each of the fieldwork "shortcuts" I enumerated earlier was and remains contested. Yet by their deployment in different combinations, the authority of the academic fieldworker-theorist was established in the years between 1920 and 1950. This peculiar amalgam of intense personal experience and scientific analysis (understood in this period as both "rite of passage" and "laboratory") emerged as a method: participant observation. Though variously understood, and now disputed in many quarters, this method remains the chief distinguishing feature of professional anthropology. Its complex subjectivity is routinely reproduced in the writing and reading of ethnographies.

$$\curlywedge$$

"Participant observation" serves as shorthand for a continuous tacking between the "inside" and "outside" of events: on the one hand grasping the sense of specific occurrences and gestures empathetically, on the other stepping back to situate these meanings in wider contexts. Particular events thus acquire deeper or more general significance, structural rules, and so forth. Understood literally, participant observation is a paradoxical, misleading formula, but it may be taken seriously if reformulated in hermeneutic terms as a dialectic of experience and interpretation. This is how the method's most persuasive recent defenders have restated it, in the tradition that leads from Wilhelm Dilthey, via Max Weber, to "symbols and meanings" anthropologists like Clifford Geertz. Experience and interpretation have, however, been accorded different emphases when presented as claims to authority. In recent years there has been a marked shift of emphasis from the former to the latter. This section and the one that follows will explore the rather different claims of experience and interpretation as well as their evolving interrelation.

The growing prestige of the fieldworker-theorist downplayed (without eliminating) a number of processes and mediators that had figured more prominently in previous methods. We have seen how language mastery was defined as a level of use adequate for amassing a discrete body of data in a limited period of time. The tasks of textual transcription and translation, along with the crucial dialogical role of interpreters and "privileged informants," were relegated to a secondary, sometimes even despised status. Fieldwork was centered in the *experience* of the participant-observing scholar. A sharp image, or narrative, made its appearance—that of an outsider entering a culture, undergoing a kind of initiation leading to "rapport" (minimally acceptance and empathy, but usually implying something akin to friendship). Out of this experience emerged, in unspecified ways, a representational text written by the participant-observer. As we shall see, this version of textual production obscures as much as it reveals. But it is worth taking seriously its principal assumption: that the experience of the researcher can serve as a unifying source of authority in the field.

Experiential authority is based on a "feel" for the foreign context, a kind of accumulated savvy and a sense of the style of a people or place. Such an appeal is frequently explicit in the texts of the early professional participant-observers. Margaret Mead's claim to grasp the underlying principle or ethos of a culture through a heightened sensitivity to form, tone, gesture, and behavioral styles, and Malinowski's stress on his life *in* the village and the comprehension derived from the "imponderabilia" of daily existence, are prominent cases in point. Many ethnographies— Colin Turnbull's *Forest People* (1962), for example—are still cast in the experiential mode, asserting prior to any specific research hypothesis or method the "I was there" of the ethnographer as insider and participant.

Of course it is difficult to say very much about experience. Like "intuition," it is something that one does or does not have, and its invocation often smacks of mystification. Nevertheless, one should resist the temptation to translate all meaningful experience into interpretation. If the two are reciprocally related, they are not identical. It makes sense to hold them apart, if only because appeals to experience often act as validations for ethnographic authority.

The most serious argument for the role of experience in the historical and cultural sciences is contained in the general notion of *Verstehen*.[6] In the influential view of Dilthey (1914) understanding others arises initially from the sheer fact of coexistence in a shared world; but this experiential world, an intersubjective ground for objective forms of knowledge, is precisely what is missing or problematic for an ethnographer entering an alien culture. Thus, during the early months in the field (and indeed throughout the research), what is going on is language learning in the broadest sense. Dilthey's "common sphere" must be established and reestablished, building up a shared experiential world in relation to which all "facts," "texts," "events," and their interpretations will be constructed.

---

6. The concept is sometimes too readily associated with intuition or empathy, but as a description of ethnographic knowledge *Verstehen* properly involves a critique of empathetic experience. The exact meaning of the term is a matter of debate among Dilthey scholars (Makreel 1975: 6–7).

This process of living one's way into an alien expressive universe is always subjective in nature, but it quickly becomes dependent on what Dilthey calls "permanently fixed expressions," stable forms to which understanding can return. The exegesis of these fixed forms provides the content of all systematic historical-cultural knowledge. Thus experience is closely linked to interpretation. (Dilthey is among the first modern theorists to compare the understanding of cultural forms to the reading of "texts.") But this sort of reading or exegesis cannot occur without an intense personal participation, an active at-homeness in a common universe.

Following Dilthey, ethnographic "experience" can be seen as the building up of a common, meaningful world, drawing on intuitive styles of feeling, perception, and guesswork. This activity makes use of clues, traces, gestures, and scraps of sense prior to the development of stable interpretations. Such piecemeal forms of experience may be classified as aesthetic and/or divinatory. There is space here for only a few words about such styles of comprehension as they relate to ethnography. An evocation of an aesthetic mode is conveniently provided by A. L. Kroeber's 1931 review of Mead's *Growing Up in New Guinea*.

> First of all, it is clear that she possesses to an outstanding degree the faculties of swiftly apperceiving the principal currents of a culture as they impinge on individuals, and of delineating these with compact pen-pictures of astonishing sharpness. The result is a representation of quite extraordinary vividness and semblance to life. Obviously, a gift of intellectualized but strong sensationalism underlies this capacity; also, obviously, a high order of intuitiveness, in the sense of the ability to complete a convincing picture from clues, for clues is all that some of her data can be, with only six months to learn a language and enter the inwards of a whole culture, besides specializing on child behavior. At any rate, the picture, so far as it goes, is wholly convincing to the reviewer, who unreservedly admires the sureness of insight and efficiency of stroke of the depiction.   (p. 248)

A different formulation is provided by Maurice Leenhardt in *Do Kamo: Person and Myth in the Melanesian World* (1937), a book that in its sometimes cryptic mode of exposition requires of its readers just the sort of aesthetic, gestaltist perception at which both Mead and Leenhardt excelled. Leenhardt's endorsement of this approach is significant since, given his extremely long field experience and profound cultivation of a

Melanesian language, his "method" cannot be seen as a rationalization for short-term ethnography: "In reality, our contact with another is not accomplished through analysis. Rather, we apprehend him in his entirety. From the outset, we can sketch our view of him using an outline or symbolic detail which contains a whole in itself and evokes the true form of his being. This latter is what escapes us if we approach our fellow creature using only the categories of our intellect" (p. 2).

Another way of taking experience seriously as a source of ethnographic knowledge is provided by Carlo Ginzburg's investigations (1980) into the complex tradition of divination. His research ranges from early hunters' interpretations of animal tracks, to Mesopotamian forms of prediction, to the deciphering of symptoms in Hippocratic medicine, to the focus on details in detecting art forgeries, to Freud, Sherlock Holmes, and Proust. These styles of nonecstatic divination apprehend specific circumstantial relations of meaning and are based on guesses, on the reading of apparently disparate clues and "chance" occurrences. Ginzburg proposes his model of "conjectural knowledge" as a disciplined, nongeneralizing, abductive mode of comprehension that is of central, though unrecognized, importance for the cultural sciences. It may be added to a rather meager stock of resources for understanding rigorously how one feels one's way into an unfamiliar ethnographic situation.

Precisely because it is hard to pin down, "experience" has served as an effective guarantee of ethnographic authority. There is, of course, a telling ambiguity in the term. Experience evokes a participatory presence, a sensitive contact with the world to be understood, a rapport with its people, a concreteness of perception. It also suggests a cumulative, deepening knowledge ("her ten years' experience of New Guinea"). The senses work together to authorize an ethnographer's real but ineffable feel or flair for "his" or "her" people. It is worth noting, however, that this "world," when conceived as an experiential creation, is subjective, not dialogical or intersubjective. The ethnographer accumulates personal knowledge of the field (the possessive form *my people* has until recently been familiarly used in anthropological circles, but the phrase in effect signifies "my experience").

木

It is understandable, given their vagueness, that experiential criteria of authority—unexamined beliefs in the "method" of participant observation, in the power of rapport, empathy, and so on—have come under criticism by hermeneutically sophisticated anthropologists. The second moment in the dialectic of experience and interpretation has received increasing attention and elaboration (see, for example, Geertz 1973, 1976; Rabinow and Sullivan 1979; Winner 1976; Sperber 1981). Interpretation, based on a philological model of textual "reading," has emerged as a sophisticated alternative to the now apparently naive claims for experiential authority. Interpretive anthropology demystifies much of what had previously passed unexamined in the construction of ethnographic narratives, types, observations, and descriptions. It contributes to an increasing visibility of the creative (and in a broad sense poetic) processes by which "cultural" objects are invented and treated as meaningful.

What is involved in looking at culture as an assemblage of texts to be interpreted? A classic account has been provided by Paul Ricoeur, in his essay "The Model of Text: Meaningful Action Considered as a Text" (1971). Clifford Geertz in a number of stimulating and subtle discussions has adapted Ricoeur's theory to anthropological fieldwork (1973: chap. 1). "Textualization" is understood as a prerequisite to interpretation, the constitution of Dilthey's "fixed expressions." It is the process through which unwritten behavior, speech, beliefs, oral tradition, and ritual come to be marked as a corpus, a potentially meaningful ensemble separated out from an immediate discursive or performative situation. In the moment of textualization this meaningful corpus assumes a more or less stable relation to a context; and we are familiar with the end result of this process in much of what counts as ethnographic thick description. For example, we say that a certain institution or segment of behavior is typical of, or a communicative element within, a surrounding culture, as when Geertz's famous cockfight (1973: chap. 15) becomes an intensely significant locus of Balinese culture. Fields of synecdoches are created in which parts are related to wholes, and by which the whole—what we often call culture—is constituted.

Ricoeur does not actually privilege part-whole relations and the specific sorts of analogies that constitute functionalist or realist representations. He merely posits a necessary relation between text and "world." A world cannot be apprehended directly; it is always inferred on the basis of its parts, and the parts must be conceptually and perceptually cut out of the flux of experience. Thus, textualization generates sense through a circular movement that isolates and then contextualizes a fact or event in its englobing reality. A familiar mode of authority is generated that claims to represent discrete, meaningful worlds. Ethnography is the interpretation of cultures.

A second key step in Ricoeur's analysis is his account of the process by which "discourse" becomes text. Discourse, in Emile Benveniste's classic discussion (1971:217–230), is a mode of communication in which the presence of the speaking subject and of the immediate situation of communication are intrinsic. Discourse is marked by pronouns (pronounced or implied) *I* and *you*, and by deictic indicators—*this, that, now,* and so on—that signal the present instance of discourse rather than something beyond it. Discourse does not transcend the specific occasion in which a subject appropriates the resources of language in order to communicate dialogically. Ricoeur argues that discourse cannot be interpreted in the open-ended, potentially public way in which a text is "read." To understand discourse "you had to have been there," in the presence of the discoursing subject. For discourse to become text it must become "autonomous," in Ricoeur's terms, separated from a specific utterance and authorial intention. Interpretation is not interlocution. It does not depend on being in the presence of a speaker.

The relevance of this distinction for ethnography is perhaps too obvious. The ethnographer always ultimately departs, taking away texts for later interpretation (and among those "texts" taken away we can include memories—events patterned, simplified, stripped of immediate context in order to be interpreted in later reconstruction and portrayal). The text, unlike discourse, can travel. If much ethnographic writing is produced in the field, actual composition of an ethnography is done elsewhere. Data constituted in discursive, dialogical conditions are appropriated only in textualized forms. Research events and encounters become field notes. Experiences become narratives, meaningful occurrences, or examples.

This translation of the research experience into a textual corpus separate from its discursive occasions of production has important consequences for ethnographic authority. The data thus reformulated need no longer be understood as the communication of specific persons. An informant's explanation or description of custom need not be cast in a form that includes the message "so and so said this." A textualized ritual or event is no longer closely linked to the production of that event by specific actors. Instead these texts become evidences of an englobing context, a "cultural" reality. Moreover, as specific authors and actors are severed from their productions, a generalized "author" must be invented to account for the world or context within which the texts are fictionally relocated. This generalized author goes under a variety of names: the native point of view, "the Trobrianders," "the Nuer," "the Dogon," as these and similar phrases appear in ethnographies. "The Balinese" function as author of Geertz's textualized cockfight.

The ethnographer thus enjoys a special relationship with a cultural origin or "absolute subject" (Michel-Jones 1978:14). It is tempting to compare the ethnographer with the literary interpreter (and this comparison is increasingly commonplace)—but more specifically with the traditional critic, who sees the task at hand as locating the unruly meanings of a text in a single coherent intention. By representing the Nuer, the Trobrianders, or the Balinese as whole subjects, sources of a meaningful intention, the ethnographer transforms the research situation's ambiguities and diversities of meaning into an integrated portrait. It is important, though, to notice what has dropped out of sight. The research process is separated from the texts it generates and from the fictive world they are made to call up. The actuality of discursive situations and individual interlocutors is filtered out. But informants—along with field notes—are crucial intermediaries, typically excluded from authoritative ethnographies. The dialogical, situational aspects of ethnographic interpretation tend to be banished from the final representative text. Not entirely banished, of course; there exist approved *topoi* for the portrayal of the research process.

We are increasingly familiar with the separate fieldwork account (a subgenre that still tends to be classified as subjective, "soft," or unscientific), but even within classic ethnographies, more-or-less stereotypic "fables of rapport" narrate the attainment of full participant-observer status. These fables may be told elaborately or in passing, naively or ironically. They normally portray the ethnographer's early ignorance, misunderstanding, lack of contact—frequently a sort of childlike status within the culture. In the *Bildungsgeschichte* of the ethnography these states of innocence or confusion are replaced by adult, confident, disabused knowledge. We may cite again Geertz's cockfight, where an early alienation from the Balinese, a confused "nonperson" status, is transformed by the appealing fable of the police raid with its show of complicity (1973:412–417). The anecdote establishes a presumption of connectedness, which permits the writer to function in his subsequent analyses as an omnipresent, knowledgeable exegete and spokesman. This interpreter situates the ritual sport as a text in a contextual world and brilliantly "reads" its cultural meanings. Geertz's abrupt disappearance into his rapport—the quasi-invisibility of participant observation—is paradigmatic. Here he makes use of an established convention for staging the attainment of ethnographic authority. As a result, we are seldom made aware of the fact that an essential part of the cockfight's construction as a text is dialogical—the author's talking face to face with particular Balinese rather than reading culture "over the[ir] shoulders" (1973:452).

木

Interpretive anthropology, by viewing cultures as assemblages of texts, loosely and sometimes contradictorally united, and by highlighting the inventive poesis at work in all collective representations, has contributed significantly to the defamiliarization of ethnographic authority. In its mainstream realist strands, however, it does not escape the general strictures of those critics of "colonial" representation who, since 1950, have rejected discourses that portray the cultural realities of other peoples without placing their own reality in jeopardy. In Michel Leiris' early critiques, by way of Jacques Maquet, Talal Asad, and many others, the unreciprocal quality of ethnographic interpretation has been called to account (Leiris 1950; Maquet 1964; Asad 1973). Henceforth neither the experience nor the interpretive activity of the scientific researcher can be considered innocent. It becomes necessary to conceive of ethnography not as the experience and interpretation of a circumscribed "other" reality, but rather as a constructive negotiation involving at least two, and usually more, conscious, politically significant subjects. Paradigms of experience and interpretation are yielding to discursive paradigms of dialogue and polyphony. The remaining sections of this chapter will survey these emergent modes of authority.

A discursive model of ethnographic practice brings into prominence the intersubjectivity of all speech, along with its immediate performative context. Benveniste's work on the constitutive role of personal pronouns and deixis highlights just these dimensions. Every use of *I* presupposes a *you,* and every instance of discourse is immediately linked to a specific, shared situation: no discursive meaning, then, without interlocution and context. The relevance of this emphasis for ethnography is evident. Fieldwork is significantly composed of language events; but language, in Bakhtin's words, "lies on the borderline between oneself and the other. The word in language is half someone else's." The Russian critic urges a rethinking of language in terms of specific discursive situations: "There are," he writes, "no 'neutral' words and forms—words and forms that can belong to 'no one'; language has been completely taken over, shot through with intentions and accents." The words of ethnographic writing, then, cannot be construed as monological, as the authoritative statement about, or interpretation of, an abstracted, textualized reality. The language of ethnography is shot through with other subjectivities and specific contextual overtones, for all language, in Bakhtin's view, is "a concrete heteroglot conception of the world" (1953:293).

Forms of ethnographic writing that present themselves in a "discursive" mode tend to be concerned with the representation of research contexts and situations of interlocution. Thus a book like Paul Rabinow's *Reflections on Fieldwork in Morocco* (1977) is concerned with the representation of a specific research situation (a series of constraining times and places) and (in somewhat fictionalized form) a sequence of individual interlocutors. Indeed an entire new subgenre of "fieldwork accounts" (of which Rabinow's is one of the most trenchant) may be situated within the discursive paradigm of ethnographic writing. Jeanne Favret-Saada's *Les mots, la mort, les sorts* (1977) is an insistent, self-conscious experiment with ethnography in a discursive mode.[7] She argues that the event of interlocution always assigns to the ethnographer a specific position in a web of intersubjective relations. There is no neutral standpoint in the power-laden field of discursive positionings, in a shifting matrix of relationships, of *I*'s and *you*'s.

A number of recent works have chosen to present the discursive processes of ethnography in the form of a dialogue between two individuals. Camille Lacoste-Dujardin's *Dialogue des femmes en ethnologie* (1977), Jean-Paul Dumont's *The Headman and I* (1978), and Marjorie Shostak's *Nisa: The Life and Words of a !Kung Woman* (1981) are noteworthy examples. The dialogical mode is advocated with considerable sophistication in two other texts. The first, Kevin Dwyer's theoretical reflections on the "dialogic of ethnology" springs from a series of interviews with a key informant and justifies Dwyer's decision to structure his ethnography in the form of a rather literal record of these exchanges (1977, 1979, 1982). The second work is Vincent Crapanzano's more complex *Tuhami: Portrait of a Moroccan*, another account of a series of interviews

---

7. Favret-Saada's book is translated as *Deadly Words* (1981); see esp. chap. 2. Her experience has been rewritten at another fictional level in Favret-Saada and Contreras 1981.

that rejects any sharp separation of an interpreting self from a textualized other (1980; see also 1977). Both Dwyer and Crapanzano locate ethnography in a process of dialogue where interlocutors actively negotiate a shared vision of reality. Crapanzano argues that this mutual construction must be at work in any ethnographic encounter, but that participants tend to assume that they have simply acquiesced to the reality of their counterpart. Thus, for example, the ethnographer of the Trobriand Islanders does not openly concoct a version of reality in collaboration with his informants but rather interprets the "Trobriand point of view." Crapanzano and Dwyer offer sophisticated attempts to break with this literary-hermeneutical convention. In the process the ethnographer's authority as narrator and interpreter is altered. Dwyer proposes a hermeneutics of "vulnerability," stressing the ruptures of fieldwork, the divided position and imperfect control of the ethnographer. Both Crapanzano and Dwyer seek to represent the research experience in ways that tear open the textualized fabric of the other, and thus also of the interpreting self.[8] (Here etymologies are evocative: the word *text* is related, as is well known, to weaving, *vulnerability* to rending or wounding, in this instance the opening up of a closed authority.)

The model of dialogue brings to prominence precisely those discursive—circumstantial and intersubjective—elements that Ricoeur had to exclude from his model of the text. But if interpretive authority is based on the exclusion of dialogue, the reverse is also true: a purely dialogical authority would repress the inescapable fact of textualization. While ethnographies cast as encounters between two individuals may successfully dramatize the intersubjective give-and-take of fieldwork and introduce a counterpoint of authorial voices, they remain *representations* of dialogue. As texts they may not be dialogical in structure, for as Steven Tyler (1981) points out, although Socrates appears as a decentered participant in his encounters, Plato retains full control of the dialogue. This displacement but not elimination of monological authority is characteristic of any

---

8. It would be wrong to gloss over the differences between Dwyer's and Crapanzano's theoretical positions. Dwyer, following Georg Lukács, translates dialogic into Marxian-Hegelian dialectic, thus holding out the possibility of a restoration of the human subject, a kind of completion in and through the other. Crapanzano refuses any anchor in an englobing theory, his only authority being that of the dialogue's writer, an authority undermined by an inconclusive narrative of encounter, rupture, and confusion. (It is worth noting that dialogic, as used by Bakhtin, is not reducible to dialectic.) For an early advocacy of dialogical anthropology see also Tedlock 1979.

approach that portrays the ethnographer as a discrete character in the fieldwork narrative. Moreover, there is a frequent tendency in fictions of dialogue for the ethnographer's counterpart to appear as a representative of his or her culture—a type, in the language of traditional realism—through which general social processes are revealed.[9] Such a portrayal reinstates the synecdochic interpretive authority by which the ethnographer reads text in relation to context, thereby constituting a meaningful "other" world. If it is difficult for dialogical portrayals to escape typifying procedures, they can, to a significant degree, resist the pull toward authoritative representation of the other. This depends on their ability fictionally to maintain the strangeness of the other voice and to hold in view the specific contingencies of the exchange.

⅄

To say that an ethnography is composed of discourses and that its different components are dialogically related is not to say that its textual form should be that of a literal dialogue. Indeed as Crapanzano recognizes in *Tuhami,* a third participant, real or imagined, must function as mediator in any encounter between two individuals (1980:147–151). The fictional dialogue is in fact a condensation, a simplified representation of complex multivocal processes. An alternative way of representing this discursive complexity is to understand the overall course of the research as an ongoing negotiation. The case of Marcel Griaule and the Dogon is well known and particularly clear-cut. Griaule's account of his instruction in Dogon cosmological wisdom, *Dieu d'eau* (1948a), was an early exercise in dialogical ethnographic narration. Beyond this specific interlocutory occasion, however, a more complex process was at work, for it is apparent that the content and timing of the Griaule team's long-term research, spanning decades, was closely monitored and significantly shaped by Dogon tribal authorities (see my discussion in Chapter 2). This is no longer news. Many ethnographers have commented on the ways, both subtle and blatant, in which their research was directed or circumscribed by their informants. In his provocative discus-

---

9. On realist "types" see Lukács 1964, passim. The tendency to transform an individual into a cultural enunciator may be observed in Marcel Griaule's *Dieu d'eau* (1948a). It occurs ambivalently in Shostak's *Nisa* (1981). For a discussion of this ambivalence and of the book's resulting discursive complexity see Clifford 1986b:103–109.

sion of this issue Ioan Lewis (1973) even calls anthropology a form of "plagiarism."

The give-and-take of ethnography is clearly portrayed in a 1980 study noteworthy for its presentation within a single work of both an interpreted other reality *and* the research process itself: Renato Rosaldo's *Ilongot Headhunting*. Rosaldo arrives in the Philippine highlands intent on writing a synchronic study of social structure; but again and again, over his objections, he is forced to listen to endless Ilongot narratives of local history. Dutifully, dumbly, in a kind of bored trance he transcribes these stories, filling notebook after notebook with what he considers disposable texts. Only after leaving the field, and after a long process of reinterpretation (a process made manifest in the ethnography), does he realize that these obscure tales have in fact provided him with his final topic, the culturally distinctive Ilongot sense of narrative and history. Rosaldo's experience of what might be called "directed writing" sharply poses a fundamental question: Who is actually the author of field notes?

The issue is a subtle one and deserves systematic study. But enough has been said to make the general point that indigenous control over knowledge gained in the field can be considerable, and even determining. Current ethnographic writing is seeking new ways to represent adequately the authority of informants. There are few models to look to, but it is worth reconsidering the older textual compilations of Boas, Malinowski, Leenhardt, and others. In these works the ethnographic genre has not coalesced around the modern interpretational monograph closely identified with a personal fieldwork experience. We can contemplate an ethnographic mode that is not yet authoritative in those specific ways that are now politically and epistemologically in question. These older assemblages include much that is actually or all but written by informants. One thinks of the role of George Hunt in Boas' ethnography, or of the fifteen "transcripteurs" listed in Leenhardt's *Documents néo-calédoniens* (1932).[10]

Malinowski is a complex transitional case. His ethnographies reflect

---

10. For a study of this mode of textual production see Clifford 1980a. See also in this context Fontana 1975, the introduction to Frank Russell, *The Pima Indians*, on the book's hidden coauthor, the Papago Indian José Lewis; Leiris 1948 discusses collaboration as coauthorship, as does Lewis 1973. For a forward-looking defense of Boas' emphasis on vernacular texts and his collaboration with Hunt see Goldman 1980.

the incomplete coalescence of the modern monograph. If he was centrally responsible for the welding of theory and description into the authority of the professional fieldworker, Malinowski nonetheless included material that did not directly support his own all-too-clear interpretive slant. In the many dictated myths and spells that fill his books, he published much data that he admittedly did not understand. The result was an open text subject to multiple reinterpretations. It is worth comparing such older compendiums with the recent model ethnography, which cites evidence to support a focused interpretation but little else.[11] In the modern, authoritative monograph there are, in effect, no strong voices present except that of the writer; but in *Argonauts* (1922) and *Coral Gardens* (1935) we read page after page of magical spells, none in any essential sense in the ethnographer's words. These dictated texts in all but their physical inscription are written by specific unnamed Trobrianders. Indeed any continuous ethnographic exposition routinely folds into itself a diversity of descriptions, transcriptions, and interpretations by a variety of indigenous "authors." How should these authorial presences be made manifest?

⅄

A useful—if extreme—standpoint is provided by Bakhtin's analysis of the "polyphonic" novel. A fundamental condition of the genre, he argues, is that it represents speaking subjects in a field of multiple discourses. The novel grapples with, and enacts, heteroglossia. For Bakhtin, preoccupied with the representation of nonhomogeneous wholes, there are no integrated cultural worlds or languages. All attempts to posit such abstract unities are constructs of monological power. A "culture" is, concretely, an open-ended, creative dialogue of subcultures, of insiders and outsiders, of diverse factions. A "language" is the interplay and struggle of regional dialects, professional jargons, generic commonplaces, the speech of different age groups, individuals, and so forth. For Bakhtin the polyphonic novel is not a tour de force of cultural or historical totalization (as realist critics such as Georg Lukács and Erich Auerbach have argued) but rather a carnivalesque arena of diversity. Bakhtin discovers a utopian tex-

---

11. James Fernandez' elaborate *Bwiti* (1985) is a self-conscious transgression of the tight, monographic form, returning to Malinowskian scale and reviving ethnography's "archival" functions.

tual space where discursive complexity, the dialogical interplay of voices, can be accommodated. In the novels of Dostoyevsky or Dickens he values precisely their resistance to totality, and his ideal novelist is a ventriloquist—in nineteenth-century parlance a "polyphonist." "He do the police in different voices," a listener exclaims admiringly of the boy Sloppy, who reads publicly from the newspaper in *Our Mutual Friend*. But Dickens the actor, oral performer, and polyphonist must be set against Flaubert, the master of authorial control, moving godlike among the thoughts and feelings of his characters. Ethnography, like the novel, wrestles with these alternatives. Does the ethnographic writer portray what natives think by means of Flaubertian "free indirect style," a style that suppresses direct quotation in favor of a controlling discourse always more or less that of the author? (Dan Sperber 1981, taking Evans-Pritchard as his example, has convincingly shown that *style indirect* is indeed the preferred mode of ethnographic interpretation.) Or does the portrayal of other subjectivities require a version that is stylistically less homogeneous, filled with Dickens' "different voices"?

Some use of indirect style is inevitable, unless the novel or ethnography is composed entirely of quotations, something that is theoretically possible but seldom attempted.[12] In practice, however, the ethnography and the novel have recourse to indirect style at different levels of abstraction. We need not ask how Flaubert knows what Emma Bovary is thinking, but the ability of the fieldworker to inhabit indigenous minds is always in doubt. Indeed this is a permanent, unresolved problem of ethnographic method. Ethnographers have generally refrained from ascribing beliefs, feelings, and thoughts to individuals. They have not, however, hesitated to ascribe subjective states to cultures. Sperber's analysis reveals how phrases such as "the Nuer think . . ." or "the Nuer sense of time" are fundamentally different from quotations or translations of indigenous discourse. Such statements are "without any specified speaker" and are literally equivocal, combining in a seamless way the ethnographer's affirmations with that of an informant or informants (1981:78). Ethnographies abound in unattributed sentences such as "The spirits re-

---

12. Such a project is announced by Evans-Pritchard in his introduction to *Man and Woman among the Azande* (1974), a late work that may be seen as a reaction against the closed, analytical nature of his own earlier ethnographies. His acknowledged inspiration is Malinowski. (The notion of a book entirely composed of quotations is a modernist dream associated with Walter Benjamin.)

turn to the village at night," descriptions of beliefs in which the writer assumes in effect the voice of culture.

At this "cultural" level ethnographers aspire to a Flaubertian omniscience that moves freely throughout a world of indigenous subjects. Beneath the surface, though, their texts are more unruly and discordant. Victor Turner's work provides a telling case in point, worth investigating more closely as an example of the interplay of monophonic and polyphonic exposition. Turner's ethnographies offer superbly complex portrayals of Ndembu ritual symbols and beliefs; and he has provided too an unusually explicit glimpse behind the scenes. In the midst of the essays collected in *The Forest of Symbols,* his third book on the Ndembu, Turner offers a portrait of his best informant, "Muchona the Hornet, Interpreter of Religion" (1967:131–150). Muchona, a ritual healer, and Turner are drawn together by their shared interest in traditional symbols, etymologies, and esoteric meanings. They are both "intellectuals," passionate interpreters of the nuances and depths of custom; both are uprooted scholars sharing "the quenchless thirst for objective knowledge." Turner compares Muchona to a university don; his account of their collaboration includes more than passing hints of a strong psychological doubling.

There is, however, a third present in their dialogue, Windson Kashinakaji, a Ndembu senior teacher at the local mission school. He brought Muchona and Turner together and shares their passion for the interpretation of customary religion. Through his biblical education he "acquired a flair for elucidating knotty questions." Newly skeptical of Christian dogma and missionary privileges, he is looking sympathetically at pagan religion. Kashinakaji, Turner tells us, "spanned the cultural distance between Muchona and myself, transforming the little doctor's technical jargon and salty village argot into a prose I could better grasp." The three intellectuals soon "settled down into a sort of daily seminar on religion." Turner's accounts of this seminar are stylized: "eight months of exhilarating quickfire talk among the three of us, mainly about Ndembu ritual." They reveal an extraordinary ethnographic "colloquy"; but significantly Turner does not make his three-way collaboration the crux of his essay. Rather he focuses on Muchona, thus transforming trialogue into dialogue and flattening a complex productive relation into the "portrait" of an "informant." (This reduction was in some degree required by the format of the book in which the essay first appeared, Joseph Casagrande's important 1960 collection of "Twenty Portraits of Anthropological Informants," *In the Company of Man.*)[13]

Turner's published works vary considerably in their discursive structure. Some are composed largely of direct quotations; in at least one essay Muchona is identified as the principal source of the overall interpretation; elsewhere he is invoked anonymously, for example as "a male ritual specialist" (1975:40–42, 87, 154–156, 244). Windson Kashinakaji is identified as an assistant and translator rather than as a source of interpretations. Overall, Turner's ethnographies are unusually polyphonic, openly built up from quotations ("According to an adept . . . ," or "One informant guesses . . ."). He does not, however, do the Ndembu in different voices, and we hear little "salty village argot." All the voices of the field have been smoothed into the expository prose of more-or-less interchangeable "informants." The staging of indigenous speech in an ethnography, the degree of translation and familiarization necessary, are complicated practical and rhetorical problems.[14] But Turner's works, by giving visible place to indigenous interpretations of custom, expose concretely these issues of textual dialogism and polyphony.

The inclusion of Turner's portrait of Muchona in *The Forest of Symbols* may be seen as a sign of the times. The Casagrande collection in which it originally appeared had the effect of segregating the crucial issue of relations between ethnographers and their indigenous collaborators. Discussion of these issues still had no place within scientific ethnographies, but Casagrande's collection shook the post-Malinowski professional taboo on "privileged informants." Raymond Firth on Pa Fenuatara, Robert Lowie on Jim Carpenter—a long list of distinguished anthropologists have described the indigenous "ethnographers" with whom they shared, to some degree, a distanced, analytic, even ironic view of custom. These individuals became valued informants because they understood, often with real subtlety, what an *ethnographic* attitude toward culture entailed. In Lowie's quotation of his Crow interpreter (and fellow "philologist") Jim Carpenter, one senses a shared outlook: "When you

---

13. For a "group dynamics" approach to ethnography see Yannopoulos and Martin 1978. For an ethnography explicitly based on native "seminars" see Jones and Konner 1976.

14. Favret-Saada's use of dialect and italic type in *Les mots, la mort, les sorts* (1977) is one solution among many to a problem that has long preoccupied realist novelists.

listen to the old men telling about their visions, you've just *got* to believe them" (Casagrande 1960:428). And there is considerably more than a wink and a nod in the story recounted by Firth about his best Tikopian friend and informant:

> On another occasion talk turned to the nets set for salmon trout in the lake. The nets were becoming black, possibly with some organic growth, and tended to rot easily. Pa Fenuatara then told a story to the crowd assembled in the house about how, out on the lake with his nets one time, he felt a spirit going among the net and making it soft. When he held the net up he found it slimy. The spirit had been at work. I asked him then if this was a traditional piece of knowledge that spirits were responsible for the deterioration of the nets. He answered, "No, my own thought." Then he added with a laugh, "My own piece of traditional knowledge." (Casagrande 1960:17–18)

The full methodological impact of Casagrande's collection remains latent, especially the significance of its accounts for the dialogical production of ethnographic texts and interpretations. This significance is obscured by a tendency to cast the book as a universalizing, humanist document revealing "a hall of mirrors . . . in full variety the endless reflected image of man" (Casagrande 1960: xii). In light of the present crisis in ethnographic authority, however, these revealing portraits spill into the oeuvres of their authors, altering the way they can be read. If ethnography is part of what Roy Wagner (1980) calls "the invention of culture," its activity is plural and beyond the control of any individual.

⋏

One increasingly common way to manifest the collaborative production of ethnographic knowledge is to quote regularly and at length from informants. (A striking example is *We Eat the Mines, the Mines Eat Us* (1979) by June Nash.) But such a tactic only begins to break up monophonic authority. Quotations are always staged by the quoter and tend to serve merely as examples or confirming testimonies. Looking beyond quotation, one might imagine a more radical polyphony that would "do the natives and the ethnographer in different voices"; but this too would only displace ethnographic authority, still confirming the final virtuoso orchestration by a single author of all the discourses in his or her text. In this sense Bakhtin's polyphony, too narrowly identified with the novel, is a domesticated heteroglossia. Ethnographic discourses are not, in any event, the speeches of invented characters. Informants are specific individuals with real proper names—names that can be cited, in altered form when tact requires. Informants' intentions are overdetermined, their words politically and metaphorically complex. If accorded an autonomous textual space, transcribed at sufficient length, indigenous statements make sense in terms different from those of the arranging ethnographer. Ethnography is invaded by heteroglossia.

This possibility suggests an alternate textual strategy, a utopia of plural authorship that accords to collaborators not merely the status of independent enunciators but that of writers. As a form of authority it must still be considered utopian for two reasons. First, the few recent experiments with multiple-author works appear to require, as an instigating force, the research interest of an ethnographer who in the end assumes an executive, editorial position. The authoritative stance of "giving voice" to the other is not fully transcended. Second, the very idea of plural authorship challenges a deep Western identification of any text's order with the intention of a single author. If this identification was less strong when Lafitau wrote his *Moeurs des sauvages ameriquains,* and if recent criticism has thrown it into question, it is still a potent constraint on ethnographic writing. Nonetheless, there are signs of movement in this domain. Anthropologists will increasingly have to share their texts, and sometimes their title pages, with those indigenous collaborators for whom the term *informants* is no longer adequate, if it ever was.

Ralph Bulmer and Ian Majnep's *Birds of My Kalam Country* (1977) is an important prototype. (Separate typefaces distinguish the juxtaposed contributions of ethnographer and New Guinean, collaborators for more than a decade.) Even more significant is the collectively produced 1974 study *Piman Shamanism and Staying Sickness (Ka:cim Mumkidag),* which lists on its title page, without distinction (though not, it may be noted, in alphabetical order): Donald M. Bahr, anthropologist; Juan Gregorio, shaman; David I. Lopez, interpreter; and Albert Alvarez, editor. Three of the four are Papago Indians, and the book is consciously designed "to transfer *to a shaman* as many as possible of the functions normally associated with authorship. These include the selection of an expository style, the duty to make interpretations and explanations, and the right to judge which things are important and which are not" (p. 7). Bahr, the initiator and organizer of the project, opts to share authority as much as possible. Gregorio, the shaman, appears as the principal source of the "theory of disease" that is transcribed and translated, at two separate levels, by Lopez and Alvarez. Gregorio's vernacular texts include compressed, often gnomic explanations, which are themselves interpreted and contextualized by Bahr's separate commentary. The book is unusual in its textual enactment of the interpretation of interpretations.

In *Piman Shamanism* the transition from individual enunciations to cultural generalizations is always visible in the separation of Gregorio's and Bahr's voices. The authority of Lopez, less visible, is akin to that of Windson Kashinakaji in Turner's work. His bilingual fluency guides Bahr through the subtleties of Gregorio's language, thus permitting the shaman "to speak at length on theoretical topics." Neither Lopez nor Alvarez appears as a specific voice in the text, and their contribution to the ethnography remains largely invisible to all but qualified Papagos, able to gauge the accuracy of the translated texts and the vernacular nuance of Bahr's interpretations. Alvarez' authority inheres in the fact that *Piman Shamanism* is a book directed at separate audiences. For most readers focusing on the translations and explanations the texts printed in Piman will be of little or no interest. The linguist Alvarez, however, corrected the transcriptions and translations with an eye to their use in language teaching, using an orthography he had developed for that purpose. Thus the book contributes to the Papagos' literary invention of their culture. This different reading, built into *Piman Shamanism,* is of more than local significance.

It is intrinsic to the breakup of monological authority that ethnographies no longer address a single general type of reader. The multiplication of possible readings reflects the fact that "ethnographic" consciousness can no longer be seen as the monopoly of certain Western cultures and social classes. Even in ethnographies lacking vernacular texts, indigenous readers will decode differently the textualized interpretations and lore. Polyphonic works are particularly open to readings not specifically intended. Trobriand readers may find Malinowski's interpretations tiresome but his examples and extended transcriptions still evocative. Ndembu will not gloss as quickly as European readers over the different voices embedded in Turner's works.

Recent literary theory suggests that the ability of a text to make sense in a coherent way depends less on the willed intentions of an originating author than on the creative activity of a reader. To quote Roland Barthes, if a text is "a tissue of quotations drawn from innumerable centers of culture," then "a text's unity lies not in its origin but in its destination" (1977:146, 148). The writing of ethnography, an unruly, multisubjective activity, is given coherence in particular acts of reading. But there is always a variety of possible readings (beyond merely individual appropriations), readings beyond the control of any single authority. One may approach a classic ethnography seeking simply to grasp the meanings that the researcher derives from represented cultural facts. Or, as I have suggested, one may also read against the grain of the text's dominant voice, seeking out other half-hidden authorities, reinterpreting the descriptions, texts, and quotations gathered together by the writer. With the recent questioning of colonial styles of representation, with the expansion of literacy and ethnographic consciousness, new possibilities for reading (and thus for writing) cultural descriptions are emerging.[15]

The textual embodiment of authority is a recurring problem for contemporary experiments in ethnography.[16] An older, realist mode—figured in the frontispiece to *Argonauts of the Western Pacific* and based on the construction of a cultural tableau vivant designed to be seen from a single vantage point, that of the writer and reader—can now be identified as only one possible paradigm for authority. Political and epistemological assumptions are built into this and other styles, assumptions the ethnographic writer can no longer afford to ignore. The modes of authority reviewed here—experiential, interpretive, dialogical, polyphonic—are available to all writers of ethnographic texts, Western and non-

---

15. An extremely suggestive model of polyphonic exposition is offered by the projected four-volume edition of the ethnographic texts written, provoked, and transcribed between 1896 and 1914 by James Walker on the Pine Ridge Sioux Reservation. Three titles have appeared so far, edited by Raymond J. DeMaille and Elaine Jahner: *Lakota Belief and Ritual* (1982a), *Lakota Society* (1982b), and *Lakota Myth* (1983). These engrossing volumes in effect reopen the textual homogeneity of Walker's classic monograph of 1917, *The Sun Dance,* a summation of the individual statements published here in translation. These statements by more than thirty named "authorities" complement and transcend Walker's synthesis. A long section of *Lakota Belief and Ritual* was written by Thomas Tyon, Walker's interpreter. The collection's fourth volume will be a translation of the writings of George Sword, an Oglala warrior and judge encouraged by Walker to record and interpret the traditional way of life. The first two volumes present the unpublished texts of knowledgeable Lakota and Walker's own descriptions in identical formats. Ethnography appears as a process of collective production. It is essential to note that the Colorado Historical Society's decision to publish these texts was stimulated by increasing requests from the Oglala community at Pine Ridge for copies of Walker's materials to use in Oglala history classes. (On Walker see also Clifford 1986a:15–17.)

16. For a very useful and complete survey of recent experimental ethnographies see Marcus and Cushman 1982; see also Webster 1982; Fahim 1982; and Clifford and Marcus 1986.

Western. None is obsolete, none pure: there is room for invention within each paradigm. We have seen how new approaches tend to rediscover discarded practices. Polyphonic authority looks with renewed sympathy to compendiums of vernacular texts—expository forms distinct from the focused monograph tied to participant observation. Now that naive claims to the authority of experience have been subjected to hermeneutic suspicion, we may anticipate a renewed attention to the subtle interplay of personal and disciplinary components in ethnographic research.

Experiential, interpretive, dialogical, and polyphonic processes are at work, discordantly, in any ethnography, but coherent presentation presupposes a controlling mode of authority. I have argued that this imposition of coherence on an unruly textual process is now inescapably a matter of strategic choice. I have tried to distinguish important styles of authority as they have become visible in recent decades. If ethnographic writing is alive, as I believe it is, it is struggling within and against these possibilities.

In fact the sociologist and his "object" form a couple where each one is to be interpreted through the other, and where the relationship *must itself be deciphered as a historical* moment.

—JEAN-PAUL SARTRE, *CRITIQUE DE LA RAISON DIALECTIQUE*

2. Power and Dialogue in Ethnography: Marcel Griaule's Initiation

M ARCEL GRIAULE cut a figure—self-confident and theatrical. He began his career as an aviator in the years just after the First World War. (Later, in 1946, as holder of the first chair in ethnology at the Sorbonne, he would lecture in his air force officer's uniform.) An energetic promotor of fieldwork, he portrayed it as the continuation—by scientific means— of a great tradition of adventure and exploration (1948c:119). In 1928, encouraged by Marcel Mauss and the linguist Marcel Cohen, Griaule spent a year in Ethiopia. He returned avid for new exploration, and his plans bore fruit two years later in the much-publicized Mission Dakar-Djibouti, which for twenty-one months traversed Africa from the Atlantic to the Red Sea along the lower rim of the Sahara. Largely a museum-collecting enterprise, the mission also undertook extended ethnographic sojourns in the French Sudan (now Mali), where Griaule first made contact with the Dogon of Sanga, and in Ethiopia (the region of Gondar), where the expedition spent five months. Among the mission's nine members (some coming and going at various points) were André Schaeffner, Deborah Lifchitz, and Michel Leiris, each of whom would make significant ethnographic contributions.

Thanks largely to the publicity sense of Georges-Henri Rivière—a well-connected jazz amateur engaged by Paul Rivet to reorganize the Trocadéro Ethnographic Museum—the Mission Dakar-Djibouti was patronized by Parisian high society. The Chamber of Deputies voted a special law of authorization, and Griaule and Rivière skillfully exploited the postwar vogue for things African in soliciting funds and personnel. The undertaking partook also of a certain technological bravado reminiscent of the period's famous expeditions, financed by Citroën, La Croisière Jaune, and La Croisière Noire, each a tour de force of mobility crossing whole continents by automobile. Griaule, an early airplane enthusiast, would be fascinated throughout his career by technological aids to ethnography: conventional and aerial photography, sound-recording devices, and even the project of a research boat–cum–laboratory for use on the Niger.

The mission's "booty," in Rivet and Rivière's term (1933:5), included among its many photos, recordings, and documents 3,500 objects destined for the Trocadéro museum, soon to become the Musée de l'Homme. The idea was only just winning acceptance in England and America, with Rockefeller funding of the International African Institute, that intensive field studies were in themselves enough to justify major subventions. Thus collecting was a financial necessity, and the mission brought back whatever authentic objects it could decently—and occasionally surreptitiously—acquire. The postwar passion for l'art nègre fostered a cult of the exotic artifact, and the carved figures and masks of West and Equatorial Africa satisfied perfectly a European fetishism nourished on cubist and surrealist aesthetics (see Chapter 4; also Jamin 1982a).

From 1935 to 1939 Griaule organized group expeditions to the French Sudan, Cameroun, and Chad, in which museum collecting played a lesser role. In annual or biannual visits to West Africa focusing increasingly on the Dogon, he worked out a distinctive ethnographic "method." For Griaule the collection of artifacts was part of the intensive documentation of a unified culture area, a region centering on the bend of the Niger, and particularly the home of the Bambara and Dogon, with whom he spent about three years over ten expeditions (Lettens 1971:504). Griaule's descriptions were cartographic and archaeological as well as ethnographic; he was concerned with variations in cultural traits, the history of migrations, and the overlay of civilizations in West Africa. Increasingly, however, his interests focused on synchronic cul-

tural patterns. Over time he established, to his own satisfaction, the existence of a ramified but coherent culture area he later portrayed as one
of three major divisions of sub-Saharan Africa: the Western Sudan, Bantu
Africa, and an intermediate zone in Cameroun and Chad. Each region
was characterized by a traditional *sophie* or *science*—a mode of knowledge inscribed in language, habitat, oral tradition, myth, technology, and
aesthetics. Griaule discerned common principles underlying the three
African epistemological fields, and this permitted him to use the Dogon
and their neighbors as privileged examples of *l'homme noir*—microcosms of "African" thought, civilization, philosophy, and religion. A
characteristic movement from parts to wholes to more inclusive wholes
was Griaule's basic mode of ethnographic representation. It mirrored,
and found confirmation in, Dogon styles of thought, with its encompass-
ing symbolic correspondences of microcosm and macrocosm, of body
and cosmos, of everyday details and patterns of myth.

A number of different approaches are subsumed under the general
label of the Griaule school.[1] The total project spans five decades, falling
roughly into two phases: before and after Ogotemmêli. In 1947, in a now
legendary series of interviews, the Dogon sage Ogotemmêli, apparently
acting on instructions from tribal elders, indoctrinated Griaule in the
deep wisdom of his people (Griaule 1948a). The first decade of research
at Sanga had been exhaustively *documentary* in character; now, with
access to the knowledge revealed by Ogotemmêli and other qualified
informants, the task became *exegetical*. Ogotemmêli's elaborate knowledge—reinforced and extended by other sources—appeared to provide
a potent "key" to Dogon culture (Griaule 1952c:548). Seen as a kind of
lived mythology, it provided a framework for grasping the Dogon world
as an integrated whole. This immanent structure—a "metaphysic," as
Griaule liked to call it—offered a purely indigenous organization of the
complex total social facts of Dogon life.

---

1. There are many personal variants, and one should distinguish the following standpoints: the "core" of the ongoing research on the Dogon and Bambara
is that of Marcel Griaule, Germaine Dieterlen, and Solange de Ganay. Genevieve
Calame-Griaule and Dominique Zahen contributed directly to the project, but
from distinct methodological standpoints. Jean-Paul Lebeuf, an early co-worker,
shared Griaule's general viewpoint, but his work was concentrated in Chad. Jean
Rouch, Luc de Heusch, and various later students remain ambivalently loyal to
the "tradition." Denise Paulme, Michel Leiris, and André Schaeffner, early contributors to the Dogon project, have always maintained a skeptical distance from
the undertaking and should not be included in the "school."

Full compilations of this *sagesse,* an enormously detailed system of symbolic and narrative correspondences, appeared only after Griaule's death in 1956. The masterpieces of the Griaule school's second period are *Le renard pâle,* written with his closest collaborator Germaine Dieterlen (1965), and *Ethnologie et langage: La parole chez les Dogon* by his daughter, the distinguished ethnolinguist Geneviève Calame-Griaule (1965). In these works one hears, as it were, two full chords of a Dogon symphony: a mythic explanation of the cosmos and a native theory of language and expressivity. More than just native explanations or theories, these superb compendia present themselves as coherent arts of life, sociomythic landscapes of physiology and personality, symbolic networks incarnate in an infinity of daily details.

The work of Griaule and his followers is one of the classic achievements of twentieth-century ethnography. Within certain areas of emphasis its depth of comprehension and completeness of detail are unparalleled. But given its rather unusual focus, the extreme nature of some of its claims, and the crucial, problematic role of the Dogon themselves as active agents in the long ethnographic process, Griaule's work has been subjected to sharp criticism from a variety of standpoints. Some have noted its idealistic bias and its lack of historical dynamism (Balandier 1960; Sarevskaja 1963). British social anthropologists have raised skeptical questions about Griaule's fieldwork, notably his lifelong reliance on translators and on a few privileged informants attuned to his interests (whose initiatory knowledge might not be readily generalizable to the rest of society). Followers of Malinowski or Evans-Pritchard have missed in Griaule's work any sustained attention to daily existence or politics as actually lived, and in general they are wary of a too perfectly ordered vision of Dogon reality (Richards 1967; Douglas 1967; Goody 1967).

Rereading the Dogon corpus closely, other critics have begun, on the basis of internal contradictions, to unravel the equilibrium of Dogon mythology and to question the processes by which an "absolute subject" (here a unified construct called "the Dogon") is constituted in ethnographic interpretation (Lettens 1971; Michel-Jones 1978). In the wake of colonialism, Griaule has been taken to task for his consistent preference for an African past over a modernizing present. Africans have criticized him for essentializing traditional cultural patterns and repressing the role of individual invention in the elaboration of Dogon myth (Hountondji 1977). After 1950 Griaule's work resonated strongly with the nègritude movement, particularly with Léopold Senghor's evocation of an African essence. But as Senghor's brand of negritude has yielded to Aimé Cé-saire's more syncretic, impure, inventive conception of cultural identity, Griaule's African metaphysic has begun to seem an ahistorical, idealized alter ego to a totalizing occidental humanism.

It is impossible here to evaluate many of the specific criticisms lev-eled at Griaule, especially in the absence of detailed restudy of the Dogon. A few methodological warnings are necessary, however, for approaching such a contested oeuvre. The historian of fieldwork is ham-pered by limited and foreshortened evidence; it is always difficult, if not impossible, to know what happened in an ethnographic encounter. (This uncertainty is at least partly responsible for the fact that the history of anthropology has tended to be a history of theory, even though the modern discipline has defined itself by reference to its distinct "method.") Usually, as in Griaule's case, one must rely heavily on the ethnographer's own ex post facto narrations, accounts that serve to confirm his authority. One can also draw on his methodological prescriptions and those of his collaborators; but these too tend to be overly systematic rationalizations composed after the fact. A scattering of relevant journals and memoirs can help somewhat (Leiris 1934; Rouch 1978b; Paulme 1977), as can a critical reading of published ethnographies and field notes—where avail-able (and comprehensible).[2] Direct evidence of the interpersonal dynam-ics and politics of research, however, is largely absent. Moreover, there is an enormous gap in all histories of fieldwork: the indigenous "side" of the story. How was the research process understood and influenced by informants, by tribal authorities, by those who did not cooperate (cf. Lewis 1973)? Griaule's story has the merit of making this part of the encounter inescapable. Yet our knowledge of Dogon influences on the ethnographic process remains fragmentary.

It is simplistic to tax Griaule with projecting onto the Dogon a sub-jective vision, with developing a research method for eliciting essentially what he was looking for (Lettens 1971:397, passim). Even the more cred-

---

2. Anyone who has tried to reinterpret field notes will know it is a problem-atic enterprise. They may be gnomic, heteroglot shorthand notes to oneself, or the sorts of "field notes" often quoted in published ethnographies—formulated summaries of events, observations, and conversations recomposed after the fact. It is well-nigh impossible to disentangle the interpretive processes at work as field notes move from one level of textualization to the next. Griaule's 173 richly detailed "fiches de terrain" for the crucial interviews with Ogotemmêli (Griaule 1946) are clearly the product of at least one rewriting, eliminating specific lin-guistic problems, the presence of the translator Kogem, and so on.

ible claim that Griaule overstressed certain parts of Dogon reality at the expense of others assumes the existence of a natural entity called Dogon culture apart from its ethnographic inventions. Even if it is true that key informants became "Griaulized," that Griaule himself was "Dogonized," that Ogotemmêli's wisdom was that of an individual "theologian," and that the "secret," initiatory nature of the revealed knowledge was systematically exaggerated, even if other priorities and methods would certainly have produced a different ethnography, it does not follow that Griaule's version of the Dogon is false. His writings, and those of his associates, express a Dogon truth—a complex, negotiated, historically contingent truth specific to certain relations of textual production. The historian asks *what kind* of truth Griaule and the Dogon he worked with produced, in what dialogical conditions, within what political limits, in what historical climate.

Masterpieces like *Le renard pâle* and *Ethnologie et langage* are elaborate inventions authored by a variety of subjects, European and African. These compendiums do not represent the way "the Dogon" think: both their enormous complexity and the absence of female informants cast doubt on any such totalizing claim. Nor is their "deep" knowledge an interpretive key to Dogon reality for anyone beyond the ethnographer and a small number of native "intellectuals." To say that these Dogon truths are specific inventions (rather than parts or distortions of "Dogon culture"), however, is to take them seriously as textual constructions, avoiding both celebration and polemic.

The Griaule tradition offers one of the few fully elaborated alternatives to the Anglo-American model of intensive participant observation. For this reason alone it is important for the history of twentieth-century ethnography—particularly with the recent discovery in America of "long-term field research" (Foster et al. 1979). Griaule's writings are also important (and here we must separate the man from his "school") for their unusual directness in portraying research as inherently agonistic, theatrical, and fraught with power. His work belongs manifestly to the colonial period. Thanks to Griaule's dramatic flair and fondness for overstatement, we can perceive clearly certain key assumptions, roles, and systems of metaphors that empowered ethnography during the thirties and forties.

⅄

One cannot speak of a French "tradition" of fieldwork, as one refers (perhaps too easily) to British and American schools. Nonetheless, if only by contrast, Griaule's ethnography does appear to be peculiarly French. We can suggest this rather elusive quality by evoking briefly two influential precursors. In Paris the most important advocates of fieldwork during the 1920s were Marcel Mauss and Maurice Delafosse, who collaborated with Lucien Lévy-Bruhl and Rivet to found the Institut d'Ethnologie. Here after 1925 a generation of "Africanist" ethnographers was trained.

In the first three decades of the century Black Africa was coming into focus, separated from the "oriental" Maghreb. By 1931, when the *Journal de la Société des Africanistes* was founded, it had become possible to speak of a field called "Africanism" (modeled on the older synthetic discipline of orientalism). The fashionable vogue for *l'art nègre* and black music contributed to the formation of a cultural object, a *civilisation* about which synthetic statements could be made. Maurice Delafosse's *Noirs de l'Afrique* and *L'ame noir* contributed to this development, along with the translated writings of Frobenius. Griaule's work unfolded within the Africanist paradigm, moving associatively from specific studies of particular populations to generalizations about *l'homme noire*, African civilization, and metaphysics (Griaule 1951, 1953).

At the Institut d'Ethnologie a regular stream of colonial officers studied ethnographic method as part of their training at the Ecole Coloniale, where Delafosse was a popular teacher before his death in 1926. As a veteran of extended duty in West Africa, Delafosse knew African languages and cultures intimately. When his health was undermined by the rigors of constant travel and research, he retired to France, becoming the first professor of Black African languages at the Ecole des Langues Orientales. A scholar of great erudition, he made contributions to African history, ethnography, geography, and linguistics. At the Ecole Coloniale, where Africans had long been considered childlike inferiors, he taught the fundamental equality (though not the similarity) of races. Different milieux produce different civilizations. If the Africans are technically and materially backward, this is a historical accident; their art, their moral life, their religions are nonetheless fully developed and worthy of esteem. He urged his students toward ethnography and the mastery of indigenous languages. His authority was concrete experience, his persona that of the *broussard*—the man of the back country, tough-minded, iconoclastic, humane, impatient with hierarchy and the artifices of polite society (Delafosse 1909; cf. Deschamps 1975:97). For a generation of young, liberally inclined colonial officers he represented an authentic, concrete way to "know" Africa and to communicate its fascination.

After Delafosse's death the principle influence on the first generation

of professional fieldworkers in France was exerted by another charis-
matic teacher, Marcel Mauss. Though he never undertood fieldwork,
Mauss consistently deplored France's backwardness in this domain
(Mauss 1913). At the Institut d'Ethnologie he taught a yearly course (ethnographie descriptive) specifically geared to fieldwork methods. Mauss
was anything but an abstract, bookish scholar; anyone who looks at his
"Techniques du corps" (1934) can see an acute power of observation, an
interest in the concrete and the experimental (cf. Condominas 1972a).
Mauss urged all his students toward ethnography; between 1925 and
1940 the Institut sponsored more than a hundred field trips (Karady
1981:176). Unlike W. H. R. Rivers, Malinowski, and later Griaule,
whose teaching reflected their own experiences in the field, he did not
propound a distinct research "method"; but if he lacked intimate experience, he did not feel compelled to rationalize or justify his own practice. Drawn from the fieldwork traditions of various nations, his course
was an inventory, classification, and critique of possible methods. Mauss
provided a sense of the complexity of "total social facts" (Mauss
1924:274) and the different means by which descriptions, recordings,
textual accounts, and collections of artifacts could be constituted. His
wide-ranging Manuel d'ethnographie (1947), a compilation of course
notes brought together by Denise Paulme shortly before his death, makes
it clear that the idea of a privileged approach was quite foreign to him.

Mauss strongly supported the general trend of modern academic
fieldwork, urging "the professional ethnographer" to adopt "the intensive
method" (1947:13). Serious comparative work depended on the completion of full local descriptions. Although the Manuel's recommendations
reflect a close knowledge of American and British techniques, there is no
emphasis on individual participant-observation. Mauss endorses team research; overall his approach is documentary rather than experiential and
hermeneutic.

This documentary concern would be reflected in the introduction to
Griaule's first major field monograph: "This work presents documents
relative to the Masks of the Dogon, collected during research trips among
the cliffs of Bandiagara" (Griaule 1938:vii).[3] It is hard to imagine an account in the Malinowskian tradition beginning in this way. Although
Griaule does considerably more in Masques Dogons than simply display

---

3. Here and throughout this book translations of foreign works are my own
unless I cite a published English translation.

collected documents, the metaphor reveals a particular empirical style (cf. Leenhardt 1932; Clifford 1982a:138–141). For Mauss, who accepted an older division of labor between the man in the field and the theorist at home, description should never be governed by explanatory concerns (Mauss 1947:389). To provide the kind of information useful to a comparative sociology, the ethnographer should avoid building too much implicit explanation into the ethnographic data in the process of its constitution. Mauss gave no special status to the idea that a synthetic portrait of a culture (something for him massively overdetermined) could be produced through the research experience of an individual subject or built around the analysis of a typical or central institution. His limiting notion of "total social facts" led him rather to recommend the deployment of multiple documentary methods by a variety of specialized observers. Working at a higher level of abstraction, the sociologist could perhaps "glimpse, measure, and hold in equilibrium" (1924:279) the different strata of "total" facts—technological, aesthetic, geographical, demographic, economic, juridical, linguistic, religious, historical, and intercultural. But the task of the ethnographer, whether alone or in a research team, was to amass as complete a corpus as possible: texts, artifacts, maps, photographs, and so forth—"documents" precisely localized and covering a broad range of cultural phenomena. Fieldworkers should construct "series and not panoplies" (p. 21). Mauss used old terms precisely: a *panoply* is a full complement of arms, a suit of armor with all its accouterments. The term suggests a functional integration of parts deployed and displayed around a coherent, effective body. Mauss did not see society or culture this way. One should be wary of reducing his concept of total social facts (reminiscent of Freud's "overdetermination") to a functionalist notion of the interrelation of parts.

Mauss's elusive concept nevertheless articulated a fundamental predicament for twentieth-century ethnographers. If every "fact" is susceptible to multiple encoding, making sense in diverse contexts and implicating in its comprehension the "total" ensemble of relations that constitutes the society under study, then this assumption can serve as encouragement to grasp the ensemble by focusing on one of its parts. Indeed this is what fieldworkers have always done, building up social wholes ("culture" in the American tradition) through a concentration on significant elements. Many different approaches have emerged: the focus on key "institutions" (Malinowski's Trobriand Kula, Evans-Pritchard's Azande witchcraft); the bringing to the foreground of "totalizing cultural performances" (Baldwin Spencer and F. Gillen's Arunta initiation, Gregory Bateson's latmul Naven, Geertz's Balinese cockfight); the identification of privileged armatures to which the whole of culture could be related (Rivers' "genealogical method" and Radcliffe-Brown's "social structure"); or even Griaule's late conception of initiatory knowledge as the key to a unified representation of West African cultures. In different ways the new generation of academic fieldworkers were all looking for what Griaule would recommend, defending his practice of teamwork in the field—a "rapid, sure method" able to grasp synthetically an over-determined cultural reality (1933:8). Thus Mauss's belief that the totality of society is implicit in its parts or organizing structures may appear as a kind of enabling charter for a broad range of fieldwork tactics (approaches to social representation in the rhetorical mode of synecdoche), without which relatively short-term professional fieldwork would be questionable—particularly research aiming at portrayals of whole cultures. Since one cannot study everything at once, one must be able to highlight parts or attack specific problems in the confidence that they evoke a wider context.

There is another side to total social facts: the idea is ambiguous and finally troubling. If it legitimates partial cultural descriptions, it offers no guidance as to which code, key, or luminous example is to be preferred. Like Nietzsche's vision of infinite interpretations, Mauss's idea sees social reality and the moral world as constructed in many possible ways, none of which may be privileged. Modern ethnography took shape in a shattered world haunted by nihilism, and Mauss in his portrayals of the constitution of collective order was acutely aware of the possibility of disorder (see Chapter 4). *The Gift* is an allegory of reconciliation and reciprocity in the wake of the First World War. As is well known, the war had a devastating impact on Mauss; its sequel in 1940 would deprive him of the will to work and think. With the breakdown of evolutionist master narratives, the relativist science of culture worked to rethink the world as a dispersed whole, composed of distinct, functioning, and inter-related cultures. It reconstituted social and moral wholeness plurally. If synecdochic ethnography argued, in effect, that "cultures" hold together, it did so in response to a pervasive modern feeling, linking the Irishman Yeats to the Nigerian Achebe, that "things fall apart."

For a committed socialist like Mauss, the study of society was a refusal of nihilism; its constructions of social wholeness served moral and political as well as scientific ends. But he was too clear-sighted and knowledgeable to espouse any sovereign method for the constitution of totalities. He contented himself with a kind of gay science; he was generous, rather than, like Nietzsche, sardonic. He presented a generation of ethnographers with an astonishing repertoire of objects for study and ways to put the world together: ethnography was a dipping of different nets in the teeming ocean, each catching its own sort of fish. Schooled in Cushing's work, he knew that the task of representing a culture was potentially endless. "You say you have spent two and a half years with one tribe," he remarked to Meyer Fortes. "Poor man, it will take you twenty years to write it up" (Fortes 1973:284).

Mauss's *Manuel* was not a *méthode* but an enormous checklist; thus one cannot speak of a "Maussian" as one can of a "Malinowskian" or a "Boasian" ethnography. (This fact may explain, in part, why French fieldwork has never assumed a distinct identity and has, in effect, been invisible to anthropologists of other traditions.) His students diverged markedly. Alfred Métraux pursued a distinguished career of American-style participant observation. Michel Leiris, while making original contributions to Dogon and Ethiopian ethnography, never stopped questioning the subjective conflicts and political constraints of cross-cultural study as such. Maurice Leenhardt, whose late entry into the University of Paris was much encouraged by Mauss, represented an older style of research whose authority was rooted in years of missionary work rather than in academic training. Charles LeCoeur, who attended Malinowski's seminar at the London School of Economics, lived among the Teda, learned their language, and formally, at least, conducted fieldwork à l'anglais. Of Mauss's other students—virtually every major French ethnographer before 1950—only Griaule developed a systematic method and a distinct tradition of research.

人

Two loose metaphoric structures govern Griaule's conception of fieldwork: a *documentary* system (governed by images of collection, observation, and interrogation) and an *initiatory* complex (in which dialogical processes of education and exegesis come to the fore). Griaule himself presented the two approaches as complementary, each requiring and building on the other. One can, however, discern a shift from the documentary to the initiatory as his career progressed and as his personal involvement with Dogon modes of thought and belief deepened. For the sake of analytic clarity I shall consider the approaches separately. It

Marcel Griaule developing photographic plates. Sanga,
October–November 1931.

should be understood, however, that both are attempts to account for a
complicated, evolving ethnographic experience—an experience traversed by influences, historical and intersubjective, beyond the control
of Griaule's metaphors.

The notion that ethnography was a process of collection dominated
the Mission Dakar-Djibouti, with its museographical emphasis. The ethnographic object—be it a tool, statue, or mask—was understood to be a
peculiarly reliable "witness" to the truth of an alien society. The Maussian
rationale is evident in a set of "Instructions for Collectors" distributed by
the mission.

> Because of the need that has always driven men to imprint the
> traces of their activity on matter, nearly all phenomena of collective

life are capable of expression in given objects. A collection of objects systematically acquired is thus a rich gathering of admissible evidence [*pièces à conviction*]. Their collection creates archives more revealing and sure than written archives, since these are authentic, autonomous objects that cannot have been fabricated for the needs of the case [*les besoins de la cause*] and that thus characterize types of civilizations better than anything else. (Mauss 1931:6–7)

"Dead," decontextualized objects, the brochure goes on to argue, can be restored to "life" by surrounding "documentation" (descriptions, drawings, photos). The links tying any object or institution to the "ensemble of society" can thus be reconstituted and the truth of the whole elicited scientifically from any one of its parts.

The recurring juridical metaphors (*pièces à conviction, besoins de la cause*) are revealing; if all the parts of a culture can in principle be made to yield the whole, what justifies an ethnographer's particular selection of revealing "evidence"? Some "witnesses" must be more reliable than others. A corollary of the value placed on objects as "authentic and autonomous," not "fabricated for the needs of the case," is the assumption that other forms of evidence, the "archives" composed on the basis of personal observation, description, and interpretation, are less pure, more infected with the contingent ethnographic encounter, its clash of interests, and partial truths. For Griaule fieldwork was a perpetual struggle for *control* (in the political and scientific senses) of this encounter.

Griaule assumed that the opposing interests of ethnographer and native could never be entirely harmonized. Relations sometimes romanticized by the term *rapport* were really negotiated settlements, outcomes of a continuous push and pull determining what could and could not be known of the society under study. The outsider was always in danger of losing the initiative, of acquiescing in a superficial modus vivendi. One could not learn what was systematically hidden in a culture simply by becoming a temporary member of a common moral community. It could be revealed only by a kind of violence: the ethnographer must keep up the pressure (Griaule 1957:14). Griaule may have had no choice: in Sudanese societies, with their long processes of initiation, one had either to force the revelation of occult traditions or to be on the scene for decades.

Of all the possible avenues to hidden truths the least reliable was speech—what informants actually said in response to questions. This was due not merely to conscious lying and resistance to inquiry; it followed from dramatistic assumptions that were a leitmotif of his work. For Griaule every informant's self-presentation (along with that of the ethnographer) was a dramatization, a putting forward of certain truths and a holding back of others. In penetrating these conscious or unconscious disguises the fieldworker had to exploit whatever advantages, whatever sources of power, whatever knowledge not based on interlocution he or she could acquire (1957:92).

Griaule looked initially to visual observation as a source of information that could be obtained without depending on uncertain oral collaboration and could provide the edge needed to provoke, control, and verify confessional discourses. Accustomed to actually looking down on things (his first job in the air force had been that of an aerial spotter and navigator), Griaule was particularly conscious of the advantages of overview, of the precise mapping of habitats and their surrounding terrain. This visual preoccupation, apparent in all his methodological works, emerges with disconcerting clarity in Les Saô légendaires, his popular account of ethnographic and archaeological work in Chad (1943):

> Perhaps it's a quirk acquired in military aircraft, but I always resent having to explore an unknown terrain on foot. Seen from high in the air, a district holds few secrets. Property is delineated as if in India ink; paths converge in critical points; interior courtyards yield themselves up; the inhabited jumble comes clear. With an aerial photograph the components of institutions fall into place as a series of things disassembled, and yielding. Man is silly: he suspects his neighbor, never the sky; inside the four walls, palisades, fences, or hedges of an enclosed space he thinks all is permitted. But all his great and small intentions, his sanctuaries, his garbage, his careless repairs, his ambitions for growth appear on an aerial photograph. In a village I know in the French Sudan, I recall having discovered four important sanctuaries at the cost of much hard land travel, along with platitudes, flattery, payoffs, and unredeemable promises. Seventeen sanctuaries appeared on an aerial photo thanks to the millet pulp spread out on their domes. All at once the openness of my informants increased to an unbelievable degree. With an airplane, one fixed the underlying structure both of topography and of minds.   (pp. 61–62)

It is not clear whether this passage should be read as enthusiastic publicity for a new scientific method (on aerial photography see Griaule 1937)

Marcel Griaule photographing from cliff top near Sanga,
October–November 1931. André Schaeffner holds him by
the ankles.

or as a somewhat disturbing fantasy of observational power. Griaule seldom had an airplane at his disposal in the field, but he adopted its panoptic viewpoint as a habit and a tactic.

The simple fact of drawing up a map could give an overview and
initial mastery of the culture inscribed on the land. Recounting the excavation of ancient funeral remains against the wishes of local inhabitants who considered the graves to be ancestral, Griaule provides an
extraordinary phenomenology of the white outsider's struggle to maintain
an edge in dealings with the native council of elders. Because their oral
tradition is a key source of information for where exactly to dig, they
must be induced to talk (1943:58). Griaule is alive to all manner of signs
in behavior and especially in the terrain that may eventually serve as

entrees into the hidden world of custom. His questions aim to provoke and confuse, to elicit unguarded responses. Having arduously mapped the landholding and habitations of the region, he is able to pose unexpectedly acute queries about incongruous sites that are in fact sacred—altars, a strange door in a wall, a curious topographic feature—traces of secrets written on the surface of the habitat. The map-making outsider holds a disconcerting authority: he seems already to know where everything is. Revelations follow. New sites are excavated.

For Griaule a map is not only a plan of work but "a base for combat" where "every inscribed position is a conquered position" (1943:66). Throughout his account he is conscious of the aggressive, disruptive power of the gaze. Investigation, looking into something, is never neutral. The researchers feel themselves under surveillance: "Hundreds of eyes follow us. We're in full view of the village; in every crack in the wall, behind every granary, an eye is attentive" (p. 64). In opposition stands their scientific observation: "To dig a hole is to commit an indiscretion, to open an eye onto the past" (p. 68). Every inquest is "a siege to be organized" (p. 60). This particular war of gazes ends with a nominal truce, a compromise permitting the collection of certain artifacts while a few especially sacred ones are spared (p. 76). The theatrical tug of war actually ends with an arrangement entirely to the advantage of the outsiders, who are able to complete their excavation, remove numerous relics, and establish ground rules for later intensive ethnography.

For Griaule the exhaustive documentation of a culture was a precondition for plumbing its "secrets" through long-term, controlled interrogation of informants. He did not, of course, believe that complete description was possible; but often—especially when defending his practice of teamwork against the Anglo-American model of individual participant observation—he would betray panoptical aspirations. His favorite example was the problem of describing a Dogon funeral ceremony, a spectacle involving hundreds of participants. An individual participant-observer would be lost in the melee, jotting down more or less arbitrary impressions, and with little grasp of the whole.

Griaule argues that the only way to document such an event adequately is to deploy a team of observers. He offers, characteristically, a map of the performance site and a set of tactics for its coverage, proceeding rather in the manner of a modern television crew reporting on an American political convention (1933:11; 1957:47–52). Observer number one is stationed atop a cliff not far from the village square with the job of photographing and noting the large-scale movements of the rite; number two is among the menstruating women to one side; three mixes with a band of young torch bearers; four observes the group of musicians; five is on the roof tops "charged with surveillance in the wings with their thousand indiscretions, and going frequently, along with number six, to the dead man's house in search of the latest news" (1957:49). Number seven observes the reactions of the women and children to the masked dances and ritual combats taking place at center stage. All observers note the exact times of their observations so that a synthetic portrait of the ritual can be constructed.

This only begins the task of adequate documentation. The synoptic outline thus constructed will later be augmented and corrected by processes of "verification" and "commentary." Witnesses must be asked for their explanations of obscure gestures. "Holes" in the fabric will be filled in, including those that are due to contingencies of a specific performance—the absence or presence of particular groups or individuals, the forgetfulness of the actors, or any divergences from the rite's "ideal harmony" (1957:50). Slowly, over a number of years, building on repeat performances if possible, an ideal type of the rite will be laboriously constructed. But this enormous "dossier" spills out in many directions, and "each part of the observation becomes the core of an enquiry that sooner or later will furnish a vast network of information" (p. 51).

Griaule's *Méthode de l'ethnographie,* from which this account is drawn, provides a rationalized version of his own research practice. It is often unclear whether the methods propounded are those Griaule actually used or ideal recommendations based on a rather more messy experience. But the *Méthode* gives a good sense of the overall assumptions and parameters of his fieldwork. In Sanga the Mission Dakar-Djibouti had in fact encountered a Dogon funeral, a dramatic, confusing rite featuring spectacular performances by masked dancers. Griaule set about its documentation: his subsequent work would center on the secret society of masks, and various of his co-workers contributed related studies (Leiris 1948; De Ganay 1941; Dieterlen 1941). By dint of repeated visits and intensive collaborative work an organized corpus of "documents" was built up.

Griaule's focus on the institution of masks did not involve a synecdochic representation of culture as a whole in the functionalist tradition (using the mask society as either an ideal-typical "institution" or its rituals as "totalizing cultural performances"). Rather, working out from this dense cluster of total social facts, he and his associates constructed a "vast network of information" as a context and control for what natives themselves said about their culture. Initially, in his "documentary" phase, Griaule used the explications of informants as commentaries on observed behavior and collected artifacts; but this attitude would change, especially after Ogotemmêli: once properly tested and qualified, informants could be trusted with research tasks. With proper control they could become regular auxiliaries and, in effect, members of the team. The network of observation and documentation could thus be dramatically extended (Griaule 1957:61–64). Teamwork was an efficient way to deal with total social facts, to produce a full documentation on a multiplicity of subjects treated in diverse manners.

As conceived by Griaule the team was much more than a makeshift collaboration of individuals. It embodied the principle underlying all modern inquiry: specialization and the division of labor. Because social reality is too complex for the single researcher, he must "rely on other specialists and try to form with them a thinking group, an element of combat, a tactical unit of research in which each person, while holding to his own personal qualities, knows he is an intelligent cog of a machine in which he is indispensable but without which he is nothing" (1957:26). Some of Griaule's early co-workers, like Leiris, Schaeffner, and Paulme, did not find enduring places within this productive mechanism. Leiris's scandalous L'Afrique fantôme (1934) was a clear breach of discipline. But others (De Ganay, Dieterlen, Lebeuf, and Calame-Griaule), if not precisely "intelligent cogs," worked freely within the developing paradigm. Griaule spoke of his ideal team in terms of organic solidarity and a quasi-military esprit de corps, and the works of the school do suggest an efficient collaborative enterprise; but as a productive mechanism the "team" could never be tightly controlled. When one includes as active agents the Dogon informants, translators, and tribal authorities, whose influence on the content and timing of the knowledge gained was crucial, it becomes apparent that the collaborative documentary experience initiated by Griaule in 1932 had by the 1950s undergone a metamorphosis.

How, before Ogotemmêli, did Griaule "choose," "identify," "interrogate," and "utilize" informants (1952c:542–547; 1957:54–61)? His methodological strictures are particularly revealing since, as his respect for African oral tradition grew, he came increasingly to center his research in close work with a limited number of collaborateurs indigènes.

The informant must first be carefully identified and located in a specific group or set of groups within the social fabric. In this way one can allow for exaggerations and for omissions related to group loyalty, taboos, and so on. He or she—in fact Griaule's informants, as he regretfully noted, were almost entirely men (1957:15)—has to be qualified to pronounce on particular subjects, whether technological, historical, legal, or religious. His "moral qualities" are to be assessed: sincerity, good faith, memory. Although many of his informants were significantly influenced by "outside" perspectives (Lettens 1971:520–535), Griaule weighed heavily the attachment to tradition, mistrusting Christians, Muslims, and individuals with too much prior contact with whites (1957:57).

Every informant, Griaule assumes, enunciates a different kind of truth, and the ethnographer must be constantly alive to its limitations, strengths, and weaknesses. In his *Méthode* he discusses various types of "liars." Indeed throughout his work he is preoccupied with lies—although not as simple untruths. Each informant, even the most sincere, experiences an "instinctive need to dissimulate particularly delicate points. He will gladly take advantage of the slightest chance to escape the subject and dwell on another" (1957:58). Native collaborators "lie" in jest or through venality, the desire to please, or the fear of neighbors and the gods (p. 56). Forgetful informants and Europeanized informants are particularly dangerous types of "liars." In an ethnographic "strategic operation" (p. 59) the investigator must break through initial defenses and dissimulations. Often an individual informant must be isolated for intensive questioning so as to remove inhibiting social pressure (p. 60). When their testimony is confronted with differing versions gained from other interviews, hard-pressed informants enunciate truths they had not intended to reveal. On one occasion Griaule permits himself to dream of an "ideal" situation: "an infinity of separated informants" (1943:62). Yet it may sometimes be profitable to pursue inquiries in public, especially over delicate problems such as land tenure, where the researcher can provoke revealing disputes with their inevitable indiscretions (1943:66–68; 1957:60).

Griaule's tactics are varied, but they have in common an active, aggressive posture not unlike the judicial process of interrogation (1952:542, 547): "The role of the person sniffing out social facts is often comparable to that of a detective or examining magistrate. The fact is the crime, the interlocutor the guilty party; all the society's members are accomplices" (1957:59). He is fascinated by the tactics of oral inquiry, the play of truth and falsehood that can lead into "labyrinths" that are "organized." Like a psychoanalyst, he begins to see patterns of resistance, forgetfulness, and omission not as mere obstacles but as signs of a deeper structuring of the truth:

> The informant, on first contact, seldom offers much resistance. He lets himself be backed into positions he has been able to organize in the course of feeling out the situation, observing the quirks, skills, and awkwardnesses of his interlocutor. The value of these positions depends on what he can make of them; he resists as best he can. And if they are taken by force? After other similar resistances he will retreat to a final position that depends neither on himself nor on his "adversary" but on the system of prohibitions of custom.   (1952c:59–60)

For Griaule the deep structure of resistances is not specific to an intersubjective encounter but derives from a general source, the rules of "custom." This hypostatized entity is the last bastion to be stormed. As we shall see, it cannot be conquered by frontal assault, by the tactical processes of observation, documentation, or interrogation. A different "initiatory" process must come into play.

Designed for beginning fieldworkers, Griaule's treatises on ethnographic technique remain largely within the "documentary" paradigm. Moreover, Griaule probably did not have time to digest fully the methodological consequences of Ogotemmêli's revelations or of the gathering critique of colonial knowledge in the decade before *Méthode* was published. It is probably best to read this rather mechanistic compendium of techniques as a less-than-successful attempt to control an unruly research process, in Georges Devereux's terms (1967), a passage from anxiety to method. Griaule's ultimate complex reciprocal involvement with the Dogon is hardly captured in section titles such as "The Detection and Observation of Human Facts" or in the portrayal of ethnographers and indigenous collaborators as builders of information networks, collectors of "documents," compilers of "dossiers." Ethnography, in Griaule's juridical language, is still akin to the process of *instruction*—in French law, the preliminary establishment of the facts of a case before the *jugement* proper (1957:51). Working among interested parties the ethnographer uses the far-reaching powers of the *juge d'instruction* (one of Griaule's favorite metaphors) to smoke out the truth (cf. Ehrmann 1976). Generally respecting the division of labor laid down by Mauss, and suspicious of abstractions and systematic cross-cultural comparison, Griaule leaves matters of theory and explanation to others outside the fray. The *juge d'instruction,* having collected enough reliable documents and having cross-checked his witnesses' versions of the facts, has in his possession everything he needs to determine the truth.

By 1950 these attitudes toward observation and interrogation were becoming generally suspect, and Griaule's early documentary metaphor was no longer adequate to a research process that was taking on a life of its own. Gradually Griaule's understanding of the Dogon was becoming indistinguishable from their increasingly elaborate explications. The originality of the ethnographic activity he set in motion was that it un-covered—and to an undetermined extent provoked—a sophisticated in-terpretation of their culture by a group of influential Dogon.

⅄

Before we consider the second phase of Griaule's work, it is worth step-ping back for a moment from his research styles and tactics to suggest their relation to the colonial situation. Griaule provides us with a kind of dramaturgy of ethnographic experience before the fifties. In an extraor-dinary passage—included in both his early and his late discussions of methodology—he evokes the gamut of power-laden roles adopted by an ethnographer eliciting information from an informant. *Ethnographie ac-tive,* he writes, is "the art of being a midwife and an examining magis-trate":

> By turns an affable comrade of the person put to cross-examination, a distant friend, a severe stranger, compassionate father, a concerned patron; a trader paying for revelations one by one, a listener affecting distraction before the open gates of the most dangerous mysteries, an obliging friend showing lively interest for the most insipid family sto-ries—the ethnographer parades across his face as pretty a collection of masks as that possessed by any museum. (1933:10; 1952c:547; 1957:59)

The passage evokes a theme infusing all of Griaule's work—that eth-nography is a theatrical undertaking. His dramaturgy does not, however, include a role popular among fieldworkers in the Anglo-American tradi-tion: the persona of the earnest learner, often cast as a child in the pro-cess of acquiring, of being taught adult knowledge. Perhaps this persona did not occur to Griaule because, seconded by interpreters and European co-workers, he never actually experienced the position of being a stammerer, helpless in an alien culture. It was only after 1950, late in his career, that he began to adopt the standoint of a student with respect to Dogon culture; but this role was always mixed with the less vulnerable authority of initiate, spokesman, and exegete. At least in his writings, Griaule never abandoned a basic confidence, a sense of ultimate control over the research and its products. But maintaining control was always a battle, at best a joking relation. Griaule never presented fieldwork as an innocent attainment of rapport analogous to friendship. Nor did he neutralize the process as an experience of education or growth (child or adolescent becoming adult) or as acceptance into an extended family (a kinship role given to the ethnographer). Rather, his accounts assumed a recurring conflict of interests, an agonistic drama resulting in mutual respect, complicity in a productive balance of power.

Griaule's writings are unusual in their sharp awareness of a structural power differential and a substratum of violence underlying all relations between whites and blacks in a colonial situation. For example in *Les flambeurs d'hommes,* an adventure story Griaule called "an objective description of certain episodes from my first trip to Abyssinia" (1934a:vi), he coolly notes a "given" of colonial life: the members of his caravan having shown themselves reluctant to attempt a tricky fording of the Nile, "there followed blows, given by the White Man and not returned; for a White is always a man of the government, and if you touch him complications ensue" (pp. 7–8). A revealing stylistic device is deployed here, as elsewhere in Griaule's accounts of fieldwork (1948a): a use of the passive voice and of generic terms for himself—"the White Man," "the European," "the Traveler," "the Nazarite," "the Foreigner." The story of the beatings suggests an automatic series of events to which all parties acquiesce. A European in Africa cannot, should not, avoid the pasts reserved for him. Griaule does not think of eluding the privileges and constraints of his ascribed status—a dream that obsesses, and to a degree paralyzes, Michel Leiris, his colleague of the Mission Dakar-Djibouti. Leiris' field journal (1934) and his later writings, both ethnological and literary, portray a slow reconciliation with a theatrical conception of the self; but his acceptance is always ambivalent, in creative conflict with a desire for immediate contact and participation (see Chapter 6). Griaule, by contrast, harbors no qualms about his own theatricality. Once this is plain, puzzling aspects of his practice become clearer—for example his ideal "coverage" of the Dogon funeral.

Griaule's elaborate panoptic plan will raise the hackles of any ethnographer schooled in participant observation. The crew he envisages must necessarily disturb and perhaps orient the course of the ceremony, but this does not seem to concern Griaule. Does he naively imagine that seven observers will not exert a considerable influence? The question is beside the point, for Griaule never thought of being an unobtrusive participant. His research was manifestly an intrusion; he made no pretense that it was otherwise. Thus, to an important degree the truth he recorded was a truth provoked *by* ethnography. One is tempted to speak of an *ethnographie vérité* analogous to the *cinéma vérité* pioneered by Griaule's later associate Jean Rouch—not a reality objectively recorded by the camera but one provoked by its active presence (Rouch 1978a).

One suspects that Griaule saw culture itself, like personality, as a performance or a spectacle. In the years following the Dakar-Djibouti mission Griaule and his teams turned up every year or so at Sanga. The arrival of these increasingly familiar outsiders was a dramatic event. Time was of the essence; informants were mobilized, rituals were acted for the cameras, and as much Dogon life as possible was recorded. In fact Griaule's early research tended to concentrate on aspects of cultural life susceptible to demonstration and performance: masks, public rituals, and games. It is significant in this regard that Sanga, the Dogon community most accustomed to ethnography, is today the region's principal tourist center, routinely performing its dances for outsiders (Imperato 1978:7–32).

Griaule's penchant for the dramatic infuses his work; for the historian this poses problems of interpretation. For example a heightened but characteristic passage in *Les Saô légendaires* exults in a breakthrough. Having maneuvered native interlocutors into giving up information they had not intended to divulge, Griaule contemplates the promise of future work in the area:

> We would be able to make asses of the old hesitators, to confound the traitors, abominate the silent. We were going to see mysteries leap like reptiles from the mouths of the neatly caught liars. We would play with the victim; we would rub his nose in his words. We'd make him smile, spit up the truth, and we'd turn out of his pockets the last secret polished by the centuries, a secret to make him who has spoken it blanch with fear.   (Griaule 1943:74)

How is one to read such a passage? Griaule always liked to provoke: a passage written to shock in 1943 is still shocking and puzzling. In the narrative to which it is a kind of climax, one watches with discomfort and with growing anger as the ethnographer bullies, cajoles, and manipulates those whose resistance interferes with his inquiry, natives who do not wish to see their ancestral remains collected in the interests of a foreign science. But Griaule will not permit us to dismiss him out of hand. If we now perceive such attitudes and acts as an embarrassment, it is thanks to Griaule that we see them so clearly. He rubs our nose in them.

Because Griaule played colonial roles with gusto and with a certain irony, the words just quoted cannot be placed neatly in their historical context and dismissed as attitudes unfortunately possible in the colonial period. It was more typical of the period to hide such violence than to bring it to the fore. Yet if the violence is, in some sense, Griaule's point, nowhere does he suggest a criticism of forced confessions in ethnography. On the contrary, his methodological writings give instructions on how to provoke them. Griaule does not express serious second thoughts about establishing dominance, finding and exploiting the weakness, disunity, and confusion of his native hosts. Thus a historical reading of such awkward passages cannot understand Griaule as either a typical participant or a self-conscious critic within the colonial situation. His position is more complex.

One is tempted to ascribe such passages to Griaule's "style"—his penchant for banter, for charged metaphors, for provocation; but this merely raises the question of how a style functions as part of a research activity and how it plays against an ideological milieu. Griaule's style is not merely, as some have assumed, a *faiblesse,* a distracting and unfortunate deviation from the scientific business at hand (Lettens 1971:12, 491). It is rather a meaningful response to a predicament, a set of roles and discursive possibilities that may be called *ethnographic liberalism.* A complex, contentious debate on anthropology and empire has largely established that ethnographers before the 1950s acquiesced in colonial regimes (Leiris 1950; Asad 1973; Copans 1974). White rule or cultural dominance was a given context for their work, and they adopted a range of liberal positions within it. Seldom "colonialists" in any direct, instrumental sense, ethnographers nonetheless accepted particular constraints while questioning them to varying degrees. This ambivalent predicament imposed certain roles.

Griaule's style of ethnographic liberalism may be understood as both a dramatic performance and a mode of irony. The most acute observers of the colonial situation, Orwell and Conrad for example, have portrayed it as a power-laden, ambiguous world of discontinuous, clashing realities. Like Orwell's young district officer who unwillingly shoots an elephant to avoid being laughed at by a crowd of Burmese, and like all the characters in *Heart of Darkness,* displaced Europeans must labor to maintain their cultural identities, however artificial these may appear. Both colonial and ethnographic situations provoke the unnerving feeling of being on stage, observed and out of place. Participants in such milieux are caught in roles they cannot choose. We have seen Griaule's heightened awareness of the masks worn as part of fieldwork's clash of wills, wits, bluffs, and strategies. He is not unique in stressing the importance of theatricality and impression management in ethnography, the sense that research relationships develop "behind many masks" (Berreman 1972). Most ethnographers have, like him, rejected the pretense of going native, of being able to shed a fundamental Europeanness; but only a few have portrayed so clearly the tactical dissimulations and irreducible violence of ethnographic work (Rabinow 1977:129–130).

Unlike Conrad, Orwell, or Leiris, Griaule seems not to be oppressed by his role playing. But although he is not critical, he is ironic. If he compares ethnography to a theater of war or a judicial proceeding, one need not assume that in the field he acted consistently as a company commander or an examining magistrate. To take Griaule's metaphors at face value is to miss their implicit analytical function. It is also to push aside his other personae: his charm, his temper, his playful banter, his growing sympathy, even love, for the Dogon.

Ethnographic liberals, of which there are many sorts, have tended to be ironic participants. They have sought ways to stand out or apart from the imperial roles reserved for them as whites. There have been frequent variations on Delafosse's *broussard.* Many have in one way or another publicly identified themselves with exotic modes of life and thought or cultivated an image of marginality. Griaule's exaggeration is another response. Ethnographic liberalism is an array of ironic positions, roles both within and at a certain remove from the colonial situation. Its complete dramaturgy remains to be written.

The political and ethical tensions visible in Griaule's writings have only recently become explicit subjects of analysis. A penetrating paragraph written in 1968 by Clifford Geertz reflects the beginning of the end of innocence in fieldwork:

> Usually the sense of being members, however temporarily, insecurely,
> and incompletely, of a single moral community, can be maintained

even in the face of the wider social realities which press in at almost every moment to deny it. It is fiction—fiction, not falsehood—that lies at the very heart of successful anthropological field research; and, because it is never completely convincing for any of the participants, it renders such research, considered as a form of conduct, continuously ironic.   (p. 154)

By the late sixties the romantic mythology of fieldwork rapport had begun to dissolve publicly. Since then a growing reflexivity in ethnographic thought and practice has deepened the recognition of its ironic structure, its reliance on improvised, historically contingent fictions. This new awareness makes possible a reading of Griaule that sees a theatrical, ironic stance as central to his ethnographic work.

大

Although Griaule's sense of the moral tension and violence inherent in fieldwork was unusually acute, he developed nonetheless an enabling fiction of reciprocal encounter with the Dogon. This fiction, not falsehood, is most clearly embodied in the work after Ogotemmêli. In Griaule's ongoing research (closely linked with that of Dieterlen) one sees the overlay of an ethnographic fiction (Dogon initiatory knowledge) by a fiction of ethnography (fieldwork as initiation). To account for this doubling we may return to Geertz's ironic fiction of moral community, which he sees as dissipating, temporarily at least, the ethical tensions inherent in fieldwork. Geertz undermines the myth of ethnographic rapport before reinstating it in an ironic mode. Like Griaule he seems to accept that all parties to the encounter recognize its elements of insincerity, hypocrisy, and self-deception. He sees this recognition as a precondition for a lived fiction (a drama in Griaule's terms) that is in some very guarded but real sense genuine. Just how this productive complicity is actually enacted is always difficult to know; but if, as Geertz suggests, such lived fictions are central to successful ethnographic research, then we may expect to find them reflected in the texts that organize, narrate, and generally account for the truths learned in fieldwork. In fact many ethnographies include some partial account of fieldwork as part of their representation of a cultural reality. But whether or not an explicit or implicit fieldwork narrative appears in the ethnography, its very shape—the definition of its topic, the horizon of what it can represesnt—is a textual expression of the performed fiction of community that has made the re-

Marcel Griaule and Michel Leiris prepare to sacrifice
chickens before the Kono altar at Kemeni, September 6, 1931,
as a condition of entering the sanctuary.

search possible. Thus, and with varying degrees of explicitness, ethnographies are fictions both of another cultural reality and of their own mode
of production. This is unusually clear in the late work of Griaule and
Dieterlen, where initiation provides the common organizing metaphor.

To say that ethnography is *like* initiation is not to recommend that
the researcher actually undergo the processes by which a native attains
the wisdom of the group. Griaule has little use for such a "comédie"
(1952c:549). The metaphor of initiation evokes, rather, the deepening of
understanding that accrues to long-term field research with repeated visits throughout the anthropologist's career. It evokes too a qualitative
change in ethnographic relationships occurring as a culmination of the

long, persistant documentary process. Initiation finally gives access to a privileged stratum of native understanding, something Griaule claimed was "a demonstration, summary but complete, of the functioning of a society." The ethnograher, rather than trying to blend into the society under study, "plays his stranger's role." A friendly but determined outsider, pressing constantly against customary interdictions, the ethnographer comes to be seen as someone who, precisely because of his or her exteriority with respect to native institutions, is unlikely to falsify them. "If he is to receive instructions and revelations that are the equivalent of, and even superior to, those enjoyed by initiates, the researcher must remain himself. He will be careful not to try to gain time by telescoping the information; rather he will follow steps parallel to those of initiation as it is practiced by the men of the society" (p. 548).

The narrative of "parallel" (or specifically *ethnographic*) initiation appears prominently in Le renard pâle and Conversations with Ogotemmêli. The first decade of documentary work at Sanga unfolded at the lowest of four stages of Dogon initiatory knowledge. All the early questions of the Griaule team were answered at a level of instruction offered by elders to beginners—the *parole de face*. But the ethnographers returned repeatedly. They proved their good faith: Griaule, for example, used his aerial photography to advise the Dogon on crucial questions of water management. Gradually the persistent researchers approached deeper, secret levels of cultural knowledge. Then, "the Dogon made a decision" (Griaule and Dieterlen 1965:54). The local patriarchs met and decided to instruct Griaule in *la parole claire*—the highest, most complete stage of initiatory knowledge. Ogotemmêli would begin the task. Others continued when he died shortly after his famous conversations with Griaule.

Taken as a whole this narrative is certainly too neat and patently self-justificatory.[4] But whether or not the "decision" by "the Dogon" was motivated in just this way, and whatever the exact status of Ogotemmêli's discourse (individual speculation or cultural knowledge), the overall initiatory paradigm does raise important questions about short- and long-

---

4. We need not go as far as Lettens (1971:509), who suggests that the entire initiatory logic of progressively revealed secrets was an invention of Griaule's to cover up the failures of his first phase of research in the light of Ogotemmêli's revelations. Letten's extreme skepticism is largely unsubstantiated and unconvincing, given widespread evidence for Sudanese initiatory systems, and given his rather rigid and literalist conception of initiatory processes.

term ethnography. There can be no doubt that Griaule's repeated visits resulted in a progressive, qualitative deepening of his understanding. Open-ended long-term study may well yield results that differ importantly from those of intensive sojourns of a year or two, followed perhaps by a later return visit to measure "change" (Foster et al. 1979). The aging of both fieldworkers and informants and the accumulated experience of cooperative work over decades produce at least the effect of a deepening knowledge. To conceive of this experience as an initiation has the merit of including indigenous "teachers" as central subjects in the process. Dogon instruction of Griaule in *la parole claire* is also an implicit criticism of the earlier "documentary" research; indeed one wonders if most ethnographies generated over a relatively narrow time span may not be *paroles de face*. The narrative of initiation sharply questions approaches that do not strive for a certain level of complexity in representing "the native point of view." Ogotemmêli's initiative need not be portrayed as a completion (in Griaule's words a "couronnement") of the earlier research. It can also be seen as a comment on it and a shifting of its epistemological basis. Here the Dogon "side" of the story remains problematic: direct evidence is lacking, and the initiatory narrative with its assumed teleology—a progress toward the most complete possible knowledge—ceases to be helpful.

It is clear that Ogotemmêli's intervention was a crucial turn in the research process. It revealed the extent of Dogon control over the kind of information accessible to the ethnographers. It announced a new style of research in which the authority of informants was more explicitly recognized. No longer untrustworthy witnesses subjected to cross-examination, the Dogon "doctors," Ogotemmêli and his successors, were now learned interlocutors. During the "documentary" phase of the research the ethnographer had been an aggressive collector of observations, artifacts, and texts. Now he or she was a transcriber of formulated lore, a translator, exegete, and commentator. In Griaule's account of their meetings Ogotemmêli is not interrogated in the manner outlined in *Méthode de l'ethnographie*. "Le blanc," "the Nazarite," as Griaule now sometimes calls himself, has become a student; the secret is communicated freely, not confessed.

The documentary and initiatory paradigms, however, are linked by important underlying assumptions. To see ethnography as either extracting confessions or undergoing initiation, one must assume the existence and importance of secrets. Cultural truth is structured in both cases as something to be revealed (Griaule's frequent work is *décelé:* disclosed, divulged, detected, uncovered). Moreover, the new paradigm incorporates the theatrical conception of fieldwork. In a "parallel" initiation the ethnographer plays the part of an initiate, the informant, an instructor. A dramatic relationship, recognized as such by both parties, becomes the enabling fiction of encounter. Indeed if all performances are controlled revelations presupposing a "back region" hidden from view where the performance is prepared and to which access is limited (Goffman 1959: 238; Berreman 1972:xxxii), then a theatrical model of relationships necessarily presupposes secrets. Thus an underlying logic of the secret unites the two phases of Griaule's career.[5] Whether the ethnographer is a relentless "judge" or a helping "midwife," the truth must always *emerge,* be brought to light. As an initiate, the researcher receives and interprets *revelations.*

This view of the emergence of truth may be contrasted with a conception of ethnography as a dialogical enterprise in which both researchers and natives are active creators or, to stretch a term, authors of cultural representations. In fact Griaule's experience with the Dogon may be better accounted for in this second perspective; but to say this presupposes a critique of initiatory authority. Dialogical, constructivist paradigms tend to disperse or share out ethnographic authority, while narratives of initiation confirm the researcher's special competence. Initiation assumes an experience of progressive, connected revelations, of getting behind half-truths and taboos, of being instructed by authentically qualified members of a community. This experience of a deepening "education" empowers the ethnographer to speak as an insider on behalf of the community's truth or reality. Though all cultural learning includes an initiatory dimension, Griaule presses this logic to the limit: "proceeding by means of successive investigations among more and more knowledgeable strata of the society, it is possible to considerably reduce a population's area of

5. Jamin (1982a:88–89) discusses this aspect of Griaule's work. For a stimulating treatment of the social functions of secrets see his *Les Lois du silence* (1977). Secrets are part of the *mise en scène sociale,* generators of group identities and of cultural meanings which, not goals to be finally attained, are "endlessly deferred and dissimulated" (p. 104). My discussion of the exegetical function of *la parole claire* draws on this general perspective, as well as on Kermode (1980). For a trenchant critique of the "cryptological" assumptions underlying Griaule's practice and that of many "symbolic anthropologists" see Sperber (1975:17–50). Perhaps the most subtle critique of the logic of secrecy is contained in Victor Segalen's *René Leys* (1922); see Chapter 5.

esoteric knowledge, the only one, to tell the truth, that is important, since it constitutes the native key to the system of thought and action" (1952c:545).

This "native key" began to emerge for Griaule and his co-workers in the late forties and early fifties. The landmark books announcing its discovery were *Dieu d'eau (Conversations with Ogotemmêli)* (1948a) and Dieterlen's *Essai sur la religion Bambara* (1951). The two works revealed a "deep thought among the blacks," "an intricate network of representations" (Dieterlen 1951:227). The "innumerable correspondences" of the Bambara and Dogon emerged as a "coherent tableau," a "metaphysic" (Griaule 1951:ix). Once Ogotemmêli had, in thirty-three days of meandering talk, enunciated the basic outlines of Dogon cosmogonic myth, an enormous work of elucidation remained. As recorded in Griaule's day-by-day account, his discourse was riddled with gaps and contradictions. The cultural master script he had sketched would require elaborate exegesis, cross-checking against other versions of myths, and attention to the script's enactment in virtually every domain of collective life.

This work was to occupy Griaule and his co-workers for decades. It would also occupy their small group of key informants, drawn from the estimated 5 percent of "completely instructed" Dogon in the Sanga region, as well as from the 15 percent of the population who possessed a fair portion of the secret knowledge (Griaule 1952a:32). There is disagreement about the precise nature of the Dogon "revelations" produced in this collaboration. Some have seen them as theological speculations by individual Dogon or as mythopoeic inventions (Goody 1967:241; Lewis 1973:16; Copans 1973:156). Griaule and Dieterlen, however, strongly reject the notion that the knowledge they report is in any significant sense the original creation of specific Dogon. In their view the uniformity of custom and the widespread behavioral articulation of the esoteric knowledge makes it unlikely that any individual could have done more than slightly inflect the enduring mythic structures. But to pose the issue as a debate between personal originality and cultural typicality (Hountondji 1977: 79–101) is probably fruitless, given our ignorance about key informants. This view is based also on a false dichotomy: all authors, whether African or European, are original only within limited resources and in restricted relations of textual production.

It is tempting to portray the late works of the Griaule school, in the words of Pierre Alexandre, as "second level ethnography—the ethnography of Dogon ethnography" (1973:4). This notion of "levels" does not do justice, however, to the way in which Griaule's version of custom and the versions enunciated by Dogon informants are dialogically implicated in one another, for it is difficult, if not impossible, to separate clearly Dogon ethnography from Griaule's ethnography. They form a common project: the textualization and exegesis of a traditional system of knowledge. The cultural "text" does not exist prior to its interpretation; it is not dictated by fully instructed informants and then explicated and contextualized at a second "level" by European ethnographers. Griaule and Dieterlen give evidence that there can in fact be no complete version of the Dogon "metaphysic." If, in Griaule's telling metaphor, it is "written" throughout the culture—in the habitat, in gestures, in the system of graphic signs—these traces are of the order of a mnemonicon rather than of a complete inscription. In fact a "fully instructed" Dogon will spend a lifetime mastering *la parole claire*. To grasp the full range of its symbolic correspondences, signs, myths, rites, and everyday gestures requires a continuous process of concrete poesis. The mythic "word" is endlessly materialized, exchanged, interpreted. Because stable order is relentlessly disrupted by the forces of disorder, incarnate in the mythic *renard pâle*, cosmos and society are constantly reinscribed.

The ethnographic encounter is one of the occasions of this reinscription, but with a significant difference. Now the Dogon dialectic of order and disorder takes place on a world stage, leading to the inscription of a new kind of totality, a Dogon essence or culture. In *Le renard pâle* we see an attempt to establish a cultural base line, to separate, for example, "commentaries" by informants from the recorded myths and variants. It is unclear, though, how rigorously such a separation can be made, for as Dieterlen says, these glosses demonstrate the Dogon propensity to "speculate on the history of creation," an ongoing "native development of thought on the basis of mythic facts" (Griaule and Dieterlen 1965:56). The development of mythic thought, as of any thought, is both structured and open-ended, but the activity of exegesis depends on the positing of a restricted set of symbols by the hermeneutical imagination. There must in principle be a stable corpus for interpretation. Griaule's "full" initiatory knowledge—which can never be expressed in its entirety—functions in this canonical manner. It provides a stopping point for the process of cultural representation. On the basis of this original master script a potentially endless exegetical discourse can be generated. *La parole claire*, like any primal text or ground of authority, acts to structure and empower interpretation.

Griaule's paradigm of initiation functioned to transform the ethnographer's role from observer and documenter of Dogon culture to exegete and interpreter. It preserved and reformulated, however, the dominant themes of his earlier practice: the logic of the secret, an aspiration to exhaustive knowledge, a vision of fieldwork as role playing. It expressed also the sense one has throughout Griaule's career of his Dogon counterparts as powerful agents in the ethnographic process, initially clever tacticians and willful resisters, later teachers and colleagues. By attaining *la parole claire* and working like any initiate to grasp the "word's" incarnation in the experiential world, Griaule becomes (always in his parallel, "ethnographic" position) one of a restricted group of "doctors" or "metaphysicians" who control and interpret Dogon knowledge. Griaule is an insider, but with a difference. It is as though the Dogon had recognized the need for a kind of cultural ambassador, a qualified representative who would dramatize and defend their culture in the colonial world and beyond. Griaule in any case acted as if this were his role.

The stance of the ethnographer who speaks as an insider on behalf of his or her people is a familiar one; it is a stock role of the ethnographic liberal. Griaule adopted this standpoint in the early fifties with confidence and authority. An active advocate and mediator in the colonial politics of the Sanga region, he effected a reconciliation between traditional Dogon authorities and the new chiefs installed by the government (Ogono d'Arou 1956:9). In a variety of forums, from the pages of *Présence africaine* to UNESCO international gatherings to the Assembly of the Union Française (where he served as president of the Commission on Cultural Affairs), he urged respect for the traditions of Africa. Fortified by Ogotemmêli's revelations, he portrayed in elaborate detail a mode of knowledge to rival or surpass the occidental legacy of the Greeks. Speaking personally, in the voice of an initiate, he could report about the Dogon that "with them, everything seems truer, more noble, that is to say more classical. This may not be the impression you have from the outside, but as for me, each day I seem to be discovering something more beautiful, more shaped, more solid" (1952b:166).

One senses in the work of Griaule and among his co-workers—especially Germaine Dieterlen—a profound, sometimes mystical engagement with the Dogon *sophie* (Rouch 1978b:11–17). But whereas Dieterlen has tended to efface her own authority behind that of the Dogon, Griaule, who lived to see only the beginnings of "decolonization," spoke in frankly paternalist accents as an advocate for African traditional cul-

tures. His late generalizations are governed by a familiar chain of synecdoches. Ogotemmêli and Sanga stand for the Dogon, the Dogon for
the traditional Sudan, the Sudan for Black Africa, Africa for *l'homme noir.*
Griaule moves freely from level to level, constructing an elemental civilization strikingly different from that of Europe; but difference is established only to be dissolved in a totalizing humanism (1952b:24). Once
traditional African essence is characterized and sympathetically defended, it is then portrayed, in the last instance, as a response to "the
same great principle, to the same great human uncertainties" that Western science and philosophy have engaged (1951:166). The ethnographer
speaks as a participant in two civilizations that by means of his initiatory
experience and special knowledge can be brought together at a "human"
level.

In the early fifties Griaule presents himself as someone who knows
Africa and who knows too what is good for Africa. Ethnographic understanding is critical in a changing colonial context: it permits one to "select those moral values which are of merit and should be preserved," to
"decide what institutions and what systems of thought should be preserved and propagated in Black Africa" (1953:372). Tradition must be
well understood so that change can be properly guided. "It is a question
of taking what's theirs that is rich and transposing it into our own situation, or into the situation we wish to make for them" (1951:163).
Griaule's "we" belongs to 1951 and the colonial Union Française, of
which he was a councilor.

The cultural riches that will somehow be preserved or transposed
are always located in the domain of tradition or "authentic" custom—an
area more or less free of European of Islamic influences. The ethnographic liberal who represents the essence of a culture against impure
"outside" forces encounters sooner or later a contradiction built into all
such discourses that resist or try to stand outside historical invention. The
most persistent critics of Griaule's defense of Africa were educated Africans, *évolués,* who rejected any reification of their cultural past, however sympathetic. Griaule tended to explain away these resistances as
unfortunate consequences of an unbalanced education: "You can't be
simultaneously at school and in the sacred grove" (1951:164; see also
Malroux 1957:15). The black intellectuals who objected to his eloquent
portrayals of their traditions were no longer authentically African but
were victims of "that kind of 'leading astray of minors' which all colonial
powers have indulged in" (1953:376).

Such statements no longer carry the authority Griaule was able to impart to them in the early fifties; in fact they were challenged even on the occasion of their enunciation (Griaule 1952b:147–166). More congenial today are the views expressed at the same time by Griaule's early colleague Michel Leiris. A brief final contrast will evoke the changing ideological situation in the years before Griaule's death, a situation in which ethnography is still enmeshed.

Leiris was perhaps the first ethnographer to confront squarely the political and epistemological constraints of colonialism on fieldwork (Leiris 1950). He viewed the ethnographer as a natural advocate for exploited peoples, and he warned against definitions of authenticity that excluded évolués and the impurities of cultural syncretism. Both Leiris and Griaule contributed essays in 1953 to a UNESCO collection entitled *Interrelations of Cultures*. The differences in their approaches are still instructive today. Griaule's essay, "The Problem of Negro Culture," argues that "traditional religions, as well as the social and legal structure and technical crafts of the black races emanate from a single, rigid system of thought—a system that provides an interpretation of the universe, as well as a philosophy enabling the tribe to carry on and the individual to lead a balanced life" (1953:361). Dogon and Bambara examples are elicited to illustrate this "metaphysical substratum," which Griaule presents throughout as characteristic of "the Negro" or of "negro culture" (p. 362). Leiris, in approaching his topic, "The African Negroes and the Arts of Carving and Sculpture," evokes a historically specific problem of intercultural translation. He begins by tracing the discovery of *art nègre* among the avant-garde early in the century—Europeans inventing an African aesthetic for their own artistic purposes. He then throws doubt on his own undertaking by pointing out the absurdity of an African attempting in a short essay to deal with the whole of "European sculpture." He proceeds to base his generalizations about "African" art not on any presumption of a common essence but on a contingent perspective. He writes as a Westerner perceiving similarities among the diverse sculptures of Africa and even presenting them as expressions of a "civilization" while understanding these ensembles to be in a sense optical illusions. The apparent unity of black art forms inheres only in a perception of the common ways in which they differ from those to which a European is accustomed. (See Chapter 9, n.3.) This refusal to represent an exotic essense—an important issue of epistemological tact—is based (in part at least) on the ways in which Leiris' ethnographic career diverged from that of his co-worker on the Mission Dakar-Djibouti. Leiris never underwent any "initiation" into an exotic form of life or belief. Indeed his work (especially *L'Afrique fantôme*) is a relentless critique of the paradigm of initiation. His literary work, largely devoted to a heterodox, endless autobiography, reinforces the ethnographic point. (See Chapter 6.) How could Leiris presume to represent another culture when he had trouble enough representing himself? Such an attitude made sustained fieldwork impossible.

Griaule's energetic confidence in cultural representation could not be farther from Leiris' tortured, lucid uncertainty. The two positions mark off the predicament of a postcolonial ethnography. Some authorizing fiction of "authentic encounter," in Geertz's phrase, seems a prerequisite for intensive research; but initiatory claims to speak as a knowledgeable insider revealing essential cultural truths are no longer credible. Fieldwork cannot appear primarily as a cumulative process of gathering "experience" or of cultural "learning" by an automonous subject. It must rather be seen as a historically contingent, unruly dialogical encounter involving to some degree both conflict and collaboration in the production of texts. Ethnographers seem to be condemned to strive for strive for true encounter while simultaneously recognizing the political, ethical, and personal cross-purposes that undermine any transmission of intercultural knowledge. Poised between Griaule's enactment and Leiris's refusal of this ironic predicament, and working at the now blurred boundaries of ethnographic liberalism, fieldworkers struggle to improvise new modes of authority.

They may perhaps find some retrospective encouragement in the Griaule tradition of ethnographic cultural invention, for the story contains elements that point beyond initiatory authority and the neocolonial context. To date the most illuminating account of how research proceeded in the wake of Ogotemmêli is Geneviève Calame-Griaule's preface to *Ethnologie et langage: La parole chez les Dogon* (1965). She tells how "the extremely precise views" she gathered from her interlocutors led to the elaboration of "a veritable Dogon 'theory' of speech" (p. 11). She introduces her four key collaborators, giving hints of their personal styles and preoccupations. We learn that one of them, Manda, was the Dogon equivalent of a "theologian" and that he guided the ethnographer toward the relations of speech and the person that became the book's organizing principle. Even the book's descriptions and interpretations of everyday behavior were the work of both ethnographer and informants, many of the latter possessing extraordinary "finesse in observation" (p. 14). While Calame-Griaule still makes a guarded claim to represent an overall Dogon "cultural orientation," her preface goes a long way toward casting the ethnographic process in specific dialogical terms. The theory of speech that Calame-Griaule has brilliantly compiled is inescapably a collaborative work, continuing her father's productive encounter with the inhabitants of Sanga. And it is an authentic creation of "Dogon thought's need in expressing itself for dialectic, for an exchange of questions and answers that interpenetrate and weave themselves together" (p. 17).

. . . the age in which we are camped, like bewildered
travelers in a garish, unrestful hotel.
                              —JOSEPH CONRAD, *VICTORY*

My whole ethics is based on the fundamental instinct of
unified personality.
                              —BRONISLAW MALINOWSKI,
                              TROBRIAND FIELD DIARY

3. On Ethnographic Self-Fashioning: Conrad and Malinowski

To SAY THAT the individual is culturally constituted has become a truism. We are accustomed to hearing that the person in Bali or among the Hopi or in medieval society is different—with different experiences of time, space, kinship, bodily identity—from the individual in bourgeois Europe or in modern America. We assume, almost without question, that a self belongs to a specific cultural world much as it speaks a native language: one self, one culture, one language. I do not wish to dispute the considerable truth contained in even so bald a formula; the idea that individuality is articulated within worlds of signification that are collective and limited is not in question. I want, however, to historicize the statement that the self is culturally constituted by examining a moment around 1900 when this idea began to make the sense it does today.

In the mid-nineteenth century to say that the individual was bound up in culture meant something quite different from what it does now. "Culture" referred to a single evolutionary process. The European bourgeois ideal of autonomous individuality was widely believed to be the natural outcome of a long development, a process that, although threatened by various disruptions, was assumed to be the basic, progressive movement of humanity. By the turn of the century, however, evolutionist confidence began to falter, and a new ethnographic conception of culture became possible. The word began to be used in the plural, suggesting a world of separate, distinctive, and equally meaningful ways of life. The ideal of an autonomous, cultivated subject could appear as a local project, not a *telos* for all humankind.[1]

The underlying causes of these ideological developments are beyond my scope here.[2] I want only to call attention to the development in the early twentieth century of a new "ethnographic subjectivity." Modern anthropology—a Science of Man linked closely to cultural description—presupposed the ironic stance of participant observation. By professionalizing fieldwork anthropology transformed a widespread predicament into a scientific method. Ethnographic knowledge could not be the property of any one discourse or discipline: the condition of off-centeredness in a world of distinct meaning systems, a state of being in culture while looking at culture, permeates twentieth-century art and writing. Nietzsche had clearly announced the new stance in his famous fragment "On Truth and Lie in an Extra-Moral Sense," asking: "What, then is truth? A mobile army of metaphors, metonyms, and anthropomorphisms—in short, a sum of human relations, which have been enhanced, transposed, and embellished poetically and rhetorically, and which after long use seem firm, canonical, and obligatory to a people" (Kaufman 1954:46). Nietzsche, perhaps more than Tylor, was the main inventor of the relativist idea of culture: this chapter could well have been called "On Truth and Lie in a *Cultural* Sense."

I have instead taken my title from Stephen Greenblatt's *Renaissance Self-Fashioning* (1980), a work that traces an emerging, bourgeois, mobile, cosmopolitan sense of the self. The ethnographic subjectivity I am concerned with may be seen as its late variant. The sixteenth-century

---

1. On the development of the concept of culture see Williams 1966, Stocking 1968, and Chapter 10. The novelty and fragility of the Western notion of the individual was noted in Mauss 1938, perhaps the first ethnographic overview of the subject.

2. A full analysis of changes in the "culture" response would presuppose those forces taken by Raymond Williams (1966) as determinants: industrialism, social conflict, the rise of mass culture. To these would be added the needs of high colonial societies to understand the increasingly accessible diversities of the planet as a dispersed totality. The mapping of the world's human arrangements as distinct cultures asserts that things hold together—separately.

figures of More, Spenser, Marlowe, Tyndale, Wyatt, and Shakespeare ex-
emplify for Greenblatt "an increased self-consciousness about the fash-
ioning of human identity as a manipulable, artful process" (p. 2). I cannot
do justice to the book's subtle and persuasive individual analyses, but I
want to note Greenblatt's own ethnographic standpoint, the complex attitude he maintains toward fashioned selves, including his own. He recognizes the extent to which recent questions about freedom, identity, and
language have shaped the version he constructs of sixteenth-century culture. He imports a modern critical approach to his material. Yet he writes
too as someone caught up with and loyal to a tradition. He expresses in
a moving epilogue his stubborn commitment to the possibility of shaping
one's own identity, even if this means only to "selfhood conceived as a
fiction" (p. 257). He is led to what Conrad approvingly called a "deliberate belief."

Greenblatt is a participant-analyst, constructing and engaging a cultural formation that is both distanced in the sixteenth century and dialec-
tically continuous with the present. His "late," reflexive version of Renaissance self-fashioning relies on a sharply articulated ethnographic
viewpoint. The fashioned, fictional self is always located with reference
to its *culture* and coded modes of expression, its *language*. Greenblatt's
study concludes that Renaissance self-fashioning was anything but the
unconstrained emergence of a new individualist autonomy. The subjectivity he finds is "not an epiphany of identity freely chosen but a cultural
artifact" (p. 256), for the self maneuvers within constraints and possibilities given by an institutionalized set of collective practices and codes.
Greenblatt invokes symbolic-interpretive anthropology, particularly the
work of Geertz (also Boon, Douglas, Duvignaud, Rabinow, and Turner);
and he knows, moreover, that cultural symbols and performances take
shape in situations of power and dominance. One hears echoes of Foucault in Greenblatt's warning: "The power to impose a shape upon oneself is an aspect of the more general power to control identity—that of
others at least as much as one's own" (p. 1). It follows that ethnographic
discourse, including Greenblatt's literary variant, works in this double
manner. Though it portrays other selves as culturally constituted, it also
fashions an identity authorized to represent, to interpret, even to believe—but always with some irony—the truths of discrepant worlds.

Ethnographic subjectivity is composed of participant observation in
a world of "cultural artifacts" linked (and this is the originality of
Nietzsche's formulation) to a new conception of language—or better,

languages—seen as discrete systems of signs. Along with Nietzsche, the thinkers who stake out my area of exploration are Boas, Durkheim, and Malinowski (inventors and popularizers of the ethnographic culture idea), and Saussure. They inaugurate an interconnected set of assumptions that are now in the last quarter of the twentieth century just becoming visible. An intellectual historian of the year 2010, if such a person is imaginable, may even look back on the first two-thirds of our century and observe that this was a time when Western intellectuals were preoccupied with grounds of meaning and identity they called "culture" and "language" (much the way we now look at the nineteenth century and perceive there a problematic concern with evolutionary "history" and "progress"). I think we are seeing signs that the privilege given to natural languages and, as it were, natural cultures, is dissolving. These objects and epistemological grounds are now appearing as constructs, achieved fictions, containing and domesticating heteroglossia. In a world with too many voices speaking all at once, a world where syncretism and parodic invention are becoming the rule, not the exception, an urban, multinational world of institutional transience—where American clothes made in Korea are worn by young people in Russia, where everyone's "roots" are in some degree cut—in such a world it becomes increasingly difficult to attach human identity and meaning to a coherent "culture" or "language."

I evoke this syncretic, "postcultural" situation only to gesture toward the standpoint (though it cannot be so easily spatialized), the condition of uncertainty from which I am writing. But my concern is not with the possible dissolution of a subjectivity anchored in culture and language. Rather, I want to explore two powerful articulations of this subjectivity in the works of Conrad and Malinowski, two displaced persons both of whom struggled in the early twentieth century with cosmopolitanism and composed their own versions of "On Truth and Lie in a Cultural Sense." Conrad may have seen more deeply into the matter, for he built into his work a vision of the constructed nature of culture and language, a serious fictionality he deliberately, almost absurdly, embraced. But a comparable grappling with culture and language may be seen in Malinowski's work, particularly in the difficult experience and literary representation of his famous Trobriand fieldwork. (This fieldwork has served as a kind of founding charter for the twentieth-century discipline of anthropology.) Conrad accomplished the almost impossible feat of becoming a great writer (his model was Flaubert) in English, a third language he began to acquire at twenty years of age. It is not surprising to find throughout his work a sense of the simultaneous artifice and necessity of cultural, linguistic conventions. His life of writing, of constantly becoming an English writer, offers a paradigm for ethnographic subjectivity; it enacts a structure of feeling continuously involved in translation among languages, a consciousness deeply aware of the arbitrariness of conventions, a new secular relativism.

Malinowski remarked, "[W. H. R.] Rivers is the Rider Haggard of Anthropology: I shall be the Conrad!" (to B. Z. Seligman, quoted in Firth 1957:6). He probably had in mind the difference between Rivers' multicultural survey methodology (collecting traits and genealogies) and his own intensive study of a single group. For Malinowski the name Conrad was a symbol of depth, complexity, and subtlety. (He invokes him in this sense in the field diary.) But Malinowski was not the Conrad of anthropology. His most direct literary model was certainly James Frazer; and in much of his own writing he was reminiscent of Zola—a naturalist presenting facts plus heightened "atmosphere," his scientific-cultural descriptions yielding morally charged humanist allegories. Anthropology is still waiting for its Conrad.

My comparison of Malinowski and Conrad focuses on their difficult accession to innovative professional expression. Heart of Darkness (1899) is Conrad's most profound meditation on the difficult process of giving himself to England and English.[3] It was written in 1898–99, just as he decisively adopted the landlocked life of writing; and it looked back to the beginning of the process, his last, most audacious voyage out to his "farthest point of navigation." On the journey up the Congo a decade earlier, Konrad Korzeniowski had carried with him the initial chapters of his first novel, Almayer's Folly, written in an awkward but powerful English. My reading of Heart of Darkness embraces a complex decade of choice, the 1890s, beginning with the African voyage and ending with its narration. The choice involved career, language, and cultural attach-

---

3. The interpretation I suggest owes a good deal to previous explicators of Conrad, most notably Edward Said and Ian Watt. In its biographical dimensions it draws on the standard works: Baines 1960; Watt 1979; Karl 1979; and Najder 1983. My focus on Heart of Darkness as an allegory of writing and of grappling with language and culture in their emergent twentieth-century definitions is, I believe, a new one, but it draws on many points well established in Conrad studies. I have not cited specific sources for biographical facts, since those I build with are not, to my knowledge, disputed in the literature.

ment. Malinowski's parallel experience is marked off by two works, which may be treated as a single expanded text: *A Diary in the Strict Sense of the Term* (1967), his intimate Trobriand journal of 1914–1918, and the classic ethnography that emerged from the fieldwork, *Argonauts of the Western Pacific* (1922).

A word of methodological caution is needed at the outset. To treat the *Diary* and *Argonauts* together need not imply that the former is a true revelation of Malinowski's fieldwork. (This is how the *Diary* was widely understood on its publication in 1967.) The Trobriand field experience is not exhausted by *Argonauts* or the *Diary* or by their combination. The two texts are partial refractions, specific experiments with writing. Recorded largely in Polish and clearly not intended for publication, the *Diary* caused a minor scandal in the public image of anthropology— although fieldworkers recognized much that was familiar. One of the discipline's founders was seen to have felt considerable anger toward his native informants. A field experience that had set the standard for scientific cultural description was fraught with ambivalence. The authoritative anthropologist in his intimate journal appeared a self-absorbed hypochondriac, frequently depressed, prey to constant fantasies about European and Trobriand women, trapped in an endless struggle to maintain his morale, to pull himself together. He was mercurial, trying out different voices, personae. The anguish, confusion, elation, and anger of the *Diary* seemed to leave little room for the stable, comprehending posture of relativist ethnography. Moreover, in its rawness and vulnerability, its unquestionable sincerity and inconclusiveness, the *Diary* seemed to deliver an unvarnished reality. But it is only one important version of a complex, intersubjective situation (which also produced *Argonauts* and other ethnographic and popular accounts). The *Diary* is an inventive, polyphonic text. It is a crucial document for the history of anthropology, not because it reveals the reality of ethnographic experience but because it forces us to grapple with the complexities of such encounters and to treat all textual accounts based on fieldwork as partial constructions.[4]

$$\overset{\displaystyle\cdot}{\textstyle\nearrow\!\!\!\!\searrow}$$

Malinowski and Conrad knew each other, and there is evidence from Malinowski's comments on the older, already well known writer that he

---

4. I juxtapose *Argonauts* and the *Diary* to highlight a critical discrepancy between the two best-known accounts of Malinowski's research process. At times

sensed a deep affinity in their predicaments. With reason: both were Poles condemned by historical contingency to a cosmopolitan European identity; both pursued ambitious writing careers in England. Drawing on Zdzislaw Najder's excellent studies of Conrad, one can speculate that the two exiles shared a peculiarly Polish cultural distance, having been born into a nation that had since the eighteenth century existed only as a fiction—but an intensely believed, serious fiction—of collective identity. Moreover, Poland's peculiar social structure, with its broadly based small nobility, made aristocratic values unusually evident at all levels of society. Poland's cultivated exiles were not likely to be charmed by Europe's reigning bourgeois values; they would keep a certain remove. This viewpoint outside bourgeois society (but maintained with a degree of artifice—rather like Balzac's standpoint in the France of the 1830s) is perhaps a peculiarly advantageous "ethnographic" position. Be that as it may, there is no doubt about Malinowski's strong affinity for Conrad. (Just before the war he presented the older man with a copy of his first book, *The Family among the Australian Aborigines,* with a Polish inscription; what Conrad made of Arunta notions of paternity remains, perhaps fortunately, unknown.) Although their acquaintance was brief, Malinowski often represented his life in Conradian terms, and in his diary he seemed at times to be rewriting themes from *Heart of Darkness.*

Nearly every commentator on the *Diary* has plausibly compared it with Conrad's African tale (see for example Stocking 1974). Both *Heart of Darkness* and the *Diary* appear to portray the crisis of an identity—a struggle at the limits of Western civilization against the threat of moral dissolution. Indeed this struggle, and the need for personal restraint, is a commonplace of colonial literature. Thus the parallel is not particularly revealing, beyond showing life (the *Diary*) imitating "literature" (*Heart of Darkness*). In addition to Kurtz's moral disintegration, however, Conrad

---

I oversimplify the course of Malinowski's research and writing; the *Diary* actually covers work done in both the Trobriands and Mailu. By concentrating on two texts I ignore other complicating ones, most notably certain unpublished and currently unavailable diaries, along with Malinowski's "Natives of Mailu" (1915) and "Baloma: The Spirits of the Dead in the Trobriand Islands" (1916). In these last two works he can be seen working out the personal and scientific ethnographic style that achieves full expression in *Argonauts.* A biographical account, or a thorough portrayal of Malinowski's fieldwork, or a depiction of Melanesian culture and history each would select a different corpus. Moreover, by stopping at 1922 I neglect Malinowski's ongoing rewriting of the dialogue with the Trobriands. In important ways his last major monograph, *Coral Gardens and Their Magic* (1935), experimentally and self-critically questions the rhetorical stance constructed in *Argonauts.*

introduces a more profound, subversive theme: the famous "lie"—actually a series of lies that in *Heart of Darkness* both undermine and somehow empower the complex truth of Marlow's narration. The most prominent of these lies is, of course, Marlow's refusal to tell Kurtz's Intended his last words, "The Horror," substituting instead words she can accept. This lie is then juxtaposed with the truth—also highly circumstantial—told to a restricted group of Englishmen on the deck of the cruising yawl *Nellie*. Malinowski's unsettled *Diary* does seem to enact the theme of disintegration. But what of the lie? The all-too-believable account? Malinowski's saving fiction, I will argue, is the classic ethnography *Argonauts of the Western Pacific*.

Heart of Darkness is notoriously interpretable; but one of its inescapable themes is the problem of truth-speaking, the *interplay* of truth and lie in Marlow's discourse. The lie to Kurtz's Intended has been exhaustively debated. Very schematically, my own position is that the lie is a saving lie. In sparing the Intended Kurtz's last words, Marlow recognizes and constitutes different domains of truth—male and female as well as the truths of the metropole and the frontier. These truths reflect elementary structures in the constitution of ordered meanings—knowledge divided by gender and by cultural center and periphery. The lie to the Intended is juxtaposed with a different truth (and it too is limited, contextual, and problematic) told on the deck of the *Nellie* to Englishmen identified only as social types—the Lawyer, the Accountant, the Director of Companies. If Marlow succeeds in communicating, it is within this limited domain. As readers, however, we identify with the unidentified person who watches Marlow's dark truths and white lies enacted on the stage of the yawl's deck. This second narrator's story is not itself undermined or limited. It represents, I propose, the ethnographic standpoint, a subjective position and a historical site of narrative authority that truthfully juxtaposes different truths. While Marlow initially "abhors a lie," he learns to lie—that is, to communicate within the collective, partial fictions of cultural life. He tells limited stories. The second narrator salvages, compares, and (ironically) believes these staged truths. This is the achieved perspective of the serious interpreter of cultures, of local, partial knowledge. The voice of Conrad's "outermost" narrator is a stabilizing voice whose words are not meant to be mistrusted.[5]

---

5. For a reading close to my own but with a different overall emphasis see J. Hillis Miller 1965. Here we find strong arguments for seeing *Heart of Darkness* not as a positive choice for the "lie of culture" but as something that undermines

Heart of Darkness offers, then, a paradigm of ethnographic subjectivity. In what follows I will be exploring specific echoes and analogies linking Conrad's situation of cultural liminality in the Congo with Malinowski's in the Trobriands. The correspondence is not exact, however. Perhaps the most important textual difference is that Conrad takes an ironic position with respect to representational truth, a stance only implicit in Malinowski's writing. The author of *Argonauts* devotes himself to constructing realistic cultural fictions, whereas Conrad, though similarly committed, represents the activity as a contextually limited practice of storytelling.[6]

---

all truth, a more tragic, dark, ultimately nihilistic text. Undoubtedly in both form and content the tale grapples with nihilism. Nonetheless, it does dramatize the successful construction of a fiction, a contingent, undermined, but finally potent story, a meaningful economy of truths and lies. Biographical evidence reinforces my suggestion that *Heart of Darkness* is a story of qualified but distinct success in truth-telling. I have already noted that the tale was written just when Conrad finally decided to stake everything on his career of writing in English. In the autumn of 1898 he left Essex and the Thames estuary (the place between land and sea) for Kent to reside near other writers—H. G. Wells, Stephen Crane, Ford Maddox Ford, Henry James. The move, immediately followed by his last recorded search for a maritime post, inaugurated his most productive years of literary work. A serious writing block was broken; *Heart of Darkness* emerged in an uncharacteristic rush. From this standpoint of decision the tale reaches back a decade to the beginning of Korzeniowski's turn to writing, when, in the Congo, his luggage contained the first chapters of *Almayer's Folly*. In the reading I am sketching out *Heart of Darkness* is centrally about writing, about telling the truth in its most alienated, nondialogical form. Conrad does succeed in becoming an English writer, a limited truth-teller. It is not surprising, then, that in the blurred cacophony of the jungle Marlow yearns for English words. Kurtz was partly educated in Britain, and his mother, we recall, was half-English. From the beginning Marlow searches for Kurtz's intimate and elemental voice; and in the end "this initiated wraith from the back of Nowhere honoured me with its amazing confidence before it vanished altogether. This was because it could speak English to me" (p. 50). I cannot here discuss the many complexities in the staging and valuing of different languages in *Heart of Darkness*.

6. In *Reading for the Plot* (1984:259–260) Peter Brooks nicely observes that *Heart of Darkness* presents its truth as a "narrative transaction" rather than a "summing up" (as in Kurtz's last words). Meaning in the narrative is not a revealed kernel; it exists outside, dialogically, in specific transmissions; it is "located in the interstices of story and frame, born of the relationship between tellers and listeners." In stressing the tale's "interminable analysis" Brooks minimizes the first narrator's stabilizing function as a special listener (reader), not named or given a limited cultural function like the others on the deck. This listener's invisibility guarantees a certain ironic authority, the possibility of seeing and not being seen, of speaking without contradiction about relative truths, or deciding their undecidability.

In comparing the experiences of Malinowski and Conrad, one is struck by their linguistic overdetermination. In each case three languages are at work, producing constant translation and interference. Conrad's predicament is extremely complex. Just before leaving for Africa he had unaccountably begun writing what would become *Almayer's Folly*. After composing the opening chapters, he ran into obstacles. Around this time he came to know a cousin by marriage, Marguerite Poradowska, with whom he became in some significant way amorously involved. She was married and a well-known French author; it was largely a literary entanglement. Conrad wrote her rather passionate and self-revelatory letters—in French. Poradowska, who lived in Brussels, was instrumental in arranging her kinsman's Congo employment. Then, in the months just before he left for Africa, Conrad returned to Poland for the first time since he had run away to sea fifteen years before. This renewed his Polish, which had remained good, and revived its association with childhood places and ambivalent feelings. From Poland (actually the Russian Ukraine) he rushed almost directly to take up his post in the Congo. There he spoke French, his most fluent acquired tongue, but kept a diary in English and may have worked on the chapters of *Almayer*. (He claims as much in his "Biographical Note" of 1900.) In Africa Conrad established a friendship with the Irishman Roger Casement and generally maintained a pose of an English nautical gentleman. His intense letters to Poradowska continued, as always, in French. His mother tongue had just been revived. The Congo experience was a time of maximal linguistic complexity. In what language was Conrad consistently thinking? It is not surprising that words and things often seem disjointed in *Heart of Darkness* as Marlow searches in the dark for meaning and interlocution.

As for Malinowski, in the field he kept his private diary in Polish and corresponded in that language with his mother, who was behind enemy lines in Austria. He wrote in English on anthropological topics to his professor, C. G. Seligman, in London. To his fiancée, "E. R. M." (Elsie R. Masson), in Australia he wrote frequently, also in English. There were, however, at least two other women, old flames, on his mind, at least one of them associated with Poland. His most intimate Polish friend, Stanislas Witkiewicz ("Stás" in the *Diary*), soon to become a major avant-garde artist and writer, also haunted his consciousness. The two had traveled together to the Pacific and had fallen out just before Malinowski's Trobriand sojourns. He yearned to set things right, but his friend was now in Russia. These powerful English and Polish associations were interrupted by a third linguistically coded world, the Trobriand universe, in which he had to live and work productively. Malinowski's daily transactions with Trobrianders were conducted in Kiriwinian, and in time his field-notes were recorded largely in the vernacular.[7]

We can suggest a tentative structure for the three active languages of Conrad's and Malinowski's exotic experiences. Between Polish, the mother tongue, and English, the language of future career and marriage, a third intervenes, associated with eroticism and violence. Conrad's French is linked with Poradowska, a problematic love object (she was both too intimidating and too intimate); French is also linked with Con-rad's reckless youth in Marseille and with the Imperial Congo, which Conrad abhorred for its violence and rapacity. Malinowski's interfering language was Kiriwinian, associated with a certain exuberance and ludic excess (which Malinowski enjoyed and portrayed sympathetically in his accounts of Kula rituals and sexual customs) and also with the erotic temptations of Trobriand women. The *Diary* struggles repeatedly with this Kiriwinian realm of desire.

So it is possible to distinguish in each case a mother tongue, a lan-guage of excess, and a language of restraint (of marriage and authorship). This is surely too neat. The languages would have interpenetrated and interfered in highly contingent ways; but enough has been said, perhaps, to make the main point. Both Conrad in the Congo and Malinowski in the Trobriands were enmeshed in complex, contradictory subjective sit-uations articulated at the levels of language, desire, and cultural affilia-tion.

⅄

In both *Heart of Darkness* and the *Diary* we see the crisis of a self at some "furthest point of navigation." Both works render an experience of lone-liness, but one that is filled with other people and with other accents and that does not permit a feeling of centeredness, coherent dialogue, or au-thentic communion. In Conrad's Congo his fellow whites are duplicitous and uncontrolled. The jungle is cacophonous, filled with too many

---

7. The "Polish" diary is extraordinarily heteroglot. Mario Bick (1967:299), whose task was to compile a glossary and generally to "sort out the linguistic melange," specifies that Malinowski wrote "in Polish with frequent use of En-glish, words and phrases in German, French, Greek, Spanish, and Latin, and of course terms from the native languages" (there were four: Motu, Mailu, Kiriwin-ian, and Pidgin).

voices—therefore mute, incoherent. Malinowski was not, of course, isolated in the Trobriands, either from natives or from local whites. But the *Diary* is an unstable *confusion* of other voices and worlds: mother, lovers, fiancée, best friend, Trobrianders, local missionaries, traders, as well as the escapist universes, the novels he can never resist. Most fieldworkers will recognize this multivocal predicament. But Malinowski experiences (or at least his *Diary* portrays) something like a real spiritual and emotional crisis: each of the voices represents a temptation; he is pulled too many ways. Thus, like Marlow in *Heart of Darkness*, Malinowski clings to his work routines, his exercises, and his diary—where confusedly, barely, he brings his divergent worlds and desires together.

A passage from the *Diary* will illustrate his predicament:

> 7.18.18 . . . *On the theory of religion.* My ethical position in relation to Mother, Stás, E. R. M. Twinges of conscience result from lack of integrated feelings and truth in relation to individuals. My whole ethics is based on the fundamental instinct of unified personality. From this follows the need to be the same in different situations (truth in relation to oneself) and the need, indispensability, of sincerity: the whole value of friendship is based on the possibility of expressing oneself, of being oneself with complete frankness. Alternative between a lie and spoiling a relationship. (My attitude to Mother, Stás, and all my friends was strained.) Love does not flow from ethics, but ethics from love. There is no way of deducing Christian ethics from my theory. But that ethics has never expressed the actual truth—love your neighbor—to the degree actually possible. The real problem is: why must you always behave as if God were watching you? (pp. 296–297)

The passage is confused; but we can extract perhaps the central issue on which it turns: the impossibility of being sincere and thus of having an ethical center. Malinowski feels the requirement of personal coherence. A punitive God is watching his every (inconsistent) move. He is thus not free to adopt different personae in different situations. He suffers from the fact that this rule of sincerity, an ethics of unified personality, means that he will have to be unpleasantly truthful to various friends and lovers. And this will mean—has already meant—losing friends: "Alternative between a lie and spoiling a relationship."

There is no way out. There must be a way out. Too much truth-telling undermines the compromises of collective life. Malinowski's solution consists of constructing two related fictions—of a self and of a culture. Although my task here is neither psychological nor biographical, let me simply suggest that the personal style—extravagant, operatic—that both charmed and irritated Malinowski's contemporaries was a response to this dilemma. He indulged in "Slavic" extremism; his revelations about himself and his work were exaggerated and ambiguously parodic. He would strike poses (he claimed to have single-handedly invented "The Functional Method"), challenging the literal-minded to see that these personal truths were in some degree fictions. His character was staged but also truthful, a pose but nonetheless authentic. One of the ways Malinowski pulled himself together was by writing ethnography. Here the fashioned wholes of a self and of a culture seem to be mutually reinforcing allegories of identity. An essay by Harry Payne, "Malinowski's Style" (1981), suggestively traces the complex combination of authority and fictionality that the narrative form of *Argonauts* enacts: "Within the immense latitude of [its] structure Malinowski can determine shifts in focus, tone, and objects; the cyclical thread will always provide a place of return. Functional therapy acts only heuristically. Since everything adheres to everything, one can wander without ever getting fully disconnected" (p. 438).[8] The literary problem of authorial point of view, the Jamesian requirement that every novel reflect a "controlling intelligence," was a painful personal problem for the Trobriand diarist. The ample, multiperspectival, meandering structure of *Argonauts* resolves this crisis of sincerity. In effect, as the scientific, persuasive author of this fiction, Malinowski can be like Flaubert's God, omnipresent in the text, arranging enthusiastic descriptions, scientific explanations, enactments of events from different standpoints, personal confessions, and so forth.

Cultural descriptions in Malinowski's style of functionalism strove for a kind of unified personality, but a convincing totalization always escaped them. Malinowski never did pull together Trobriand culture; he produced no synthetic portrait, only densely contextualized monographs on important institutions. Moreover, his obsessive inclusion of data, "imponderabilia," and vernacular texts may be seen as a desire to unmake as well as to make a whole; such additive, metonymic empiricism undermines the construction of functional, synecdochic representations. Malinowski's ethnographies—unlike Radcliffe-Brown's spare, analytic, functional portraits—were multifarious, loose, but rhetorically success-

---

8. There is an interesting slip between this passage and its footnote: functionalist "therapy" becomes functionalist "theory."

ful narrative forms (Payne 1981:420–421). Fictional expressions of a culture and of a subjectivity, they provided a way out of the bind of sincerity and wholeness, the Conradian problematic of the lie at issue in the *Diary*.

There are more specific echoes of *Heart of Darkness* in Malinowski's intimate Polish text. Speaking of his Trobriand informants who will not cooperate with his research, he damns them in Kurtz's terms: "At moments I was furious at them, particularly because after I gave them their portions of tobacco they all went away. On the whole my feelings toward the natives are decidedly tending to '*Exterminate the brutes,*' " (p. 69). Malinowski flirted with various colonial white roles—Kurtz-like excess included. Here the ironic invocation provides him with a fictional grasp of the stresses of fieldwork and the violence of his feelings. In the *Diary*, like Marlow in his ambivalent doubling with Kurtz, Malinowski often faces the inseparability of discourse and power. He must struggle for control in the ethnographic encounter.

Another nonironic echo of *Heart of Darkness* is heard in Malinowski's grief-stricken response to the news of his mother's death, which shatters the *Diary*'s last pages: "The terrible mystery that surrounds the death of someone dear, close to you. The unspoken last word—something that was to cast light is buried, the rest of life lies half hidden in darkness" (p. 293). Malinowski feels he has been denied Marlow's rescued talisman, an ambiguously illuminating, potent last word breathed in the moment of death.

Beyond the more-or-less direct citations in the *Diary* one notes also more general thematic and structural parallels with *Heart of Darkness*. Both books are records of white *men* at the frontier, at points of danger and disintegration. In both sexuality is at issue: both portray an other that is conventionally feminized, at once a danger and a temptation. Feminine figures in the two texts fall into either spiritual (soft) or sensual (hard) categories. There is a common thematization of the pull of desire or excess barely checked by some crucial restraint. For Malinowski the restraint is embodied by his fiancée, linked in his mind to an English academic career, to an elevated love, and to marriage. "Thought of E. R. M. . . ." is the *Diary*'s censor for lascivious thoughts about women, native or white: "I must not betray E. R. M. mentally, i.e., recall my previous relations with women, or think about future ones . . . Preserve the essential inner personality through all difficulties and vicissitudes: I must never sacrifice moral principles or essential work to 'posing' to convivial *Stimmung*, etc. My main task must be work. Ergo: work!" (p. 268).

Like Conrad's protagonist, the ethnographer struggles constantly to maintain an essential inner self-reliance—his "own true stuff," as Marlow puts it. The pull of dangerous others, the disintegrating frontier, is resisted by methodical, disciplined work. For Marlow obsessive attentions to his steamboat and its navigation provide the "surface wisdom" needed to hold his personality in place. As invoked in the *Diary,* Malinowski's scientific labors serve a similar purpose. Restrained, ethical personality is relentlessly achieved through work. This structure of feeling can be located with some precision in the historical predicament of late Victorian high colonial society, and it is closely related to the emergence of ethnographic culture.

Victorian social critics discerned a pervasive crisis for which Mathew Arnold's title *Culture and Anarchy* provided the basic diagnosis: against the fragmentation of modern life stood the order and wholeness of culture. Raymond Williams (1966) has offered a subtle account of these humanist responses to the unprecedented technological and ideological transformations at work in the mid-nineteenth century. George Eliot's strange affirmation is characteristic: of the three words "God," "Immortality," and "Duty," she pronounced, "with terrible earnestness, how inconceivable was the *first,* how unbelievable was the *second,* and yet how peremptory and absolute the *third!*" (quoted in Houghton 1957:43). Duty had become a deliberate belief, a willed fidelity to aspects of convention and to *work* (Carlyle's solution). Ian Watt has persuasively tied Conrad to this response (1979:148–151). Marlow, in the middle of Africa, clings for dear life to his steamboat, to the routine duties of its maintenance and navigation. And the structure persists in Malinowski's *Diary,* with its constant self-exhortations to avoid loose distractions and get down to work. In the culture and anarchy problematic (which persists in plural, anthropological culture concepts that privilege order and system over disorder and conflict), personal and collective essences must continuously be *maintained.* The ethnographic standpoint that concerns us here stands half-outside these processes, observing their local, arbitrary, but indispensable workings.

Culture, a collective fiction, is the ground for individual identity and freedom. The self, Marlow's "own true stuff," is a product of work, an ideological construction that is nonetheless essential, the foundation of ethics. But once culture becomes visible as an object and ground, a system of meaning among others, the ethnographic self can no longer take root in unmediated identity. Edward Said has said of Conrad that his principal struggle, reflected in his writing, was "the achievement of character" (1966:13). Indeed he reconstructed himself quite carefully in the persona of an "English" author, the character who speaks in the "Author's Note" he would later add to each of his works. This construction of a self was both artificial and deadly serious. (We can see the process parodied by the accountant in *Heart of Darkness,* who seems literally to be held together by his ridiculously formal but somehow admirable get-up.) All of this gives special poignancy to the sentence that ends the published *Diary:* "Truly I lack real character."

Malinowski did, however, rescue a self from the disintegration and depression. That self was to be tied, like Conrad's, to the process of writing. In this context it is worth exploring another region of similarity between the *Diary* and *Heart of Darkness:* The role of incongruous written texts. The fragmented subjectivity manifested in both works is that of a writer, and the pull of different desires and languages is manifested in a number of discrepant inscriptions. The most famous example in *Heart of Darkness* is Kurtz's strident essay on the suppression of savage customs, abruptly canceled by his own scrawled comment, "Exterminate all the brutes." But another equally significant text loose in Conrad's jungle is a strange book Marlow discovers on one of only two perilous departures from the deck of his steamboat (on the other he wrestles Kurtz back from the wilderness). In a shack by the riverbank he falls into an almost mystical reverie:

> There remained a rude table—a plank on two posts; a heap of rubbish reposed in a dark corner, and by the door I picked up a book. It had lost its covers, and the pages had been thumbed into a state of extremely dirty softness; but the back had been lovingly stitched afresh with white cotton thread, which looked clean yet. It was an extraordinary find. Its title was, *An Inquiry Into Some Points of Seamanship,* by a man Towser, Towson—some such name—Master in His Majesty's Navy. The matter looked dreary reading enough, with illustrative diagrams and repulsive tables of figures, and the copy was sixty years old. I handled this amazing antiquity with the greatest possible tenderness, lest it should dissolve in my hands. Within, Towson or Towser was inquiring earnestly into the breaking strain of ships' chains and tackle, and other such matters. Not a very enthralling book; but at the first glance you could see there a singleness of intention, an honest concern for the humble pages, thought out so many years ago, luminous with another than a professional light. The simple old sailor, with his

talk of chains and purchases, made me forget the jungle and the pilgrims in a delicious sensation of having come upon something unmis-
takably real. Such a book being there was wonderful enough; but still
more astounding were the notes pencilled in the margin, and plainly
referring to the text. I couldn't believe my eyes! They were in cipher!
Yes, it looked like cipher. Fancy a man lugging with him a book of that
description into this nowhere and studying it—in cipher at that! It was
an extraagant mystery.   (pp. 38–39)[9]

The passage has religious overtones—a miraculous relic, an abrupt
movement in imagery from dirt and decay to transcendence and light
and thence into mystery, the naive witnessing of a moment of faith. We
must be careful not to interpret the *Inquiry*'s appeal to Marlow simply as
nostalgia for the sea, though that is part of its charm. The Russian "harlequin" who turns out to be the book's owner seems to read the treatise
primarily in this way; for he takes careful notes, presumably on the
book's content, as if he were studying seamanship. For Marlow, however,
the inspiration of the book proceeds in some way directly out of the
writing itself, which, transcending the chains and ships and tackle, is
"luminous with another than a professional light." Marlow heeds not the
content but the language. He is interested in the old sailor's painstaking
craft; his way of making the book and his "talk" seem concrete—even to
the abstract numerical tables.

What charms Marlow is not primarily the possibility of sincere authorship. The old salt, "Towser or Towson—some such name—Master in
His Majesty's Navy," is personally elusive; it is not his being that counts
but his language. The man seems to dissolve into vague typicality; what
matters is his plain English. Significantly, though, the text fails to unite its
two equally devout readers; for when they finally meet, the Russian is
overjoyed to greet a fellow seaman, whereas Marlow is disappointed not
to find an Englishman. Readership is in question. The same physical
book provokes different, equally reverent reactions. I cannot explore
here the biographical significance of the disjuncture: Conrad had just
shed his official Russian citizenship for British nationality, and arguably
the harlequin is connected with the young wanderer, Korzeniowski, who
was becoming Conrad. It is enough to notice the radical relativity: the
distance between two readings. The "cipher" makes the point graphi-
cally, and if the marginalia turn out later to be in a European language,

---

9. Page references here and elsewhere are from the 1971 Norton edition.

that in no way diminishes the graphic image of a separateness. (It is reminiscent of the sense of unease one experiences on finding strange markings in a book and then recognizing having made them oneself—another person—in a previous reading.)

What persists is the text itself—barely. Worn by thumbing and cut loose from its covers—which may symbolize the context of its original publication—the written text must resist decay as it travels through space and time. After sixty years—a human lifetime—the moment of disintegration has come. The author's creation faces oblivion, but a reader stitches the pages lovingly back together. Then the book is abandoned to its death somewhere on a strange continent, its nautical content run aground in the absence of context—and once more a reader to the rescue. Rescue is one of Conrad's key images for his work; the act of writing always reaches toward rescue in an imagined act of reading. Significantly the text that means most in *Heart of Darkness* is the one with the least reference to the situation at hand.

Malinowski's fieldwork experience is filled with discrepant inscriptions: his detailed field notes, written in English and Kiriwinian; vernacular texts, often recorded on the back of letters from abroad; his Polish (actually heteroglot) diary; the multilingual correspondence; and finally a corpus worth lingering on for a moment, the novels he cannot resist. These last contain whole narrated worlds that seem at times more real (in any case more desirable) than the day-to-day business of research, with its many incomplete, contradictory notes, impressions, data that must be made to cohere. Malinowski catches himself "escaping from" Trobriand actuality "to the company of Thackeray's London snobs, following them eagerly around the streets of the big city." (The escapist reading of ethnographers in the field may require an essay of its own.)

Malinowski's novels suggest a revealing though imperfect parallel with Towser's *Inquiry*—another wonderfully compelling fiction in the midst of confusing experience. Towser's book shows the possibility of personally and authentically speaking the truth; and it points toward writing (a miraculous presence in absence) as salvation. But Towser is also a temptation, like Malinowski's novels, drawing Marlow away from his work, his steamboat, into a kind of vertiginous reverie. Such readings are desired communions, places where a coherent subjectivity can be recovered in fictional identification with a whole voice or world. Towser and the novels do suggest a viable path beyond fragmentation, not for the charmed reader but for the hard-working, constructive writer. For Malinowski rescue lies in creating realist cultural fictions, of which *Argonauts* is his first fully realized success. In both novels and ethnographies the self as author stages the diverse discourses and scenes of a believable world.

人

The loose texts in *Heart of Darkness* and the *Diary* are scraps of worlds; like field notes they are incongruent. They must be *made* into a probable portrait. To unify a messy scene of writing it is necessary to select, combine, rewrite (and thus efface) these texts. The resulting true fictions for Malinowski are *Argonauts* and the whole series of Trobriand ethnographies, for Conrad *Almayer's Folly* and the long process of learning to write English books, culminating in his first masterpiece, *Heart of Darkness*. Obviously these are different writing experiences: ethnographies are both like and unlike novels. But in an important general way the two experiences enact the process of fictional self-fashioning in relative systems of culture and language that I call ethnographic. *Heart of Darkness* enacts and ironically calls attention to the process. *Argonauts* is less reflexive, but it does both produce a cultural fiction and announce the emergence of an authoritative persona: Bronislaw Malinowski, new-style anthropologist. This persona, endowed with what Malinowski called "the ethnographer's magic," a new kind of insight and experience, was not, properly speaking, constructed in the field. The persona does not represent but rationalizes a research experience. The *Diary* shows this clearly, for the fieldwork, like most similar research, was ambivalent and unruly. The confused subjectivity it records is sharply different from that staged and recounted in *Argonauts*. When the *Diary* was first published in 1967, the discrepancy was shocking, for the authoritative participant-observer, a locus of sympathetic understanding of the other, is simply not visible in the *Diary*. Conversely, what is visible, a pronounced ambivalence toward the Trobrianders, empathy mixed with desire and aversion, is nowhere in *Argonauts*, where comprehension, scrupulousness, and generosity reign.

One is tempted to propose that ethnographic comprehension (a coherent position of sympathy and hermeneutic engagement) is better seen as a creation of ethnographic *writing* than a consistent quality of ethnographic *experience*. In any event what Malinowski achieved in writing was simultaneously (1) the fictional invention of the Trobrianders from a mass of field notes, documents, memories, and so forth, and (2) the construction of a new public figure, the anthropologist as fieldworker, a persona that would be further elaborated by Margaret Mead and others. It is worth noting that the persona of the participant-observer anthropologist was not the professional image about which Malinowski fantasized in the *Diary* (which involved knighthoods, "Royal Societies," "New Humanisms," and the like). Rather it was an artifact of the version he constructed retrospectively in *Argonauts*. In fusing anthropology with fieldwork Malinowski made the most, the best story, of what circumstance had obliged him to attempt.

Such considerations lead us to a problem in discussing Malinowski's—and indeed nearly all—ethnographic production. Thanks to a growing number of confessional and analytic accounts, we know more and more about fieldwork experiences and their constraints. But the actual writing of ethnographies remains obscure and unanalyzed. We know something about Malinowski's Trobriand research of 1914 and 1918 but virtually nothing of what he was doing in the Canary Islands during 1920 and 1921. (He was writing *Argonauts of the Western Pacific*.)

The *Diary* leaves us hanging. There is a sudden gap in the writing that, as we learn from small revelations when the text struggles to resume, signals the arrival of word that his mother has died. Then the desperate envoi: "Truly I lack real character." Silence. Three years later Malinowski reappears as the author of *Argonauts*, the charter of the new fieldworker-anthropologist. What has intervened? Like Conrad in the period between the rout of his African adventure and the success of *Heart of Darkness* he has accepted three major commitments: (1) to writing, (2) to marriage, and (3) to a limited audience, language, and culture.

The Canary Islands are an intriguing scene for Malinowski's writing cure. He goes there for his health, but the choice is overdetermined. One is tempted to see this place as a liminal site at the outer edge of Europe, propitious for a displaced Pole writing Pacific ethnography. More important, however, is the fact that he had earlier vacationed in the Canaries with his mother. Now he is there again with his new wife, completing his first major work. He is fully in the realm of substitution, of a series of compromises and replacements. For Malinowski, as for Conrad, three such substitutions are crucial: (1) family, with mother replaced by wife; (2) language, with the mother tongue abandoned for English; and (3) writing, with inscriptions and texts substituted for immediate oral experience. The arbitrary code of one language, English, is finally given precedence. The mother tongue recedes, and (here the personal and the political coincide) English dominates—represents and interprets—Kiriwinian. Cultural attachment is enacted as marriage. The yearning for sincere interlocutory speech gives way to a play on written substitutes.

Some of these transitions and replacements were surely at stake in the successful writing on the Canary Islands. Malinowski's *Diary* ends with the death of a mother; *Argonauts* is a rescue, the inscription of a culture.[10]

⼊

A few final reflections on the current status of the ethnographic author: When Malinowski's *Diary* was first published, it seemed scandalous. The quintessential anthropologist of *Argonauts* did not, in fact, always maintain an understanding, benevolent attitude toward his informants; his state of mind in the field was anything but coolly objective; the story of ethnographic research included in the finished monograph was stylized and selective. These facts, once entered into the public record of anthropological science, shook the fiction of cultural relativism as a stable subjectivity, a standpoint for a self that understands and represents a cultural other. In the wake of the *Diary* cross-cultural comprehension appeared a rhetorical construct, its balanced comprehension traversed by ambivalence and power.

We recall the fate of Kurtz's violent scrawl in *Heart of Darkness,* "Exterminate all the brutes." Marlow tears off the damning, truthful supplement when he gives Kurtz's disquisition on savage customs to the Belgian press. It is a telling gesture, and it suggests a troubling question about Malinowski and anthropology: What is always torn off, as it were, to construct a public, believable discourse? In *Argonauts* the *Diary* was excluded, written over, in the process of giving wholeness to a culture (Trobriand) and a self (the scientific ethnographer). Thus the discipline of fieldwork-based anthropology, in constituting its authority, constructs and reconstructs coherent cultural others and interpreting selves. If this ethnographic self-fashioning presupposes lies of omission and of rhetoric, it also makes possible the telling of powerful truths. But like Marlow's account aboard *Nellie,* the truths of cultural descriptions are meaningful to specific interpretive communities in limiting historical circumstances. Thus the "tearing off," Nietzsche reminds us, is simultaneously an act of censorship *and* of meaning creation, a suppression of incoherence and contradiction. The best ethnographic fictions are, like Malinowski's, in-

---

10. It would be interesting to analyze systematically how, out of the heteroglot encounters of fieldwork, ethnographers construct texts whose prevailing language comes to override, represent, or translate other languages. Here Talal Asad's conception of a persistent, structured inequality of languages gives political and historical content to the apparently neutral process of cultural translation (Asad 1986).

tricately truthful; but their facts, like all facts in the human sciences, are classified, contextualized, narrated, and intensified.

In recent years new forms of ethnographic realism have emerged, more dialogical and open-ended in narrative style. Self and other, culture and its interpreters, appear less confident entities. Among those who have revised ethnographic authority and rhetoric from within the discipline I shall mention just three (whom Clifford Geertz has marked off for critique in a series of provocative lectures on the writing of ethnography): Paul Rabinow, Kevin Dwyer, and Vincent Crapanzano.[11] (For their sins of self-display Geertz calls them "Malinowski's Children.") These three can stand for many others currently engaged in a complex field of textual experiments at the limits of academic ethnography.[12] I have said that anthropology still awaits its Conrad. In various ways the recent experimentalists are filling that role. They teeter productively, as Conrad did— and as, more ambivalently, Geertz himself balances—between realism and modernism. The experimentalists reveal in their writings an acute sense of the fashioned, contingent status of all cultural descriptions (and of all cultural describers).

These self-reflexive writers occupy ironic positions within the general project of ethnographic subjectivity and cultural description. They stand, as we all do, on an uncertain historical ground, a place from which we can begin to analyze the ideological matrix that produced ethnography, the plural definition of culture, and a self positioned to mediate between discrepant worlds of meaning. (To say that this historical ground is, for example, postcolonial or postmodern is not to say much— except to name what one hopes no longer to have to be.) In fact most of the self-conscious hermeneutic ethnographers writing today get about as far as Conrad did in *Heart of Darkness,* at least in their presentations of narrative authority. They now gesture toward the problematic other narrator on the deck of the *Nellie* as they say, with Marlow: "Of course in this you fellows see more than I did then. You see me, whom you know."

11. Geertz's lectures (1983), "Works and Lives: The Anthropologist as Author," were not yet published as of this writing. In the section of the oral presentation I am discussing he refers primarily to Rabinow 1977; Crapanzano 1980; and Dwyer 1982.

12. The discursive field cannot, of course, be limited to the discipline of anthropology or its frontiers; nor is it adequately captured in terms like *reflexive* or *dialogical.* For provisional surveys see Marcus and Cushman 1982; Clifford 1986a; and Chapter 1.

Store, avenue des Gobelins. 1920s. Photograph by Eugène Atget.

Part Two ⚓ Displacements

The coupling of two realities, irreconcilable in appearance,
upon a plane which apparently does not suit them . . .
—MAX ERNST, "WHAT IS THE MECHANISM OF COLLAGE?"

4. On Ethnographic Surrealism

ANDRÉ BRETON often insisted that surrealism was not a body of doctrines or a definable idea but an activity. This chapter is an exploration of ethnographic activity set, as it must always be, in specific cultural and historical circumstances. I will be concentrating on ethnography and surrealism in France between the two world wars. To discuss these activities together—at times, indeed, to permit them to merge—is to question a number of common distinctions and unities. I am concerned less with charting intellectual or artistic traditions than with following some of the byways of what I take to be a crucial modern orientation toward cultural order. If I sometimes use familiar terms against the grain, my aim is to cut across retrospectively established definitions and to recapture, if possible, a situation in which ethnography is again something unfamiliar and surrealism not yet a bounded province of modern art and literature.

The orientation toward cultural order that I evoke cannot be neatly defined. It is more properly called modernist than modern, taking as its problem—and opportunity—the fragmentation and juxtaposition of cultural values. From this disenchanted viewpoint stable orders of collective

117

meaning appear to be constructed, artificial, and indeed often ideological or repressive. The sort of normality or common sense that can amass empires in fits of absent-mindedness or wander routinely into world wars is seen as a contested reality to be subverted, parodied, and transgressed. I will suggest reasons for linking ethnographic activity to this set of critical attitudes, dispositions usually associated with the artistic avant-garde. In France particularly the modern human sciences have not lost contact with the world of literature and art, and in the hothouse milieu of Parisian cultural life no field of social or artistic research can long remain indifferent to influences or provocations from beyond its disciplinary boundaries. In the twenties and thirties, as we shall see, ethnography and surrealism developed in close proximity.

I am using the term *surrealism* in an obviously expanded sense to circumscribe an aesthetic that values fragments, curious collections, unexpected juxtapositions—that works to provoke the manifestation of extraordinary realities drawn from the domains of the erotic, the exotic, and the unconscious. This set of attitudes cannot, of course, be limited to Breton's group; and the surrealist movement narrowly defined—with its manifestoes, schisms, and excommunications—is not the concern here. Indeed the figures I will be discussing were at best fellow travelers or dissidents who broke with Breton. They partook nonetheless of the general attitude I call surrealist,[1] a tangled disposition foreshortened here in an attempt to disengage its ethnographic dimension. Ethnography and surrealism are not stable unities; my subject is not, therefore, an overlapping of two clearly distinguishable traditions.[2] Moreover, I have tried not to think of my topic as a conjuncture restricted to French culture of the twenties and thirties. The boundaries of art and science (especially the human sciences) are ideological and shifting, and intellectual history is itself enmeshed in these shifts. Its genres do not remain firmly anchored. Changing definitions of art or science must provoke new retrospective

---

1. My broad use of the term roughly coincides with Susan Sontag's (1977) view of surrealism as a pervasive—perhaps dominant—modern sensibility. For a treatment that distinguishes the specific tradition I am discussing from the surrealism of Breton's movement see Jamin 1980. A "corrective" to this chapter, reasserting strict definitions of both surrealism and ethnography, can be found in Jamin 1986.

2. Research on the common ground of twentieth-century social science and the avant-garde is still undeveloped. Thus my discussion is very preliminary. On the French context see Boon 1972; Duvignaud 1979; Hollier 1979; Jamin 1979, 1980; Lourau 1974; and Tiryakian 1979.

unities, new ideal types for historical description. In this sense ethnographic surrealism is a utopian construct, a statement at once about past and future possibilities for cultural analysis.

The Ethnographic Surreal

In "The Storyteller" Walter Benjamin describes the transition from a traditional mode of communication based on continuous oral narrative and shared experience to a cultural style characterized by bursts of "information"—the photograph, the newspaper clip, the perceptual shocks of a modern city. Benjamin begins his essay with the First World War:

> A generation that had gone to school on a horse-drawn streetcar now stood under the open sky in a countryside in which nothing remained unchanged but the clouds, and beneath the clouds, in a field of force of destructive torrents and explosions, was the tiny, fragile human body. (1969:84)

Reality is no longer a given, a natural, familiar environment. The self, cut loose from its attachments, must discover meaning where it may—a predicament, evoked at its most nihilistic, that underlies both surrealism and modern ethnography. Earlier literary and artistic refractions of Benjamin's modern world are well known: the experience of Baudelaire's urban *flâneur*, Rimbaud's systematic sensual derangements, the analytic decomposition of reality begun by Cézanne and completed by the cubists, and especially Lautréamont's famous definition of beauty, "the chance encounter on a dissecting table of a sewing machine and an umbrella." To see culture and its norms—beauty, truth, reality—as artificial arrangements susceptible to detached analysis and comparison with other possible dispositions is crucial to an ethnographic attitude.

In his classic *History of Surrealism* (1965) Maurice Nadeau stressed the formative impact of wartime experiences on the founders of the surrealist movement—Breton, Eluard, Aragon, Péret, Soupault. After Europe's collapse into barbarism and the manifest bankruptcy of the ideology of progress, after a deep fissure had opened between the experience of the trenches and the official language of heroism and victory, after the romantic rhetorical conventions of the nineteenth century had proved themselves incapable of representing the reality of the war, the world was permanently surrealist. Fresh from the trenches, Guillaume Apollinaire coined the term in a letter of 1917. His *Calligrammes* (1918:341) with their fractured form and heightened attention to the perceived world, announced the postwar aesthetic:

> The Victory above all will be
> To see clearly at a distance
> To see everything
> Near at hand
> And may all things bear a new name.

While for Fernand Léger:

> The war had thrust me, as a soldier, into the heart of a mechanical atmosphere. Here I discovered the beauty of the fragment. I sensed a new reality in the detail of a machine, in the common object. I tried to find the plastic value of these fragments of our modern life.[3]

Before the war Apollinaire had decorated his study with African "fetishes," and in his long poem "Zone" these objects would be invoked as "des Christ d'une autre forme et d'une autre croyance." For the Paris avant-garde, Africa (and to a lesser degree Oceania and America) provided a reservoir of other forms and other beliefs. This suggests a second element of the ethnographic surrealist attitude, a belief that the other (whether accessible in dreams, fetishes, or Lévy-Bruhl's *mentalité primitive*) was a crucial object of modern research. Unlike the exoticism of the nineteenth century, which departed from a more-or-less confident cultural order in search of a temporary *frisson,* a circumscribed experience of the bizarre, modern surrealism and ethnography began with a reality deeply in question. Others appeared now as serious human alternatives; modern cultural relativism became possible. As artists and writers set about after the war putting the pieces of culture together in new ways, their field of selection expanded dramatically. The "primitive" societies of the planet were increasingly available as aesthetic, cosmological, and scientific resources. These possibilities drew on something more than an older Orientalism; they required modern ethnography. The postwar context was structured by a basically ironic experience of culture. For every local custom or truth there was always an exotic alternative, a possible juxtaposition or incongruity. Below (psychologically) and

---

3. Quoted in Sontag 1977:204. Paul Fussell's incisive study *The Great War and Modern Memory* (1975) also stresses the First World War's initiation of a generation into a fragmented, "modernist" world.

beyond (geographically) ordinary reality there existed another reality. Surrealism shared this ironic situation with relativist ethnography.

The term *ethnography* as I am using it here is evidently different from the empirical research technique of a human science that in France was called ethnology, in England social anthropology, and in America cultural anthropology. I am referring to a more general cultural predisposition that cuts through modern anthropology and that this science shares with twentieth-century art and writing. The ethnographic label suggests a characteristic attitude of participant observation among the artifacts of a defamiliarized cultural reality. The surrealists were intensely interested in exotic worlds, among which they included a certain Paris. Their attitude, while comparable to that of the fieldworker who strives to render the unfamiliar comprehensible, tended to work in the reverse sense, making the familiar strange. The contrast is in fact generated by a continuous play of the familiar and the strange, of which ethnography and surrealism are two elements. This play is constitutive of the modern cultural situation I am assuming as the ground for my account.

The world of the city for Louis Aragon's *Payson de Paris* or for Breton in *Nadja* was a source of the unexpected and the significant—significant in ways that suggested beneath the dull veneer of the real the possibility of another more miraculous world based on radically different principles of classification and order. The surrealists frequented the Marché aux Puces, the vast flea market of Paris, where one could rediscover the artifacts of culture, scrambled and rearranged. With luck one could bring home some bizarre or unexpected object, a work of art with nowhere to go—"ready-mades" such as Marcel Duchamp's bottle rack, and *objets sauvages*, African or Oceanian sculptures. These objects—stripped of their functional context—were necessary furnishings for the avant-garde studio.

It is best to suspend disbelief in considering the practices—and the excesses—of surrealist "ethnographers." And it is important to understand their way of taking culture seriously, as a contested reality—a way that included the ridiculing and reshuffling of its orders. This much is necessary if one is to penetrate the milieu that spawned and oriented the emerging French scholarly tradition. More generally, it is advisable not to dismiss surrealism too quickly as frivolous, in contrast with the *sérieux* of ethnographic science. The connections between anthropological research and research in literature and the arts, always strong in this century, needed to be more fully explored. Surrealism is ethnography's secret sharer—for better or worse—in the description, analysis, and extension of the grounds of twentieth-century expression and meaning.

Mauss, Bataille, Métraux

Paris 1925: the *Revue nègre* enjoys a smash season at the Theâtre des Champs-Elysées, following on the heels of W. H. Wellmon's Southern Syncopated Orchestra. Spirituals and *le jazz* sweep the avant-garde bourgeoisie, which haunts Negro bars, sways to new rhythms in search of something primitive, *sauvage* . . . and completely modern. Stylish Paris is transported by the pulsing strum of banjos and by the sensuous Josephine Baker "abandoning herself to the rhythm of the Charleston" (Leiris 1968:33).

Paris 1925: a nucleus of University scholars—Paul Rivet, Lucien Lévy-Bruhl, and Marcel Mauss—establishes the Institut d'Ethnologie. For the first time in France there exists an organization whose primary concern is the training of professional fieldworkers and the publication of ethnographic scholarship.

Paris 1925: in the wake of the First Surrealist Manifesto the movement begins to make itself notorious. France is engaged in a minor war with anticolonial rebels in Morocco; Breton and company sympathize with the insurgents. At a banquet in honor of the symbolist poet Saint-Pol-Roux, a melee erupts between the surrealists and conservative patriots. Epithets fly; "Vive l'Allemagne!" rings out; Philippe Soupault swings from a chandelier, kicking over bottles and glasses. Michel Leiris is soon at an open window, denouncing France to the growing crowd. A riot ensues; Leiris, nearly lynched, is arrested and manhandled by the police (Nadeau 1965:112–114).

The three events were connected by more than a coincidence of date. For example when Leiris, whose evocation of Josephine Baker I have just quoted, defected from the surrealist movement in the late twenties seeking a more concrete application for his subversive literary talents, it seemed natural for him to study with Mauss at the Institut d'Ethnologie and to become an ethnographer of Africa—a participant in France's first major fieldwork expedition, the Mission Dakar-Djibouti of 1931–1933. Scientific, or at least academic ethnography had not yet come of age. Its development in the early thirties, through successes like that much-publicized Dakar-Djibouti expedition, was continuous with the surrealism of the twenties. The organizational energies of Rivet and the teaching of Mauss were dominant factors. I shall discuss Rivet's institutional accomplishments later in this chapter, notably his creation of the Musée de l'Homme. Mauss's pervasive influence is harder to pin down since it took the form of oral inspiration in his teaching at the Ecole Pratique des Hautes Etudes and the Institut d'Ethnologie.

Nearly every major French ethnographer before the mid-fifties— with the notable exception of Lévi-Strauss—was the beneficiary of Mauss's direct stimulation. From the perspective of today's intellectual regime, where publication is at a premium and where any idea of value tends to be guarded for the next article or monograph, it is astonishing, indeed moving, to note the tremendous energies that Mauss poured into his teaching at Hautes Etudes. A glance through the school's *Annuaire*, where course summaries are recorded, reveals the extraordinary wealth of learning and analysis made available to a few students, year in and year out, without repetition, much of which never saw print. Mauss gave courses on topics from Siberian shamanism to Australian oral poetry to Polynesian and West Coast Indian ritual, bringing to bear his profound knowledge of oriental religions and classical antiquity. Readers of Mauss's essays—the pages half-devoured by footnotes—will recognize the breadth of references; they will miss, however, the wit and verve, the give-and-take of his oral performances.

Mauss was a research scholar. He taught a select group. In the thirties a band of devotees, some of them amateurs of the fashionable exotic, others ethnographers preparing to leave for the field (some of the former in the process of becoming the latter), would follow Mauss from hall to hall. At Hautes Etudes, the Institut d'Ethnologie, and later the Collège de France they reveled in his erudite, loquacious, and always provocative tours through the world's cultural diversities. Mauss's lectures were not theoretical demonstrations. They stressed, in their divagating way, concrete ethnographic fact; he had a sharp eye for the significant detail. Though he never did fieldwork himself, Mauss was effective in pressing his students toward firsthand research (see Condominas 1972a, b; Mauss 1947).

His essay "Techniques of the Body" (1934) gives a hint of Mauss's oral style. Here are a few lines from what is essentially a long list of the things people in different parts of the world do with their bodies:

> It's normal for children to squat. We no longer know how to squat. I consider this to be an absurdity and inferiority of our races, civilizations, societies.

> The notion that sleeping is something natural is completely inexact.

Nothing is more dizzying than to see a Kabylie come downstairs with *babouches* on. How can he stand without losing his slippers? I've tried to watch, to do it. I don't see how. And I don't understand either how women can walk on their high heels.

Hygiene of natural body functions. Here I could list numberless facts.

Finally, it must be understood that dancing while embracing is a product of modern European civilization. This should show you that things quite natural for us are historical; they may horrify everyone else in the world except us. (pp. 374, 378, 381, 383)

The prehistorian André Leroi-Gourhan remembers his teacher as a man of "inspired confusion." In an interview he is asked what he recalls of his teacher's speech:

His silences, if I may put it thus. I can't provide an imitation; so many years have passed, and I have an idealized image of Mauss; but he constructed his sentences in a way that suggested things without declaring them inflexibly. His discourse was all articulations and elasticity. Most of his sentences came up empty, but it was an emptiness that invited you to build. That's why I said the most characteristic things were his silences.

He was especially amazing when he did textual explications on authors who had worked in Siberia on the Giliaks or Goldies. I remember sessions at Hautes Etudes—there were never more than ten of us, and yet! We gathered around a table like this one, not quite so long; Mauss translated from German to French with commentaries that drew comparisons from every corner of the globe. His erudition was fantastic, and we took it in without really being able to say afterwards how he had managed to be so engrossing. (1982:32)

Mauss did not write books. His *Oeuvres* (1968–69) is composed of essays, scholarly articles, interventions at meetings, countless book reviews. Compressed classics such as *The Gift* (1923) and *A General Theory of Magic* (1902) were published in the *Année sociologique*. His magnum opus, a dissertation on prayer, remained a collection of drafts, essays, scraps, and notes. So did other synthetic works on money and the nation. Perhaps because so much was connected in his mind, Mauss could easily be sidetracked; and he was profligate with commitments and loyalties. He lectured constantly and spent years bringing work by deceased colleagues (Durkheim, Robert Hertz, Henri Hubert) to completion. A Dreyfusard and socialist in the tradition of Jaurès, he wrote for *L'humanité* and took part in strikes, elections, and the popular university movement. Unlike Durkheim, his rather austere uncle, Mauss was gregarious, bohemian, and something of a bon vivant.

Some recall Mauss as a loyal Durkheimian. Others see a forerunner of structuralism. Some see primarily an anthropologist, others a historian. Still others, citing his rabbinical roots, his training in Sanskrit, and his lifelong interest in ritual, ally him with students of religion such as his friends Marcel Granet, Hubert, and Leenhardt. Some stress Mauss's iconoclasm, others his coherent socialist-humanist vision. Some see a brilliant armchair theorist. Others remember a sharp empirical observer. The different versions of Mauss are not irreconcilable, but they do not quite add up. People reading and remembering him always seem to find something of themselves (from Leroi-Gourhan 1982:32–33):

> For a period of two years when I was attending nearly all his courses it was agreed that a comrade and I—a Russian Jew, Deborah Lifchitz who died in the Nazi deportation—would take notes in turn and in a way that would let us compare them to determine the real content of Mauss's teaching. We never managed to construct anything coherent because it was too rich and always ended up at the horizon. Later a record of his course was published by a group of former students. Well, there was a total divergence between what they noted and what Deborah and I took down! This is the secret, I believe, of the real spell he cast on his followers.

An example of how Mauss's peculiar brand of intellectual stimulation got around is provided by the great fieldworker Alfred Métraux, who was his student during the mid-twenties (Bing 1964:20–25). Being of a careful, empirical temperament, Métraux soon distrusted the fast-and-loose way that ethnographic fact was being used by the early surrealists. He devoted his life to firsthand research, becoming, in the words of Sidney Mintz (1972:2), the "fieldworker's fieldworker." But he remained in touch with the avant-garde. While a student at the Ecole des Chartes, Métraux had established a lasting friendship with Georges Bataille, the idiosyncratic scholar, essayist, and pornographer, whose influence has been so pervasive on the present generation of radical critics and writers in Paris. The work of the two friends could not be more different: the one restrained, almost puritanical in tone, though with a flair for isolating the telling detail; the other provocative, far-flung, Nietzschean. Yet in a curious, compelling way the two are complementary: while Bataille was steadied by Métraux's erudition, Métraux found his passion for ethnography confirmed by his friend's willingness to express what, according to Leiris, they had in common—"a violent ardor for life combined with a pitiless awareness of its absurdity" (Leiris 1966a:252; see also Bataille 1957:14; and Métraux 1963:677–684). The lifelong association between Bataille and Métraux can be seen as emblematic of that enduring contiguity, if not always similarity, that has kept French ethnography on speaking terms with the avant-garde.

Bataille's most influential book was his late treatise *L'erotisme* (1957). Its orientation, and that of Bataille's work generally, can be traced to Mauss by way of Métraux's report of a lecture around 1925. In *L'erotisme* Bataille introduces the book's key chapter, on transgression, with the phrase "Transgression does not negate an interdiction, it transcends and completes it." Métraux specifies that his characteristic formula is only a paraphrase of "one of those profound aphorisms, often obscure, that Marcel Mauss would throw out without worrying about the confusion of his students." Métraux had heard Mauss say in a lecture, "Taboos are made to be violated." This theme, which Bataille would often repeat, became a key to his thinking. Culture is ambivalent in structure. One may refrain from murder, or one may go to war; both acts are, for Bataille, generated by the interdiction on killing. Cultural order includes both the rule and the transgression. This logic applies to all manner of rules and freedoms—for example to sexual normality and its partner the perversions. In Métraux's words, "Mauss's proposition, in the apparent absurdity of its form, manifests the inevitable connection of conflicting emotions: [quoting Bataille] 'Under the impact of negative emotion, we must obey the interdiction. We violate it if the emotion is positive' " (Métraux 1963:682–683; Bataille 1957:72–73).

Bataille's lifelong project was to demystify and valorize this "positive emotion" of transgression in all its various forms, and in this he was true to his surrealist beginnings. (In the twenties Bataille was first an associate then a critic of the Breton group.) One of his first published texts was part of a collection on pre-Columbian art, in which he collaborated with Métraux and Rivet. His appreciation of human sacrifice ("For the Aztecs death was nothing") juxtaposes in surrealist fashion the beautiful and the ugly, the normal and the repugnant. Thus Tenochtitlán is simultaneously a "human slaughterhouse" and a gorgeous "Venice" of canals and flowers. The sacrificial victims dance in perfumed garlands; the swarms of flies that gather on the running blood are beautiful (Bataille 1930:13). "All writing is garbage," said Antonin Artaud, another renegade surrealist, who would flee France to his own dream of Mexico—courting madness among the Tarahumara Indians (Artaud 1976). The exotic was a primary court of appeal against the rational, the beautiful, the normal of the West. But Bataille's interest in the world's cultural systems, however, finally went well beyond mere delectation or escapism. Unlike most surrealists he worked toward a more rigorous theory of collective order based on the double logic of interdiction. Always au courant with ethnographic scholarship, he continued to draw heavily on Mauss—La part maudite (1949) is an elaborate extrapolation of The Gift—and later on Lévi-Strauss. The logic developed by Bataille, which I cannot pursue here, has provided an important continuity in the ongoing relation between cultural analysis and early surrealism in France. It links the twenties' context to a later generation of radical critics, including Michel Foucault, Roland Barthes, Jacques Derrida, and the Tel Quel group.[4]

It is worth noting that the collection of essays in which Métraux, Rivet, and Bataille collaborated was part of the first popular exhibition of pre-Columbian art in France. The exhibit had been organized by Georges-Henri Rivière, a music student and amateur of jazz who would become France's most energetic ethnographic museologist. Rivière was well connected socially, Rivet politically. The latter understood perfectly that the creation of anthropological research institutions required a fashionable enthusiasm for things exotic. Such a vogue could be exploited financially and channeled in the interests of science and public instruction. Rivet, impressed by Rivière's successful pre-Columbian show, hired him on the spot to reorganize the Trocadéro museum, whose collections were in a state of disorganization and disrepair. This was the beginning of a productive collaboration between the two chief *animateurs* of French ethnographic institutions, one that would result in the Musée de

---

4. The tradition is visible in "Hommage à Georges Bataille," published in 1963 by *Critique*, which includes essays by Alfred Métraux, Michel Leiris, Raymond Queneau, André Masson, and Jean Wahl of the prewar generation, and by Michel Foucault, Roland Barthes, and Philippe Sollers of the emerging critical tradition. (Another outgrowth of ethnographic surrealism that cannot be pursued here is its connection with Third World modernism and nascent anticolonial discourse. It is enough to mention a few prominent names: Aimé Cesaire (a longtime friend of Leiris), Octavio Paz, and Alejo Carpentier, who was a collaborator on the journal *Documents*.)

l'Homme and in Rivière's Musée des Arts et Traditions Populaires (see Rivière 1968, 1979).

Before the full deployment of these institutions, in the early years of the Institut d'Ethnologie, Mauss's courses remained the crucial forum for an emerging ethnography. This teaching was a curious scholarly instrument, not fundamentally at odds with surrealism and capable of stimulating the likes of both Métraux and Bataille. It is revealing to consider in this light a well-known evocation of Mauss:

> In his work, and still more in his teaching, unthought-of comparisons flourish. While he is often obscure by the constant use of antitheses, shortcuts, and apparent paradoxes which, later on, prove to be the result of a deeper insight, he gratifies his listener, suddenly, with fulgurating intuitions, providing the substance for months of fruitful thinking. In such cases, one feels that one has reached the bottom of the social phenomenon and has, as he says somewhere, "hit the bedrock." This constant striving toward the fundamental, this willingness to sift, over and over again, a huge mass of data until the purest material only remains, explains Mauss's preference for the essay over the book, and the limited size of his published work.   (Lévi-Strauss 1945:527)

This account from the pen of Lévi-Strauss suffers perhaps from a tendency in its final sentences to portray Mauss as a protostructuralist.[5] The drive to reach bedrock, to grasp only the purest underlying material is an aspiration more characteristic of Lévi-Strauss than of Mauss, who published relatively little not because he had distilled elemental truths but because he was preoccupied with teaching, editing, and politics, and because, knowing so much, he found that the truth had become too complex. As Louis Dumont recalls, "He had too many ideas to be able to give complete expression to any of them" (1972:12). Lévi-Strauss's description of the great teacher's provocative use of antithesis and paradox in the presentation of ethnographic knowledge rings true, however, in the context I have been discussing. Ethnographic truth for Mauss was restlessly subversive of surface realities. Its principal task was to discover, in his famous phrase, the many "lunes mortes," pale moons in the "firmament of

---

5. Lévi-Strauss's most elaborate attempt in this vein is his brilliant "Introduction à l'oeuvre de Marcel Mauss" (1950). For a good corrective see Maurice Leenhardt 1950.

reason" (1924:309). There is no better summary of the task of ethnographic surrealism, for the "reason" referred to is not a parochial Western rationality but the full human potential for cultural expression.

Taxonomies

In an avant-garde periodical's "Homage to Picasso" one is not surprised to find a statement from Mauss (1930). The journal in question, *Documents,* was a glossy review edited by Georges Bataille. It offers a revealing case of ethnographic surrealist collaboration. Bataille had left Breton's surrealist movement along with Robert Desnos, Leiris, Artaud, Raymond Queneau, and various others during the schisms of 1929, and his journal functioned as a forum for dissident views. It had, moreover, a distinctly ethnographic bent, which would attract the collaboration of future fieldworkers such as Griaule, André Schaeffner, and Leiris, as well as Rivière and Rivet. Griaule, Schaeffner, and Leiris would depart for Africa on the Mission Dakar-Djibouti soon after the demise of *Documents* in 1930. If *Documents* appears today as a rather strange context for purveying ethnographic knowledge, in the late twenties it was a perfectly appropriate—that is, outré—forum.

Indeed, it requires an effort of imagination to recapture the sense, or senses, of the word *ethnography* as it was used in the surrealist twenties. A defined social science with a discernible method, a set of classic texts, and university chairs was not yet fully formed. Examining the word's uses in a publication like *Documents,* we see how ethnographic evidence and an ethnographic attitude could function in the service of a subversive cultural criticism. In the subtitle of *Documents*—"Archéologie, Beaux Arts, Ethnographie, Variétés"—the wild card was "Ethnographie." It denoted a radical questioning of norms and an appeal to the exotic, the paradoxical, the *insolite*. It implied too a leveling and a reclassification of familiar categories. "Art," spelled with a capital *A,* had already succumbed to dada's heavy artillery. "Culture," having barely survived this postwar barrage, was now resolutely lower-case, a principle of relative order in which the sublime and the vulgar were treated as symbols of equal significance. Since culture was perceived by the collaborators of *Documents* as a system of moral and aesthetic hierarchies, the radical critic's task was one of semiotic decoding, with the aim of deauthenticating and then expanding or displacing the common categories. The cubists' break with the canons of realism had set the pace for a general assault on the normal. Ethnography, which shares with surrealism an abandonment of the distinction between high and low culture, provided both a fund of non-Western alternatives and a prevailing attitude of ironic participant observation among the hierarchies and meanings of collective life.

It is instructive to attempt an inventory of ethnographic perspectives as revealed by their use in *Documents*. Before one has caught the drift, one is surprised, for example, to come upon an article by Carl Einstein— author of *Negerplastik* (1915), a pioneering account of African sculpture viewed in the light of cubism—entitled "André Masson, étude ethnologique." What did it mean in 1929 to study an avant-garde painter "ethnologically"? From the outset Einstein sounds the cubist-surrealist battle cry:

> One thing is important: to shake what is called reality by means of nonadapted hallucinations so as to alter the value hierarchies of the real. Hallucinatory forces create a breach in the order of mechanistic processes; they introduce blocs of "a-causality" in this reality which had been absurdly given as such. The uninterrupted fabric of this reality is torn, and one inhabits the tension of dualisms.   (1929:95)

The "hallucinatory forces" of Masson's painting represent, according to Einstein, "the return of mythological creation, the return of a psychological archaism as opposed to a purely imitative archaism of forms" (p. 100). Einstein describes this mythic psychology as "totemic." To grasp the significance of Masson's metamorphoses and unexpected animal-human combinations, "it is enough to recall the primitive mask-costumes that incite identifications with animals, ancestors, etc." (p. 102). Einstein's casual allusion *en passant* to masks (African? Oceanian? Alaskan? His audience will know what he means) suggests a context in which exotic or archaic possibilities are never far from the surface of consciousness, are ever ready to offer confirmation for any and all breaks opened in the Western order of things. In Einstein's essay two key elements of ethnographic surrealism are noticeable: first, the corrosive analysis of a reality now identified as local and artificial; and second, the supplying of exotic alternatives.

There is a third aspect of this attitude that springs to one's attention as one leafs through the pages of *Documents*. Marcel Griaule provides a clear statement in an essay ridiculing the aesthetic assumptions of primitive-art amateurs who doubt the purity of a Baoule drum because the figure carved on it is holding a rifle. The ethnographic surrealist, unlike either the typical art critic or anthropologist of the period, delights in cultural impurities and disturbing syncretisms. Griaule equates the European's delectation of African art with the African's taste for textiles, gas cans, alcohol, and firearms. If Africans do not choose to imitate our high-cultural products, *tant pis!* He concludes:

> Ethnography—it is quite tiresome to have to keep repeating this—is interested in the *beautiful* and the *ugly,* in the European sense of these absurd words. It has, however, a tendency to be suspicious of the beautiful, which is rather often a rare—that is monstrous—occurrence in a civilization. Ethnography is suspicious too of itself—for it is a white science, i.e., stained with prejudices—and it will not refuse aesthetic value to an object because it is up-to-date or mass-produced. (1930:46)

André Schaeffner urges a similar point in a scholarly survey of "Les instruments de musique dans un museé d'ethnographie." His strictures are now an anthropological commonplace. Read, however, in the surrealist context of *Documents,* they recover their full subversive effect.

> Whoever says ethnography admits necessarily that no object designed to produce sound or music, however "primitive" or formless it may seem, no musical instrument—whether its existence is accidental or essential—shall be excluded from a methodical classification. For this purpose any percussive procedure, on a wooden box or on the earth itself, is of equal importance with the melodic or polyphonic means available to a violin or a guitar. (1929:248)

Schaeffner, an early authority on Stravinsky, would come, by way of jazz, to study the music of the Dogon and later to found the ethnomusicology section of the Musée de l'Homme.

The "ethnographic" attitude provided a style of scientifically validated cultural leveling, the redistribution of value-charged categories such as "music," "art," "beauty," "sophistication," "cleanliness," and so forth. The extreme relativism, even nihilism, latent in the ethnographic approach did not go unexploited by the more extreme collaborators of *Documents.* Their view of culture did not feature conceptions of organic structure, functional integration, wholeness, or historical continuity.

Their conception of culture can be called, without undue anachronism, semiotic. Cultural reality was composed of artificial codes, ideological identities, and objects susceptible to inventive recombination and juxtaposition: Lautréamont's umbrella and sewing machine, a violin and a pair of hands slapping the African dirt.

The conception, highlighted in Schaeffner's title, of an "ethnographic museum" is of more than passing importance here. The fragmentation of modern culture perceived by Benjamin, the dissociation of cultural knowledge into juxtaposed "citations," is presupposed by *Documents*. The journal's title, of course, is indicative. Culture becomes something to be collected, and *Documents* itself is a kind of ethnographic display of images, texts, objects, labels, a playful museum that simultaneously collects and reclassifies its specimens.

The journal's basic method is juxtaposition—fortuitous or ironic collage. The proper arrangement of cultural symbols and artifacts is constantly placed in doubt. High art is combined with hideously enlarged photographs of big toes; folk crafts; *Fantômas* (a popular mystery series) covers; Hollywood sets; African, Melanesian, pre-Columbian, and French carnival masks; accounts of music hall performances; descriptions of the Paris slaughterhouses. *Documents* poses, for the culture of the modern city, the problem facing any organizer of an ethnographic museum: What belongs with what? Should masterpieces of sculpture be isolated as such or displayed in proximity with cooking pots and ax blades? (see Leiris 1966b.) The ethnographic attitude must continually pose these sorts of questions, composing and decomposing culture's "natural" hierarchies and relationships. Once everything in a culture is deemed worthy in principle of collection and display, fundamental issues of classification and value are raised.

In *Documents* we observe the use of ethnographic juxtaposition for the purpose of perturbing commonplace symbols. A regular section of the journal is a so-called dictionary of unexpected definitions. The entry for the word *homme* is characteristic. It recites a researcher's breakdown of the chemical composition of the average human body: enough iron to make a nail, enough sugar for one cup of coffee, magnesium sufficient to take a photograph, and so on—market value twenty-five francs. The body, a privileged image of order, is a favorite target. Together with a variety of other "natural" entities, it is recoded, and in the process it is thrown in doubt. Robert Desnos contributes a disconcerting inventory of rhetorical forms concerning the eye, and his entry for the mobile symbol "nightingale" begins, "Except in special cases, this does not have to do with a bird" (Desnos 1929:117).

Crachat, "spittle," is redefined by Griaule using black African and Islamic evidence with the result that spit becomes associated with the soul, and with both good and evil spirits. In Europe, naturally, to spit in someone's face is an absolute dishonor; in West Africa it can be a mode of blessing. "Spittle acts like the soul: balm or garbage" (Griaule 1929). The ethnographer, like the surrealist, is licensed to shock. Leiris takes up Griaule's definition and goes further: spittle is the permanent spermlike sullying of the noble mouth, an organ associated in the West with intelligence and language. Spit thus resymbolized denotes a condition of inescapable sacrilege (Leiris 1929). In this newly recomposed definition to talk or to think is also to ejaculate.

An approach to representation by means of juxtaposition or collage was a familiar surrealist tack (Matthews 1977). Its intent was to break down the conventional "bodies"—objects, identities—that combine to produce what Barthes would later call "the effect of the real" (1968). In Documents the juxtaposition of the contributions, and especially of their photographic illustrations, was designed to provoke this defamiliarization. The first issue of 1929 begins, for example, with an article by Leiris, "Picasso's Recent Canvases," profusely illustrated with photographs. (These were years when Picasso seemed to be breaking and bending, almost savagely, the normal shape of the human frame.) These deformed images are followed by "The Outcasts of Nature" by Bataille, a characteristic appreciation of freaks, illustrated by full-page eighteenth-century engravings of Siamese twins. Next an illustrated review of an exhibition of African sculpture provides further visual dislocation of the "natural" body as realistically conceived in the West. The body, like a culture semiotically imagined, is not a continuous whole but an assemblage of conventional symbols and codes.

Documents, particularly in its use of photographs, creates the order of an unfinished collage rather than that of a unified organism. Its images, in their equalizing gloss and distancing effect, present in the same plane a Châtelet show advertisement, a Hollywood movie clip, a Picasso, a Giacometti, a documentary photo from colonial New Caledonia, a newspaper clip, an Eskimo mask, an Old Master, a musical instrument— the world's iconography and cultural forms presented as evidence or data. Evidence of what? Evidence, one can only say, of surprising, declassified cultural orders and of an expanded range of human artistic invention. This odd museum merely documents, juxtaposes, relativizes—a perverse collection.

The museum of ethnographic surrealism was to be improved and channeled into more stable, continuous institutions. In 1930 *Documents*, which had become less and less recognizably a review of art, was abandoned by its chief financial backer. Three years later a reconstituted category, easily identifiable today as modern art, would be incarnated in the legendary *Minotaure*. A thing of beauty, *Minotaure* interspersed no photographs of slaughterhouses, Movietone Follies, or big toes among its lavishly reproduced Picassos, Dalis, or Massons. After turning over its second issue to the Dakar-Djibouti team for a handsomely illustrated report on their African research (Griaule 1934b), *Minotaure* did not subsequently reserve any significant place for ethnographic evidence. The artifacts of otherness were replaced, generally, by Breton's category of the surreal—located in the mythic or psychoanalytic unconscious and all too easily co-opted by romantic notions of artistic genius or inspiration. The concrete cultural artifact was no longer called upon to play a disruptive, illuminatory role. Modern art and ethnography had emerged as fully distinct positions, in communication to be sure, but from a distance.

I have dwelt on *Documents* because it exemplifies with unusual clarity the chief areas of convergence between ethnography and surrealism during the twenties and because a number of its contributors went on to become influential fieldworkers and museum organizers. *Documents* reveals too in its subversive, nearly anarchic documentary attitude an epistemological horizon for twentieth-century cultural studies. If *Documents* was, as Leiris recalls, "impossible," it would be hasty to dismiss it as an aberration, a personal creation of the "impossible" Georges Bataille (Leiris 1963). It attracted the participation of too many serious scholars and artists to be written off as merely self-indulgent or nihilistic. It exemplified, rather, an extreme sensitivity (more characteristic of the French ethnographic tradition than is often recognized) to the overdetermined character of what Mauss had called "total social facts" (1924:76–77). Reality, after the surrealist twenties, could never again be seen as simple or continuous, describable empirically or through induction. It was Mauss who best exemplified the underlying attitude when he remarked, as he liked to: "Ethnology is like the ocean. All you need is a net, any kind of net; and then if you step into the sea and swing your net about, you're sure to catch some kind of fish" (Fortes 1973:284).

In the Museum of Man

The history of French ethnography between the world wars can be told as a tale of two museums. The old Trocadéro museum and the new Musée de l'Homme exerted significant influences, both practical and ideological, on the course of research and the comprehension of its results. If the "Troca" of the twenties, with its mislabeled, misclassified objets d'art, corresponded with the aesthetics of ethnographic surrealism, the completely modern Palais de Chaillot incarnated the emerging scholarly paradigm of ethnographic humanism. The scientific gains represented by the Musée de l'Homme were considerable. It provided both needed technical facilities and the equally necessary delineation of a field for study—the "human," in all its physical, archaeological, and ethnographic manifestations. The coalescence of a research paradigm creates the possibility of an accumulation of knowledge and thus the phenomenon of scholarly progress. What is less often recognized, for the human sciences at least, is that any consolidation of a paradigm depends on the exclusion or relegation to the status of "art" of those elements of the changing discipline that call the credentials of the discipline itself into question, those research practices that, like *Documents,* work at the edges of disorder.

Before 1930 the Trocadéro was a jumble of exotica. Its arrangements emphasized "local color" or the evocation of foreign settings: costumed mannequins, panoplies, dioramas, massed specimens. A journalist could write that a visit was like "un voyage en pleine barbarie" (Diaz 1985:378). Since the collection lacked an up-to-date scientific, pedagogical vision, its disorder made the museum a place where one could go to encounter curiosities, fetishized objects. It was there that Picasso, around 1908, began to make a serious study of *l'art nègre.*

> When I went for the first time, at Derain's urging, to the Trocadéro Museum, the smell of dampness and rot there stuck in my throat. It depressed me so much I wanted to get out fast, but I stayed and studied.   (Gilot 1964:266)

"Le Troca" was a curious Byzanto-Moorish structure, unheated, unlit. Its lack of coherent scientific contextualization encouraged the appreciation of its objects as detached works of art rather than as cultural artifacts. After the First World War, as the enthusiasm for things primitive blossomed, the scandalous museum became temporarily a museum of "art."

As Rivière's improvements of the early thirties progressed, the museum began to feature a number of exhibitions of African, Oceanian, and Eskimo art. The display of objects collected by the Dakar-Djibouti expedition would, to a large degree, fall into this category. A devoted group of volunteers—prospective ethnographers like Denise Paulme and fashionable sixteenth-arrondissement ladies, amateurs of the exotic—helped with the renovations. The museum was becoming chic. At the opening of a new Oceanian exhibition hall models from the great Parisian fashion houses went on parade exotically and alluringly attired. The Mission Dakar-Djibouti drew its funds, beyond government and Rockefeller Foundation subventions, from private patrons of the arts (among them the wealthy protosurrealist author of *Impressions d'Afrique*, Raymond Roussel). Before the departure of Griaule's team for its twenty-month reconnaissance, a gala fund-raiser was organized by Rivière at the Cirque d'Hiver, a boxing event featuring the "African" featherweight champ Al Brown and attended by *le tout Paris* in evening attire. According to legend the champion shadowboxed with Marcel Mauss, a legend not entirely improbable (the great scholar was a good athlete and a practitioner of *savate*).[6]

These anecdotes give a sense of the Trocadéro's extrascientific ambiance around 1930. The museum was riding the crest of the wave of enthusiasm for *l'art nègre*.[7] During the twenties the term *nègre* could embrace modern American jazz, African tribal masks, voodoo ritual, Oceanian sculpture, and even pre-Columbian artifacts. It had attained the proportions of what Edward Said has called an "orientalism"—a knitted-together collective representation figuring a geographically and historically vague but symbolically sharp exotic world (1978a).[8] If the notion of the African "fetish" had any meaning in the twenties, it described not a mode of African belief but rather the way in which exotic artifacts were consumed by European aficionados. A mask or statue or any shred of black culture could effectively summon a complete world

6. My account is based largely on personal communications from Georges-Henri Rivière and on his two memoirs (1968, 1979). See also Paulme 1977 and Jamin 1982a.

7. On this *négrophilie* see Laude 1968:528–539; also Leiris 1968 and Blachère 1981. For a particularly revealing example see *Le nègre* by Philippe Soupault (1927). Soupault's *nègre* is a kind of destructive-regenerative force, more Nietzschean than Afro-American.

8. Said's account underplays the positive valuations of the exotic frequently associated with such projections. See Chapter 11.

of dreams and possibilities—passionate, rhythmic, concrete, mystical, unchained: an "Africa."

By the time of the Mission Dakar-Djibouti this interest in Africa had become a fully developed *exotisme*. The public and the museums were eager for more of an aestheticized commodity, and it was in this climate that the French legislature was prevailed upon to enact a special law underwriting an expedition whose chief official task was to enrich the nation's collections. The Mission Dakar-Djibouti satisfied the demand; it brought back data that could be counted and displayed (Jamin 1982a).[9]

The ethnographers departed in 1931 with a structured aesthetic in mind, a vision of Africa, and a certain (essentially fetishist) conception of how "it" should be collected and represented. They did not, in the manner of English and American fieldworkers of the time, set out to experience and interpret discrete cultural wholes. Fieldwork rapport in Leiris' account (1934) emerges as little more than a romantic fantasy; and in Griaule's report (1933) ethnography is portrayed as a process fraught with role playing and manipulation, in which power is centrally at stake (see Chapters 2 and 6). Even in the later work of Griaule and his collaborators, which looks far beyond the museum collecting that dominated the early mission, there is little attempt to present a unified version of an African reality (Griaule strongly emphasized multiperspectival group research) free of the gaps and discontinuities of a documentary, exegetical presentation.

The research process that began with the Mission Dakar-Djibouti has produced one of the most complete descriptions of a tribal group (the Dogon and their neighbors) on record anywhere. Yet, as Mary Douglas (1967) has complained, the picture is curiously skewed. We can never grasp, for instance, just how daily life is conducted, how circumstantial political decisions are actually made.[10] There is an overemphasis on

---

9. According to Rivet and Rivière's proud calculations in *Minotaure* no. 2 (1933), 3,500 "ethnographic objects" were collected, along with six thousand photographs, a large collection of Abyssinian paintings, three hundred manuscripts and amulets, notations of thirty languages and dialects, and hundreds of recordings, "ethnographic observations," botanical specimens, and so on. This, the mission's "booty," in Rivet and Rivière's words, was the public measure of a successful mission. Barthes (1957:140) dissects the word *mission:* an imperial "mana term," he calls it, which can be applied to any and all colonial undertakings, giving them as required a heroic, redemptive aura.

10. This account should serve as a corrective to Douglas' tendency to portray Griaule and the French tradition generally as formalistic and enamored of

elaborately cross-referenced native theories of the way things are or should be—a mythic conception of cosmic order that aspires to embrace every gesture and detail of the profane world. The extraordinary beauty and conceptual power of Dogon wisdom, known in its fullness to only a small group of elders, never satisfies the nagging question: What are the Dogon really like? The Griaule tradition gives us a scrupulously explicated ensemble of documents, the most important of which, the cosmogonic myth, is manifestly composed by Dogon. Little effort is expended on a naturalistic account in the manner of, say, Malinowski's *Argonauts;* indeed, in the wake of surrealist fragmentation what would be the point?

If the Mission Dakar-Djibouti brought back considerable quantities of "art" for display at the Trocadéro, its objects found their permanent home in a rather different museum. No sooner had Rivière completed his restorations in 1934 than Rivet announced the approval of a grandiose new plan. The old Byzantine structure was to be razed to make way for a dream building that would sublimate the anarchic cosmopolitanism of the twenties into a monumental unity: "humanity." The Musée de l'Homme, a name that has only recently become multiply ironic, was in the mid-thirties an admirable ideal, at once scientific and political in significance. The new institution combined under a single roof the technical laboratories from the Musée d'Histoire Naturelle and the Institut d'Ethnologie, formerly housed at the Sorbonne. The museum brought together a liberal, synthetic image of "man," a vision conceived by Rivet, which wove together in a powerful symbolic ensemble a number of the ideological threads I have been tracing. Rivet had gathered together a talented group of ethnologists including Métraux, Leroi-Gourhan, Leenhardt, Griaule, Leiris, Schaeffner, Dieterlen, Paulme, Louis Dumont, and Jacques Soustelle. He provided the institutional support that, along with Mauss's teaching, formed a center for an emerging fieldwork tradition. For most of these scholars the connection between art and ethnography was crucial.

Mauss and Rivet's brand of humanism envisaged an expansion and an opening-out of local conceptions of human nature. No one time or

---

abstract systems. It should also reinforce her suggestive rapprochement between Dogon culture and surrealism. On this correspondence see also Guy Davenport's (1979) imaginative placement of the Dogon, along with Charles Fourier, in 1920s Paris.

culture could claim to incarnate the mankind on display at the Musée de l'Homme. The species in its totality would be represented there, beginning with biological evolution, moving through the archaeological remains of early civilizations, and ending with a full array of actual cultural alternatives. The different races and cultures of the planet were to be successively displayed, arranged in galleries organized synthetically on one side, analytically on the other. Mauss's *homme total* would be brought together for the first time for the edification of the public. Also for the instruction of the scientist the Musée de l'Homme contained extensive research laboratories and scholarly collections. Less than 10 percent of its total collection was on display at any given moment (see Rivière 1968, 1979; Rivet 1948:110–118).

The wedding of science and public education within a progressivist humanism suited Rivet's world view perfectly. He was a socialist with a vision—and with the political and social connections necessary to realize it. The Musée de l'Homme was conceived as part of the International Exhibition of 1937, a symbol of Popular Front ideals. Rivet, whose specialty was American archaeology and prehistory, tended to see mankind in an evolutionary, diffusionist frame, stressing long-term biocultural development and the reconstruction of historical sequences through the extensive collection and comparison of traits. In an early article on method, which appeared in *Documents*, he announced the underlying themes of his dream museum (Rivet 1929). In the study of man, he writes, the boundaries between ethnography, archaeology, and prehistory are "absolutely artificial." (In a later version he would add physical anthropology to the mixture.) Equally artificial are classifications of human realities according to the divisions of political geography. "Humanity is an indivisible whole, in space and time." "The science of man" no longer need be subdivided arbitrarily. "It [is] high time to break down the barriers. And that is what the Musée de l'Homme has tried to do" (Rivet 1948:113). The political message for 1937 was clear.

The Musée de l'Homme provided a liberal, productive environment for the growth of French ethnographic science. Its guiding values were cosmopolitan, progressive, and democratic; one of the first cells of the Resistance formed within its walls in 1940 (Blumenson 1977). The museum encouraged international understanding and global values, an orientation that would continue after the Second World War with the involvement of Rivière, Rivet, Griaule, Leiris, Métraux, and other ethnol-

ogists in UNESCO.[11] Theirs was a cosmopolitan tradition that had remained congruent, in important ways, with the ethnographic surrealism
of the twenties. It should be remembered that surrealism has been a genuinely international phenomenon with branches on every continent. It
has sought the articulation less of cultural differences than of human differences. The same can be said overall of French ethnography.[12] But
though it shared the scope of surrealism, the ethnographic humanism of
the Musée de l'Homme did not adopt an earlier surrealism's corrosive,
defamiliarizing attitude toward cultural reality. The aim of science was
rather to collect ethnographic artifacts and data and to display them in
reconstituted, easily interpretable contexts. This entailed losses as well
as gains. Indeed it is possible to imagine an ethnographic surrealist critique of the Museum of Man pointing tentatively at the shape—or rather
at the activity—of a more supple and less authoritative humanism.

The Musée de l'Homme's African sculptures were displayed regionally along with related objects, their significance functionally interpreted. They did not find a place beside the Picassos of the Musée d'Art
Moderne, located a few streets away. As we have seen, the emerging
domains of modern art and ethnology were more distinct in 1937 than a
decade before.[13] It is not merely whimsical to question these apparently
natural classifications. At issue is the loss of a disruptive and creative play
of human categories and differences, an activity that does not simply
display and comprehend the diversity of cultural orders but openly ex-
pects, allows, indeed desires its own disorientation.

Such an activity is lost in the consolidation and display of a stable
ethnographic knowledge. In the twenties the knowledge brandished by
a younger ethnography allied with surrealism was more eccentric, un-

---

11. Two characteristic UNESCO publications are *Interrelations of Cultures*
(1953), with contributions by Griaule and Leiris, and *Race and History* by Claude
Lévi-Straus (1952).

12. An implicitly surrealist ("anthropological") conception of mind as a creative source capable of generating the entire range of human expressions—both
existing and potential, both mythic and rational—finds perhaps its most pro-
grammatic expression in Lévi-Strauss's structuralist *ésprit humain*. See Chapter
10, section 3.

13. The distinction was not achieved without conscious effort. According
to Michel Leiris (personal communication) in the Musée de l'Homme Rivet issued
a formal injunction against treating artifacts aesthetically. The new institution had
to purge the legacy of the Trocadéro and the twenties, a period when the contexts
of science and art bled into each other. Rivet's taboo remained in effect until the
1960s.

formed, and willing to dislocate the orders of its own culture—the culture that built great museums of ethnographic science and modern art.

The Musée de l'Homme opened its doors to the public in June 1938. During the previous summer a curious alternative had been created by Bataille, Leiris, Roger Caillois, and a loose collection of avant-garde intellectuals (some of them students of Mauss) who called themselves the Collège de Sociologie. While the name suggests the tradition of Durkheim, the group's renewed interest in the *Année sociologique* involved a considerable degree of reinvention. Their turn toward sociology (less sharply distinguished from ethnology than in England or the United States) signaled a rejection of what they saw as surrealism's overidentification with literature and art, its excessive subjectivism and concern with automatic writing, individual dream experience, and depth psychology. The Collège de Sociologie—which met for two years in the dining room of a Latin Quarter café then folded because of internal dissension and the outbreak of war—was an attempt to reintegrate scientific rigor with personal experience in the study of cultural processes. Like the author of *Elementary Forms of the Religious Life,* the founders of the Collège were preoccupied with those ritual moments when experiences outside the normal flow of existence can find collective expression, moments when cultural order is both transgressed and rejuvenated. They adopted the Durkheimian concept of the sacred to circumscribe this recreative domain.

If Durkheim discovered the roots of social solidarity in displaced ethnographic examples such as the "collective effervescence" of aboriginal rites, Bataille envisaged collective expressions of transgression and excess in contemporary Paris. He was obsessed with the power of sacrifice and with the place de la Concorde, which he hoped to reclaim as a site for ritual acts organized by the Collège. Caillois, more temperate, was engaged in the research that would result in *L'homme et le sacré* (1939). He would lecture to the Collège on "la fête," a tour of the world's cultures, drawing on his teachers Mauss, Georges Dumézil, and Marcel Granet, as well as on the ethnographers A. P. Elkin, Daryll Forde, and Maurice Leenhardt. Caillois' diverse *sacré* included ritual expressions of primordial chaos, excess, cosmogony, fertility, debauchery, incest, sacrilege, and parodies of all sorts. While they shared Durkheim's interest in the constitution of collective order, the members of the Collège de Sociologie tended to focus on the regenerative processes of disorder and the necessary irruptions of the sacred in everyday life. From this standpoint the subversive critical activities of the avant-garde could be seen as essential for the life of society; the circumscribed position of "art" in modern culture could be transcended, at least programmatically.

It is hard to generalize about the Collège, a body so short-lived and idiosyncratic in its membership. Leiris, for example, was preoccupied not with collective rites but rather with those autobiographical moments in which the articulation of self and society can be brought to consciousness. To this end he cultivated a kind of methodical clumsiness, a permanent inability to fit. His own chief contribution to the Collège (before resigning because of qualms about loose standards of evidence and the danger of founding a coterie) was an essay entitled "The Sacred in Everyday Life" (1938b). In this text, a bridge between ethnography and self-portraiture, Leiris sketched many of the topics he later developed in *La règle du jeu* (1948–1976). Objects of unusual attraction (his father's revolver), dangerous zones (the racetrack), taboo sites (the parental bedroom), secret spots (the W.C.), words and phrases with a special magical resonance—these sorts of data would evoke "that ambiguous attitude tied to the approach of something both attractive and dangerous, prestigious and rejected, that mixture of respect, desire, and terror that can be taken as the psychological mark of the sacred" (Leiris 1938b:60).

In *L'Afrique fantôme* (1934) Leiris sharply questioned certain scientific distinctions between "subjective" and "objective" practices. Why, he wondered, are my own reactions (my dreams, bodily responses, and so on) not important parts of the "data" produced by fieldwork? In the Collège de Sociologie he glimpsed the possibility of a kind of ethnography, analytically rigorous *and* poetic, focused not on the other but on the self, its peculiar system of symbols, rituals, and social topographies. The exception would be made to illuminate the rule without confirming it. Building on the work of Robert Hertz, Leiris and his colleagues cultivated a *gauche,* or left-handed, sense of the sacred. In Leiris' case this attitude generated a lifework of self-portraiture, an awkward and forever-imperfect process of socialization whose title, *La règle du jeu,* would express the ambiguous two-sidedness of order the Collège was concerned to investigate. From the late thirties on, however, Leiris held his literary and ethnographic work rigorously apart. His provocative field journal, *L'Afrique fantôme,* remains an isolated example of surrealist ethnography. (see Chapter 6).[14]

---

14. An essay that highlights the "ethnographic" dimensions of Leiris' career is Clifford 1986c, from which parts of this discussion are adapted. Chaney and

The Collège de Sociologie was frequented by a diverse public that included Jean Wahl, Pierre Klossowski, Alexandre Kojève, Jean Paulhan, Jules Monnerot, and Walter Benjamin. Long a subject of legend and misinformation, the Collège can now be discussed with some degree of confidence thanks to the labors of Denis Hollier (1979), who has brought together virtually every surviving documentary trace of its existence.[15] The picture is complex and in many ways still mysterious; it is enough here to enumerate those concerns of the Collège that resonate with what I have been calling ethnographic surrealism—concerns that still occupy the margins of the human sciences.

The members of the Collège struggled in an exemplary way against the opposition of individual and social knowledge (Duvignaud 1979:91). Although they never successfully resolved a tension between scientific rigor and the claims of activism, they nevertheless resisted any easy compromise with one side or the other. The Collège envisaged a critical "ethnology of the quotidian," as Jean Jamin puts it, which could react simultaneously on society and on a group of activist researchers constituted as a kind of vanguard or initiatory body. In Jamin's summary:

> The notions of distantiation, exoticism, representation of the other, and difference are inflected, reworked, readjusted as a function of criteria no longer geographical or cultural but methodological and even epistemological in nature: to make foreign what appears familiar; to study the rituals and sacred sites of contemporary institutions with the mi-

---

Pickering (1986a,b) offer a rich account of another possible example of "surrealist ethnography": Mass Observation, the British social documentary project of 1937–1943. Instigated by Charles Madge, a journalist and surrealist writer, Tom Harrisson, an ethnographer and ornithologist, and Humphrey Jennings, a documentary film maker and surrealist painter, Mass Observation envisaged a comprehensive ethnography of British popular culture conceived as a defamiliarized, exotic world. Its goal was to mobilize ethnographers from all classes in a democratic expansion of social consciousness and a constant interchange of observations. As Madge and Jennings put it, these observations, "though subjective, became objective because the subjectivity of the observer is one of the facts under observation" (quoted in Chaney and Pickering 1986a:47). The project anticipated later conceptions of reflexive ethnography and anthropology as cultural criticism. (See Chapter 1; also Marcus and Fischer 1986; Jackson 1987.) The specific mixtures of social, aesthetic, and scientific aims in the interwar "documentary" movements of France, England, and the United States deserve systematic comparison. (See also Stott 1973.)

15. The collection includes texts by Bataille, Caillois, Guastalla, Klossowski, Kojève, Leiris, Lewitsky, Mayer, Paulhan, and Wahl, with extensive commentaries by the editor. On the Collège see also Lourau 1974 and an excellent account in Jamin 1980.

nute attention of an "exotic" ethnographer, and using his methods; to become observers observing those others who are ourselves—and at the limit, this other who is oneself . . . The irruption of the sociologist in the field of his research, the interest devoted to his experience, probably constitutes the most original aspect of the Collège. (1980:16)

The Collège de Sociologie, in its conception of an avant-garde, activist science, in its dedication to breaking through the veneer of the profane, in its gaucherie, and in its sometimes grandiose ambitions, was a late emanation of the surrealist twenties. It offers a particularly striking example of that dimension of surrealism that struggled against the grain of both modern art and science to deploy a fully ethnographic cultural criticism.

If the Collège was unstable, ad hoc, and amateurish, the Musée de l'Homme bore all the marks of an officially sanctioned, scientific, monumental learning. In an ambivalent report on the opening of the institution where he would be employed for the next three decades, Leiris dwelt on the paradox of a museum devoted to the arts of life. The danger, he wrote, was that "in the service of those two abstractions called Art and Science, everything that is living fermentation" would be "systematically excluded." While praising the humanist, progressive aims of the new ethnographic museology, Leiris allowed himself a regretful glance backward to the old Trocadéro museum, with its distinctive ambiance and a "certain familiar air (lacking didactic rigidity)" (1938a:344).

On the high parapet of the Musée de l'Homme, in gold letters, are engraved words by Paul Valéry (while below stands the statue of a muscular man subduing a buffalo):

> Every man creates without knowing it, as he breathes. But the artist is
> aware of himself creating. His act engages his entire being. He is for-
> tified by his well-loved pain.

Art, now a universal essence, is displayed and approved by an idealistic, confident good sense. A particular version of human authenticity, featuring personal interiority and romantic agony, is projected onto the rest of the planet. All people create, love, work, worship. A stable, complete "humanity" is confirmed.[16] Such a whole presupposes an omission,

---

16. For a stinging critique of these assumptions see "La grande famille des hommes," in Barthes 1957.

the excluded source of the projection. What was not displayed in the Musée de l'Homme was the modern West, its art, institutions, and techniques. Thus the orders of the West were everywhere present in the Musée de l'Homme, except on display. An important impact was lost in the well-classified halls, for the museum encouraged the contemplation of mankind as a whole, seen, as it were, from a distance, coolly, tolerantly. The identity of the West and its "humanism" was never exhibited or analyzed, never openly at issue.

To speak of "man" and the "human" is to run the risk of reducing contingent differences to a system of universal essences. Moreover, the authority arrogated by the humanist too often goes unquestioned. As Maurice Merleau-Ponty would point out: "In its own eyes, Western humanism is the love of humanity, but to others it is merely the custom and institution of a group of men, their password, and sometimes their battle cry" (1947:182). The problems associated with a humanist (or anthropological) vision have lately become all too apparent. Third-world voices now call into question the right of any local intellectual tradition to construct a museum of mankind (see, for example, Adotevi 1972–73); and in France radical cultural critics have announced with equanimity the death of man. I cannot dwell here on the ambiguities of such analyses of the humanist West and its global discourses (see Chapter 11). One should be wary, in any event, of abandoning too quickly the vision of a Mauss or a Rivet—a humanism that still offers grounds for resistance to oppression and a necessary counsel of tolerance, comprehension, and mercy.

Culture/Collage

To stress, as I have, the paradoxical nature of ethnographic knowledge is not necessarily to abandon the assumption of human connectedness, although it does mean questioning any stable or essential grounds of human similarity. Anthropological humanism and ethnographic surrealism need not be seen as mutually exclusive; they are perhaps best understood as antinomies set within a transient historical and cultural predicament. To state the contrast schematically, anthropological humanism begins with the different and renders it—through naming, classifying, describing, interpreting—comprehensible. It familiarizes. An ethnographic surrealist practice, by contrast, attacks the familiar, provoking the irruption of otherness—the unexpected. The two attitudes presuppose each other; both are elements within a complex process that

generates cultural meanings, definitions of self and other. This process—
a permanent ironic play of similarity and difference, the familiar and the
strange, the here and the elsewhere—is, as I have argued, characteristic
of global modernity.

In exploring this predicament I have dwelt on the practice of ethnographic surrealism, paying less attention to its converse, surrealist ethnography. Let me offer a few hypotheses concerning the latter. There are
no pure examples, except perhaps Leiris' *L'Afrique fantôme;* but I would
like to suggest that surrealist procedures are always present in ethnographic works, though seldom explicitly acknowledged. (For example
see the addendum to this chapter.) I have noted some of them in Griaule's
documentary approach. More generally the mechanism of collage can
serve as a helpful paradigm. In every introductory anthropology course,
and in most ethnographies, moments are produced in which distinct cultural realities are cut from their contexts and forced into jarring proximity.
For example in Malinowski's Trobriand Islands behavior we label economics or trade is identified with canoe magic and myth. Ritual exchange valuables, *vaygu'a* (shell necklaces), are juxtaposed with the English crown jewels. Even to bring an alien kinship system into the
conceptual domain of Western marriage is to provoke a defamiliarizing
effect; but it is essential to distinguish this moment of metonymic juxtaposition from its normal sequel, a movement of metaphorical comparison in which consistent grounds for similarity and difference are elaborated.

The surrealist moment in ethnography is that moment in which the
possibility of comparison exists in unmediated tension with sheer incongruity. This moment is repeatedly produced and smoothed over in the
process of ethnographic comprehension. But to see this activity in terms
of collage is to hold the surrealist moment in view—the startling co-
presence on Lautréamont's dissecting table. Collage brings to the work
(here the ethnographic text) elements that continually proclaim their for-
eignness to the context of presentation. These elements—like a newspaper clipping or a feather—are marked as real, as collected rather than
invented by the artist-writer. The procedures of (a) cutting out and (b)
assemblage are of course basic to any semiotic message; here they *are*
the message. The cuts and sutures of the research process are left visible;
there is no smoothing over or blending of the work's raw data into a
homogeneous representation. To write ethnographies on the model of
collage would be to avoid the portrayal of cultures as organic wholes or
as unified, realistic worlds subject to a continuous explanatory discourse.

(Gregory Bateson's *Naven* is an early and, in the genre, unclassifiable example of what I am suggesting here. On *Naven* as an experiment in ethnographic writing see Marcus 1980:509 and 1985.) The ethnography as collage would leave manifest the constructivist procedures of ethnographic knowledge; it would be an assemblage containing voices other than the ethnographer's, as well as examples of "found" evidence, data not fully integrated within the work's governing interpretation. Finally it would not explain away those elements in the foreign culture that render the investigator's own culture newly incomprehensible.

The surrealist elements of modern ethnography tend to go unacknowledged by a science that sees itself engaged in the reduction of incongruities rather than, simultaneously, in their production. But is not every ethnographer something of a surrealist, a reinventor and reshuffler of realities? Ethnography, the science of cultural jeopardy, presupposes a constant willingness to be surprised, to unmake interpretive syntheses, and to value—when it comes—the unclassified, unsought other.

Ethnographic surrealism and surrealist ethnography are utopian constructs; they mock and remix institutional definitions of art and science. To think of surrealism as ethnography is to question the central role of the creative "artist," the shaman-genius discovering deeper realities in the psychic realm of dreams, myths, hallucinations, automatic writing. This role is rather different from that of the cultural analyst, interested in the making and unmaking of common codes and conventions. Surrealism coupled with ethnography recovers its early vocation as critical cultural politics, a vocation lost in later developments (Max Ernst devoting his energies to designing an oneiric double bed for Nelson and Happy Rockefeller, the general production of "art" for the "art world").

Ethnography combined with surrealism can no longer be seen as the empirical, descriptive dimension of anthropology, a general science of the human. Nor is it the interpretation of cultures, for the planet cannot be seen as divided into distinct, textualized ways of life. Ethnography cut with surrealism emerges as the theory and practice of juxtaposition. It studies, and is part of, the invention and interruption of meaningful wholes in works of cultural import-export.

Two final examples (parables) of juxtaposition and invention in the modern world system: both call for an ethnographic surrealist attitude. The first is perhaps too familiar. Around 1905 Picasso acquires a West African mask. It is beautiful, all planes and cylinders. He discovers cubism. (Other versions of the story locate the epiphany in the old "Troca.") Much ink has been spilled in trying to account for the role of African sculpture in the emergence of cubism. Did Picasso recognize primarily a formal affinity? Was *l'art nègre* essentially "raisonnable," as he once put it? Or was he moved—as he intimated much later—by a quasi-religious "magic" felt in African art? The debate continues (see Rubin 1984b:268– 336; Foster 1985:181–208). Whatever inspirations and affinities may be retrospectively constructed by and for Picasso it seems clear that the exotic objects he collected were tools suited for doing specific jobs: the projecting cylindrical eyes of a Grebo mask, for example, suggesting the sound hole of a metal guitar construction. A cubist solution to various problems of composition would doubtless have emerged without the masks; but the fact that Picasso, Derain, and others noticed and appreciated African artifacts at this historical moment is significant. Something new was occurring in the presence of something exotic. It is a common process; for example Monet's house at Giverny overflowed with Japanese prints. Around 1920 when *l'art nègre* was in vogue, an inquest would be sponsored on the subject. Picasso replied in a famous sally: "L'art nègre? Connais pas!" Indeed he had little interest in Africa per se. There had been nothing essentially *nègre* about the masks he found powerful and instructive fifteen years earlier. They had come in handy for making a difference.

My second example comes from the Trobriand Islands. It occurs in the classic ethnographic film made by Jerry Leach and Gary Kildea in collaboration with a local Trobriand political movement: *Trobriand Cricket: An Ingenious Response to Colonialism.* The gentleman's game, brought by British missionaries about the time Malinowski was on the scene, has been taken over and made new. Now it is ludic warfare, extravagant sexual display, political competition and alliance, parody. Something amazing has been concocted from elements of tradition, building on the missionaries' game which has been "rubbished," working in symbols drawn from the military occupation of the islands during the Second World War. The film takes us into a staged swirl of brightly painted, feathered bodies, balls, and bats. In the midst of all this on a chair sits the umpire, calmly influencing the game with magical spells. He is chewing betel nut, which he shares out from a stash held on his lap. It is a bright blue plastic Adidas bag. It is beautiful.

Perhaps an acquaintance with ethnographic surrealism can help us see the blue plastic Adidas bag as part of the same kind of inventive cultural process as the African-looking masks that in 1907 suddenly appeared attached to the pink bodies of the *Demoiselles d'Avignon.*

Dada Data—An Addendum

One was free to go and stand on another man's shadow.

Excerpt from J. H. M. C. Boelaars, *Headhunters about Themselves: An Ethnographic Report from Irian Jaya. Indonesia.* The Hague: Martinus Nijoff, 1981, pp. 67–69.

Here follows a list of notes about the various parts of the human body.

1. The hair, *muku-rumb,* was paid attention to when somebody was ill and during the age ceremony for the children. In both cases the hair was shaved off but in the latter case replaced by ornaments. The hair of a captured head was used to decorate spears and to make waist-bands, *qowa,* for the great headhunters.

2. The face might be painted for celebrations. They made use of a butterfly pattern, *rur-dokák.* By painting the parts around the eyes in bright colours the eyes looked like the black dots on the wings of a butterfly.

3. The eyes, *kind,* may represent a person as is stressed in the advice: "The wedding sago should be given under the eyes of the sun, *tapaq-kind-kan.*"

4. The ear is associated with using one's brains. A stupid person is a person without ears, *mono-ain-mbék.* The expression *mono-koame,* there is an ear, means, "we too are able to think."

5. The nose, *tamangk,* was specially adorned by pieces of a shell and claws of birds. *Tamangk qana,* hard nose, is a sombre and determined face.

6. The mouth, *mèm,* is always associated with eating. *Mèm rènggèmbak,* big mouth, does not refer to an impudent person but to a glutton. The mouth has a special function in the custom of taking a mouthful of water and sprinkling this over the face of a person who has lost consciousness. The gestures of putting out one's tongue or of spitting on the ground in front of somebody's feet are insults, which lead to fights. The tongue is also said to be a delicacy (just as is the ball of the thumb) for cannibals.

7. Shrugging one's shoulders was not an expression of ignorance but of fear. In the presence of men, women may stand together with hunched shoulders as a token of decency, but the men know better. They say, "If

they were alone with a man, they would all too much like to have sexual intercourse."

8. Chin rubbing or nose rubbing, as among the Asmat, is not a Jaqaj custom of greeting. They used to lay their right hand in the left hand of the other, who then clasped the first man's fingers. Men kiss each other on the cheeks but do not kiss any women, not even their own wives. Women usually do not kiss one another.

9. Breath is not associated with the notion of spirit. Breathing proves that somebody is still alive.

10. Women adorn their upper arms and the place between the breasts with scarifications. The girls gladly suffered any pain in order to have these marks. The men are greatly interested in the breasts, *abur*, and in the size of the female genitals, *jo*. The women in turn gossiped about the bellies, *kandöm*, and the anuses, *mo*, of the men. These parts of the body always turned up in my list of words of abuse.

11. Children were not allowed to touch the inside of their mother's thighs. The "inside of the thighs of his wife" was the place where the ancestor *Kapaqait* took the seeds for planting vegetables. The pubic hair of women and the fibres of their perineal bands were smoked in the peace pipe. They said that the hymen should remain untouched until after the first menstruation. Sperm and urine could be used as medicine. The myth of *Ujoqot* relates how he created a human being by smearing his sperm on a coconut.

12. The anus, *mo*, had a special cover, a tail, *èk*, of fibres. Whenever a man was ill, he would always ask whether he was lying decently. To touch a man's anus was either an appeal to his strength or a very serious insult. Breaking wind proved that one had eaten too much. If it happened in the presence of men only it did not matter, but in the presence of women, especially in the presence of one's own wife, it could be perilous for them or her. Women incurred the risk of being killed if they looked at the excrements of their husbands. Husbands feared their endless reproaches about eating too much.

13. The penis, *paqadi*, or the pubic hair of a man drew less attention. They did not wear any shame cover. The term *paqadi*, penis, was often heard as an expletive. The most stupid thing a person could do, they said, was to hurt his own anus or penis.

14. The fluid oozing out of a decaying corpse was not used for any special purpose. The only thing that happened after a corpse had decayed was that children were told to trample the ground where the burial

platform had been. This was done so that they might become the worthy successors of the deceased.

15. Body odour, especially that of the armpits, was believed to have a special defensive power against spirits. A person's shadow did not get any attention. One was free to go and stand on another man's shadow.

NOTES

1. I am grateful to Renato Rosaldo for bringing Boelaars' list to my attention. "Borges," he said, "could not have improved on this one."

2. Malinowski was interested by what he called the "coefficient of weirdness" in cross-cultural descriptions. It had always to be balanced, however, by the "coefficient of reality." Other ways of life should be made real and comprehensible while at the same time preserving a sense of their strangeness and difference. One way of preserving this strangeness was to include data not fully contextualized—random, odd facts, "imponderabilia." Realist ethnographies, Malinowski thought, should maintain a productive balance between the coefficients of weirdness and reality, leaving readers to circle hermeneutically (happily) between plausibility and surprise, coherence and small bits of data. But the interpretive balance sometimes slips; and when it does, the image of the other disintegrates into partial collections of facts and juxtaposed statements from heterogeneous sources. The listing, selecting, sorting processes by which certain kinds of information emerge as significant become suddenly visible.

3. Ethnographic lists tend to induce reverie, the way Joseph Cornell's partitioned "hotels," "habitats," and "museums" do: birds and clocks, star charts, ball bearings, pipes, body parts . . . An unexpected beauty can be found in classifications or in sentences like "The fluid oozing out of a decaying corpse was not used for any special purpose." "To touch a man's anus was either an appeal to his strength or a very serious insult."

4. Boelaars was a missionary-ethnographer and linguist (Father of the Sacred Heart) for nearly ten years in Indonesian New Guinea.

5. Ethnographies generate multiple readings. For example Trobrianders are free to read Malinowski's accounts of their culture as parodies. By selecting out individual sentences from any cultural description, one can easily produce series like Boelaars'.

6. When the "coefficient of weirdness" floats free from the "coefficient of reality," the result is a new sort of exoticism. The strangeness that's produced does not inhere in the culture or world of the peoples represented. This exoticism is different from earlier varieties—romantic, Orientalist, and poetic—for what has become irreducibly curious is no longer the other but cultural description itself.

7. "At 10 I went to Tegava, where I took pictures of a house, a group of girls, and the *wasi,* and studied construction of a new house" (Malinowski's Trobriand diary).

8. What's called for, then, is an ethno (GRAPHIC) poetics . . .

. . . dire, non pas tout crûment sa vision, mais par un
transfert *instantané, constant, l'écho de sa présence.*
—VICTOR SEGALEN, *ESSAI SUR L'*EXOTISME

5. A Poetics of Displacement: Victor Segalen

T HE FIRST DETAILED account of Paul Gauguin's last weeks was sent to Paris from the Marquesas by a young naval doctor who had arrived just too late to meet the great recluse. It was a significant missed rendezvous, for Victor Segalen was to become an important contributor to what may be called a postsymbolist poetics of displacement. This poetics, dramatized by Gauguin's flight from Europe, had already sent Arthur Rimbaud to Abyssinia. It would propel Blaise Cendrars around the globe, Leiris to Africa, Artaud to the Tarahumaras. The new poetics rejected established exoticisms—those for example of a Pierre Loti—and it differed from Paul Claudel's quest for a profound, "inside" *Connaissance de l'est.* The new poetics reckoned with more troubling, less stable encounters with the exotic.

Born in Brittany in 1878, Segalen voyaged widely in Polynesia from 1902 to 1905 and in China, where he spent nearly five years before his death in 1919. A poet, novelist, archaeologist, and travel writer, Segalen participated in the Paris literary milieu of late symbolism—but from a distance. His work is hard to define. An expanded genre of travel litera-

ture comes closest but cannot finally accommodate the full range. Segalen would have been most content to be called a writer of exoticism; but
the word would first need to be cleansed of its myriad connections with
swaying palms, beaches, teeming markets, Tibetan monasteries, dangerous (African, Malaysian, Amazonian) jungles, "the wisdom of the East,"
the pleasures and ironies of travel by rail or on shipboard, and so forth.
Segalen redefines exoticism as an "aesthetic of the diverse." This is the
subtitle of his long essay on the subject, begun many times but never
finished. In it he attacks the predictable narratives and décor of most
travel writing (Loti is his chief target). His own writing substitutes troubling encounters with the unexpected, the strangely familiar, the unformed. Exoticism emerges as an extension of his friend Jules de Gaul-
tier's "Law of Bovaryism": in Segalen's paraphrase, "Every being in
conceiving of itself conceives itself as necessarily other than it is"
(1978:23–24). Making the most of modern anomie, Segalen's exoticist
extends and rediscovers an identity by means of a perpetual series of
detours, of encounters with "le Divers."

His own life of travel was an incomplete quest for a self among the
others—in Polynesia and, most troublingly, in China. By the time he died
at the age of forty-one, wasted by an undiagnosed illness, he had produced the elements of a major "exoticist" oeuvre, most of it unpublished.
Over the years Segalen has enjoyed a secret reputation, nourished by the
publication of new *inédits*. Recently, with a growing sensitivity to the
epistemological problems of writing across cultural boundaries, Segalen's meditations on his exotic encounters have acquired fresh resonance
for a wide range of modern cultural studies. (For discussions extending
his significance, see Jamin 1979 and Gilsenan 1986.) More than twenty
titles are now in print, making it possible finally to perceive the variety
and development of his writing, its growing reflexivity, and the troubled
questioning of the exoticist project.

木

A traveler's phenomenological "body" can sometimes be rather precisely
located. Certain writers are happiest with the view and conversation organized by a compartment on a moving train. Saul Steinberg liked America as seen from a Greyhound bus (the old model, without tinted glass);
it gave him, he said, a "cavalier's" perspective. This was close to Segalen's viewpoint, particularly in China—a distance both aesthetic and po-

litical from which to engage the other. Segalen did not warm to the Chinese. He felt none of the instinctive sympathy and erotic attraction he had for Tahitians. For aristocratic Chinese perhaps; but here he lacked social access. Segalen preferred China's monuments and what he could imaginatively rescue from an imperial tradition that seemed menaced after 1910 by mass violence, rebellion, and headlong modernization (Segalen and Manceron (1985:92,120,137).

Traveling through China (as portrayed in his texts), he seldom looks into people's intimate lives, like a candid photographer, or rubs elbows with the crowd; he is seldom face to face with individuals. Segalen often seems to be on horseback—walking, in physical contact with the uneven ground, but at a certain height. The mounted traveler sees out over things while avoiding the map maker's commanding overview. In a world of gates, portals, and courts, the horseman rides through Chinese places but without presuming to be "inside China." He rejects Claudelian participation, knowledge of the East as co-birth ("co-naissance"). Segalen does not experience and reveal the deep, hidden truths of China. Mounted and mobile, he moves over and around its surfaces. The surfaces are complex, looping.

木

In his first book, *Les immémoriaux* (1907a), Segalen tried realistically to evoke indigenous experience, what ethnographers of the time were beginning to call the native point of view. This is probably his best-known and least characteristic work. It speaks eloquently on behalf of traditional Polynesia—and it falls rather too easily into an elegiac lament for the vanishing primitive. The novel's standpoint is that of Térii, a *récitant,* or oral performer of genealogies and myths. It begins with a crisis: Térii forgets, falters in the midst of an important recitation. This rupture of oral tradition is tied to the arrival of European ships in Tahiti, the presence of a new, confusing power. The novel follows Térii's disgrace and flight, his travels, his encounters with missionaries; and it ends with a tragic prognosis: the death of "Maori Civilization." *Les immémoriaux* is a rather successful ethnographic novel. Segalen was a sensitive observer of the cultural situation in French Polynesia around the turn of the century, and his discriptions of traditional ritual are based on the best scholarship available at the time. In addition there is a happy correspondence between Segalen's own symbolist fascination for the orphic power of oral expression, the musical Word, and a Polynesian emphasis on cosmogonic speech.

> And it's the business of the night-walkers, the *haèrè-po* with long memories, to pass on from altar to altar, from priest to disciple the primal stories and exploits that must never die. And so as soon as night falls the *haèrè-po* hurry about their task; from every one of the divine terraces, from every *maraè* built on the circle of beaches, a monotonous murmur rises in the darkness, mixing with the howling voice of the surf and surrounding the island with a girdle of prayers.   (1907a:11)

But if *Les immémoriaux* touched a romantic chord among its (European) readers, certain of its deepest associations may have been problematic for its author. The doomed tradition of Polynesia is rendered as a sonorous world, an environment of spoken and heard intimacies. Such presences were strongly but dangerously attractive to Segalen. One of his short fictions, "Dans un monde sonore" (1907b), imagines a man who chooses to live in a darkened room filled with subtle sounds, who touches and apprehends space acoustically. Sight in this world seems crude and intrusive. The tale's protagonist is beautifully insane. Moreover the sonorous world of *Les immémoriaux* is associated with an inevitable cultural death. In China Segalen moved away from this style of cultural evocation, but he felt a constant nostalgia for the sensuous absorption associated with sound. His last, fragmentary poems were a series of long-lined odes—*Thibet* (he clung to the aspirated spelling)—songs of the most exotic place, a pure, transcendent echochamber (1979). Segalen never reached Tibet, the ultimate, deferred goal of all his expeditions.

⼂

The move from Tahiti to China was a shift from the sonorous and oral to the visual and written. Segalen, who played the piano, composed a bit, and even collaborated with Debussy, found China an acoustic desert. Its music and song repelled him (1985:143–144). Chinese speech is barely evoked in his writings, but inscriptions—characters, gestures, architecture, paintings—abound. It is no longer a question of evocation, of Segalen merging his voice with that of the other. As he put it in a letter to Debussy, "In the end, I came here looking for neither Europe nor China but for a vision of China" (Bouiller 1961:100). Segalen's other is a construct of desire and a manifest fiction—like its recent analogue, the "Japan" of Roland Barthes in *Empire of Signs* (1970).

Though he was a scholar and connoisseur of things Chinese, Segalen often portrayed an uncertain reality—multiform, shifting, giving way. His collection of travel observations written in 1910, *Briques et tuiles* (1975), is a series of discrete encounters, notes, and prose poems that enact the movement of a traveler through a country that is, to adapt Breton's phrase, an "érosion fixe." His fascination with ruins is a positive aesthetic of movement and process. China appears as light surfaces and crumbling forms, walls and doors with nothing behind. Segalen walks—rides—through this country, entranced by its wooden structures, the decay accepted and built in. (Could not a French traveler see the same today among California's ruins?) He mocks Europe, where stone cathedrals are built as if for the ages: "Duration does not come from solidity; immutability lives not in your dwellings but in you, slow men, ongoing men!" (1975:47).

He wrote to his friend Henry Manceron: "I think I've hit upon a rather satisfactory formula for the art of Chinese monuments by simply replacing the stasis the Egyptians and Greeks have taught us to put there with a kind of dynamism that must not be stripped of its perpetually nomadic character. Houses and temples are still tents and platforms, just waiting for the procession to depart" (1985:91).

This feeling for the dynamism of Chinese monuments provoked a corresponding movement on the part of the traveler, abandoning any fixed place of "observation." From *Briques et tuiles* (Segalen's ellipses register the bumpy motion):

> Palaces, immobile by accident and against your nature; light construc-
> tions . . . can't return you to the swaying of the platform bearers . . .
> It's I that will move toward you; and the undulation of my walking,
> with each of your courtyards a station, will return to you the shoulders'
> rhythms and the oscillations by which you once were animated. I will
> walk to you.   (p. 32)

Segalen's Chinese landscape is barely stopped motion. Mountains are "frozen waves." He rides with fascination over the "yellow country" of the north ("Image de la Chine?" he wonders), a furrowed, cut land, yellow dust in the wind and water constantly moving; everything erodes. His road maneuvers across the land, tacking to skirt each new cave-in or alteration of a stream's course. Segalen writes the modern experience of displacement: self and other a sequence of encounters, detours, with the stable identity of each at issue.

⼊

Segalen's China is a multiform allegory, a source of increasingly personal (if carefully equivocal) meanings. *Stèles* (1912), poems written in the manner of funerary inscriptions, do not so much translate a Chinese cultural content as provide their author with an impersonal, official voice, a disguise allowing him a degree of expressive freedom. Segalen is not given to personal statements of emotion; but his *Peintures* (1916), poems describing a series of Chinese paintings, are facets of an intimate imagination. The "paintings" are inscribed on silk, porcelain, wool, water, even in the air by a moving fan. Some unroll as long scrolls. In the opaque gaze of a woman, the feel of a tapestry, the cold surface of a vase, Segalen explores a gallery of personal fascinations and fears.

The painting that comes next isn't one that hangs high up but is to be opened with a touch of thumb and index, like the half-moon fan carried in Autumn and Spring . . . and actually it's called:

FLYING FAN

Don't give it any rest: don't try to inspect it laid out flat, or count the ivory inlays; but give it movement, always; stroke the air and secretly, out of the corner of an eye, look into each gentle breath it sends, bit by bit guess at the furtive scenes: the background, black and shining. Suddenly a battlement opens: wings beat: eyes roll: a skull caves in: out comes a pagoda, with a single spurt spreading to the open sky . . .

Did you see it? Fan, keep fanning.

A figure composes itself: a naked monk, ecstatic. Just two eyes are left of his entire body, but they're very much alive. (The rest is dry or rotted.) He lets us know that what's seen, alone, is good. Fan, keep fanning . . .

Now a wide-open face stares out at you; so magically and deeply that it will fix itself to your features and may become *your face* if you don't, still fanning, change it to something else less questioning: the curved stroke of a Painter's horizon; the vast undulation of the sea; slow wing-beat of the great rose goose in the sky; the gathered, stripped, spare caress of every desire . . . Fan, keep fanning . . .

But the painted face evokes itself again, with insolence, clearer at every turn. It gazes from too close. What can it mean? Are you provoking it? Met anywhere else: what an intolerable experience! Like the appearance of an overly insistent friend, like a too-faithful regret, like a mute wanting to ask a question.

But we don't inhabit the true world. We can reject what offends or troubles us, effaced more easily than a regret, with a quick flick of the hand.

So close up your fingers: at once, the face is gone . . .   (pp. 34–36)

The sequence of Chinese paintings is controlled by a consciousness that moves through an exotic but intimate *imaginaire*. As Segalen wrote in a letter, "The transfer from the Empire of China to the Empire of the self is constant" (Bouiller 1961:10). Reading his later works, one begins to suspect why he never finished the long-planned essay on exoticism, "an aesthetic of the diverse." China had confounded the exoticist's quest for diversity. Segalen's China was more distant and mysterious than the sensuous, acoustically present world of Tahiti. But distance and mystery would not be paths to "le Divers." They would provoke the endless construction of doubles and allegories of the self.

人

Segalen never wrote a coherent theory of his exotic encounters. Instead he engaged in a series of writing experiments, self-conscious fictional excursions that probed and questioned the search for diversity. Theory, as the word's etymology might imply, was inseparable from displacement, transfer, and travel.

Segalen's novel *René Leys* (1922) is perhaps his most sustained self-reflexive work. This brilliant mystery story about the imperial Forbidden City undermines the classic exoticist topography of barriers and thresholds surrounding a "secret." *René Leys* is a subtle meditation on depth—truth, its disclosure, and the endless will to know. The narrator, named Segalen (the novel is loosely based on real events he witnessed in Peking during 1912, the last days of the Ch'ing dynasty), is obsessed with the Forbidden City and with the hidden center of China, the emperor. He must know everything possible about "The Within." (Segalen in fact dreamed of writing a large book on China as seen by the emperor, *Le fils du ciel*.) A young Belgian named René Leys who has grown up in Peking and is a master of languages (and of role playing) serves as intermediary. The youth passes in and out of the walled compound, revealing to the avid narrator more and more amazing stories of seduction and intrigue. In an echo of Loti's famous seduction of Aziyadé, violating the Turkish harem, René Leys becomes the secret lover of the empress. In a forbidden place the ultimate (female) other is possessed.

Soon, however, this familiar Orientalist drama goes awry. Segalen's knowledge is vicarious. He and René Leys are doubles, secret sharers. A too-intimate understanding unites them, makes them complicit—we are led to suspect—in the very invention and revelation of the exotic "Within." The narrative begins to unravel. Doubts emerge; stories become contradictory. We begin to question the existence of any secret or central truth inside the palace, a world that emerges as multifarious and labyrinthine, where no one, especially not the emperor, can know all that goes on. At the same time we are unable to dismiss what we hear as lies and fantasy. The story has too much historical specificity, following very closely as it does the overthrow of the empire. René Leys is finally killed for his "inside" activities: there must have been something; it cannot all have been made up.

René Leys maintains a subtle uncertainty as to what if anything goes on within the palace. We are finally brought to see the seductive, even lethal force of the narrator's desire for knowledge, penetration, and disclosure. Indeed the parable resonates widely: countless stories of concealment, revelation, and initiation are structured by a similar desire that posits secrets in order to reveal them, imagines an other with a true "within." By the end of *René Leys* there are no more ultimate depths: the search for revelations is shown to be endless. What remains are surfaces, mirrors, doubles—an ethnography of signs without essential content.

⋏

Segalen's imaginary detours through China would become more and more obviously personal. By the end of his life the search for diversity returned him relentlessly to himself, to his familiar obsessions. Several late texts dramatize this short circuit of "le Divers." The death of Segalen's young confidant in *René Leys* signifies, among other things, the end of that part of his being that could "pass" within an exotic Forbidden City, that could believe in the possibility of sharing other lives, of erotically possessing the other, of shedding a given identity. Little remains of the exoticist project. The novel's ending is infused with lucid sadness, a poi-

gnant sense of loss. (Perhaps appropriately Segalen's own life would end
in uncertainty. His strange final illness, linked to a spiritual crisis, remains
obscure. Claudel would urge him toward a reconciliation with Catholicism, without success. Rumors of suicide persist.)

Segalen's last finished work was *Equipée* (1929); the title means
something between "trek" and "escapade." It records his longest archaeological expedition, just before the First World War, a journey that approached but did not cross into Tibet. Subtitled "Voyage au pays du réel,"
Equipée is Segalen's most directly personal work of travel writing. The
first-person singular prevails. But this *je* is far from simple: it moves
through the Chinese landscape in two distinct registers. *Equipée* records
a permanent alternation between "imaginary" and "real"—"between the
summit conquered by a metaphor and heights arduously gained by the
legs" (p. 12), between what one seeks and what is grasped. This is not
simply a matter of illusion versus reality or of "mental" against "physical"
events. Rather it is a process of desire, a forever-unsatisfied quest for
diversity constituting the body and subjectivity of the traveler.

In the mountainous landscapes of the south, so distant from the
world around Peking, Segalen unlearns much of what he knew of China.
But he seldom describes the places and people he meets, as if they could
be held at a distance, pictured in detail. *Equipée* provides instead a subjective rhythm—the perceptions and feelings of a body moving through
a space that is both real and visionary. If at times it is unclear whether
what is evoked is an external perception or a dream, the narrative still
preserves an irreducible concreteness. This quality inheres in its beautifully articulated steps—the variable stages of the journey, each a negotiation with the real.

For Segalen true diversity is not what has been precoded as exotic
or "Chinese" but rather the sensations and desires that surprise him and
seek him out. In the mountains near Tibet the exhausted narrator of *Equipée* finally encounters the *Autre*, spelled now with a capital *A*—the end
of his long "initiation au réel" (p. 121). This Other sends him back on his
tracks. Met on the path a strangely familiar man, blond, fifteen years
younger, wandering, "ready for anything, ready for other places, ready
to live other possibilities . . . ." Victor Segalen starting out for Tahiti.

木

Is Segalen's quest for diversity finally trapped by a field of subjective
desires? Yes and no. His writing departs in search of the Diverse, only to

confront the Same in new guises. Each time, however, there is a small difference. Segalen encounters doubles and reflections, but the mirrors are never perfect. A displacement occurs. By the end of his career the self, not the other, has become exotic. It is this opening of a fissure in the subject, however slight—a passage in time, a surprising angle of vision—that constitutes "le Divers."

Segalen sometimes writes in stereotypic terms about the tropics. In a letter from China he dreams of a return to Polynesia, remembering its sensuous ease: "The whole island came to me like a woman. And indeed woman out there gave me gifts that whole countries can't give anymore . . . I knew caresses and rendez-vous, liberties that required nothing more than a voice, eyes, a mouth, and lovely childish words" (1985:106). This vision of the other as feminized and childish is an obvious projection. The exotic is domesticated to male yearning.

Even familiar Orientalist visions refract strangely in Segalen. He presses his desire to an impossible limit and thus to its possible subversion. Sexual possession and easy eroticism are not his ultimate goals. His "veritable amoureuse" is a young girl, a virgin: "My *Essai sur l'exotisme* will say it: the young girl is farthest from us, thus incomparably precious to all devotees of the Diverse" (pp. 106–107). The most distant, inaccessible, tabooed object provokes his strongest desire, a desire that does not aim at penetration or possession. In 1912 he wrote from Tientsin that his wife would soon be giving birth to "a child I hope will be of the feminine sex, for pure reasons of exoticism" (p. 119). Segalen's exotic "amoureuse" was not simply the childish woman of color, of the harem, René Leys's empress, the yielding female, a forbidden place to be entered. This object was more complex.

What follows is another

REFLECTION IN THE EYES

of a girl, plainly;—this hair style, this carriage! Even these eyes looking straight at you and me . . . or perhaps over our shoulders into the space behind? (Don't turn around.)

This face reveals no emotion. The delicate brow is smooth; the eyebrows sedately arched; the lids pursed or open . . . Look again: this chaste curve of the shoulders, and the hands clasped around the stomach from decency and a good education, as if for a bow she's about to make, or to hide an encumbering pregnancy. All in all, a great purity.

Still, you'd like to know what vision or turn of mind gives her whole young body this discreet demeanor . . .

Very well! Look her straight in the eyes, as she seems to be doing to us. If the Painter is equal to the masters (to the one who enclosed in the pupil of a cowherd the perfect image of a cow, with spots, hide, and halter), if the Painter has been skilled and clever, the REFLECTION IN THE EYES should contain everything they see or dream. So gaze into them, from very close . . .

Oh—this minute mirage, marvelous and magically enclosed in the shining little shield! According to the commentary, we discern "two girls, naked from breast to foot, one on the knees of the other who cradles and caresses her." (We can even distinguish the finger-tips!) What integrity in the Painter's craft! So this is the scene the pure face reflects, decently contemplates.

But the eyes are still riveted to our own. So what's the source of the reflection?

Our *own* eyes? The space behind us?   (1916:41–43)

The last line of "Reflection in the Eyes" suggests a crucial uncertainty. Does Segalen see in the masklike face something of his own psyche projected, its "deep" wishes, a perverse unconscious revealed? Or does he discern something hidden by the gesture of *turning* toward that particular face, the act of positioning a self vis-à-vis an other? Is the self composed of inner depths or of specific encounters with alterity that produce areas of blindness and potential insight? Understood psychologically, the imagined painting reflects repressed feelings about sexuality. The onlooker sees only what is already in his own eyes, and the other becomes a screen for projected desires. Segalen's vision of two naked girls is a cliché of pornographic voyeurism.

We are left, however, with a question rather than a revelation. The scene's possible displacement suggests that the painting registers not a psychic projection but something hidden "behind" the self in the specific act of imagining an enigmatic woman. In his turn *toward* a feminine other the heterosexual male turns *away* from lesbian eroticism. What is occulted is not a phantom or hidden desire but the real possibility of a female sexuality independent of the male. Glimpsed as a reflection in the other's eyes, this imagined *reality* confuses the dominant historical category: woman as opposite sex, mystery, and object of man's desire. The heterosexual exotic wavers.

Segalen's program of exoticism is a failure. There is no escape; neither is there a stable home. The failure enacted in Segalen's poetics of displacement is both an epitome and a critique of the white man's relentless quest for himself.

Postface

Several years ago, while doing archival research on the history of ethnographic photographs, I found in a file a face that stuck like "an overly insistent friend, like a too-faithful regret, like a mute wanting to ask a question." No amount of flipping through other files—countless images of Indians, Africans, Melanesians, Eskimos—could fan this face away. Nor could I penetrate its fixed, eloquent silence.

The archive's caption records an "Igorot Man" (brought from the Philippine Highlands to be exhibited at the 1904 World's Fair in St. Louis). If we look intimately into this face, what disturbances appear behind? (Don't turn around.)

Igorot man, Philippines, exhibited at the 1904 St. Louis World's Fair.

Guinée, de ton cri, de ta main, de ta patience
il nous reste toujours des terres arbitraires.

—AIMÉ CÉSAIRE

6. Tell about Your Trip: Michel Leiris

L'AFRIQUE FANTÔME is a monster: 533 dense pages of ethnography, travel diary, self-exploration, "oneirography." Take the book's *prière d'insérer*, a publicity flyer slipped between the pages of the finished work. Throughout his career Michel Leiris has cultivated this microscopic genre: the cool essay that describes a book to which it is both intimately and barely attached, leading or misleading its readers, permitting the writer to cover his tracks. Of late the *prière d'insérer* has come to be printed on the back, or jacket flap, of published books—an immobilization Leiris regrets. That of the first edition of *L'Afrique fantôme* (1934) was a loose sheet:

> Sick of his life in Paris, viewing travel as poetic adventure, a method of concrete knowledge, an ordeal, a symbolic way to stop growing old, to deny time by crossing space, the author, interested in ethnography for the value he gives that science in the clarification of human relations, joins a scientific expedition crossing Africa.
>
> What does he find?

Few adventures, research that initially excites him but soon reveals itself too inhuman to be satisfying, an increased erotic obsession, an emotional void of growing proportions. Despite his distaste for civilized people and for the life of metropolitan cities, by the end of his journey he yearns for the return.

His attempted escape has been a complete failure, and anyway he no longer believes in the value of escape. Even with capitalism's increasing tendency to render all true human contacts impossible, isn't it within his own civilization that a Westerner can find opportunities for self-realization at the emotional level? In any case he will learn again that here as everywhere else man cannot escape his isolation: the result being that he will start out again, one day or another, caught up in new phantoms—but this time without illusions. Such is the schema of the work the author would perhaps have written if, concerned above all to offer as objective and sincere a document as possible, he had not stuck to his travel notebook, publishing it as is.

This schema is perceptible, at least in latent form, throughout a journal in which are noted, pell-mell, events, observations, feelings, dreams, ideas.

It's up to the reader to discover the germs of a coming to consciousness attained only well after the return, while at the same time following the author among peoples, sites, vicissitudes from the Atlantic to the Red Sea.   (Leiris 1966a:54–55)

The *prière d'insérer* is unbound, neither preface nor conclusion, written for readers without the time to read—journal editors, booksellers, distributors, reviewers. (The customs agents of genre: where to place this awkward *Afrique?*) And for the curious turners of pages a small sheet fluttering out into wastebaskets. The author describes pages destined for anonymous readers: a chance to start them on the right track, to tell what (whom) the book is about, to give the pages, finally, a subject. A last chance to say what was being said, to evoke a schema, the story he'd intended to write. (But this author describes the story he had not intended and that he refused to write.) A chance to begin writing again . . .

Fifty years later, with the help of a new introductory explanation and yet another "Préambule," it is still hard to know what to *make* of the 638 entries of this book that isn't one: "It's up to the reader to discover the germs of a coming to consciousness attained only well after the return, while at the same time following the author among peoples, sites, vicissitudes . . ." An impossible double reading: for if we keep in mind the narrative shape offered (always) by hindsight, we cannot follow the journal's multidirectional periplus; and if we do give ourselves to these ad hoc wanderings, then the creation of any story to account for them becomes problematic. The author refuses to narrate the scraps of experience, publishing them *tel quel*, in chronological series—as if this could solve the ultimate dilemma of giving public form to personal experiences without betraying their peculiar lived authenticity. Leiris to reader: "Warning—this book is unreadable."

". . . as objective and sincere a document as possible." *L'Afrique fantôme* will not amass its objects as if they were artifacts destined for waiting museum cases. Its ethnographic collecting is without clear guidelines, aesthetic or scientific. Nor can its pages reflect an authoritative viewpoint or adopt a dispassionate tone: they must contradict one another. And they will be strangely meticulous: "My boots are muddy, my hair long, my nails dirty. But I enjoy this filth, where everything I love becomes so pure and distant" (p. 287). By excess of subjectivity, a kind of objectivity is guaranteed—that (paradoxically) of a personal ethnography. The realist imagination, fabricator of the *vraisemblable,* is refused in favor of an impossibly sincere record of the real: perceptions, moods, facts.

In Africa Leiris begins to keep field notes on himself, or more precisely on an uncertain existence. These notes, on carefully collated cards, will form the data for *L'age d'homme* (*Manhood,* translated by Richard Howard) and four volumes of *La règle du jeu:* not autobiographies but collections of "facts and images which I refused to exploit by letting my imagination work on them; in other words, the negation of a novel. To reject all fables . . . nothing but these facts and all these facts" (1946:156).

"Rien que ces faits." "But a voyage must be told. It cannot be a heap of observations, notes, souvenirs—the pieces are displayed in sequences. A journey *makes sense* as a "coming to consciousness"; its story hardens around an identity. (Tell us about your trip!) But what if one refuses to tell? (Like every child Leiris has learned to tell a proper story. What did you do in school? No, it's not important to say just what happened, that you went to the classroom, that it was hot and boring, there were flies, you sharpened your pencil, went to the blackboard. And you don't have to recall all the little things that were lovely or that set you on edge: a bird's wing through the windowpane, an ugly turd in the lavatory.) "From the start, writing this journal, I've struggled against a poison: the idea of publication" (1934:215).

Would it be enough to return from Africa, like Conrad's Marlow, with only a single potent word? What sorts of erasures, lies, are necessary to make an acceptable story? Or could one outmaneuver narrative and somehow tell all, transcribing with equal rigor the boring, the passionate, the interesting, the unexpected, the banal? Another way of telling: as if a thousand snapshots could testify to the real in their own way: *this was*. *Ça a été. Et ça, ça, ça.* "To be in facts like a child. That's where I'd like to get" (1934:234). Desire for a regression to existence before the need to collect oneself, to account for things and one's life.

But *L'Afrique fantôme* portrays the surrealist-ethnographer enmeshed in writing—himself through the others. Toward the end of an intense period of research on *zâr* possession in Ethiopia, a sacrifice is made specifically for Leiris. His journal records that he tasted the blood of the animal but did not perform the *gourri,* the dance of the possessed. We see him seated among the *zâr* adepts, the room thick with incense, sweat, and perfume. His head is smeared with butter, and—as required by ritual—the dead animal's entrails are coiled around his brow. He does not, however, interrupt his note taking.

Leiris holds the superb title of "secretary-archivist" for the Dakar-Djibouti mission. As such he is expected to produce a history of the expedition and its historic crossing of the Dark Continent; but this story is, in effect, already inscribed before he has taken down a single note or written out his first identification card for one of the 3,600 objects the mission will acquire. A narrative is implicit in the very name of the undertaking: Mission Dakar-Djibouti. *Mission* functions as an all-purpose term for any redemptive colonial errand, whether military, evangelical, educational, medical, or ethnographic (see Barthes 1979). It suggests hundreds of other voyages, all of them heroic, confident gestures of a stable subject who conquers, instructs, converts, decribes, admires, represents . . . other people and their worlds.

"Ne visitez pas l'Exposition Coloniale" (surrealist slogan of 1931).

Just as the Dakar-Djibouti team is preparing for its departure, an enormous panoply of exotic worlds is being laid out in the bois de Vincennes. Pavilions from all the colonies, costumes, statues, masks, curiosities of every sort, "savage dances" regale the traveler in a land of well-ordered enchantment. Official marked paths lead the visitor without confusion from one outpost of progress to the next—Indochina, French West Africa, Madagascar, New Caledonia, Guinea, Martinique, Reunion. A history of the Mission Dakar-Djibouti, the one Leiris is expected to write, of an expedition passing through thirteen African countries of which ten are under French domination risks appearing to be this kind of series.

Then Ethiopia, never colonized, interrupts the expedition's smooth progress and provokes the longest, most troubled pages from the pen of its *secretaire-archiviste*. Here the mission encounters the first serious obstacles to its authority; it must alter its course, make the best of a tense political situation. At Gondar Leiris grapples with the shifting roles, deceptions; and undomesticated eroticism of his work with the *zâr* adepts; and he loses for good whatever shreds remain of the confidence needed to shape an authoritative story about Africa. The narrative implied in the mission's name unravels in the day-to-day ephemera of his journal.

To be replaced by what? Leiris has for some time been struggling against certain narrative positions, standpoints firmly assigned to whites in the colonies, whatever their personal political or aesthetic proclivities. Early in the trip at a performance of drumming and dancing: "I remain for a moment, lost in the crowd, then, seeing that a seat is reserved for me beside the administrator, I decide, with many hesitations, to take it" (1934:32).

If the colonial standpoint can be recognized and, to a degree, held at a distance, others are less perceptible. It is not until late in the voyage that Leiris breaks with the alternative, liberal stance offered by scientific ethnography, a discursive position that "understands" Africa, its peoples, and its cultures, in their own terms if possible. Ethnography studies its objects sympathetically, systematically. "Intense work, to which I give myself with a certain assiduousness, but without an ounce of passion. I'd rather be possessed than study possessed people, have carnal knowledge of a 'zarine,' rather than scientifically know all about her. For me, abstract knowledge will never be anything but a second best" (1934:324).

Still another position from which, confidently, to tell a story is offered by the voyager who goes native and returns to evoke initiation, loss of self, terror, enlightenment. Before leaving for Africa Leiris had been impressed by William Seabrook's adventure story of Haitian voodoo, *The*

Magic Island (translated into French in 1929). Seabrook appears in a photograph beside a voodoo altar with a cross in blood on his brow, the sign of his initiation. Leiris rereads the traveler's fantastic African tale *Les secrets de la jungle* (1931) during an interminable delay at the border of the Anglo-Egyptian Sudan. Again he is seduced by this "rather brilliant fantasy" (1934:202). But a certain *pudeur* always seems to restrain Leiris, who, in any event, appears to derive as much inspiration from *Notes and Queries on Anthropology* (reading W. H. R. Rivers on Freud's and Jung's theories of dreams, he is guided in his ongoing self-ethnography) and from *Pickwick Papers,* found by chance in a guest house.

Stuck at the Ethiopian border, reading whatever turns up and scribbling to fill the time, Leiris becomes preoccupied with the kind of narrative he is collecting. Which of all the possible enunciative positions should the reluctant historian adopt and which avoid? How not write the travelogue, the adventure story, the *grand reportage,* the utopia, the pilgrimage, the ecstatic (or ironic) access to wisdom, the ethnographic fable of rapport, the humanist rite of passage, the scientific myth of discovery, the quest (for woman, for the bizarre, for suffering, for art, for renewal, for an authentic voice)? We come across lists of "imagerie africaine" (to be forgotten)—Prester John, death of Livingston, Fachoda, Rimbaud, Kitchener, Raymond Roussel's *Impressions d'Afrique,* "les amazones de Behanzin" . . . (p. 294).

Leiris passes the slack days drafting prefaces (two of which appear in the midst of *L'Afrique fantôme*). In addition to issues of genre and narrative form he worries about principles of inclusion and exclusion. He defends a rigorous subjectivity, the right (the duty) to record the course of a dream or a bowel movement—along with observations of the locale, events of the mission, and scientific inquiries. He will leave his text open to objective chance, recording whatever ideas, problems, or fantasies impose themselves.

⅄

Leiris continues to search, however, for a satisfactory way of telling—of collecting and displaying—an existence. The last pages of *L'Afrique fantôme* contains a sketch for a novel centering on a patent alter ego, a character named after Axel Heyst from Conrad's *Victory.* Heyst enacts Leiris' various sexual obsessions and fears—his worries about the imminent return to Europe, reunification with his wife, the eternal problem of measuring up to an obscure, punitive standard of manhood. The convolutions of the plot are intriguing, if inconclusive (pp. 499–504). More important is the implicit narrative model for the work, which prefigures Leiris' later literary productions.

The novel's projected form owes less to Conrad's *Victory* than to *Heart of Darkness,* a tale Leiris much admired (p. 196). Like Conrad he portrays the death of a mysterious colonial figure (Heyst/Kurtz) as seen by a second character ("le docteur"/Marlow) who pieces together his story from fragments—letters, documents, hearsay, and an elusive personal contact. Once a plausible account of the protagonist's death is established, the second figure fabricates a false version for use in a particular context where it will be believable. The enacted process of collecting and telling a personal story becomes itself the focus of narration. Leiris' novel outline includes the laborious *documentation* of a life story, the *lie* of any single version of it, and the interplay of character, writer, and audience in its *mise en scène.*

A theatrical conception of the subject appears later in Leiris' scholarly reckoning with his *zâr* research, its ambiguous, disturbing play of roles: *La possession et ses aspects théâtraux chez les Ethiopiens de Gondar* (1958). Indeed his literary works always manifest their "aspects théâtraux," giving frequent glimpses behind the scene of writing. Leiris' practice resembles that of a disciplined actor, combining simultaneously dissimulation and sincerity in a quest for presence that never quite comes off.

This discipline is visible in the sequel to *L'Afrique fantôme. Manhood* (1946) adopts a narrative form that successfully draws on both the intimate journal and the novelistic fiction while falling into neither genre. In the book's first *prière d'insérer* (inserted in a later prefatory essay, "On Literature Considered as a Bullfight") the author still seeks a way to "speak of himself with a maximum of lucidity and sincerity." He does this paradoxically, though, by avoiding forms that present themselves as *expressions* of a self-revelatory subject. Leiris turns our attention away from an authentic voice to "l'objet fabriqué," a blatant self-creation that he offers, deadpan, to the public. *Manhood,* a novel of education, ends with the emergence not of an identity but of a personage. It stops short, unfinished, with words quoted from a dream: "I explain to my mistress how necessary it is to construct a wall around oneself by means of clothing."

The "sincerity" Leiris seeks has as little to do with the romantic notion of confession (an unmediated true speech) as the "objectivity" he cultivates has to do with scientific detachment. In each case the author seems to accept a rule of public comportment but then, by pressing it rigorously, elaborately to its limit, exposes the proceeding as yet another ruse of a subjectivity in process, forever telling and retelling itself. ("Ruse" is not quite right, for there is always another turn by which Leiris convinces us somehow of the simplicity of the undertaking.) "The undissimulated use of rhetoric," Leiris' phrase applied to Raymond Queneau (preface to *Contes et propos,* 1981), describes equally his own narrative constructions of and around himself—clothes that make the man.

L'Afrique fantôme, stubbornly naive, holds off acceptable forms of narrative while hinting at their necessity (in its *prière d'insérer*). *Manhood* goes beyond the journal's antinarrative, the merely chronological collection of citations and snapshots. It constructs its story, Leiris tells us, on the model of photomontage (1946:15). This arranged anthology of the self still cultivates a photographic viewpoint—a documentary, quasi-scientific, but also surreal tone. There is no attempt—as in the anti-rhetoric of romanticism—to speak without artifice or from the heart. Leiris's "objective," "sincere" stance obsessively reveals itself as an effect of style, largely through a systematically clumsy and complicated staging of the text for which the various elaborate explanations, supplementary notes, hidden prefaces, and *prières d'insérer* are props.

What is most inexplicable about *L'Afrique fantôme,* however, is not its awkwardness, its dada ideas of data, its refusals, even its boredom (a form of *disponibilité*). Nor is it the persistent disappointment that the journal enacts. (If something luminous occurs, it tends quickly to appear as a shabby spectacle, a commercial transaction, a further occasion for ambivalence, depression, and so on.) After Conrad we are accustomed to the *tristes tropiques* with their fables of disenchantment. What remains most inexplicable is the strange childlike innocence emerging somehow, each time, *after* experience. It is incredible that Leiris keeps on writing, and that we keep on reading, dipping in and out of these pages. Yet every day the journal's scrupulous entries appear—long, short, elaborate, terse—each promising that *something* will somehow happen and that soon we will see what the relentless series is leading to. We never do. No moment of truth: *Afrique fantôme* is only a pen starting up each day.

We recall afterward the intensities, the confrontations, the incidents of self-doubt, the diatribes against colonialism and ethnography, as if they marked a thread, the progress of the tale. We forget all the tiny beginnings, entries: "Coup de théâtre sur coup de théâtre" . . . "Slept

badly" . . . "Intense work, to which I give myself with a certain assiduousness" . . . "We're bored, all of us" . . . "The masks' mothers used to
be offered human sacrifices; this is Tabyon's story" . . . "Departure from
Bordeaux at 5:50 P.M." . . . "Another night at Malkam Ayahou's" . . .
"We're approaching Malakal. Green grasses. Yellow grasses."

Leiris' life of writing combines an acute sense of the futility of existence with a tenacious desire to salvage its meaningful details—quotation, perception, memory. He returns to his field notes. His 1981 work,
Le ruban au cou d'Olympia, adopts once again a fragmentary form—
collected textual evidences of an existence. Its *prière d'insérer* records a
double goal: "for a moment, to give the protagonist of this sort of, sometimes open sometimes disguised, public confession the intoxicated feeling of living a second life; to make the receiver perceive what, speaking
of an actor and his play [*son jeu*] he'd call 'presence.' "

Prière d'insérer—loose somewhere between the written book, the
desired reader. Starting up. The next Leiris . . .

⁂

L'Afrique fantôme begins a writing process that will endlessly pose and
recompose an identity. Its poetics is one of incompletion and process,
with space for the extraneous. Interrupting the smooth ethnographic story
of an access to Africa, it undermines the assumption that self and other
can be gathered in a stable narrative coherence. Leiris' strange, open-
ended "book" may be situated within a new, heterogeneous historical
situation. Leiris would become a friend of Aimé Césaire in the crucial
decade after the Second World War, when surrealism, as cultural-
political criticism, returned to its native land, Paris, but now speaking
the accents of negritude. (Leiris was perhaps the first professional ethnographer to name and analyze colonialism, in 1950, as an inescapable
ideological ground.) It is becoming common to distinguish two negri-
tudes. Senghor's looks back to tradition and eloquently gathers up a collective "African" essence. Césaire's is more syncretic, modernist, and
parodic—Caribbean in its acceptance of fragments and in its appreciation of the mechanism of collage in cultural life.

We are all Caribbeans now in our urban archipelagos. "Guinea" (old
Africa, writes Césaire) "from your cry from your hand from your patience/
we still have some arbitrary lands" (1983:207). Perhaps there's no return
for anyone to a native land—only field notes for its reinvention. The
Guyanese novelist and critic Wilson Harris recommends a "principle of

juxtaposition" as a way to account for "the making of tradition . . . the heterogeneous groundwork of authentic community." He is interested in something he calls "the jigsaw of nature, and the dialogue of reality" (1973:7, 9, 81). We can recognize in this vision the jagged setting for modern ethnography and ethnopoetics. Beginning with Césaire's unsettling irony (1983:51):

And you know the rest

That 2 and 2 are 5
that the forest meows
that the tree plucks the maroons from the fire
that the sky strokes its beard
etc etc . . .

Who and what are we?
A most worthy question!

Two cultures seem to intermingle in a fascinating, ambiguous embrace only so that each can inflict on the other a more visible denial.

—MICHEL LEIRIS, *FRÊLE BRUIT*

7. A Politics of Neologism: Aimé Césaire

"VEERITION"? The last word of Aimé Césaire's "Notebook of a Return to the Native Land" brings the whole incredible poem to an impossible term—or turn. The "Notebook" is a tropological landscape in which syntactic, semantic, and ideological transformations occur. Césaire's poems make demands. To engage this writing (the best English translation to date is by Clayton Eshleman and Annette Smith) is an active work of rethinking.[1] How does one grasp, translate a language that is blatantly making itself up? Eshleman and Smith have gone to great lengths of accuracy and daring; but Césaire still sends readers to dictionaries in several tongues, to encyclopedias, to botanical reference works, histories, and atlases. He is attached to the obscure, accurate term and to the new word. He makes readers confront the limits of their language, or of any single language. He forces them to *construct* readings from a debris of historical and future possibilities. His world is Caribbean—hybrid and heteroglot.

---

1. All poetry by Césaire is quoted from the 1983 Eshleman and Smith translation (Césaire 1973).

Césaire's poems *veer*. This requires a special page; and the page itself is questioned by his verse. Nowhere are the size and format of "the book" so standardized as in France. On the narrow pages of earlier editions Césaire's exorbitant lines were stubbed. Lengthy continuations separated into discrete units. Where these had hardened into printing errors, Eshleman and Smith, with Césaire's help, have corrected the prosody. Their edition provides an unusually large page, giving the poetry the space it needs to swerve extravagantly between vertical and horizontal momentums. For example the famous ending of the "Notebook":

> then, strangling me with your lasso of stars
> rise,
> Dove
> rise
> rise
> rise
> I follow you who are imprinted on my ancestral white cornea
> rise sky licker
> and the great black hole where a moon ago I wanted to drown it is
> there I will now fish the malevolent tongue of the night in its
> motionless veerition!

No page can really accommodate the final horizontal rush of words from "and the great" to "veerition." Eshleman and Smith print it as a continuous unit, running out of page only once (before "malevolent"). By contrast the French of the "definitive" *Présence africaine* edition breaks this long sequence into two syntactically and spatially distinct lines. Emile Snyder's well-known translation opts for three separate lines, while John Berger's Penguin version carves out four, moving even farther in the wrong direction of imagistic compression. After the plummeting vertical sequence of "rise"s, Eshleman and Smith stay with Césaire's final ecstatic run-on sentence. On a page accommodating one hundred horizontal characters (*Présence africaine*, Snyder forty-five characters, Berger fifty-five) the "line" zooms across and off—a long expulsion.

The poem "stops" on a coinage, itself a new turn. Césaire's great lyric about finding a voice, about returning to native ground, strands us, finally, with a made-up, Latinate, abstract-sounding question mark of a word. So much for expectations of direct, immediate linguistic "authenticity." With Césaire we are involved in a poetics of cultural *invention*.

Eshleman and Smith have done well—as well as possible—with the poem's various neologisms (*rhizulate, effarade, desencastration* . . .); but as they write in their introduction: "Only Césaire himself was in a position to reveal (in a private communication) that 'verrition' which preceding translators and scholars had interpreted as 'flick' and 'swirl' had been coined on a Latin verb, 'verri,' meaning 'to sweep,' 'to scrape a surface,' and ultimately 'to scan.' Our rendition ('veerition') attempts to preserve the turning motion (set against its oxymoronic modifier) as well as the Latin sound of the original—thus restituting the long-lost meaning of an important passage" (p. 26). The translators may be forgiven their claim to have restored a "long-lost meaning." In fact radical indeterminacy is the essence of neologism. No dictionary or etymology can nail down the significance, nor can an inventor's (remembered) intention. The real strength of Césaire's last word is that it forces open again the semantic universe of the "Notebook"—just as it is about to close. Césaire does not restore the "meanings" of language, culture, and identity; he gives them a turn.

人

Césaire's most famous neologism, *négritude,* has by now lost its newness. It is too familiar as a literary movement and as a set of "positions" in an ongoing debate about black identity, essentialism, and oppositional consciousness. Negritude, in many of its senses, has become what Césaire never wanted it to be, an abstraction and an ideology. When the word first appeared in the "Notebook," it was sheer political, poetical invention. Any neologism, perceived as such, announces itself as *made.* Negritude is less an enduring fact or condition to be discovered and named than it is a historical creation, a language process. In an interview with René Depestre (1980) Césaire declines to define his coinage in any way except historically and contingently: "There's been a lot of theorizing about negritude. I've kept out of it, from personal discretion. But if you ask me how I conceive of negritude I'll say that in my opinion negritude is primarily a concrete, not abstract, coming to consciousness." He goes on to recall a generation's response to the dominant "atmosphere of assimilation" in the thirties and forties. Speaking with Lilyan Kesteloot, Césaire is even more careful in his handling of the term:

> It's an obvious fact: negritude has brought dangers. It has tended to become a school, to become a church, to become a theory, an ideology. I'm in favor of negritude seen as a literary phenomenon, and as a personal ethic, but I'm against building an ideology on negritude . . .

> If negritude means a kind of prophecy, well then no, because I strongly believe there's a class struggle, for example, and there are other elements, philosophical elements, that certainly determine us. I absolutely refuse any sort of confused, idyllic pan-Africanism . . . As a result, although I don't reject negritude, I look on it with an extremely critical eye. Critical, that's basically what I mean: lucidity and discernment, not confusedly mixing everything. In addition, my conception of negritude is not biological, it's cultural and historical. I think there's always a certain danger in basing something on the black blood in our veins, the three drops of black blood.   (Depestre 1980:144–145)

Two of those who participated in the early creation of negritude as a movement (and who would both sharply criticize it from a standpoint of Marxist humanism) have now published important books that look back reflectively on the phenomenon. The title of René Depestre's collection of essays, *Bonjour et adieu à la négritude,* is indicative of a clear distance taken. Similarly René Ménil's *Tracées* (1981) reflects a desire to place negritude in a historical context and to see it as part of a general New World predicament.

Ménil, who was Césaire's main contact with surrealism in the thirties and who participated in both of the formative group endeavors, *Légitime défense* and *Tropiques,* has republished a selection of essays from his long career, including a subtle rereading of Césaire's "Notebook." Here the negritude of Léopold Senghor and that of Césaire are clearly distinguished. The former elaborates a "backward-looking idealism," a falsely naturalized, consistent African mentality that tends to reinscribe the categories of a romantic, sometimes racialist European ethnography. Césaire's Caribbean negritude, by contrast, rejects all essentialist evocations. Instead, in the *Notebook,* according to Ménil, "antiphrasis and ellipsis are constantly brought to the service of poetic condensation. The poet consistently holds himself at a distance from what he is and from what he says, in order to produce *the literary effect of derision*" (p. 80, emphasis in the original). Irony is inherent in the West Indian predicament:

> It can be said that our West Indian consciousness is necessarily parodic, since it's caught in a game of doubling and redoubling, mirroring and separation, in the face of a French colonial consciousness embodied in ruling institutions and the mass media. For this kind of divided, worried consciousness, naiveté in art is forbidden. This is the source

of those dissonances in our art that, as Baudelaire said in the nine-teenth century, are agreeable to modern ears.   (pp. 223–224)

Depestre too in his "adieu" to negritude merges it with a broader modernism, with "the essential *créolité* of the Caribbean and of Latin America" (p. 151). To be "American" is to be hybrid, *métis;* and in De-pestre's vision the true heirs of negritude are writers like Carpentier, Guil-lén, Amado, Vallejo, Cortázar, Márquez. Again negritude is transmuted; it is no longer about roots but about present process in a polyphonous reality.

With this in mind it is good to return to the word's original coinage in the "Notebook" (p. 67), where we see not the elaboration of a broad black identity but rather very specific affirmations and negations. "*My negritude is not . . .*"

> my negritude is not a stone, its deafness hurled against the clamor
>   of the day
> my negritude is not a leukoma of dead liquid over the earth's dead
>   eye
> my negritude is neither tower nor cathedral
> it takes root in the red flesh of the soil
> it takes root in the ardent flesh of the sky
> it breaks through the opaque prostration with its upright patience

人

Césaire writes "in" French, but . . ."Marronnerons-nous Depestre mar-ronnerons-nous?" The line appears in a poem of 1955 entitled "The Verb 'Marronner'/for René Depestre, Haitian Poet." Here neologism defeats the best of translators, for the only possible equivalent of the coined *mar-ronner* is "to maroon," which, though derived from the same root, is dominated by images of shipwreck and abandonment. The noun *marron-age* has been adopted by anglophone scholars of maroon societies in the Guianas, Brazil, and the Caribbean; but the verb, Césaire's invention, is still without translation. The source is old Spanish: *cima,* or "mountain-top" (thus a place of escape), leading to the later *cimarrón,* "wild," "run-away" (thus the maroon, or fugitive slave). Césaire's *marronner* invokes escape and something more.

Recent studies of maroon societies have made apparent the very complex mix of ingredients that combined in original ways to form resil-ient, flexible cultures. The ties with Africa were real, but notions of a "collective memory" or of cultural "survivals" could not fully account for the specific Afro-American forms constructed from diverse tribal traditions, from the new "slave cultures," from various creolizing processes, and from local, properly historical experiences. (See Price 1973, 1983.)

Césaire's new verb *marronner* itself changes significantly in successive revisions of the poem for Depestre. In its first version, dated 1955, the work was called "Réponse à Depestre, poète haitien: Eléments d'un art poétique." Depestre, then exiled in Brazil, had recently rallied, in the pages of *Présence africaine,* to the French Communist party's emerging conservative line on poetic experimentation. In the wake of surrealism, Louis Aragon was pressing for a return to more traditional prosody, to simpler forms and messages, linking these with the interests of revolutionary workers. Free verse and radical innovation of many kinds were now proscribed as "formal individualism." Césaire's reply to Depestre, also published in *Présence africaine,* rejected the conservative trend and prepared his own break with French communism a year later in his *Letter to Maurice Thorez.* "Is it true this season that they're polishing up sonnets?" he asks Depestre, and immediately ties the new constraints to Haiti's colonial sugar mills (1983:369):

> when slow skinny oxen make their rounds to the whine
> of mosquitos
>
> Bah! Depestre the poem is not a mill for
> grinding sugar cane absolutely not
> and if the rhymes are flies on ponds
>   without rhymes
>   for a whole season
> away from ponds
>   under my persuasion
> let's laugh drink and escape like slaves
> [rions buvons et marronnons]

The first and second printings of the "Reply to Depestre" contain a specific reference to Aragon: "To hell with it Depestre to hell with it let Aragon talk." The reference would be dropped from Césaire's *Oeuvres complètes* (1976), the source for Eshleman and Smith. This movement away from a specific controversy is reflected in a more significant textual change. In 1955 Césaire had exhorted Depestre: "Marronnons-les Depestre marronnons-les / comme jadis nous marronnions nos maîtres à fouet" (Let's escape them Depestre let's escape them / as in the past we escaped our whip-wielding masters). In the later version the exhortation, once cast in a transitive form, "let's escape *them*" (the slave drivers, the party line), has been altered to an interrogative future form in which the play of sound becomes a slightly glossolalic ripple of *n*'s and *r*'s. "Marronnerons-nous Depestre marronnerons-nous?" The reference to "whip-wielding masters" is gone, and *marronage* is now a less limited and ongoing act of escape. In the poem it is enacted as the mixing up of sound and sense, the running away with language. Thus *marronage* is no longer about simply escaping (*them*). It is also about reflexive possibility and poesis. Césaire makes rebellion and the remaking of culture—the historical maroon experience—into a *verb*. A necessary new verb names the New World poetics of continuous transgression and cooperative cultural activity ("Marronnerons-*nous* Depestre"). Fugitive slaves who created cultures in the swamps of the Guianas represented distinct African traditions. Living together they took over, used, and altered one another's customs, words, and pasts. So Césaire, born in Martinique, invokes incidents of Haitian history in his letter to Depestre, while pressing a poetic radicalism derived from Rimbaud and surrealism. The final lines of "The Verb 'Marronner' " are scattered with words and place names from West Africa, France, Hispanic America, Brazil, Haiti. Césaire veers among the traditions that history has offered to and imposed on a Caribbean identity. His being and his poetics are elements of "A Freedom in Passage" (the last poem of the collection):

> helped so much by birds
> whose mission is by means of pollen

We still need a *verb marronner.*

8. The Jardin des Plantes: Postcards

Paris, 9/2/84

Dear A,

Around the Jardin des Plantes: boules played in the old Roman space . . . remember? Arènes de Lutèce, hidden behind buildings of the rue Monge; Mouftard and its market (gentrified); or the mosque, where you can still take a steam bath and drink mint tea from gold trays. This year the gardens are lush—blur of blossoms from everywhere, going to seed. People scattered on green chairs observe the plants. And statues: Bernardin de Saint-Pierre smiles down in bluish bronze at the mythic kids Paul et Virginie. Buffon, back turned to everyone: a pigeon twitches on his metal head. Over near the zoo and the Seine Lamarck in an attitude of thought—above a rising sun (science? nature?). See you at the end of the month . . .

9/3/84

Dear P,

NATURE/CULTURE NATURE/CULTURE NATURE/CULTURE: it's still the most beautiful, intense, funny, etc. etc. exhibit in Paris: "Les Plus Beaux Insectes du Monde" (Institute of Entomology, rue Buffon, afternoons). One bright room . . . pinned fireworks, faces, masks, eyes, bones, skin . . . then suddenly four exactly torn leaves (with antennae), a band of *tricolores*, the dusty subtlety of moths (Braque, Klee), touched up, sprayed, day-glo, lacquer, ceramic, microchip . . . laugh of classifications. Bougainville, Borneo, Sumatra, Java; with wings, without wings; "Hercules," gold metal, blackblue, neongreen . . . Didn't Lévi-Strauss write somewhere that modern art should be inspired by butterflies, not Picasso?

9/4/84

Dear S,

Tall tree, SOPHORA JAPONICA, planted by B. Jussieu, 1747, in the Jardin du Roy, seed sent from China by R. P. d'Incarville, . . . or another, brought from "The Levant." Strange things, *alive and historical* (not at all like those sequoia rings with dates, 1492, 1776, 1914; or "the bed Napoleon slept in"). They're living in planetary-human time and space . . . the Age of Discovery transplanted. Outliving us. By the way, there's a new bookstore with a pretty good poetry section, Mouftard and Pot de Fer: "L'Arbre Voyageur." Will you be passing through California this winter?

9/5/84

Dear T,

Inhuman *Robinsonade*—

ROBINIER de ROBIN (Robina Pseudo Accacia Linné)

The first subject introduced into Europe from seeds originating in NORTH AMERICA by Jean ROBIN in his garden of the place Dauphine in 1601. Transplanted to this spot in the Royal Garden in 1636 by Vespasier ROBIN, son of the above.

9/6/84

Dear B,

You won't have forgotten the fantastic, long, dappled alleyways of Tilleul. But maybe you didn't see a little rock garden where they cultivate shrubs, flowers, cacti, and herbs from China, the Caucasus, Corsica, New Zealand, Morocco, the Himalayas, Pyrenees, Balkans, Arctic, Japan . . . Continents beside each other in hundreds of beds. On a trunk supported by an iron post:

PISTACHER (Pistacia Vera L.)

Planted in the seedling garden around 1700

(the present Alpine Garden).
Permitted Sebastian Vaillant to discover the
sexuality of plants in 1716.
So what's become of M. Vaillant? Or the sexuality of plants? The pistachio tree lives. With love . . .

9/7/84

Dear N,
"Primitive" painting by Haitians is a recent avocation. (But you know all about this.) And they took to it so "naturally." A friend tells me he once saw a Haitian artist painting the complex forests of "Guinée" (place of origin) with Henri Rousseau reproductions at hand. There are no African jungles in Haiti. And the Douanier hadn't seen them either but copied his in Paris from tropical specimens at the Jardin. Right now I'm looking in at the entrance to one of the old dreamlike greenhouses. A tyger? Behind tall panes . . . fabulous, sharp, sagging leaves. Fable of our "Caribbean" selves?

9/7/84

Dear L,
About the view from your hotel, rue Linné . . . I can imagine the ivy-drenched gate of the Jardin, and within, dark walls of the "Labyrinth." (Its rising circular paths, assignations, strangers . . .) And isn't this near the great Cedar of Lebanon where around 1860 (in an old print) people with top hats and long dresses strolled to admire the superb, spreading form and to marvel at the gathered imperial universe? They must have heard—as one still does—noises from the zoo, animals that would be devoured some years later by besieged citizens of the Commune. Please stay in touch.

9/9/84

Dear C,
Thanks for sending me the new book by Alicia Dujovne Ortiz, *Buenos Aires*. One of those miracles of travel, the *vertige horizontal*. Jews from Moldavia marrying Argentinians (immigrants: Spanish, Italian, Albanian . . .), then a daughter: *porteña*, in Paris, writing French, remembering. I like her ambivalent glimpses of Borges and the tango. Also, especially, her love for the city's Jardin Botanico—giant plants visited by cats and old ladies with bags of liver. The zoo's "hindu place inhabited by a dusty

elephant . . . " Transplanted civilization. "But if I have no roots, why have my roots hurt me so?"

9/10/84

Dear J,

Paris of the *rentrée:* streets filling again, tempo picking up. The low sun has an artificial glaze. In the Jardin des Plantes, they're building a new "Zoothèque," underground. Pruning has begun. Contemplating winter. I'm infatuated yet again with the palms of the Luxembourg Gardens ("Autour d'une meme place / l'ample palme ne se lasse . . . "), symmetrical, perfect, in boxes with iron feet. Vegetable extraterrestrials . . . six inches of air between the path and their . . . earth.

Indian woman spinning yarn and rocking cradle with a cord tied to her foot. In the background Franz Boas and George Hunt help compose the picture.

Part Three ⋏ Collections

You do not stand in one place to watch a masquerade.
—AN IGBO SAYING

9. Histories of the Tribal and the Modern

D URING THE WINTER of 1984–85 one could encounter tribal objects in an unusual number of locations around New York City. This chapter surveys a half-dozen, focusing on the most controversial: the major exhibition held at the Museum of Modern Art (MOMA), "'Primitivism' in 20th Century Art: Affinity of the Tribal and the Modern." The chapter's "ethnographic present" is late December 1984.

The "tribal" objects gathered on West Fifty-third Street have been around. They are travelers—some arriving from folklore and ethnographic museums in Europe, others from art galleries and private collections. They have traveled first class to the Museum of Modern Art, elaborately crated and insured for important sums. Previous accommodations have been less luxurious: some were stolen, others "purchased" for a song by colonial administrators, travelers, anthropologists, missionaries, sailors in African ports. These non-Western objects have been by turns curiosities, ethnographic specimens, major art creations. After 1900 they began to turn up in European flea markets, thereafter moving between avant-garde studios and collectors' apartments. Some came to rest in the unheated basements or "laboratories" of anthropology museums, surrounded by objects made in the same region of the world. Others encountered odd fellow travelers, lighted and labeled in strange display cases. Now on West Fifty-third Street they intermingle with works by European masters—Picasso, Giacometti, Brancusi, and others. A three-dimensional Eskimo mask with twelve arms and a number of holes hangs beside a canvas on which Joan Miró has painted colored shapes. The people in New York look at the two objects and see that they are alike.

Travelers tell different stories in different places, and on West Fifty-third Street an origin story of modernism is featured. Around 1910 Picasso and his cohort suddenly, intuitively recognize that "primitive" objects are in fact powerful "art." They collect, imitate, and are affected by these objects. Their own work, even when not directly influenced, seems oddly reminiscent of non-Western forms. The modern and the primitive converse across the centuries and continents. At the Museum of Modern Art an exact history is told featuring individual artists and objects, their encounters in specific studios at precise moments. Photographs document the crucial influences of non-Western artifacts on the pioneer modernists. This focused story is surrounded and infused with another—a loose allegory of relationship centering on the word *affinity*. The word is a kinship term, suggesting a deeper or more natural relationship than mere resemblance or juxtaposition. It connotes a common quality or essence joining the tribal to the modern. A Family of Art is brought together, global, diverse, richly inventive, and miraculously unified, for every object displayed on West Fifty-third Street looks modern.

The exhibition at MOMA is historical and didactic. It is complemented by a comprehensive, scholarly catalogue, which includes divergent views of its topic and in which the show's organizers, William Rubin and Kirk Varnedoe, argue at length its underlying premises (Rubin 1984). One of the virtues of an exhibition that blatantly makes a case or tells a story is that it encourages debate and makes possible the suggestion of other stories. Thus in what follows different histories of the tribal and the modern will be proposed in response to the sharply focused history on display at the Museum of Modern Art. But before that history can be seen for what it is, however—a specific story that excludes other stories—the universalizing allegory of affinity must be cleared away.

This allegory, the story of the Modernist Family of Art, is not rigorously argued at MOMA. (That would require some explicit form of either an archetypal or structural analysis.) The allegory is, rather, built into the exhibition's form, featured suggestively in its publicity, left uncontradicted, repetitiously asserted—"Affinity of the Tribal and the Modern." The allegory has a hero, whose virtuoso work, an exhibit caption tells us, contains more affinities with the tribal than that of any other pioneer modernist. These affinities "measure the depth of Picasso's grasp of the informing principles of tribal sculpture, and reflect his profound identity of spirit with the tribal peoples." Modernism is thus presented as a search for "informing principles" that transcend culture, politics, and history. Beneath this generous umbrella the tribal is modern and the modern more richly, more diversely human.

⋏

The power of the affinity idea is such (it becomes almost self-evident in the MOMA juxtapositions) that it is worth reviewing the major objections to it. Anthropologists, long familiar with the issue of cultural diffusion versus independent invention, are not likely to find anything special in the similarities between selected tribal and modern objects. An established principle of anthropological comparative method asserts that the greater the range of cultures, the more likely one is to find similar traits. MOMA's sample is very large, embracing African, Oceanian, North American, and Arctic "tribal" groups.[1] A second principle, that of the "limitation of possibilities," recognizes that invention, while highly diverse, is not infinite. The human body, for example, with its two eyes, four limbs, bilateral arrangement of features, front and back, and so on, will be represented and stylized in a limited number of ways.[2] There is thus a priori no reason to claim evidence for affinity (rather than mere

---

1. The term *tribal* is used here with considerable reluctance. It denotes a kind of society (and art) that cannot be coherently specified. A catchall, the concept of tribe has its source in Western projection and administrative necessity rather than in any essential quality or group of traits. The term is now commonly used instead of *primitive* in phrases such as *tribal art*. The category thus denoted, as this essay argues, is a product of historically limited Western taxonomies. While the term was originally an imposition, however, certain non-Western groups have embraced it. Tribal status is in many cases a crucial strategic ground for identity. In this essay my use of *tribe* and *tribal* reflects common usage while suggesting ways in which the concept is systematically distorting. See Fried 1975 and Sturtevant 1983.

2. These points were made by William Sturtevant at the symposium of anthropologists and art historians held at the Museum of Modern Art in New York on November 3, 1984.

resemblance or coincidence) because an exhibition of tribal works that seem impressively "modern" in style can be gathered. An equally striking collection could be made demonstrating sharp dissimilarities between tribal and modern objects.

The qualities most often said to link these objects are their "conceptualism" and "abstraction" (but a very long and ultimately incoherent list of shared traits, including "magic," "ritualism," "environmentalism," use of "natural" materials, and so on, can be derived from the show and especially from its catalogue). Actually the tribal and modern artifacts are similar only in that they do *not* feature the pictorial illusionism or sculptural naturalism that came to dominate Western European art after the Renaissance. Abstraction and conceptualism are, of course, pervasive in the arts of the non-Western World. To say that they share with modernism a rejection of certain naturalist projects is not to show anything like an affinity.[3] Indeed the "tribalism" selected in the exhibition to resemble modernism is itself a construction designed to accomplish the task of resemblance. Ife and Benin sculptures, highly naturalistic in style, are excluded from the "tribal" and placed in a somewhat arbitrary category of "court" society (which does not, however, include large chieftanships). Moreover, pre-Columbian works, though they have a place in the catalogue, are largely omitted from the exhibition. One can question other selections and exclusions that result in a collection of only "modern"-looking tribal objects. Why, for example, are there relatively few "impure" objects constructed from the debris of colonial culture contacts? And is there not an overall bias toward clean, abstract forms as against rough or crude work?

The "Affinities" room of the exhibition is an intriguing but entirely problematic exercise in formal mix-and-match. The short introductory

---

3. A more rigorous formulation than that of affinity is suggested in Leiris 1953. How, Leiris asks, can we speak of African sculpture as a single category? He warns of "a danger that we may underestimate the variety of African sculpture; as we are less able to appreciate the respects in which cultures or things unfamiliar to us differ from one another than the respects in which they differ from those to which we are used, we tend to see a certain resemblance between them, which lies, in point of fact, merely in their common differentness" (p. 35). Thus, to speak of African sculpture one inevitably shuts one's eyes "to the rich diversity actually to be found in this sculpture in order to concentrate on the respects in which it is *not* what our own sculpture generally is." The affinity of the tribal and the modern is, in this logic, an important optical illusion—the measure of a *common differentness* from artistic modes that dominated in the West from the Renaissance to the late nineteenth century.

text begins well: "AFFINITIES presents a group of tribal objects notable for their appeal to modern taste." Indeed this is all that can rigorously be said of the objects in this room. The text continues, however, "Selected pairings of modern and tribal objects demonstrate common denominators of these arts that are independent of direct influence." The phrase *common denominators* implies something more systematic than intriguing resemblance. What can it possibly mean? This introductory text, cited in its entirety, is emblematic of the MOMA undertaking as a whole. Statements carefully limiting its purview (specifying a concern only with modernist primitivism and not with tribal life) coexist with frequent implications of something more. The affinity idea itself is wide-ranging and promiscuous, as are allusions to universal human capacities retrieved in the encounter between modern and tribal or invocations of the expansive human mind—the healthy capacity of modernist consciousness to question its limits and engage otherness.[4]

Nowhere, however, does the exhibition or catalogue underline a more disquieting quality of modernism: its taste for appropriating or redeeming otherness, for constituting non-Western arts in its own image, for discovering universal, ahistorical "human" capacities. The search for similarity itself requires justification, for even if one accepts the limited task of exploring "modernist primitivism," why could one not learn as much about Picasso's or Ernst's creative processes by analyzing the *differences* separating their art from tribal models or by tracing the ways their art moved *away* from, gave new twists to, non-Western forms?[5] This side of the process is unexplored in the exhibition. The prevailing viewpoint is made all too clear in one of the "affinities" featured on the catalogue's cover, a juxtaposition of Picasso's *Girl before a Mirror* (1932) with a Kwakiutl half-mask, a type quite rare among Northwest Coast creations. Its task here is simply to produce an effect of resemblance (an effect actually created by the camera angle). In this exhibition a universal message, "Affinity of the Tribal and the Modern," is produced by careful selection and the maintenance of a specific angle of vision.

The notion of affinity, an allegory of kinship, has an expansive, cel-

---

4. See, for example, Rubin's discussion of the mythic universals shared by a Picasso painting and a Northwest Coast half-mask (Rubin 1984:328–330). See also Kirk Varnedoe's association of modernist primitivism with rational, scientific exploration (Rubin 1984:201–203, 652–653).

5. This point was made by Clifford Geertz at the November 3, 1984, symposium at the Museum of Modern Art (see n.2).

(a)   (b)

The Making of an Affinity
(a) *Pablo Picasso,* Girl before a
Mirror, *1932 (detail)*
(b) *Kwakiutl mask*
(c) *Picasso,* Girl before a Mirror
*The detail from the Picasso paint-
ing and the Kwakiutl mask were
juxtaposed on the cover of the exhibition catalog* "Primitivism"
in 20th Century Art: Affinity
of the Tribal and the Modern,
volume I.

(c)

ebratory task to perform. The affinities shown at MOMA are all on modernist terms. The great modernist "pioneers" (and their museum) are shown promoting formerly despised tribal "fetishes" or mere ethnographic "specimens" to the status of high art and in the process discovering new dimensions of their ("our") creative potential. The capacity of art to transcend its cultural and historical context is asserted repeatedly (Rubin 1984:x, 73). In the catalogue Rubin tends to be more interested in a recovery of elemental expressive modes, whereas Varnedoe stresses the rational, forward-looking intellect (which he opposes to an unhealthy primitivism, irrational and escapist). Both celebrate the generous spirit of modernism, pitched now at a global scale but excluding—as we shall see—Third World modernisms.

At West Fifty-third Street modernist primitivism is a going Western concern. It is, Varnedoe tells us, summing up in the last sentence of the catalogue's second volume, "a process of revolution that begins and ends in modern culture, and because of that—not in spite of it—can continually expand and deepen our contact with that which is remote and different from us, and continually threaten, challenge, and reform our sense of self" (Rubin 1984: 682). A skeptic may doubt the ability of the modernist primitivism exhibited at MOMA to threaten or challenge what is by now a thoroughly institutionalized system of aesthetic (and market) value; but it is appropriate, and in a sense rigorous, that this massive collection spanning the globe should end with the word *self*.

Indeed an unintended effect of the exhibition's comprehensive catalogue is to show once and for all the incoherence of the modern Rorschach of "the primitive." From Robert Goldwater's formalism to the transforming "magic" of Picasso (according to Rubin); from Lévy-Bruhl's mystical *mentalité primitive* (influencing a generation of modern artists and writers) to Lévi-Strauss's *pensée sauvage* (resonating with "systems art" and the cybernetic binarism of the minimalists); from Dubuffet's fascination with insanity and the childish to the enlightened rational sense of a Gauguin, the playful experimentalism of a Picasso or the new "scientific" spirit of a James Turrell (the last three approved by Varnedoe but challenged by Rosalind Krauss, who is more attached to Bataille's decapitation, *bassesse*, and bodily deformations[6]); from fetish to icon and back

---

6. The clash between Krauss's and Varnedoe's dark and light versions of primitivism is the most striking incongruity within the catalogue. For Krauss the crucial task is to shatter predominant European forms of power and subjectivity; for Varnedoe the task is to expand their purview, to question, and to innovate.

again; from aboriginal bark paintings (Klee) to massive pre-Columbian monuments (Henry Moore); from weightless Eskimo masks to Stonehenge—the catalogue succeeds in demonstrating not any essential affinity between tribal and modern or even a coherent modernist attitude toward the primitive but rather the restless desire and power of the modern West to collect the world.

⅄

Setting aside the allegory of affinity, we are left with a "factual," narrowly focused history—that of the "discovery" of primitive art by Picasso and his generation. It is tempting to say that the "History" section of the exhibition is, after all, the rigorous part and the rest merely suggestive association. Undeniably a great deal of scholarly research in the best *Kunstgeschichte* tradition has been brought to bear on this specific history. Numerous myths are usefully questioned; important facts are specified (what mask was in whose studio when); and the pervasiveness of tribal influences on early modernist art—European, English, and American—is shown more amply than ever before. The catalogue has the merit of including a number of articles that dampen the celebratory mood of the exhibition: notably the essay by Krauss and useful contributions by Christian Feest, Philippe Peltier, and Jean-Louis Paudrat detailing the arrival of non-Western artifacts in Europe. These historical articles illuminate the less edifying imperialist contexts that surrounded the "discovery" of tribal objects by modernist artists at the moment of high colonialism.

If we ignore the "Affinities" room at MOMA, however, and focus on the "serious" historical part of the exhibition, new critical questions emerge. What is excluded by the specific focus of the history? Isn't this factual narration still infused with the affinity allegory, since it is cast as a story of creative genius recognizing the greatness of tribal works, discovering common artistic "informing principles"? Could the story of this intercultural encounter be told differently? It is worth making the effort to extract another story from the materials in the exhibition—a history not of redemption or of discovery but of reclassification. This other history assumes that "art" is not universal but is a changing Western cultural category. The fact that rather abruptly, in the space of a few decades, a large class of non-Western artifacts came to be redefined as art is a taxonomic shift that requires critical historical discussion, not celebration. That this construction of a generous category of art pitched at a global scale occurred just as the planet's tribal peoples came massively under European political, economic, and evangelical dominion cannot be irrelevant. But there is no room for such complexities at the MOMA show. Obviously the modernist appropriation of tribal productions as art is not simply imperialist. The project involves too many strong critiques of colonialist, evolutionist assumptions. As we shall see, though, the scope and underlying logic of the "discovery" of tribal art reproduces hegemonic Western assumptions rooted in the colonial and neocolonial epoch.

Picasso, Léger, Apollinaire, and many others came to recognize the elemental, "magical" power of African sculptures in a period of growing *négrophilie,* a context that would see the irruption onto the European scene of other evocative black figures: the jazzman, the boxer (Al Brown), the *sauvage* Josephine Baker. To tell the history of modernism's recognition of African "art" in this broader context would raise ambiguous and disturbing questions about aesthetic appropriation of non-Western others, issues of race, gender, and power. This other story is largely invisible at MOMA, given the exhibition's narrow focus. It can be glimpsed only in the small section devoted to "La création du monde," the African cosmogony staged in 1923 by Léger, Cendrars, and Milhaud, and in the broadly pitched if still largely uncritical catalogue article by Laura Rosenstock devoted to it. Overall one would be hard pressed to deduce from the exhibition that all the enthusiasm for things *nègre,* for the "magic" of African art, had anything to do with race. Art in this focused history has no essential link with coded perceptions of black bodies—their vitalism, rhythm, magic, erotic power, etc.—as seen by whites. The modernism represented here is concerned only with artistic invention, a positive category separable from a negative primitivism of the irrational, the savage, the base, the flight from civilization.

A different historical focus might bring a photograph of Josephine Baker into the vicinity of the African statues that were exciting the Parisian avant-garde in the 1910s and 1920s; but such a juxtaposition would be unthinkable in the MOMA history, for it evokes different affinities from those contributing to the category of great art. The black body in Paris of the twenties was an ideological artifact. Archaic Africa (which came to Paris by way of the future—that is, America) was sexed, gendered, and invested with "magic" in specific ways. Standard poses adopted by "La Bakaire," like Léger's designs and costumes, evoked a recognizable "Africanity"—the naked form emphasizing pelvis and buttocks, a segmented stylization suggesting a strangely mechanical vitality. The inclusion of so ideologically loaded a form as the body of Josephine Baker among the figures classified as art on West Fifty-third Street would suggest a different account of modernist primitivism, a different analysis of the category *nègre* in *l'art nègre,* and an exploration of the "taste" that was something more than just a backdrop for the discovery of tribal art in the opening decades of this century.[7]

Such a focus would treat art as a category defined and redefined in specific historical contexts and relations of power. Seen from this angle and read somewhat against the grain, the MOMA exhibition documents a *taxonomic* moment: the status of non-Western objects and "high" art are importantly redefined, but there is nothing permanent or transcendent about the categories at stake. The appreciation and interpretation of tribal objects takes place within a modern "system of objects" which confers value on certain things and withholds it from others (Baudrillard 1968). Modernist primitivism, with its claims to deeper humanist sympathies and a wider aesthetic sense, goes hand-in-hand with a developed market in tribal art and with definitions of artistic and cultural authenticity that are now widely contested.

Since 1900 non-Western objects have generally been classified as either primitive art *or* ethnographic specimens. Before the modernist revolution associated with Picasso and the simultaneous rise of cultural anthropology associated with Boas and Malinowski, these objects were dif-

---

7. On *négrophilie* see Laude 1968; for parallel trends in literature see Blachère 1981 and Levin 1984. The discovery of things "nègre" by the European avant-garde was mediated by an imaginary America, a land of noble savages simultaneously standing for the past and future of humanity—a perfect affinity of primitive and modern. For example, jazz was associated with primal sources (wild, erotic passions) and with technology (the mechanical rhythm of brushed drums, the gleaming saxophone). Le Corbusier's reaction was characteristic: "In a stupid variety show, Josephine Baker sang 'Baby' with such an intense and dramatic sensibility that I was moved to tears. There is in this American Negro music a lyrical 'contemporary' mass so invincible that I could see the foundation of a new sentiment of music capable of being the expression of the new epoch and also capable of classifying its European origins as stone age—just as has happened with the new architecture" (quoted in Jencks 1973:102). As a source of modernist inspiration for Le Corbusier, the figure of Josephine Baker was matched only by monumental, almost Egyptian, concrete grain elevators, rising from the American plains and built by nameless "primitive" engineers (Banham 1986:16). The historical narrative implicit here has been a feature of twentieth-century literary and artistic innovation, as a redemptive modernism persistently "discovers" the primitive that can justify its own sense of emergence.

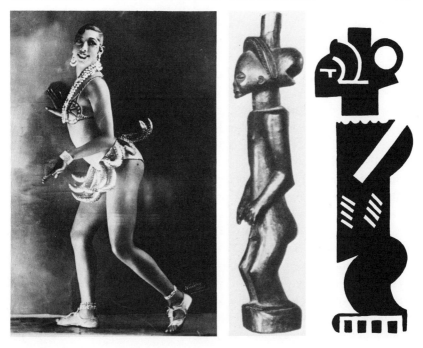

Affinities Not Included in the MOMA "Primitivism" Show.
1. Bodies
(a) Josephine Baker in a famous pose, Paris, ca. 1929
(b) Wooden figure (Chokwe, Angola)
(c) Fernand Léger, costume design for The Creation of
the World, *1922–23*

ferently sorted—as antiquities, exotic curiosities, orientalia, the remains of early man, and so on. With the emergence of twentieth-century modernism and anthropology figures formerly called "fetishes" (to take just one class of object) became works either of "sculpture" or of "material culture." The distinction between the aesthetic and the anthropological was soon institutionally reinforced. In art galleries non-Western objects were displayed for their formal and aesthetic qualities; in ethnographic museums they were represented in a "cultural" context. In the latter an African statue was a ritual object belonging to a distinct group; it was displayed in ways that elucidated its use, symbolism, and function. The institutionalized distinction between aesthetic and anthropological discourses took form during the years documented at MOMA, years that saw the complementary discovery of primitive "art" and of an anthropo-

logical concept of "culture" (Williams 1966).[8] Though there was from
the start (and continues to be) a regular traffic between the two domains,
this distinction is unchallenged in the exhibition. At MOMA treating
tribal objects as art means excluding the original cultural context. Consideration of context, we are firmly told at the exhibition's entrance, is
the business of anthropologists. Cultural background is not essential to
correct aesthetic appreciation and analysis: good art, the masterpiece, is
universally recognizable.[9] The pioneer modernists themselves knew little
or nothing of these objects' ethnographic meaning. What was good
enough for Picasso is good enough for MOMA. Indeed an ignorance of
cultural context seems almost a precondition for artistic appreciation. In
this object system a tribal piece is detached from one milieu in order to
circulate freely in another, a world of art—of museums, markets, and
connoisseurship.

Since the early years of modernism and cultural anthropology non-
Western objects have found a "home" either within the discourses and
institutions of art or within those of anthropology. The two domains have
excluded and confirmed each other, inventively disputing the right to
contextualize, to represent these objects. As we shall see, the aesthetic-
anthropological opposition is systematic, presupposing an underlying set
of attitudes toward the "tribal." Both discourses assume a primitive world
in need of preservation, redemption, and representation. The concrete,
inventive existence of tribal cultures and artists is suppressed in the process of either constituting authentic, "traditional" worlds or appreciating
their products in the timeless category of "art."

人

Nothing on West Fifty-third Street suggests that good tribal art is being
produced in the 1980s. The non-Western artifacts on display are located

---

8. The twentieth-century developments traced here redeploy these ideas in
an intercultural domain while preserving their older ethical and political charge.
See Chapter 10, section 2.

9. On the recognition of masterpieces see Rubin's confident claims
(1984:20–21). He is given to statements such as the following on tribal and modern art: "The solutions of genius in the plastic arts are all essentially instinctual"
(p. 78, n.80). A stubborn rejection of the supposed views of anthropologists (who
believe in the collective production of works of tribal art) characterizes Rubin's
attempts to clear out an autonomous space for aesthetic judgment. Suggestions
that he may be projecting Western aesthetic categories onto traditions with different definitions of art are made to seem simplistic (for example p. 28).

either in a vague past (reminiscent of the label "nineteenth-twentieth century" that accompanies African and Oceanian pieces in the Metropolitan Museum's Rockefeller Wing) or in a purely conceptual space defined by "primitive" qualities: magic, ritualism, closeness to nature, mythic or cosmological aims (see Rubin 1984:10, 661–689). In this relegation of the tribal or primitive to either a vanishing past or an ahistorical, conceptual present, modernist appreciation reproduces common ethnographic categories.

The same structure can be seen in the Hall of Pacific Peoples, dedicated to Margaret Mead, at the American Museum of Natural History. This new permanent hall is a superbly refurbished anthropological stopping place for non-Western objects. In *Rotunda* (December 1984), the museum's publication, an article announcing the installation contains the following paragraph:

> Margaret Mead once referred to the cultures of Pacific peoples as "a world that once was and now is no more." Prior to her death in 1978 she approved the basic plans for the new *Hall of Pacific Peoples*.   (p. 1)

We are offered treasures saved from a destructive history, relics of a vanishing world. Visitors to the installation (and especially members of *present* Pacific cultures) may find a "world that is no more" more appropriately evoked in two charming display cases just outside the hall. It is the world of a dated anthropology. Here one finds a neatly typed page of notes from Mead's much-disputed Samoan research, a picture of the fieldworker interacting "closely" with Melanesians (she is carrying a child on her back), a box of brightly colored discs and triangles once used for psychological testing, a copy of Mead's column in *Redbook*. In the Hall of Pacific Peoples artifacts suggesting change and syncretism are set apart in a small display entitled "Culture Contact." It is noted that Western influence and indigenous response have been active in the Pacific since the eighteenth century. Yet few signs of this involvement appear anywhere else in the large hall, despite the fact that many of the objects were made in the past 150 years in situations of contact, and despite the fact that the museum's ethnographic explanations reflect quite recent research on the cultures of the Pacific. The historical contacts and impurities that are part of ethnographic work—and that may signal the life, not the death, of societies—are systematically excluded.

The tenses of the hall's explanatory captions are revealing. A recent color photograph of a Samoan *kava* ceremony is accompanied by the words: "STATUS and RANK were [sic] important features of Samoan society," a statement that will seem strange to anyone who knows how important they remain in Samoa today. Elsewhere in the hall a black-and-white photograph of an Australian Arunta woman and child, taken around 1900 by the pioneer ethnographers Spencer and Gillen, is captioned in the *present* tense. Aboriginals apparently must always inhabit a mythic time. Many other examples of temporal incoherence could be cited—old Sepik objects described in the present, recent Trobriand photos labeled in the past, and so forth.

The point is not simply that the image of Samoan *kava* drinking and status society presented here is a distortion or that in most of the Hall of Pacific Peoples history has been airbrushed out. (No Samoan men at the *kava* ceremony are wearing wristwatches; Trobriand face painting is shown without noting that it is worn at cricket matches.) Beyond such questions of accuracy is an issue of systematic ideological coding. To locate "tribal" peoples in a nonhistorical time and ourselves in a different, historical time is clearly tendentious and no longer credible (Fabian 1983). This recognition throws doubt on the perception of a vanishing tribal world, rescued, made valuable and meaningful, either as ethnographic "culture" or as primitive/modern "art." For in this temporal ordering the real or genuine life of tribal works always precedes their collection, an act of salvage that repeats an all-too-familiar story of death and redemption. In this pervasive allegory the non-Western world is always vanishing and modernizing—as in Walter Benjamin's allegory of modernity, the tribal world is conceived as a ruin. (Benjamin 1977). At the Hall of Pacific Peoples or the Rockefeller Wing the actual ongoing life and "impure" inventions of tribal peoples are erased in the name of cultural or artistic "authenticity." Similarly at MOMA the production of tribal "art" is entirely in the past. Turning up in the flea markets and museums of late nineteenth-century Europe, these objects are destined to be aesthetically redeemed, given new value in the object system of a generous modernism.

⅄

The story retold at MOMA, the struggle to gain recognition for tribal art, for its capacity "like all great art . . . to show images of man that transcend the particular lives and times of their creators" (Rubin 1984:73), is taken for granted at another stopping place for tribal travelers in Manhattan, the Center for African Art on East Sixty-eighth Street. Susan Vogel, the executive director, proclaims in her introduction to the catalogue of its inaugural exhibition, "African Masterpieces from the Musée de l'Homme," that the "aesthetic-anthropological debate" has been resolved. It is now widely accepted that "ethnographic specimens" can be distinguished from "works of art" and that within the latter category a limited number of "masterpieces" are to be found. Vogel correctly notes that the aesthetic recognition of tribal objects depends on changes in Western taste. For example it took the work of Francis Bacon, Lucas Samaras, and others to make it possible to exhibit as art "rough and horrifying [African] works as well as refined and lyrical ones" (Vogel 1985:11). Once recognized, though, art is apparently art. Thus the selection at the Center is made on aesthetic criteria alone. A prominent placard affirms that the ability of these objects "to transcend the limitations of time and place, to speak to us across time and culture . . . places them among the highest points of human achievement. It is as works of art that we regard them here and as a testament to the greatness of their creators."

There could be no clearer statement of one side of the aesthetic anthropological "debate" (or better, *system*). On the other (anthropological) side, across town, the Hall of Pacific Peoples presents collective rather than individual productions—the work of "cultures." But within an institutionalized polarity interpenetration of discourses becomes possible. Science can be aestheticized, art made anthropological. At the American Museum of Natural History ethnographic exhibits have come increasingly to resemble art shows. Indeed the Hall of Pacific Peoples represents the latest in aestheticized scientism. Objects are displayed in ways that highlight their formal properties. They are suspended in light, held in space by the ingenious use of Plexiglas. (One is suddenly astonished by the sheer weirdness of a small Oceanic figurine perched atop a three-foot-tall transparent rod.) While these artistically displayed artifacts are scientifically explained, an older, functionalist attempt to present an integrated picture of specific societies or culture areas is no longer seriously pursued. There is an almost dadaist quality to the labels on eight cases devoted to Australian aboriginal society (I cite the complete series in order): "CEREMONY, SPIRIT FIGURE, MAGICIANS AND SORCERERS, SACRED ART, SPEAR THROWERS, STONE AXES AND KNIVES, WOMEN, BOOMERANGS." Elsewhere the hall's pieces of culture have been recontextualized within a new cybernetic, anthropological discourse. For instance flutes and stringed instruments are captioned: "MUSIC is a system of organized

Affinities Not Included in the MOMA "Primitivism" Show.
2. Collections
(a) Interior of Chief Shake's House, Wrangel, Alaska, 1909

sound in man's [sic] aural environment" or nearby: "COMMUNICATION is an important function of organized sound."

In the anthropological Hall of Pacific Peoples non-Western objects still have primarily scientific value. They are in addition beautiful.[10] Conversely, at the Center for African Art artifacts are essentially defined as "masterpieces," their makers as great artists. The discourse of connoisseurship reigns. Yet once the story of art told at MOMA becomes dogma,

---

10. At the November 3, 1984, symposium (see n.2) Christian Feest pointed out that the tendency to reclassify objects in ethnographic collections as "art" is in part a response to the much greater amount of funding available for art (rather than anthropological) exhibitions.

(b) View of the Margaret Mead Hall of Pacific Peoples

it is possible to reintroduce and co-opt the discourse of ethnography. At the Center tribal contexts and functions are described along with individual histories of the objects on display. Now firmly classified as masterpieces, African objects escape the vague, ahistorical location of the "tribal" or the "primitive." The catalogue, a sort of *catalogue raisonné*, discusses each work intensively. The category of the masterpiece individuates: the pieces on display are not typical; some are one of a kind. The famous Fon god of war or the Abomey shark-man lend themselves to precise histories of individual creation and appropriation in visible colonial situations. Captions specify *which* Griaule expedition to West Africa in the 1930s acquired each Dogon statue (see Leiris 1934 and Chapter 2). We learn in the catalogue that a superb Bamileke mother and child was carved by an artist named Kwayep, that the statue was bought by the colonial administrator and anthropologist Henri Labouret from King

N'Jike. While tribal names predominate at MOMA, the Rockefeller Wing, and the American Museum of Natural History, here personal names make their appearance.

In the "African Masterpieces" catalogue we learn of an ethnographer's excitement on finding a Dogon hermaphrodite figure that would later become famous. The letter recording this excitement, written by Denise Paulme in 1935, serves as evidence of the aesthetic concerns of many early ethnographic collectors (Vogel and N'diaye 1985:122). These individuals, we are told, could intuitively distinguish masterpieces from mere art or ethnographic specimens. (Actually many of the individual ethnographers behind the Musée de l'Homme collection, such as Paulme, Michel Leiris, Marcel Griaule, and André Schaeffner, were friends and collaborators of the same "pioneer modernist" artists who, in the story told at MOMA, constructed the category of primitive art. Thus the intuitive aesthetic sense in question is the product of a historically specific milieu. See Chapter 4.) The "African Masterpieces" catalogue insists that the founders of the Musée de l'Homme were art connoisseurs, that this great anthropological museum never treated all its contents as "ethnographic specimens." The Musée de l'Homme was and is secretly an art museum (Vogel 1985:11). The taxonomic split between art and artifact is thus healed, at least for self-evident "masterpieces," entirely in terms of the aesthetic code. Art is art in any museum.

In this exhibition, as opposed to the others in New York, information can be provided about each individual masterpiece's history. We learn that a Kiwarani antelope mask studded with mirrors was acquired at a dance given for the colonial administration in Mali on Bastille Day 1931. A rabbit mask was purchased from Dogon dancers at a gala soirée in Paris during the Colonial Exhibition of the same year. These are no longer the dateless "authentic" tribal forms seen at MOMA. At the Center for African Art a different history documents both the artwork's uniqueness and the achievement of the discerning collector. By featuring rarity, genius, and connoisseurship the Center confirms the existence of autonomous artworks able to circulate, to be bought and sold, in the same way as works by Picasso or Giacometti. The Center traces its lineage, appropriately, to the former Rockefeller Museum of Primitive Art, with its close ties to collectors and the art market.

In its inaugural exhibition the Center confirms the predominant aesthetic-ethnographic view of tribal art as something located in the past, good for being collected and given aesthetic value. Its second show (March 12–June 16, 1985) is devoted to "Igbo Arts: Community and Cosmos." It tells another story, locating art forms, ritual life, and cosmology in a specific, changing African society—a past *and* present heritage. Photographs show "traditional" masks worn in danced masquerades around 1983. (These include satiric figures of white colonists.) A detailed history of cultural change, struggle, and revival is provided. In the catalogue Chike C. Aniakor, an Igbo scholar, writes along with co-editor Herbert M. Cole of "the continually evolving Igbo aesthetic": "It is illusory to think that which we comfortably label 'traditional' art was in an earlier time immune to changes in style and form; it is thus unproductive to lament changes that reflect current realities. Continuity with earlier forms will always be found; the present-day persistence of family and community values ensures that the arts will thrive. And as always, the Igbo will create new art forms out of their inventive spirit, reflecting their dynamic interactions with the environment and their neighbors and expressing cultural ideals" (Cole and Aniakor 1984:14).

Cole and Aniakor provide a quite different history of "the tribal" and "the modern" from that told at the Museum of Modern Art—a story of invention, not of redemption. In his foreword to the catalogue Chinua Achebe offers a vision of culture and of objects that sharply challenges the ideology of the art collection and the masterpiece. Igbo, he tells us, do not like collections.

> The purposeful neglect of the painstakingly and devoutly accomplished *mbari* houses with all the art objects in them as soon as the primary mandate of their creation has been served, provides a significant insight into the Igbo aesthetic value as *process* rather than *product*. Process is motion while product is rest. When the product is preserved or venerated, the impulse to repeat the process is compromised. Therefore the Igbo choose to eliminate the product and retain the process so that every occasion and every generation will receive its own impulse and experience of creation. Interestingly this aesthetic disposition receives powerful endorsement from the tropical climate which provides an abundance of materials for making art, such as wood, as well as formidable agencies of dissolution, such as humidity and the termite. Visitors to Igboland are shocked to see that artifacts are rarely accorded any particular value on the basis of age alone.   (Achebe 1984:ix)

Achebe's image of a "ruin" suggests not the modernist allegory of redemption (a yearning to make things whole, to think archaeologically)

The Earth Deity, Ala, *with her "children" in her* mbari
house. Obube Ulakwo, southeast Nigeria, 1966.

but an acceptance of endless seriality, a desire to keep things apart, dynamic, and historical.

᛭

The aesthetic-anthropological object systems of the West are currently under challenge, and the politics of collecting and exhibiting occasionally become visible. Even at MOMA evidence of living tribal peoples has not been entirely excluded. One small text breaks the spell. A special label explains the absence of a Zuni war god figure currently housed in the Berlin Museum für Völkerunde. We learn that late in its preparations for the show MOMA "was informed by knowledgeable authorities that Zuni people consider any public exhibition of their war gods to be sacrilegious." Thus, the label continues, although such figures are routinely displayed elsewhere, the museum decided not to bring the war god (an influence on Paul Klee) from Berlin. The terse note raises more questions than it answers, but it does at least establish that the objects on display may in fact "belong" somewhere other than in an art or an ethnographic museum. Living traditions have claims on them, contesting (with a distant but increasingly palpable power) their present home in the institutional systems of the modern West.[11]

Elsewhere in New York this power has been made even more visible. "Te Maori," a show visiting the Metropolitan, clearly establishes that the "art" on display is still sacred, on loan not merely from certain New Zealand museums but also from the Maori people. Indeed tribal art is political through and through. The Maori have allowed their tradition to be exploited as "art" by major Western cultural institutions and their corporate sponsors in order to enhance their own international prestige and

---

11. The shifting balance of power is evident in the case of the Zuni war gods, or Ahauuta. Zuni vehemently object to the display of these figures (terrifying and of great sacred force) as "art." They are the only traditional objects singled out for this objection. After passage of the Native American Freedom of Religion Act of 1978 Zuni initiated three formal legal actions claiming return of the Ahauuta (which as communal property are, in Zuni eyes, by definition stolen goods). A sale at Sotheby Parke-Bernet in 1978 was interrupted, and the figure was eventually returned to the Zuni. The Denver Art Museum was forced to repatriate its Ahauutas in 1981. A claim against the Smithsonian remains unresolved as of this writing. Other pressures have been applied elsewhere in an ongoing campaign. In these new conditions Zuni Ahauuta can no longer be routinely displayed. Indeed the figure Paul Klee saw in Berlin would have run the risk of being seized as contraband had it been shipped to New York for the MOMA show. For general background see Talbot 1985.

Affinities Not Included in the MOMA "Primitivism" Show.
3. Appropriations
(a) Mrs. Pierre Loeb in her family apartment with modern
and tribal works, rue Desbordes-Valmore, Paris, 1929

thus contribute to their current resurgence in New Zealand society (Mead 1984).[12] Tribal authorities gave permission for the exhibition to travel, and they participated in its opening ceremonies in a visible, distinctive manner. So did Asante leaders at the exhibition of their art and culture at the Museum of Natural History (October 16, 1984–March 17, 1985). Although the Asante display centers on eighteenth- and nineteenth-century artifacts, evidence of the twentieth-century colonial suppression and recent renewal of Asante culture is included, along with color photos

12. An article on corporate funding of the arts in the *New York Times,* Feb. 5, 1985, p. 27, reported that Mobil Oil sponsored the Maori show in large part to please the New Zealand government, with which it was collaborating on the construction of a natural gas conversion plant.

(b) New Guinea girl with photographer's flash bulbs

of modern ceremonies and newly made "traditional" objects brought to
New York as gifts for the museum. In this exhibition the *location* of the
art on display—the sense of where, to whom, and in what time(s) it belongs—is quite different from the location of the African objects at
MOMA or in the Rockefeller Wing. The tribal is fully historical.

Still another representation of tribal life and art can be encountered
at the Northwest Coast collection at the IBM Gallery (October 10–December 29, 1984), whose objects have traveled downtown from the Museum of the American Indian. They are displayed in pools of intense light
(the beautifying "boutique" decor that seems to be modernism's gift to
museum displays, both ethnographic and artistic). But this exhibition of
traditional masterpieces ends with works by living Northwest Coast artists. Outside the gallery in the IBM atrium two large totem poles have
been installed. One is a weathered specimen from the Museum of the
American Indian, and the other has been carved for the show by the

Kwakiutl Calvin Hunt. The artist put the finishing touches on his creation where it stands in the atrium; fresh wood chips are left scattered around the base. Nothing like this is possible or even thinkable at West Fifty-third Street.

The organizers of the MOMA exhibition have been clear about its limitations, and they have repeatedly specified what they do not claim to show. It is thus in a sense unfair to ask why they did not construct a differently focused history of relations between "the tribal" and "the modern." Yet the exclusions built into any collection or narration are legitimate objects of critique, and the insistent, didactic tone of the MOMA show only makes its focus more debatable. If the non-Western objects on West Fifty-third Street never really question but continually confirm established aesthetic values, this raises questions about "modernist primitivism's" purportedly revolutionary potential. The absence of any examples of Third World modernism or of recent tribal work reflects a pervasive "self-evident" allegory of redemption.

The final room of the MOMA exhibition, "Contemporary Explorations," which might have been used to refocus the historical story of modernism and the tribal, instead strains to find contemporary Western artists whose work has a "primitive feel."[13] Diverse criteria are asserted: a use of rough or "natural" materials, a ritualistic attitude, ecological concern, archaeological inspiration, certain techniques of assemblage, a conception of the artist as shaman, or some familiarity with "the mind of primitive man in his [sic] science and mythology" (derived perhaps from reading Lévi-Strauss). Such criteria, added to all the other "primitivist" qualities invoked in the exhibition and its catalogue, unravel for good the category of the primitive, exposing it as an incoherent cluster of qualities that at different times have been used to construct a source, origin, or alter ego confirming some new "discovery" within the territory of the Western self. The exhibition is at best a historical account of a certain moment in this relentless process. By the end the feeling created is one of claustrophobia.

---

13. In places the search becomes self-parodic, as in the caption for works by Jackie Winsor: "Winsor's work has a primitivist feel, not only in the raw physical presence of her materials, but also in the way she fabricates. Her labor—driving nails, binding twine—moves beyond simple systematic repetition to take on the expressive character of ritualized action."

The non-Western objects that excited Picasso, Derain, and Léger broke into the realm of official Western art from outside. They were quickly integrated, recognized as masterpieces, given homes within an anthropological-aesthetic object system. By now this process has been sufficiently celebrated. We need exhibitions that question the boundaries of art and of the art world, an influx of truly indigestible "outside" artifacts. The relations of power whereby one portion of humanity can select, value, and collect the pure products of others need to be criticized and transformed. This is no small task. In the meantime one can at least imagine shows that feature the impure, "inauthentic" productions of past and present tribal life; exhibitions radically heterogeneous in their global mix of styles; exhibitions that locate themselves in specific multicultural junctures; exhibitions in which nature remains "unnatural"; exhibitions whose principles of incorporation are openly questionable. The following would be my contribution to a different show on "affinities of the tribal and the postmodern." I offer just the first paragraph from Barbara Tedlock's superb description of the Zuni Shalako ceremony, a festival that is only part of a complex, living tradition (1984:246):

> Imagine a small western New Mexican village, its snow-lit streets lined with white Mercedes, quarter-ton pickups and Dodge vans. Villagers wrapped in black blankets and flowered shawls are standing next to visitors in blue velveteen blouses with rows of dime buttons and voluminous satin skirts. Their men are in black Stetson silver-banded hats, pressed jeans, Tony Lama boots and multicolored Pendleton blankets. Strangers dressed in dayglo orange, pink and green ski jackets, stocking caps, hiking boots and mittens. All crowded together they are looking into newly constructed houses illuminated by bare light bulbs dangling from raw rafters edged with Woolworth's red fabric and flowered blue print calico. Cinderblock and plasterboard white walls are layered with striped serapes, Chimayó blankets, Navajo rugs, flowered fringed embroidered shawls, black silk from Mexico and purple, red and blue rayon from Czechoslovakia. Rows of Hopi cotton dance kilts and rain sashes; Isleta woven red and green belts; Navajo and Zuni silver concha belts and black mantas covered with silver brooches set with carved lapidary, rainbow mosaic, channel inlay, turquoise needlepoint, pink agate, alabaster, black cannel coal and bakelite from old '78s, coral, abalone shell, mother-of-pearl and horned oyster hang from poles suspended from the ceiling. Mule and

white-tailed deer trophy-heads wearing squash-blossom, coral and chunk-turquoise necklaces are hammered up around the room over rearing buckskins above Arabian tapestries of Martin Luther King and the Kennedy brothers, The Last Supper, a herd of sheep with a haloed herder, horses, peacocks.

There is a Third World in every First World, and vice-versa.
—TRINH T. MINH-HA, "DIFFERENCE," *DISCOURSE* 8

10. On Collecting Art and Culture

T HIS CHAPTER is composed of four loosely connected parts, each concerned with the fate of tribal artifacts and cultural practices once they are
relocated in Western museums, exchange systems, disciplinary archives,
and discursive traditions. The first part proposes a critical, historical approach to collecting, focusing on subjective, taxonomic, and political
processes. It sketches the "art-culture system" through which in the last
century exotic objects have been contextualized and given value in the
West. This ideological and institutional system is further explored in the
second part, where cultural description is presented as a form of collecting. The "authenticity" accorded to both human groups and their artistic
work is shown to proceed from specific assumptions about temporality,
wholeness, and continuity. The third part focuses on a revealing moment
in the modern appropriation of non-Western works of "art" and "culture,"
a moment portrayed in several memoirs by Claude Lévi-Strauss of his
wartime years in New York. A critical reading makes explicit the
redemptive metahistorical narrative these memoirs presuppose. The
general art-culture system supported by such a narrative is contested

throughout the chapter and particularly in the fourth part, where alternative "tribal" histories and contexts are suggested.

Collecting Ourselves

Entering
You will find yourself in a climate of nut castanets,
A musical whip
From the Torres Straits, from Mirzapur a sistrum
Called Jumka, "used by Aboriginal
Tribes to attract small game
On dark nights," coolie cigarettes
And mask of Saagga, the Devil Doctor,
The eyelids worked by strings.

James Fenton's poem "The Pitt Rivers Museum, Oxford" (1984:81–84), from which this stanza is taken, rediscovers a place of fascination in the ethnographic collection. For this visitor even the museum's descriptive labels seem to increase the wonder (". . . attract small game / on dark nights") and the fear. Fenton is an adult-child exploring territories of danger and desire, for to be a child in this collection ("Please sir, where's the withered / Hand?") is to ignore the serious admonitions about human evolution and cultural diversity posted in the entrance hall. It is to be interested instead by the claw of a condor, the jaw of a dolphin, the hair of a witch, or "a jay's feather worn as a charm / in Buckinghamshire." Fenton's ethnographic museum is a world of intimate encounters with inexplicably fascinating objects: personal fetishes. Here collecting is inescapably tied to obsession, to recollection. Visitors "find the landscape of their childhood marked out / Here in the chaotic piles of souvenirs . . . boxroom of the forgotten or hardly possible."

Go
As a historian of ideas or a sex-offender,
For the primitive art,
As a dusty semiologist, equipped to unravel
The seven components of that witch's curse
Or the syntax of the mutilated teeth. Go
In groups to giggle at curious finds.
But do not step into the kingdom of your promises

To yourself, like a child entering the forbidden
Woods of his lonely playtime.

Do not step in this tabooed zone "laid with the snares of privacy and
fiction / And the dangerous third wish." Do not encounter these objects
except as *curiosities* to giggle at, *art* to be admired, or *evidence* to be
understood scientifically. The tabooed way, followed by Fenton, is a path
of too-intimate fantasy, recalling the dreams of the solitary child "who
wrestled with eagles for their feathers" or the fearful vision of a young
girl, her turbulent lover seen as a hound with "strange pretercanine eyes."
This path through the Pitt Rivers Museum ends with what seems to be a
scrap of autobiography, the vision of a personal "forbidden woods"—
exotic, desired, savage, and governed by the (paternal) law:

He had known what tortures the savages had prepared
For him there, as he calmly pushed open the gate
And entered the wood near the placard: "TAKE NOTICE MEN
MEN-TRAPS AND SPRING-GUNS ARE SET ON THESE
PREMISES."
For his father had protected his good estate.

Fenton's journey into otherness leads to a forbidden area of the self. His
intimate way of engaging the exotic collection finds an area of desire,
marked off and policed. The law is preoccupied with *property*.

C. B. Macpherson's classic analysis of Western "possessive individualism" (1962) traces the seventeenth-century emergence of an ideal self
as owner: the individual surrounded by accumulated property and
goods. The same ideal can hold true for collectivities making and remaking their cultural "selves." For example Richard Handler (1985) analyzes
the making of a Québécois cultural "patrimoine," drawing on Macpherson to unravel the assumptions and paradoxes involved in "having a culture," selecting and cherishing an authentic collective "property." His
analysis suggests that this identity, whether cultural or personal, presupposes acts of collection, gathering up possessions in arbitrary systems of
value and meaning. Such systems, always powerful and rule governed,
change historically. One cannot escape them. At best, Fenton suggests,
one can transgress ("poach" in their tabooed zones) or make their self-
evident orders seem strange. In Handler's subtly perverse analysis a system of retrospection—revealed by a Historic Monuments Commission's
selection of ten sorts of "cultural property"—appears as a taxonomy wor-

thy of Borges' "Chinese encyclopedia": "(1) commemorative monuments; (2) churches and chapels; (3) forts of the French Regime; (4) windmills; (5) roadside crosses; (6) commemorative inscriptions and plaques; (7) devotional monuments; (8) old houses and manors; (9) old furniture; (10) 'les choses disparues'" (1985:199). In Handler's discussion the collection and preservation of an authentic domain of identity cannot be natural or innocent. It is tied up with nationalist politics, with restrictive law, and with contested encodings of past and future.

⼑

Some sort of "gathering" around the self and the group—the assemblage of a material "world," the marking-off of a subjective domain that is not "other"—is probably universal. All such collections embody hierarchies of value, exclusions, rule-governed territories of the self. But the notion that this gathering involves the accumulation of possessions, the idea that identity is a kind of wealth (of objects, knowledge, memories, experience), is surely not universal. The individualistic accumulation of Melanesian "big men" is not possessive in Macpherson's sense, for in Melanesia one accumulates not to hold objects as private goods but to give them away, to redistribute. In the West, however, collecting has long been a strategy for the deployment of a possessive self, culture, and authenticity.

Children's collections are revealing in this light: a boy's accumulation of miniature cars, a girl's dolls, a summer-vacation "nature museum" (with labeled stones and shells, a hummingbird in a bottle), a treasured bowl filled with the bright shavings of crayons. In these small rituals we observe the channelings of obsession, an exercise in how to make the world one's own, to gather things around oneself tastefully, appropriately. The inclusions in all collections reflect wider cultural rules—of rational taxonomy, of gender, of aesthetics. An excessive, sometimes even rapacious need to *have* is transformed into rule-governed, meaningful desire. Thus the self that must possess but cannot have it all learns to select, order, classify in hierarchies—to make "good" collections.[1]

---

1. On collecting as a strategy of desire see the highly suggestive catalogue (Hainard and Kaehr 1982) of an exhibition entitled "Collections passion" at the Musée d'Ethnographie, Neuchâtel, June to December 1981. This analytic collection of collections was a tour de force of reflexive museology. On collecting and desire see also Donna Haraway's brilliant analysis (1985) of the American Museum of Natural History, American manhood, and the threat of decadence be-

Whether a child collects model dinosaurs or dolls, sooner or later she or he will be encouraged to keep the possessions on a shelf or in a special box or to set up a doll house. Personal treasures will be made public. If the passion is for Egyptian figurines, the collector will be expected to label them, to know their dynasty (it is not enough that they simply exude power or mystery), to tell "interesting" things about them, to distinguish copies from originals. The good collector (as opposed to the obsessive, the miser) is tasteful and reflective.[2] Accumulation unfolds in a pedagogical, edifying manner. The collection itself—its taxonomic, aesthetic structure—is valued, and any private fixation on single objects is negatively marked as fetishism. Indeed a "proper" relation with objects (rule-governed possession) presupposes a "savage" or deviant relation (idolatry or erotic fixation).[3] In Susan Stewart's gloss, "The boundary between collection and fetishism is mediated by classification and display in tension with accumulation and secrecy" (1984:163).

Stewart's wide-ranging study *On Longing* traces a "structure of desire" whose task is the repetitious and impossible one of closing the gap that separates language from the experience it encodes. She explores certain recurrent strategies pursued by Westerners since the sixteenth century. In her analysis the miniature, whether a portrait or doll's house, enacts a bourgeois longing for "inner" experience. She also explores the

---

tween 1908 and 1936. Her work suggests that the passion to collect, preserve, and display is articulated in gendered ways that are historically specific. Beaucage, Gomilia, and Vallée (1976) offer critical meditations on the ethnographer's complex experience of objects.

2. Walter Benjamin's essay "Unpacking My Library" (1969:59–68) provides the view of a reflective devotee. Collecting appears as an art of living intimately allied with memory, with obsession, with the salvaging of order from disorder. Benjamin sees (and takes a certain pleasure in) the precariousness of the subjective space attained by the collection. "Every passion borders on the chaotic, but the collector's passion borders on the chaos of memories. More than that: the chance, the fate, that suffuse the past before my eyes are conspicuously present in the accustomed confusion of these books. For what else is this collection but a disorder to which habit has accommodated itself to such an extent that it can appear as order? You have all heard of people whom the loss of their books has turned into invalids, of those who in order to acquire them became criminals. These are the very areas in which any order is a balancing act of extreme precariousness." (p. 60)

3. My understanding of the role of the fetish as a mark of otherness in Western intellectual history—from DeBrosses to Marx, Freud, and Deleuze—owes a great deal to the largely unpublished work of William Pietz; see "The Problem of the Fetish, I" (1985).

strategy of gigantism (from Rabelais and Gulliver to earthworks and the billboard), the souvenir, and the collection. She shows how collections, most notably museums—create the illusion of adequate representation of a world by first cutting objects out of specific contexts (whether cultural, historical, or intersubjective) and making them "stand for" abstract wholes—a "Bambara mask," for example, becoming an ethnographic metonym for Bambara culture. Next a scheme of classification is elaborated for storing or displaying the object so that the reality of the collection itself, its coherent order, overrides specific histories of the object's production and appropriation (pp. 162–165). Paralleling Marx's account of the fantastic objectification of commodities, Stewart argues that in the modern Western museum "an illusion of a relation between things takes the place of a social relation" (p. 165). The collector discovers, acquires, salvages objects. The objective world is given, not produced, and thus historical relations of power in the work of acquisition are occulted. The *making* of meaning in museum classification and display is mystified as adequate *representation*. The time and order of the collection erase the concrete social labor of its making.

Stewart's work, along with that of Phillip Fisher (1975), Krzysztof Pomian (1978), James Bunn (1980), Daniel Defert (1982), Johannes Fabian (1983), and Rémy Saisselin (1984), among others, brings collecting and display sharply into view as crucial processes of Western identity formation. Gathered artifacts—whether they find their way into curio cabinets, private living rooms, museums of ethnography, folklore, or fine art—function within a developing capitalist "system of objects" (Baudrillard 1968). By virtue of this system a world of *value* is created and a meaningful deployment and circulation of artifacts maintained. For Baudrillard collected objects create a structured environment that substitutes its own temporality for the "real time" of historical and productive processes: "The environment of private objects and their possession—of which collections are an extreme manifestation—is a dimension of our life that is both essential and imaginary. As essential as dreams" (1968:135).

入

A history of anthropology and modern art needs to see in collecting both a form of Western subjectivity and a changing set of powerful institutional practices. The history of collections (not limited to museums) is central to an understanding of how those social groups that invented anthropology and modern art have *appropriated* exotic things, facts, and meanings. (*Appropriate:* "to make one's own," from the Latin *proprius,* "proper," "property.") It is important to analyze how powerful discriminations made at particular moments constitute the general system of objects within which valued artifacts circulate and make sense. Far-reaching questions are thereby raised.

What criteria validate an authentic cultural or artistic product? What are the differential values placed on old and new creations? What moral and political criteria justify "good," responsible, systematic collecting practices? Why, for example, do Leo Frobenius' wholesale acquisitions of African objects around the turn of the century now seem excessive? (See also Cole 1985 and Pye 1987.) How is a "complete" collection defined? What is the proper balance between scientific analysis and public display? (In Santa Fe a superb collection of Native American art is housed at the School of American Research in a building constructed, literally, as a vault, with access carefully restricted. The Musée de l'Homme exhibits less than a tenth of its collections; the rest is stored in steel cabinets or heaped in corners of the vast basement.) Why has it seemed obvious until recently that non-Western objects should be preserved in European museums, even when this means that no fine specimens are visible in their country of origin? How are "antiquities," "curiosities," "art," "souvenirs," "monuments," and "ethnographic artifacts" distinguished—at different historical moments and in specific market conditions? Why have many anthropological museums in recent years begun to display certain of their objects as "masterpieces"? Why has tourist art only recently come to the serious attention of anthropologists? (See Graburn 1976, Jules-Rosette 1984.) What has been the changing interplay between natural-history collecting and the selection of anthropological artifacts for display and analysis? The list could be extended.

The critical history of collecting is concerned with what from the material world specific groups and individuals choose to preserve, value, and exchange. Although this complex history, from at least the Age of Discovery, remains to be written, Baudrillard provides an initial framework for the deployment of objects in the recent capitalist West. In his account it is axiomatic that all categories of meaningful objects—including those marked off as scientific evidence and as great art—function within a ramified system of symbols and values.

To take just one example: the *New York Times* of December 8, 1984, reported the widespread illegal looting of Anasazi archaeological sites in the American Southwest. Painted pots and urns thus excavated in good condition could bring as much as $30,000 on the market. Another article in the same issue contained a photograph of Bronze Age pots and jugs salvaged by archaeologists from a Phoenician shipwreck off the coast of Turkey. One account featured clandestine collecting for profit, the other scientific collecting for knowledge. The moral evaluations of the two acts of salvage were sharply opposed, but the pots recovered were all meaningful, beautiful, and old. Commercial, aesthetic, and scientific worth in both cases presupposed a given system of value. This system finds intrinsic interest and beauty in objects from a past time, and it assumes that collecting everyday objects from ancient (preferably vanished) civilizations will be more *rewarding* than collecting, for example, decorated thermoses from modern China or customized T-shirts from Oceania. Old objects are endowed with a sense of "depth" by their historically minded collectors. Temporality is reified and salvaged as origin, beauty, and knowledge.

This archaizing system has not always dominated Western collecting. The curiosities of the New World gathered and appreciated in the sixteenth century were not necessarily valued as antiquities, the products of primitive or "past" civilizations. They frequently occupied a category of the marvelous, of a present "Golden Age" (Honour 1975; Mullaney 1983; Rabasa 1985). More recently the retrospective bias of Western appropriations of the world's cultures has come under scrutiny (Fabian 1983; Clifford 1986b). Cultural or artistic "authenticity" has as much to do with an inventive present as with a past, its objectification, preservation, or revival.

λ

Since the turn of the century objects collected from non-Western sources have been classified in two major categories: as (scientific) cultural artifacts or as (aesthetic) works of art.[4] Other collectibles—mass-produced commodities, "tourist art," curios, and so on—have been less systemati-

---

4. For "hard" articulations of ethnographic culturalism and aesthetic formalism see Sieber 1971, Price and Price 1980, Vogel 1985, and Rubin 1984. The first two works argue that art can be understood (as opposed to merely appreciated) only in its original context. Vogel and Rubin assert that aesthetic qualities transcend their original local articulation, that "masterpieces" appeal to universal or at least transcultural human sensibilities. For a glimpse of how the often incompatible categories of "aesthetic excellence," "use," "rarity," "age," and so

cally valued; at best they find a place in exhibits of "technology" or "folk-lore." These and other locations within what may be called the "modern art-culture system" can be visualized with the help of a (somewhat procrustian) diagram.

A. J. Greimas' "semiotic square" (Greimas and Rastier 1968) shows us "that any initial binary opposition can, by the operation of negations and the appropriate syntheses, generate a much larger field of terms which, however, all necessarily remain locked in the closure of the initial system" (Jameson 1981:62). Adapting Greimas for the purposes of cultural criticism, Fredric Jameson uses the semiotic square to reveal "the limits of a specific ideological consciousness, [marking] the conceptual points beyond which that consciousness cannot go, and between which it is condemned to oscillate" (1981:47). Following his example, I offer the following map (see diagram) of a historically specific, contestible field of meanings and institutions.

Beginning with an initial opposition, by a process of negation four terms are generated. This establishes horizontal and vertical axes and between them four semantic zones: (1) the zone of authentic masterpieces, (2) the zone of authentic artifacts, (3) the zone of inauthentic masterpieces, (4) the zone of inauthentic artifacts. Most objects—old and new, rare and common, familiar and exotic—can be located in one of these zones or ambiguously, in traffic, between two zones.

The system classifies objects and assigns them relative value. It establishes the "contexts" in which they properly belong and between which they circulate. Regular movements toward positive value proceed from bottom to top and from right to left. These movements select artifacts of enduring worth or rarity, their value normally guaranteed by a "vanishing" cultural status or by the selection and pricing mechanisms of the art market. The value of Shaker crafts reflects the fact that Shaker society no longer exists: the stock is limited. In the art world work is recognized as "important" by connoisseurs and collectors according to criteria that are more than simply aesthetic (see Becker 1982). Indeed, prevailing definitions of what is "beautiful" or "interesting" sometimes change quite rapidly.

An area of frequent traffic in the system is that linking zones 1 and

on are debated in the exercise of assigning authentic value to tribal works, see the richly inconclusive symposium on "Authenticity in African Art" organized by the journal *African Arts* (Willett et al. 1976).

THE ART–CULTURE SYSTEM
A Machine for Making Authenticity

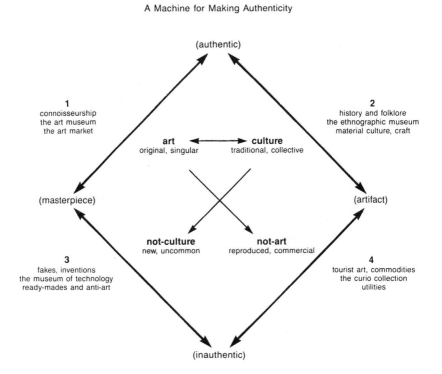

2. Objects move in two directions along this path. Things of cultural or historical value may be promoted to the status of fine art. Examples of movement in this direction, from ethnographic "culture" to fine "art," are plentiful. Tribal objects located in art galleries (the Rockefeller Wing at the Metropolitan Museum in New York) or displayed anywhere according to "formalist" rather than "contextualist" protocols (Ames 1986:39–42) move in this way. Crafts (Shaker work collected at the Whitney Museum in 1986), "folk art," certain antiques, "naive" art all are subject to periodic promotions. Movement in the inverse direction occurs whenever art masterworks are culturally and historically "contextualized," something that has been occurring more and more explicitly. Perhaps the most dramatic case has been the relocation of France's great impressionist collection, formerly at the Jeu de Paume, to the new Museum of the Nineteenth Century at the Gare d'Orsay. Here art masterpieces take their

place in the panorama of a historical-cultural "period." The panorama includes an emerging industrial urbanism and its triumphant technology, "bad" as well as "good" art. A less dramatic movement from zone 1 to zone 2 can be seen in the routine process within art galleries whereby objects become "dated," of interest less as immediately powerful works of genius than as fine examples of a period style.

Movement also occurs between the lower and upper halves of the system, usually in an upward direction. Commodities in zone 4 regularly enter zone 2, becoming rare period pieces and thus collectibles (old green glass Coke bottles). Much current non-Western work migrates between the status of "tourist art" and creative cultural-artistic strategy. Some current productions of Third World peoples have entirely shed the stigma of modern commercial inauthenticity. For example Haitian "primitive" painting—commercial and of relatively recent, impure origin— has moved fully into the art-culture circuit. Significantly this work entered the art market by association with zone 2, becoming valued as the work not simply of individual artists but of *Haitians*. Haitian painting is surrounded by special associations with the land of voodoo, magic and negritude. Though specific artists have come to be known and prized, the aura of "cultural" production attaches to them much more than, say, to Picasso, who is not in any essential way valued as a "Spanish artist." The same is true, as we shall see, of many recent works of tribal art, whether from the Sepik or the American Northwest Coast. Such works have largely freed themselves from the tourist or commodity category to which, because of their modernity, purists had often relegated them; but they cannot move directly into zone 1, the art market, without trailing clouds of authentic (traditional) culture. There can be no direct movement from zone 4 to zone 1.

Occasional travel occurs between zones 4 and 3, for example when a commodity or technological artifact is perceived to be a case of special inventive creation. The object is selected out of commercial or mass culture, perhaps to be featured in a museum of technology. Sometimes such objects fully enter the realm of art: "technological" innovations or commodities may be contextualized as modern "design," thus passing through zone 3 into zone 1 (for example the furniture, household machines, cars, and so on displayed at the Museum of Modern Art in New York).

There is also regular traffic between zones 1 and 3. Exposed art forgeries are demoted (while nonetheless preserving something of their original aura). Conversely various forms of "anti-art" and art parading its unoriginality or "inauthenticity" are collected and valued (Warhol's soup can, Sherrie Levine's photo of a photo by Walker Evans, Duchamp's urinal, bottle rack, or shovel). Objects in zone 3 are all potentially collectible within the general domain of art: they are uncommon, sharply distinct from or blatantly cut out of culture. Once appropriated by the art world, like Duchamp's ready-mades, they circulate within zone 1.

The art-culture system I have diagramed excludes and marginalizes various residual and emergent contexts. To mention only one: the categories of art and culture, technology and commodity are strongly secular. "Religious" objects can be valued as great art (an altarpiece by Giotto), as folk art (the decorations on a Latin American popular saint's shrine), or as cultural artifact (an Indian rattle). Such objects have no individual "power" or mystery—qualities once possessed by "fetishes" before they were reclassified in the modern system as primitive art or cultural artifact. What "value," however, is stripped from an altarpiece when it is moved out of a functioning church (or when its church begins to function as a museum)? Its specific power or sacredness is relocated to a general aesthetic realm. (See Chapter 9, n.11, on a recent challenge by Zuni tribal authorities to such secular contextualizations.)

⼊

It is important to stress the historicity of this art-culture system. It has not reached its final form: the positions and values assigned to collectible artifacts have changed and will continue to do so. Moreover a synchronic diagram cannot represent zones of contest and transgression except as movements or ambiguities among fixed poles. As we shall see at the end of this chapter, much current "tribal art" participates in the regular art-culture traffic *and* in traditional spiritual contexts not accounted for by the system (Coe 1986). Whatever its contested domains, though, generally speaking the system still confronts any collected exotic object with a stark alternative between a second home in an ethnographic or an aesthetic milieu. The modern ethnographic museum and the art museum or private art collection have developed separate, complementary modes of classification. In the former a work of "sculpture" is displayed along with other objects of similar function or in proximity to objects from the same cultural group, including utilitarian artifacts such as spoons, bowls, or spears. A mask or statue may be grouped with formally dissimilar objects and explained as part of a ritual or institutional complex. The names of individual sculptors are unknown or suppressed. In art museums a sculpture is identified as the creation of an individual: Rodin, Giacometti, Barbara Hepworth. Its place in everyday cultural practices (including the market) is irrelevant to its essential meaning. Whereas in the ethnographic museum the object is culturally or humanly "interesting," in the art museum it is primarily "beautiful" or "original." It was not always thus.

Elizabeth Williams (1985) has traced a revealing chapter in the shifting history of these discriminations. In nineteenth-century Paris it was difficult to conceive of pre-Columbian artifacts as fully "beautiful." A prevailing naturalist aesthetic saw *ars Americana* as grotesque or crude. At best pre-Columbian work could be assimilated into the category of the antiquity and appreciated through the filter of Viollet-le-Duc's medievalism. Williams shows how Mayan and Incan artifacts, their status uncertain, migrated between the Louvre, the Bibliothèque Nationale, the Musée Guimet, and (after 1878) the Trocadéro, where they seemed at last to find an ethnographic home in an institution that treated them as scientific evidence. The Trocadéro's first directors, Ernest-Théodore Hamy and Rémy Verneau, showed scant interest in their aesthetic qualities.

The "beauty" of much non-Western "art" is a recent discovery. Before the twentieth century many of the same objects were collected and valued, but for different reasons. In the early modern period their rarity and strangeness were prized. The "cabinet of curiosities" jumbled everything together, with each individual object standing metonymically for a whole region or population. The collection was a microcosm, a "summary of the universe" (Pomian 1978). The eighteenth century introduced a more serious concern for taxonomy and for the elaboration of complete series. Collecting was increasingly the concern of scientific naturalists (Feest 1984:90), and objects were valued because they exemplified an array of systematic categories: food, clothing, building materials, agricultural tools, weapons (of war, of the hunt), and so forth. E. F. Jomard's ethnographic classifications and A. H. L. F. Pitt Rivers' typological displays were mid-nineteenth-century culminations of this taxonomic vision (Chapman 1985:24-25). Pitt Rivers' typologies featured developmental sequences. By the end of the century evolutionism had come to dominate arrangements of exotic artifacts. Whether objects were presented as antiquities, arranged geographically or by society, spread in panoplies, or arranged in realistic "life groups" and dioramas, a story of human development was told. The object had ceased to be primarily an exotic "curiosity" and was now a source of information entirely integrated in the universe of Western Man (Dias 1985:378–379). The value of exotic objects was their ability to testify to the concrete reality of an earlier stage of human Culture, a common past confirming Europe's triumphant present.

With Franz Boas and the emergence of relativist anthropology an emphasis on placing objects in specific lived contexts was consolidated. The "cultures" thus represented could either be arranged in a modified evolutionary series or dispersed in synchronous "ethnographic presents." The latter were times neither of antiquity nor of the twentieth century but rather representing the "authentic" context of the collected objects, often just prior to their collection or display. Both collector and salvage ethnographer could claim to be the last to rescue "the real thing." Authenticity, as we shall see, is produced by removing objects and customs from their current historical situation—a present-becoming-future.

With the consolidation of twentieth-century anthropology, artifacts contextualized ethnographically were valued because they served as objective "witnesses" to the total multidimensional life of a culture (Jamin 1982a:89–95; 1985). Simultaneously with new developments in art and literature, as Picasso and others began to visit the "Troca" and to accord its tribal objects a nonethnographic admiration, the proper place of non-Western objects was again thrown in question. In the eyes of a triumphant modernism some of these artifacts at least could be seen as universal masterpieces. The category of "primitive art" emerged.

This development introduced new ambiguities and possibilities in a changing taxonomic system. In the mid-nineteenth century pre-Columbian or tribal objects were grotesques or antiquities. By 1920 they were cultural witnesses and aesthetic masterpieces. Since then a controlled migration has occurred between these two institutionalized domains. The boundaries of art and science, the aesthetic and the anthropological, are not permanently fixed. Indeed anthropology and fine arts museums have recently shown signs of interpenetration. For example the Hall of Asian Peoples at the New York Museum of Natural History reflects the "boutique" style of display, whose objects could never seem out of place as "art" on the walls or coffee tables of middle-class living rooms. In a complementary development downtown the Museum of Modern Art has expanded its permanent exhibit of cultural artifacts: furniture, automobiles, home appliances, and utensils—even hanging from the ceiling, like a Northwest Coast war canoe, a much-admired bright green helicopter.

入

While the object systems of art and anthropology are institutionalized and powerful, they are not immutable. The categories of the beautiful, the cultural, and the authentic have changed and are changing. Thus it is important to resist the tendency of collections to be self-sufficient, to suppress their own historical, economic, and political processes of production (see Haacke 1975; Hiller 1979). Ideally the history of its own collection and display should be a visible aspect of any exhibition. It had been rumored that the Boas Room of Northwest Coast artifacts in the American Museum of Natural History was to be refurbished, its style of display modernized. Apparently (or so one hopes) the plan has been abandoned, for this atmospheric, dated hall exhibits not merely a superb collection but a moment in the history of collecting. The widely publicized Museum of Modern Art show of 1984, "'Primitivism' in Twentieth-Century Art" (see Chapter 9), made apparent (as it celebrated) the precise circumstance in which certain ethnographic objects suddenly became works of universal art. More historical self-consciousness in the display and viewing of non-Western objects can at least jostle and set in motion the ways in which anthropologists, artists, and their publics collect themselves and the world.

At a more intimate level, rather than grasping objects only as cultural signs and artistic icons (Guidieri and Pellizzi 1981), we can return to them, as James Fenton does, their lost status as fetishes—not specimens of a deviant or exotic "fetishism" but *our own* fetishes.[5] This tactic, necessarily personal, would accord to things in collections the power to fixate rather than simply the capacity to edify or inform. African and Oceanian artifacts could once again be *objets sauvages,* sources of fascination with the power to disconcert. Seen in their resistance to classification they could remind us of our *lack* of self-possession, of the artifices we employ to gather a world around us.

---

5. For a post-Freudian positive sense of the fetish see Leiris 1929a, 1946; for fetish theory's radical possibilities see Pietz 1985, which draws on Deleuze; and for a repentant semiologist's perverse sense of the fetish (the "punctum") as a place of strictly personal meaning unformed by cultural codes (the "studium") see Barthes 1980. Gomila (1976) rethinks ethnographic material culture from some of these surrealist-psychoanalytic perspectives.

Culture Collecting

Found in *American Anthropologist*, n.s. 34 (1932):740:

NOTE FROM NEW GUINEA
Aliatoa, Wiwiak District, New Guinea

April 21, 1932

We are just completing a culture of a mountain group here in the lower Torres Chelles. They have no name and we haven't decided what to call them yet. They are a very revealing people in spots, providing a final basic concept from which all the mother's brothers' curses and father's sisters' curses, etc. derive, and having articulate the attitude toward incest which Reo [Fortune] outlined as fundamental in his Encyclopedia article. They have taken the therapeutic measures which we recommended for Dobu and Manus—having a devil in addition to the neighbor sorcerer, and having got their dead out of the village and localized. But in other ways they are annoying: they have bits and snatches of all the rag tag and bob tail of magical and ghostly belief from the Pacific, and they are somewhat like the Plains in their receptivity to strange ideas. A picture of a local native reading the index to the *Golden Bough* just to see if they had missed anything, would be appropriate. They are very difficult to work, living all over the place with half a dozen garden houses, and never staying put for a week at a time. Of course this offered a new challenge in method which was interesting. The difficulties incident upon being two days over impossible mountains have been consuming and we are going to do a coastal people next.

Sincerely yours,

MARGARET MEAD

"Cultures" are ethnographic collections. Since Tylor's founding definition of 1871 the term has designated a rather vague "complex whole" including everything that is learned group behavior, from body techniques to symbolic orders. There have been recurring attempts to define culture more precisely (see Kroeber and Kluckhohn 1952) or, for example, to distinguish it from "social structure." But the inclusive use persists. For there are times when we still need to be able to speak holistically of Japanese or Trobriand or Moroccan culture in the confidence that we are designating something real and differentially coherent. It is increasingly clear, however, that the concrete activity of representing a culture, subculture, or indeed any coherent domain of collective activity is always strategic and selective. The world's societies are too systematically interconnected to permit any easy isolation of separate or independently functioning systems (Marcus 1986). The increased pace of historical change, the common recurrence of stress in the systems under study, forces a new self-consciousness about the way cultural wholes and boundaries are constructed and translated. The pioneering *élan* of Margaret Mead "completing a culture" in highland New Guinea, collecting a dispersed population, discovering its key customs, naming the result— in this case "the Mountain Arapesh"—is no longer possible.

To see ethnography as a form of culture collecting (not, of course, the *only* way to see it) highlights the ways that diverse experiences and facts are selected, gathered, detached from their original temporal occasions, and given enduring value in a new arrangement. Collecting— at least in the West, where time is generally thought to be linear and irreversible—implies a rescue of phenomena from inevitable historical decay or loss. The collection contains what "deserves" to be kept, remembered, and treasured. Artifacts and customs are saved out of time.[6] Anthropological culture collectors have typically gathered what seems "traditional"—what by definition is opposed to modernity. From a complex historical reality (which includes current ethnographic encounters) they select what gives form, structure, and continuity to a world. What is hybrid or "historical" in an emergent sense has been less commonly collected and presented as a system of authenticity. For example in New Guinea Margaret Mead and Reo Fortune chose not to study groups that were, as Mead wrote in a letter, "badly missionized" (1977:123); and it had been self-evident to Malinowski in the Trobriands that what most

---

6. An exhibition, "Temps perdu, temps retrouvé," held during 1985 at the Musée d'Ethnographie of Neuchâtel systematically interrogated the temporal predicament of the Western ethnographic museum. Its argument was condensed in the following text, each proposition of which was illustrated museographically: "Prestigious places for locking things up, museums give value to things that are outside of life: in this way they resemble cemeteries. Acquired by dint of dollars, the memory-objects participate in the group's changing identity, serve the powers that be, and accumulate into treasures, while personal memory fades. Faced with the aggressions of everyday life and the passing of phenomena, memory needs objects—always manipulated through aesthetics, selective emphasis, or the mixing of genres. From the perspective of the future, what from the present should be saved?" (Hainard and Kaehr 1986:33; also Hainard and Kaehr 1985.)

deserved scientific attention was the circumscribed "culture" threatened by a host of modern "outside" influences. The experience of Melanesians becoming Christians for their own reasons—learning to play, and play with, the outsiders' games—did not seem worth salvaging.

Every appropriation of culture, whether by insiders or outsiders, implies a specific temporal position and form of historical narration. Gathering, owning, classifying, and valuing are certainly not restricted to the West; but elsewhere these activities need not be associated with accumulation (rather than redistribution) or with preservation (rather than natural or historical decay). The Western practice of culture collecting has its own local genealogy, enmeshed in distinct European notions of temporality and order. It is worth dwelling for a moment on this genealogy, for it organizes the assumptions being arduously unlearned by new theories of practice, process, and historicity (Bourdieu 1977, Giddens 1979, Ortner 1984, Sahlins 1985).

A crucial aspect of the recent history of the culture concept has been its alliance (and division of labor) with "art." Culture, even without a capital c, strains toward aesthetic form and autonomy. I have already suggested that modern culture ideas and art ideas function together in an "art-culture system." The inclusive twentieth-century culture category— one that does not privilege "high" or "low" culture—is plausible only within this system, for while in principle admitting all learned human behavior, this culture with a small c orders phenomena in ways that privilege the coherent, balanced, and "authentic" aspects of shared life. Since the mid-nineteenth century, ideas of culture have gathered up those elements that seem to give continuity and depth to collective existence, seeing it whole rather than disputed, torn, intertextual, or syncretic. Mead's almost postmodern image of "a local native reading the index to *The Golden Bough* just to see if they had missed anything" is not a vision of authenticity.

Mead found Arapesh receptivity to outside influences "annoying." *Their* culture collecting complicated hers. Historical developments would later force her to provide a revised picture of these difficult Melanesians. In a new preface to the 1971 reprint of her three-volume ethnography *The Mountain Arapesh* Mead devotes several pages to letters from Bernard Narokobi, an Arapesh then studying law in Sydney, Australia. The anthropologist readily admits her astonishment at hearing from him: "How was it that one of the Arapesh—a people who had had such a light hold on any form of collective style—should have come further than any individual among the Manus, who had moved as a group into the modern world in the years between our first study of them, in 1928, and the beginning of our restudy, in 1953?" (Mead 1971:ix). She goes on to explain that Narakobi, along with other Arapesh men studying in Australia, had "moved from one period in human culture to another" as "individuals." The Arapesh were "less tightly bound within a coherent culture" than Manus (pp. ix–x). Narakobi writes, however, as a member of his "tribe," speaking with pride of the values and accomplishments of his "clansfolk." (He uses the name Arapesh sparingly.) He articulates the possibility of a new multiterritorial "cultural" identity: "I feel now that I can feel proud of my tribe and at the same time feel I belong not only to Papua–New Guinea, a nation to be, but to the world community at large" (p. xiii). Is not this modern way of being "Arapesh" already prefigured in Mead's earlier image of a resourceful native paging through *The Golden Bough?* Why must such behavior be marginalized or classed as "individual" by the anthropological culture collector?

Expectations of wholeness, continuity, and essence have long been built into the linked Western ideas of culture and art. A few words of recent background must suffice, since to map the history of these concepts would lead us on a chase for origins back at least to the Greeks. Raymond Williams provides a starting point in the early nineteenth century—a moment of unprecedented historical and social disruption. In *Culture and Society* (1966), *Keywords* (1976), and elsewhere Williams has traced a parallel development in usage for the words *art* and *culture.* The changes reflect complex responses to industrialism, to the specter of "mass society," to accelerated social conflict and change.[7]

According to Williams in the eighteenth century the word *art* meant predominantly "skill." Cabinetmakers, criminals, and painters were each in their way artful. *Culture* designated a tendency to natural growth, its uses predominantly agricultural and personal: both plants and human individuals could be "cultured." Other meanings also present in the eighteenth century did not predominate until the nineteenth. By the 1820s *art* increasingly designated a special domain of creativity, spontaneity, and purity, a realm of refined sensibility and expressive "genius." The

---

7. Although Williams' analysis is limited to England, the general pattern applies elsewhere in Europe, where the timing of modernization differed or where other terms were used. In France, for example, the words *civilisation* or, for Durkheim, *société* stand in for *culture.* What is at issue are general qualitative assessments of collective life.

"artist" was set apart from, often against, society—whether "mass" or "bourgeois." The term *culture* followed a parallel course, coming to mean what was most elevated, sensitive, essential, and precious—most uncommon—in society. Like art, culture became a general category; Williams calls it a "final court of appeal" against threats of vulgarity and leveling. It existed in essential opposition to perceived "anarchy."

Art and culture emerged after 1800 as mutually reinforcing domains of human *value*, strategies for gathering, marking off, protecting the best and most interesting creations of "Man."[8] In the twentieth century the categories underwent a series of further developments. The plural, anthropological definition of culture (lower-case c with the possibility of a final s) emerged as a liberal alternative to racist classifications of human diversity. It was a sensitive means for understanding different and dispersed "whole ways of life" in a high colonial context of unprecedented global interconnection. *Culture* in its full evolutionary richness and authenticity, formerly reserved for the best creations of modern Europe, could now be extended to all the world's populations. In the anthropological vision of Boas' generation "cultures" were of equal value. In their new plurality, however, the nineteenth-century definitions were not entirely transformed. If they became less elitist (distinctions between "high" and "low" culture were erased) and less Eurocentric (every human society was fully "cultural"), nevertheless a certain body of assumptions were carried over from the older definitions. George Stocking (1968:69–90) shows the complex interrelations of nineteenth-century humanist and emerging anthropological definitions of culture. He suggests that anthro-

---

8. As Virginia Dominguez has argued, the emergence of this new subject implies a specific historicity closely tied to ethnology. Drawing on Foucault's *Order of Things* (1966) and writing of the scramble for ethnographic artifacts during the "Museum Age" of the late nineteenth century, she cites Douglas Cole's summation of the prevailing rationale: "It is necessary to use the time to collect before it is too late" (Cole 1985:50). "Too late for what?" Dominguez asks. "There is a historical consciousness here of a special sort. We hear an urgency in the voices of the collectors, a fear that we will no longer be able to get our hands on these objects, and that this would amount to an irretrievable loss of the means of preserving our own historicity. There is a twofold displacement here. Objects are collected no longer because of their intrinsic value but as metonyms for the people who produced them. And the people who produced them are the objects of examination not because of their intrinsic value but because of their perceived contribution to our understanding of our own historical trajectory. It is a certain view of 'man' and a certain view of 'history' that make this double displacement possible" (Dominguez 1986:548).

pology owes as much to Matthew Arnold as to its official founding father, E. B. Tylor. Indeed much of the vision embodied in *Culture and Anarchy* has been transferred directly into relativist anthropology. A powerful structure of feeling continues to see culture, wherever it is found, as a coherent *body* that lives and dies. Culture is enduring, traditional, structural (rather than contingent, syncretic, historical). Culture is a process of ordering, not of disruption. It changes and develops like a living organism. It does not normally "survive" abrupt alterations.

In the early twentieth century, as *culture* was being extended to all the world's functioning societies, an increasing number of exotic, primitive, or archaic objects came to be seen as "art." They were equal in aesthetic and moral value with the greatest Western masterpieces. By midcentury the new attitude toward "primitive art" had been accepted by large numbers of educated Europeans and Americans. Indeed from the standpoint of the late twentieth century it becomes clear that the parallel concepts of art and culture did successfully, albeit temporarily, comprehend and incorporate a plethora of non-Western artifacts and customs. This was accomplished through two strategies. First, objects reclassified as "primitive art" were admitted to the imaginary museum of human creativity and, though more slowly, to the actual fine arts museums of the West. Second, the discourse and institutions of modern anthropology constructed comparative and synthetic images of Man drawing evenhandedly from among the world's authentic ways of life, however strange in appearance or obscure in origin. Art and culture, categories for the best creations of Western humanism, were in principle extended to all the world's peoples.

It is perhaps worth stressing that nothing said here about the historicity of these cultural or artistic categories should be construed as claiming that they are false or denying that many of their values are worthy of support. Like any successful discursive arrangement the art-culture authenticity system articulates considerable domains of truth and scientific progress as well as areas of blindness and controversy. By emphasizing the transience of the system I do so out of a conviction (it is more a feeling of the historical ground moving underfoot) that the classifications and generous appropriations of Western art and culture categories are now much less stable than before. This instability appears to be linked to the growing interconnection of the world's populations and to the contestation since the 1950s of colonialism and Eurocentrism. Art collecting and culture collecting now take place within a changing field of counterdiscourses, syncretisms, and reappropriations originating both outside and inside "the West." I cannot discuss the geopolitical causes of these developments. I can only hint at their transforming consequences and stress that the modern genealogy of culture and art that I have been sketching increasingly appears to be a local story. "Culture" and "art" can no longer be simply *extended* to non-Western peoples and things. They can at worst be *imposed,* at best *translated*—both historically and politically contingent operations.

Before I survey some of the current challenges to Western modes of collection and authentication, it may be worth portraying the still-dominant form of art and culture collecting in a more limited, concrete setting. The system's underlying historical asumptions will then become inescapable. For if collecting in the West salvages things out of non-repeatable time, what is the assumed direction of this time? How does it confer rarity and authenticity on the varied productions of human skill? Collecting presupposes a story; a story occurs in a "chronotope."

A Chronotope for Collecting

> *Dans son effort pour comprendre le monde, l'homme dispose*
> *donc toujours d'un surplus de signification.*
> —CLAUDE LÉVI-STRAUSS

T HE TERM *chronotope,* as used by Bakhtin, denotes a configuration of spatial and temporal indicators in a fictional setting where (and when) certain activities and stories *take place.*[9] One cannot realistically situate historical detail—putting something "in its time"—without appealing to explicit or implicit chronotopes. Claude Lévi-Strauss's pointed, nostalgic recollections of New York during the Second World War can serve as a chronotope for modern art and culture collecting. The setting is elaborated in an essay whose French title, "New York post-et préfiguratif"

---

9. *Chronotope:* literally "time-space" with no priority to either dimension (Bakhtin 1937). The chronotope is a fictional setting where historically specific relations of power become visible and certain stories can "take place" (the bourgeois salon in nineteenth-century social novels, the merchant ship in Conrad's tales of adventure and empire). As Bakhtin puts it: "In the literary artistic chronotope, spatial and temporal indicators are fused into one carefully thought-out, concrete whole. Time, as it were, thickens, takes on flesh, becomes artistically visible; likewise space becomes charged and responsive to the movements of time, plot and history" (p. 84).

(1983), suggests its underlying spatio-temporal predicament more strongly than the published English translation, "New York in 1941" (1985). The essay falls within a microgenre of Lévi-Strauss's writing, one he developed with virtuosity in *Tristes tropiques*. Specific places—Rio, Fire Island, new Brazilian cities, Indian sacred sites—appear as moments of intelligible human order and transformation surrounded by the destructive, entropic currents of global history.

In what follows I have supplemented the essay on New York with passages from other texts written by Lévi-Strauss either during the war years or in recollection of them. In reading them as a unified chronotope, one ought to bear in mind that these are not historical records but complex literary commemorations. The time-space in question has been retrospectively composed by Lévi-Strauss and recomposed, for other purposes, by myself.

人

A refugee in New York during the Second World War, the anthropologist is bewildered and delighted by a landscape of unexpected juxtapositions. His recollections of those seminal years, during which he invented structural anthropology, are bathed in a magical light. New York is full of delightful incongruities. Who could resist

> the performances that we watched for hours at the Chinese opera under the first arch of the Brooklyn Bridge, where a company that had come long ago from China had a large following. Every day, from mid-afternoon until past midnight, it would perpetuate the traditions of classical Chinese opera. I felt myself going back in time no less when I went to work every morning in the American room of the New York Public Library. There, under its neo-classical arcades and between walls paneled with old oak, I sat near an Indian in a feather headdress and a beaded buckskin jacket—who was taking notes with a Parker pen. (1985:266)

As Lévi-Strauss tells it, the New York of 1941 is an anthropologist's dream, a vast selection of human culture and history.[10] A brief walk or subway ride will take him from a Greenwich Village reminiscent of Bal-

---

10. It still is. Returning to the neighborhood where I grew up on the Upper West Side and walking between 116th and 86th Streets, I invariably encounter several races, cultures, languages, a range of exotic smells, "Cuban-Chinese"

zac's Paris to the towering skyscrapers of Wall Street. Turning a corner in this jumble of immigrants and ethnic groups, the stroller suddenly enters a different world with its own language, customs, cuisine. Everything is available for consumption. In New York one can obtain almost any treasure. The anthropologist and his artistic friends André Breton, Max Ernst, André Masson, Georges Duthuit, Yves Tanguy, and Matta find masterpieces of pre-Columbian, Indian, Oceanic, or Japanese art stuffed in dealers' closets or apartments. Everything somehow finds it way here. For Lévi-Strauss New York in the 1940s is a wonderland of sudden openings to other times and places, of cultural matter out of place:

> New York (and this is the source of its charm and its peculiar fascination) was then a city where anything seemed possible. Like the urban fabric, the social and cultural fabric was riddled with holes. All you had to do was pick one and slip through it if, like Alice, you wanted to get to the other side of the looking glass and find worlds so enchanting that they seemed unreal.   (p. 261)

The anthropological *flâneur* is delighted, amazed, but also troubled by the chaos of simultaneous possibilities. This New York has something in common with the early-century dada-surrealist flea market—but with a difference. Its *objets trouvés* are not just occasions for reverie. This they surely are, but they are also signs of vanishing worlds. Some are treasures, works of great art.

Lévi-Strauss and the refugee surrealists were passionate collectors. The Third Avenue art dealer they frequented and advised, Julius Carlebach, always had several Northwest Coast, Melanesian, or Eskimo pieces on hand. According to Edmund Carpenter, the surrealists felt an immediate affinity with these objects' predilection for "visual puns"; their selections were nearly always of a very high quality. In addition to the art dealers another source for this band of primitive-art connoisseurs was the Museum of the American Indian. As Carpenter tells it: "The Surrealists began to visit the Bronx warehouse of that Museum, selecting for themselves, concentrating on a collection of magnificent Eskimo masks. These huge visual puns, made by the Kuskokwim Eskimo a century or more ago, constituted the greatest collection of its kind in the world. But

restaurants, and so on. It is enough to seriously smudge at least the spatial distinction between First and Third Worlds, center and periphery in the modern world system.

the Museum Director, George Heye, called them 'jokes' and sold half for $38 and $54 each. The Surrealists bought the best. Then they moved happily through Heye's Northwest Coast collection, stripping it of one masterwork after another" (Carpenter 1975:10). In 1946 Max Ernst, Barnett Newman, and several others mounted an exhibit of Northwest Coast Indian painting at the Betty Parsons Gallery. They brought together pieces from their private collections and artifacts from the American Museum of Natural History. By moving the museum pieces across town, "the Surrealists declassified them as scientific specimens and reclassified them as art" (Carpenter 1975:11).

The category of primitive art was emerging, with its market, its connoisseurship, and its close ties to modernist aesthetics. What had begun with the vogue for *l'art nègre* in the twenties would become institutionalized by the fifties and sixties; but in wartime New York the battle to gain widespread recognition for tribal objects was not yet won. Lévi-Strauss recalls that as cultural attaché to the French Embassy in 1946 he tried in vain to arrange a trade: for a massive collection of American Indian art a few Matisses and Picassos. But "the French authorities turned a deaf ear to my entreaties, and the Indian collections wound up in American museums" (1985:262). The collecting of Lévi-Strauss and the surrealists during the forties was part of a struggle to gain aesthetic status for these increasingly rare masterworks.

人

New York seemed to have something unusual, valuable, and beautiful for everyone. Franz Boas liked to tell his European visitors about a Kwakiutl informant who had come to work with him in the city. As Roman Jakobson recalls:

> Boas loved to depict the indifference of this man from Vancouver Island toward Manhattan skyscrapers ("we built houses next to one another, and you stack them on top of each other"), toward the Aquarium ("we throw such fish back in the lake") or toward the motion pictures which seemed tedious and senseless. On the other hand, the stranger stood for hours spellbound in the Times Square freak shows with their giants and dwarfs, bearded ladies and fox-tailed girls, or in the Automats where drinks and sandwiches appear miraculously and where he felt transferred into the universe of Kwakiutl fairy-tales. (Jakobson 1959:142)

In Lévi-Strauss's memory brass balls on staircase bannisters also figure in the collection of fascinating phenomena (1960:27).

⚹

For a European New York's sheer space is vertiginous:

> I strode up and down miles of Manhattan avenues, those deep chasms over which loomed skyscrapers' fantastic cliffs. I wandered randomly into cross streets, whose physiognomy changed drastically from one block to the next: sometimes poverty-stricken, sometimes middle-class or provincial, and most often chaotic. New York was decidedly not the ultra-modern metropolis I had expected, but an immense, horizontal and vertical disorder attributable to some spontaneous upheaval of the urban crust rather than to the deliberate plans of builders. (Lévi-Strauss 1985:258)

Lévi-Strauss's New York is a juxtaposition of ancient and recent "strata," chaotic remnants of former "upheavals." As in *Tristes tropiques* metaphors from geology serve to transform empirical surface incongruities or faults into legible history. For Lévi-Strauss the jumble of Manhattan becomes intelligible as an overlay of past and future, legible as a story of cultural development. Old and new are side by side. The European refugee encounters scraps of his past as well as a troubling prefiguration of common destiny.

New York is a site of travel and reverie unlike the oneiric city of Breton's *Nadja* or Aragon's *Paysan de Paris*. For Parisian emigrés finding their feet on its streets and avenues it is never a known place, something to be made strange by a certain surrealist and ethnographic attention. Instead they are ambushed by the familiar—an older Paris in Greenwich Village, glimpses of the European world in immigrant neighborhoods, medieval buildings reassembled at the Cloisters. But these reminders are masks, survivals, mere collectibles. In New York one is permanently away from home, *dépaysé*, both in space and in time. Post- and prefigurative New York is fantastically suspended between a jumble of pasts and a uniform future.

> Whoever wanted to go hunting needed only a little culture, and flair, for doorways to open in the wall of industrial civilization and reveal other worlds and other times. Doubtless nowhere more than in New York at that time were there such facilities for escape. Those possibili-

ties seem almost mythical today when we no longer dare to dream of doors: at best we may wonder about niches to cower in. But even these have become the stake in a fierce competition among those who are not willing to live in a world without friendly shadows or secret shortcuts known only to a few initiates. Losing its old dimensions one after another, this world has pushed us back into the one remaining dimension: one will probe it in vain for secret loopholes. (1985:262)

The resigned "entropologist" of *Tristes tropiques* remembers New York as the final glow and prophetic disintegration of all real cultural differences. Soon even the loopholes will be gone. Millennia of human diversity and invention seem to have been shipwrecked here, remnants and broken shards, good to evoke in escapist reveries, good to collect as art (or antiques), and "good to think with" in salvaging the cultural structures of a transhistorical *esprit humain*. The chronotope of New York prefigures anthropology.

Structuralist anthropology at least was conceived and written there. It is hard to imagine a better setting. Among New York's jumble of cultures, arts, and traditions, as a professor at the Ecole Libre des Hautes Etudes, Lévi-Strauss attended Roman Jakobson's celebrated lectures on sound and meaning. On many occasions he has testified to their revolutionary impact. Jakobson's demonstration that the bewildering diversity of meaningful human sounds could be reduced to discrete differential systems through the application of phonemic analysis offered an immediate model for studying the plethora of human kinship systems. More generally Jakobson's approach suggested a research program—that of discovering elementary cognitive structures behind the many "language-like" productions of human culture. Amid the cultural-historical jumble of wartime New York—too much in the same place at the same time—Lévi-Strauss glimpsed an underlying order.

The Elementary Structures of Kinship was researched in the New York Public Library reading room, where, beside what seemed to be a parody of a feathered Indian with a Parker pen, Lévi-Strauss pored over accounts of tribal marriage rules. The founding text of structural anthropology was drafted in a small, dilapidated studio in Greenwich Village, down the street from Yves Tanguy and a few yards (through the walls) from Claude Shannon, who, unknown to his neighbor, "was creating cybernetics" (1985:260).

Uptown at the American Museum of Natural History Lévi-Strauss could
wander and wonder among the intimate, hyperreal dioramas of African
animal species. Or he could marvel in the Hall of Northwest Coast Indians, where Kwakiutl and Tlingit masks in their glass cases whispered to
him of Baudelairean *correspondances* (Lévi-Strauss 1943:180). Indeed
by the 1940s a deep correspondence between primitive and modern art
was widely assumed in avant-garde milieux. The anthropologist friend of
the surrealists saw these magical, archaic objects as luminous examples
of human creative genius. He wrote in 1943 for the *Gazette des beaux
arts:*

> These objects—beings transformed into things, human animals, living
> boxes—seem as remote as possible from our own conception of art
> since the time of the Greeks. Yet even here one would err to suppose
> that a single possibility of the aesthetic life had escaped the prophets
> and virtuosos of the Northwest Coast. Several of those masks and stat-
> ues are thoughtful portraits which prove a concern to attain not only
> physical resemblance but the most subtle spiritual essence of the soul.
> The sculptor of Alaska and British Columbia is not only the sorcerer
> who confers upon the supernatural a visible form but also the creator,
> the interpreter who translates into eternal *chefs d'oeuvre* the fugitive
> emotions of man.   (1943:181)

Human artistic creation transcends location and time. To communicate the incredible inventiveness he sees in the Northwest Coast Hall,
Lévi-Strauss finds a revealing comparison: "This incessant renovation,
this sureness which in no matter what direction guarantees definite and
overwhelming success, this scorn of the beaten path, this ceaseless driving toward new feats which infallibly ends in dazzling results—to know
this our civilization had to await the exceptional destiny of a Picasso. It
is not futile to emphasize that the daring ventures of a single man which
have left us breathless for thirty years, were known and practiced during one hundred and fifty years by an entirely indigenous culture"
(1943:175). The passage is undoubtedly adapted to its occasion: the
need to promote tribal works for an art-world public. (Elsewhere Lévi-
Strauss would stress the systems limiting and making possible inventions
by any local group or individual creator.) Here he insists only that tribal
works are as inventive as that modern paragon of creativity, Picasso. Implicit in the conceit was a vision of human cultures as comparable to

creative artists. As I have already argued, the twentieth-century categories of art and culture presupposed each other.

The categories were, however, institutionally separated. If the surrealists could reclassify tribal objects by moving them across town from an anthropology museum to an art gallery, the end points of the traffic were not thereby undermined. The discourses of anthropology and art were developing on separate but complementary paths. Their evolving relationship may be seen in a legendary surrealist journal of 1942–43 edited by David Hare and dominated by its "editorial advisers" André Breton, Max Ernst, and Marcel Duchamp. *VVV,* according to its subtitle, aspired to cover the fields of "poetry, plastic arts, anthropology, sociology, psychology." In fact it did justice to the first two, with a sprinkling of the third. (Only four issues of *VVV* appeared in two years.) Number 1 contained two short articles by Lévi-Strauss, one on Kaduveo Indian face painting, the other an obituary for Malinowski. The following number contained a note by Alfred Métraux on two ancestral figurines from Easter Island. And in the final issue Robert Allerton Parker fancifully interpreted complex line drawings from the New Hebrides (extracted from A. B. Deacon's ethnography) under the title "Cannibal Designs." In general material from non-Western cultures was included as exoticism or naive art. There were occasional photos of an Alaskan mask or a kachina.

In *VVV* anthropology was part of the décor of avant-garde art and writing. Serious cultural analysis made no real inroads into what were by now canonical surrealist notions of genius, inspiration, the irrational, the magical, the exotic, the primitive. Few of those around Breton (with the possible exception of Max Ernst) had any systematic interest in ethnological science. Lévi-Strauss's contributions to *VVV* seem out of place. Essentially a journal of art and literature, *VVV* was preoccupied with dreams, archetypes, genius, and apocalyptic revolution. It engaged in little of the unsettling, reflexive ethnography practiced by the dissidents of the earlier journal *Documents* (see Chapter 4). "Mainstream" surrealism did not typically bring cultural analysis to bear on its own categories.

Surrealist art and structural anthropology were both concerned with the human spirit's "deep" shared springs of creativity. The common aim was to transcend—not, as in *Documents,* to describe critically or subvert—the local orders of culture and history. Surrealism's subject was an international and elemental humanity "anthropological" in scope. Its object was Man, something it shared with an emerging structuralism. But a conventional division of labor was solidifying. Within the project of probing and extending humanity's creative esprit, the two methods diverged, one playing art to the other's science.

⋏

Modern practices of art and culture collecting, scientific and avantgarde, have situated themselves at the end of a global history. They have occupied a place—apocalyptic, progressive, revolutionary, or tragic—from which to gather the valued inheritances of Man. Concretizing this temporal setup, Lévi-Strauss's "post- and prefigurative" New York anticipates humanity's entropic future and gathers up its diverse pasts in decontextualized, collectible forms. The ethnic neighborhoods, the provincial reminders, the Chinese Opera Company, the feathered Indian in the library, the works of art from other continents and eras that turn up in dealers' closets: all are survivals, remnants of threatened or vanished traditions. The world's cultures appear in the chronotope as shreds of humanity, degraded commodities, or elevated great art but always functioning as vanishing "loopholes" or "escapes" from a one-dimensional fate.

In New York a jumble of humanity has washed up in one vertiginous place and time, to be grasped simultaneously in all its precious diversity and emerging uniformity. In this chronotope the pure products of humanity's pasts are rescued by modern aesthetics only as sublimated art. They are salvaged by modern anthropology as consultable archives for thinking about the range of human invention. In Lévi-Strauss's setting the products of the present-becoming-future are shallow, impure, escapist, and "retro" rather than truly different—"antiques" rather than genuine antiquities. Cultural invention is subsumed by a commodified "mass culture" (1985:264–267).

The chronotope of New York supports a global allegory of fragmentation and ruin. The modern anthropologist, lamenting the passing of human diversity, collects and values its survivals, its enduring works of art. Lévi-Strauss's most prized acquisition from a marvelous New York where everything seemed available was a nearly complete set of volumes 1 through 48 of the *Annual Reports* of the Bureau of American Ethnology. These were, he tells us in another evocation of the war years, "sacrosanct volumes, representing most of our knowledge about the American Indians . . . It was as though the American Indian cultures had suddenly come alive and become almost tangible through the physical contact that these books, written and published before these cultures' definite extinction, established between their times and me" (Lévi-Strauss 1976:50).

These precious records of human diversity had been recorded by an eth-nology still in what he calls its "pure" rather than "diluted" state (Lévi-Strauss 1960:26). They would form the authentic ethnographic material from which structuralism's metacultural orders were constructed.

Anthropological collections and taxonomies, however, are con-stantly menaced by temporal contingencies. Lévi-Strauss knows this. It is a disorder he always holds at bay. For example in *Tristes tropiques* he is acutely aware that focusing on a tribal past necessarily blinds him to an emergent present. Wandering through the modern landscape of New York, far from encountering less and less to know, the anthropologist is confronted with more and more—a heady mix-and-match of possible human combinations. He struggles to maintain a unified perspective; he looks for order in deep "geological" structures. But in Lévi-Strauss's work generally, the englobing "entropological" narrative barely contains a cur-rent history of loss, transformation, invention, and emergence.

Toward the end of his brilliant inaugural lecture at the Collège de France, "The Scope of Anthropology," Lévi-Strauss evokes what he calls "anthropological doubt," the inevitable result of ethnographic risk-taking, the "buffetings and denials directed at one's most cherished ideas and habits by other ideas and habits best able to rebut them" (1960:26). He poignantly recalls Boas's Kwakiutl visitor, transfixed by the freaks and automats of Times Square, and he wonders whether anthropology may not be condemned to equally bizarre perceptions of the distant societies and histories it seeks to grasp. New York was perhaps Lévi-Strauss's only true "fieldwork": for once he stayed long enough and mastered the local language. Aspects of the place, such as Boas's Kwakiutl, have continued to charm and haunt his anthropological culture collecting.

But one New York native sits with special discomfort in the chrono-tope of 1941. This is the feathered Indian with the Parker pen working in the Public Library. For Lévi-Strauss the Indian is primarily associated with the past, the "extinct" societies recorded in the precious Bureau of Amer-ican Ethnology *Annual Reports*. The anthropologist feels himself "going back in time" (1985:266). In modern New York an Indian can appear only as a survival or a kind of incongruous parody.

Another historical vision might have positioned the two scholars in the library differently. The decade just preceding Lévi-Strauss's arrival in New York had seen a dramatic turnaround in federal policy. Under John Collier's leadership at the Bureau of Indian Affairs a "New Indian Policy" actively encouraged tribal reorganization all over the country. While

Lévi-Strauss studied and collected their pasts, many "extinct" Native American groups were in the process of reconstituting themselves cultur- ally and politically. Seen in this context, did the Indian with the Parker pen represent a "going back in time" or a glimpse of another future? That is a different story. (See Chapter 12.)

Other Appropriations

To tell these other stories, local histories of cultural survival and emergence, we need to resist deep-seated habits of mind and systems of authenticity. We need to be suspicious of an almost-automatic tendency to relegate non-Western peoples and objects to the pasts of an increas- ingly homogeneous humanity. A few examples of current invention and contestation may suggest different chronotopes for art and culture col- lecting.

Anne Vitart-Fardoulis, a curator at the Musée de l'Homme, has pub- lished a sensitive account of the aesthetic, historical, and cultural dis- courses routinely used to explicate individual museum objects. She dis- cusses a famous intricately painted animal skin (its present name: M.H. 34.33.5), probably originating among the Fox Indians of North America. The skin turned up in Western collecting systems some time ago in a "cabinet of curiosities"; it was used to educate aristocratic children and was much admired for its aesthetic qualities. Vitart-Fardoulis tells us that now the skin can be decoded ethnographically in terms of its combined "masculine" and "feminine" graphic styles and understood in the context of a probable role in specific ceremonies. But the meaningful contexts are not exhausted. The story takes a new turn:

> The grandson of one of the Indians who came to Paris with Buffalo Bill was searching for the [painted skin] tunic his grandfather had been forced to sell to pay his way back to the United States when the circus collapsed. I showed him all the tunics in our collection, and he paused before one of them. Controlling his emotion, he spoke. He told the meaning of this lock of hair, of that design, why this color had been used, the meaning of that feather . . . This garment, formerly beautiful and interesting but passive and indifferent, little by little became mean- ingful, active testimony to a living moment through the mediation of someone who did not observe and analyze but who lived the object and for whom the object lived. It scarcely matters whether the tunic is really his grandfather's. (Vitart-Fardoulis 1986:12)

Whatever is happening in this encounter, two things are clearly *not* happening. The grandson is not replacing the object in its original or "authentic" cultural context. That is long past. His encounter with the painted skin is part of a modern recollection. And the painted tunic is not being appreciated as art, as an aesthetic object. The encounter is too specific, too enmeshed in family history and ethnic memory.[11] Some aspects of "cultural" and "aesthetic" appropriation are certainly at work, but they occur within a *current tribal history,* a different temporality from that governing the dominant systems I diagrammed earlier. In the context of a present-becoming-future the old painted tunic becomes newly, traditionally meaningful.

The currency of "tribal" artifacts is becoming more visible to non-Indians. Many new tribal recognition claims are pending at the Department of the Interior. And whether or not they are formally successful matters less than what they make manifest: the historical and political reality of Indian survival and resurgence, a force that impinges on Western art and culture collections. The "proper" place of many objects in museums is now subject to contest. The Zuni who prevented the loan of their war god to the Museum of Modern Art (see Chapter 9) were challenging the dominant art-culture system, for in traditional Zuni belief war god figures are sacred and dangerous. They are not ethnographic artifacts, and they are certainly not "art." Zuni claims on these objects specifically reject their "promotion" (in all senses of the term) to the status of aesthetic or scientific treasures.

I would not claim that the only true home for the objects in question

---

11. In his wide-ranging study "Ethnicity and the Post-Modern Arts of Memory" (1986) Michael Fischer identifies general processes of cultural reinvention, personal search, and future-oriented appropriations of tradition. The specificity of some Native American relations with collected "tribal" objects is revealed in a grant proposal to the National Endowment for the Humanities by the Oregon Art Institute (Monroe 1986). In preparation for a reinstallation of the Rasmussen Collection of Northwest Coast works at the Portland Art Museum a series of consultations is envisioned with the participation of Haida and Tlingit elders from Alaska. The proposal makes clear that great care must be given "to matching specific groups of objects in the collection to the clan membership and knowledge base of specific elders. Northwest Coast Natives belong to specific clans who have extensive oral traditions and histories over which they have ownership. Elders are responsible for representing their clans as well as their group" (Monroe 1986:8). The reinstallation "will present *both the academic interpretation of an object or objects and the interpretation of the same material as viewed and understood by Native elders and artists*" (p. 5; original emphasis).

is in "the tribe"—a location that, in many cases, is far from obvious. My
point is just that the dominant, interlocking contexts of art and anthropology are no longer self-evident and uncontested. There are other contexts, histories, and futures in which non-Western objects and cultural
records may "belong." The rare Maori artifacts that in 1984–85 toured
museums in the United States normally reside in New Zealand museums.
But they are controlled by the traditional Maori authorities, whose permission was required for them to leave the country. Here and elsewhere
the circulation of museum collections is significantly influenced by resurgent indigenous communities.

What is at stake is something more than conventional museum programs of community education and "outreach" (Alexander 1979:215).
Current developments question the very status of museums as historical-
cultural theaters of memory. Whose memory? For what purposes? The
Provincial Museum of British Columbia has for some time encouraged
Kwakiutl carvers to work from models in its collection. It has lent out old
pieces and donated new ones for use in modern potlatches. Surveying
these developments, Michael Ames, who directs the University of British
Columbia Museum, observes that "Indians, traditionally treated by museums only as objects and clients, add now the role of patrons." He continues: "The next step has also occurred. Indian communities establish
their own museums, seek their own National Museum grants, install their
own curators, hire their own anthropologists on contract, and call for
repatriation of their own collections" (Ames 1986:57). The Quadra Island Kwakiutl Museum located in Quathraski Cove, British Columbia,
displays tribal work returned from the national collections in Ottowa.
The objects are exhibited in glass cases, but arranged according to their
original family ownership. In Alert Bay, British Columbia, the U'mista
Cultural Centre displays repatriated artifacts in a traditional Kwakiutl "big
house" arranged in the sequence of their appearance at the potlatch ceremony. The new institutions function both as public exhibits and as cultural centers linked to ongoing tribal traditions. Two Haida museums
have also been established in the Queen Charlotte Islands, and the
movement is growing elsewhere in Canada and the United States.

Resourceful Native American groups may yet appropriate the Western museum—as they have made their own another European institution, the "tribe." Old objects may again participate in a tribal present-
becoming-future. Moreover, it is worth briefly noting that the same thing
is possible for written artifacts collected by salvage ethnography. Some

of these old texts (myths, linguistic samples, lore of all kinds) are now being recycled as local history and tribal "literature."[12] The objects of both art and culture collecting are susceptible to other appropriations.

This disturbance of Western object systems is reflected in a recent book by Ralph Coe, *Lost and Found Traditions: Native American Art: 1965–1985* (1986). (On inventive tribal work see also Macnair, Hoover, and Neary 1984; Steinbright 1986; Babcock, Monthan, and Monthan 1986). Coe's work is a collector's tour de force. Once again a white authority "discovers" true tribal art—but with significant differences. Hundreds of photographs document very recent works, some made for local use, some for sale to Indians or white outsiders. Beautiful objects—many formerly classified as curios, folk art, or tourist art—are located in ongoing, inventive traditions. Coe effectively questions the widespread assumption that fine tribal work is disappearing, and he throws doubt on common criteria for judging purity and authenticity. In his collection among recognizably traditional kachinas, totem poles, blankets, and plaited baskets we find skillfully beaded tennis shoes and baseball caps, articles developed for the curio trade, quilts, and decorated leather cases (peyote kits modeled on old-fashioned toolboxes).

Since the Native American Church, in whose ceremonies the peyote kits are used, did not exist in the nineteenth century, their claim to traditional status cannot be based on age. A stronger historical claim can in fact be made for many productions of the curio trade, such as the beaded "fancies" (hanging birds, mirror frames) made by Matilda Hill, a Tuscarora who sells at Niagara Falls:

> "Just try telling Matilda Hill that her 'fancies' (cat. no. 46) are tourist curios," said Mohawk Rick Hill, author of an unpublished paper on the subject. "The Tuscarora have been able to trade pieces like that bird or beaded frame (cat. no. 47) at Niagara since the end of the War

---

12. The archives of James Walker, produced before 1910, have become relevant to the teaching of local history by Sioux on the Pine Ridge Reservation (see Chapter 1; n. 15, and Clifford 1986a:15–17). Also a corpus of translated and untranslated Tolowa tales and linguistic texts collected by A. L. Kroeber and P. E. Goddard are important evidence in a planned petition for tribal recognition. The texts were gathered as "salvage ethnography" to record the shreds of a purportedly vanishing culture. But in the context of Tolowa persistence, retranslated and interpreted by Tolowa elders and their Native American lawyer, the texts yield evidence of tribal history, territorial limits, group distinctness, and oral tradition. They are Tolowa "literature" (Slagle 1986).

of 1812, when they were granted exclusive rights, and she wouldn't take kindly to anyone slighting her culture!"

"Surely," Coe adds, "a trade privilege established at Niagara Falls in 1816 should be acceptable as tradition by now" (1986:17). He drives the general point home[13]: "Another misconception derives from our failure to recognize that Indians have always traded both within and outside their culture; it is second nature to the way they operate in all things. Many objects are, and always have been, created in the Indian world without a specific destination in mind. The history of Indian trading predates any white influence, and trading continues today unabated. It is a fascinating instrument of social continuity, and in these modern times its scope has been greatly enlarged" (p. 16).

Coe does not hesitate to commission new "traditional" works, and he spends considerable time eliciting the specific meaning of objects both as individual possessions and as tribal art. We see and hear particular artists; the coexistence of spiritual, aesthetic, and commercial forces is always visible. Overall Coe's collecting project represents and advocates ongoing art forms that are both related to and separate from dominant systems of aesthetic-ethnographic value. In *Lost and Found Traditions* authenticity is something produced, not salvaged. Coe's collection, for all its love of the past, gathers futures.

A long chapter on "tradition" resists summary, for the diverse statements quoted from practice artists, old and young, do not reproduce prevailing Western definitions. "Whites think of our experience as the past," says one of a group of students discussing the topic. "We know it is right here with us" (p. 49).

---

13. The common presumption that tribal art is *essentially* noncommercial ("sacred," "spiritual," "environmental," and so on) is of questionable value everywhere. A revealing case is the New Guinea Sepik region, where customary objects and lore have long been traded, bought, and sold. To a significant degree the involvement of local groups in the art markets of a wider world can be "traditional." Indigenous commodity systems interact with outside capitalist forces; they do not simply give way to them. The world system is thus dynamically and locally organized. A persistent tendency to see non-Western societies as lacking historical agency is corrected by a growing number of academic studies; for example Rosaldo 1980, R. Price 1983, and Sahlins 1985. These works undermine the binary ("Orientalist") division of human groups into historical and mythical, "hot" and "cold," diachronic and synchronic, modern and archaic. Sally Price (1986) draws attention to the diverse *historical visions* of non-Western, "tribal" peoples and to the role of art in articulating these visions.

"We always begin our summer dances with a song that repeats only four words, over and over. They don't mean much of anything in English, 'young chiefs stand up.' To us those words demonstrate our pride in our lineage and our happiness in always remembering it. It is a happy song. Tradition is not something you gab about . . . It's in the doing." (p. 46)

"Your tradition is 'there' always. You're flexible enough to make of it what you want. It's always with you. I pray to the old pots at the ruins and dream about making pottery. I tell them I want to learn it. We live for today, but never forget the past." (p. 47)

"Our job as artists is to go beyond, which implies a love of change, [always accomplished with] traditions in mind, by talking to the elders of the tribe and by being with your grandparents. The stories they tell are just amazing. When you become exposed to them, everything becomes a reflection of those events. There's a great deal of satisfaction being an artist of traditions." (p. 47)

"We've always had charms: everything that's new is old with us." (p. 79)

Inside a Hopi kiva.

Part Four ⋏ Histories

There are many different kinds of Palestinian experience, which cannot all be assembled into one. One would therefore have to write parallel histories of the communities in Lebanon, the occupied territories, and so on. That is the central problem. It is almost impossible to imagine a single narrative: it would have to be the kind of crazy history that comes out in Midnight's Children, *with all those little strands coming in and out.*

—EDWARD SAID, "ON PALESTINIAN IDENTITY, A CONVERSATION WITH SALMAN RUSHDIE"

11. On *Orientalism*

IN 1939 Aimé Césaire published his searing long poem "Cahier d'un retour au pays natal." In it he wrote of his native Martinique, of colonial oppression, of rediscovered African sources; he coined the term *nègritude.* His poem was written in the language of Lautréamont and Rimbaud, but it was a French spattered with neologisms, punctuated by new rhythms. For Césaire a "native land" was something complex and hybrid, salvaged from a lost origin, constructed out of a squalid present, articulated within and against a colonial tongue.

By the early 1950s the negritude movement was in full swing, thrusting an alternative humanism back at Europe; and in this new context it became possible to question European ideological practices in radical ways. Michel Leiris, who was a friend and collaborator of Césaire's, composed the first extended analysis of the relationship between anthropological knowledge and colonialism (Leiris 1950). His discourse opened a debate that has continued, with varying degrees of intensity, during the subsequent decades. How has European knowledge about the rest of the planet been shaped by a Western will to power? How have Western writers, both imaginative and scientific, been enmeshed in co-

255

lonial and neocolonial situations? How, concretely, have they ignored, resisted, and acquiesced in these enduring conditions of inequality? Leiris pointed to a basic imbalance. Westerners had for centuries studied and spoken for the rest of the world; the reverse had not been the case. He announced a new situation, one in which the "objects" of observation would begin to write back. The Western gaze would be met and scattered. Since 1950 Asians, Africans, Arab orientals, Pacific islanders, and Native Americans have in a variety of ways asserted their independence from Western cultural and political hegemony and established a new multivocal field of intercultural discourse. What will be the long-term consequences of such a situation—if it endures? How has it already altered what one can know about others, the ways such knowledge may be formulated? It is still early to judge the depth and extent of the epistemological changes that may be under way. (The literature on anthropology and colonialism is quite large. A few important works are Maquet 1964; Hymes 1969; Asad 1973; Firth 1977; Copans 1974, 1975; Leclerc 1972; and Nash 1975. In the field of Oriental and Islamic studies see Tibawi 1963; Abdel-Malek 1963; Hourani 1967; and Khatibi 1976.)

⋏

Edward Said's *Orientalism* (1978a), a critical study of Western knowledge about the exotic, occupies this indeterminate historical context. If it presents itself as part of the general "writing back" against the West that Leiris announced, *Orientalism*'s predicament is an ambiguous one that should be seen not in terms of a simple anti-imperialism but rather as a symptom of the uncertainties generated by the new global situation. It is important to situate Said's book within this wide perspective, for it would be all too easy to dismiss *Orientalism* as a narrow polemic dominated by immediate ideological goals in the Middle East struggle. It could be seen too as merely the personal protest of a Palestinian deprived of his homeland by a "uniquely punishing destiny," suffering from his externally imposed, abstract identity as "an Oriental," oppressed by "an almost unanimous consensus that politically he does not exist" (pp. 26–27). Indeed Said writes forthrightly and eloquently of this, his own predicament; and he writes also from a conviction that "pure" scholarship does not exist. Knowledge in his view is inextricably tied to power. When it becomes institutionalized, culturally accumulated, overly restrictive in its definitions, it must be actively opposed by a counterknowledge. *Orientalism* is polemical, its analysis corrosive; but Said's book operates in a number of registers, and it would be wrong to restrict its significance unduly. *Orientalism* is at once a serious exercise in textual criticism and, most fundamentally, a series of important if tentative epistemological reflections on general styles and procedures of cultural discourse.

Said's topic is usually thought of as a rather old-fashioned scholarly discipline allied with nineteenth-century philology and concerned with the collection and analysis of texts in Eastern languages. Raymond Schwab's encyclopedic *Renaissance orientale* (1950) is of course the classic history of this ensemble, which included Sinologists, Islamicists, Indo-Europeanists, literati, travelers, and an eclectic host of aficionados. Said does not attempt to revise or extend Schwab's work, for his approach is not historicist or empirical but deductive and constructivist. His study undertakes a simultaneous expansion and formalization of the field, transforming Orientalism into a synecdoche for a much more complex and ramified totality. Said calls this totality a "discourse," following Foucault. I shall discuss Said's adoption of a Foucauldian methodology and its hazards. For the moment, though, it is enough to say that the Orientalist "discourse" is characterized by an oppressive systematicity, a "sheer knitted-together strength" (p. 6) that Said sets out to reveal through a reading of representative texts and experiences.

Although Said discovers "Orientalism" in Homer, Aeschylus, the *Chanson de Roland,* and Dante, he situates its modern origins in Barthélémy d'Herblot's *Bibliothèque orientale.* This compendium of oriental knowledge is criticized by Said for its cosmological scope and for its construction as a "systematic" and "rational" oriental panorama. It is significant that Said's reading of Herblot's seventeenth-century work makes no attempt to analyze it as Foucault would in *Les mots et les choses*— that is, "archaeologically"—in relation to a synchronic epistemological field. The approach of *Orientalism* is thus clearly indicated as genealogical. Its central task is to describe retrospectively and continuously the structures of an Orientalism that achieved its classical form in the nineteenth and early twentieth centuries. Said's two criticisms of Herblot are constitutive of his object: Orientalism is always too broadly and abstractly pitched, and it is always overly systematic.

Said proceeds to apply these reproaches, with varying degrees of plausibility, to a diverse range of authors, institutions, and typical experiences. There are analyses of Sylvestre de Sacy, Ernest Renan and the Napoleonic expedition to Egypt's scholarly product, the massive *Description de l'Egypte.* The speeches of politicians such as Balfour and

Cromer (juxtaposed with Henry Kissinger); the Indian journalism of Marx; the oriental voyages of Chateaubriand, Lamartine, Nerval, and Flaubert; the adventures of Burton and Lawrence; the scholarship of H. A. R. Gibb and Louis Massignon are all woven into an intertextual unity. This ensemble—though it leaves some room for historical mutation, different national traditions, personal idiosyncrasies, and the genius of "great" writers—is designed to emphasize the systematic and invariant nature of the Orientalist discourse. There is no way to summarize the complex interweavings of Said's critical method—associative, sometimes brilliant, sometimes forced, and in the end numbingly repetitive. It succeeds at least in isolating and discrediting an array of "oriental" stereotypes: the eternal and unchanging East, the sexually insatiable Arab, the "feminine" exotic, the teeming marketplace, corrupt despotism, mystical religiosity. Said is particularly effective in his critical analysis of Orientalist "authority"—the paternalist privileges unhesitatingly assumed by Western writers who "speak for" a mute Orient or reconstitute its decayed or dismembered "truth," who lament the passing of its authenticity, and who know more than its mere natives ever can. This methodical suspicion of the reconstitutive procedures of writing about others could be usefully extended beyond Orientalism to anthropological practice generally.

If Orientalism, as Said describes it, has a structure, this resides in its tendency to *dichotomize* the human continuum into we-they contrasts and to *essentialize* the resultant "other"—to speak of the oriental mind, for example, or even to generalize about "Islam" or "the Arabs." All of these Orientalist "visions" and "textualizations," as Said terms them, function to suppress an authentic "human" reality. This reality, he implies, is rooted in oral encounter and reciprocal speech, as opposed to the processes of writing or of the visual imagination. Said's limited polemical goal is well served by such an analysis. "Authentic" human encounter can be portrayed as subjugated to the dead book. (Flaubert does not, for example, really experience Egypt as much as he recopies a passage from earlier "voyages to the East.") The theoretical issues raised by *Orientalism* as a case study of a cultural discourse cannot be disposed of, however, by means of any simple contrast between experience and textuality.

Said is not a simple polemicist. His critical approach is restless and mordant, repeatedly pushing its analyses to epistemological limits. Behind the immediate influence of Foucault lies an ambivalent admiration for Nietzsche. At various moments in his book Said is led to argue that all cultural definitions must be restrictive, that all knowledge is both powerful and fictional, that all language distorts. He suggests that "authenticity," "experience," "reality," "presence" are mere rhetorical conventions. The general influence of the French theory that Said has done so much to interpret for American readers is here most apparent (see particularly his "Abcdarium Culturae" in Said 1975:277–344). While he cites Lévi-Strauss and Barthes as well as Foucault, at the same time Said makes frequent appeals to an old-fashioned existential realism. In the multivocal world situation I have outlined this sort of uncertainty is crucial. Should criticism work to counter sets of culturally produced images such as those of Orientalism with more "authentic" or more "human" representations? Or if criticism must struggle against the procedures of representation itself, how is it to begin? How, for example, is an oppositional critique of Orientalism to avoid falling into "Occidentalism"? These are fundamental issues—inseparably political and epistemological—raised by Said's work.

$$\downarrow\!\!\!\uparrow$$

Said never defines Orientalism but rather qualifies and designates it from a variety of distinct and not always compatible standpoints. The book begins by postulating three loose "meanings" of Orientalism, "historical generalizations" that comprise the "backbone" of his subsequent analyses. First, Orientalism is what Orientalists do and have done. An Orientalist is "anyone who teaches, writes about, or researches the Orient . . . either in its specific or its general aspects." Included in this group are academics and government experts: philologists, sociologists, historians, and anthropologists. Second, Orientalism is a "style of thought based upon an ontological and epistemological distinction made between 'the Orient' and (most of the time) 'the Occident'" (p. 2). Any writing, Said goes on to suggest, at any period in the history of the Occident that accepts as its starting point a basic dichotomy between East and West and that makes essentialist statements about "the Orient, its people, customs, 'mind,' destiny, and so on" is Orientalist. Finally, Orientalism is a "corporate institution for dealing with the Orient," which, during the colonial period following roughly the late eighteenth century wields the power of "dominating, restructuring, and having authority over the Orient" (p. 3). This third designation, unlike the other two, is pitched at a rigorously transindividual, cultural level and suggests "an enormously systematic" mechanism capable of organizing and largely determining whatever may be said or written about the Orient.

One notices immediately that in the first and third of Said's "meanings" Orientalism is concerned with something called the Orient, while in the second the Orient exists merely as the construct of a questionable mental operation. This ambivalence, which sometimes becomes a confusion, informs much of Said's argument. Frequently he suggests that a text or tradition distorts, dominates, or ignores some real or authentic feature of the Orient. Elsewhere, however, he denies the existence of any "real Orient," and in this he is more rigorously faithful to Foucault and the other radical critics of representation whom he cites. Indeed the absence of anything more than a brief allusion to the "brute reality" of the "cultures and nations whose location is in the East . . . their lives, histories and customs" represents a significant methodological choice on his part. Orientalist inauthenticity is not answered by any authenticity. Yet Said's concept of a "discourse" still vacillates between, on the one hand, the status of an ideological distortion of lives and cultures that are never concretized and, on the other, the condition of a persistent structure of signifiers that, like some extreme example of experimental writing, refers solely and endlessly to itself. Said is thus forced to rely on nearly tautological statements, such as his frequent comment that Orientalist discourse "orientalizes the Orient," or on rather unhelpful specifications such as: "Orientalism can thus be regarded as a manner of regularized (or Orientalized) writing, vision, and study, dominated by imperatives, perspectives, and ideological biases ostensibly suited to the Orient" (p. 202).

If redundancy haunts Said's account, this is not, I think, merely the result of a hermeneutical short circuit in which the critic discovers in his topic what he has already put there. Nor is it simply an effect of his insistence on the sheer knitted-togetherness of a textual unity that is constantly in danger of decomposing into its discontinuous functions, authors, institutions, histories, and epistemologically distinct epochs. Beyond these problems (faced by any interpreter of constructed, complex cultural ensembles) lies a substantial and disquieting set of questions about the ways in which distinct groups of humanity (however defined) imagine, describe, and comprehend each other. Are such discourses ultimately condemned to redundancy, the prisoners of their own authoritative images and linguistic protocols? Orientalism—"enormously systematic," cosmological in scope, incestuously self-referential—emerges as much more than a mere intellectual or even ideological tradition. Said at one point calls it "a considerable dimension of modern political-intellectual culture." As such it "has less to do with the Orient than it does with 'our' world" (p. 12).

The quotation marks placed by Said around *our* may be understood to have generated his entire study. The reasons for this are not simply personal but lead us to what Said rightly identifies as "the main intellectual issue raised by Orientalism. Can one divide human reality, as indeed human reality seems to be genuinely divided, into clearly different cultures, histories, traditions, societies, even races, and survive the consequences humanly?" (p. 45). The result of such distinctions, he argues, is to create invidious and imperially useful oppositions that serve to "limit the human encounter between different cultures, traditions, and societies" (p. 46). (It is worth noting in passing that we-they distinctions of the kind Said condemns are also useful to anti-imperialism and national liberation movements.) The key theoretical issue raised by *Orientalism* concerns the status of *all* forms of thought and representation for dealing with the alien. Can one ultimately escape procedures of dichotomizing, restructuring, and textualizing in the making of interpretive statements about foreign cultures and traditions? If so, how? Said frankly admits that alternatives to orientalism are not his subject. He merely attacks the discourse from a variety of positions, and as a result his own standpoint is not sharply defined or logically grounded. Sometimes his analysis flirts with a critique of representation as such; but the most constant position from which it attacks Orientalism is a familiar set of values associated with the Western anthropological human sciences—existential standards of "human encounter" and vague recommendations of "personal, authentic, sympathetic, humanistic knowledge" (p. 197).

In Said's discussion of the Orientalist as humanist these assumptions are thrown into sharp relief. There has, of course, been a sympathetic, nonreductive Orientalist tradition, a strand that Said downplays. He does, however, on one occasion grapple with this "good" Orientalism in the person of its most representative figure, Louis Massignon. Massignon must stand for those Orientalists—one thinks of scholars such as Sylvain Lévi, Marcel Mauss, Henry Corbin—whose involvement with the foreign traditions they studied evolved into a deep personal and dialogical quest for comprehension. Such writers have characteristically presented themselves as spokesmen for oriental or primitive "wisdom" and also as democratic reformers and humanist critics of imperialism.

Said's discussion of Massignon, the most interesting in his book, is a crucial test case for the theory of Orientalism as a pervasive and coercive cultural discourse. Here Said can no longer generalize sweepingly and categorically about "the Orientalist" and "Orientalism." (Indeed his critical manner sometimes appears to mimic the essentializing discourse it attacks.) Said gives full and generous recognition to Massignon's profound empathy with Islamic mysticism, to his subtlety and range of expression, and to his political commitment on behalf of exploited orientals; but he argues that the great scholar's work is still finally defined within a restricted "discursive consistency." He deploys his most Nietzschean arguments to the effect that any representation must be "implicated, intertwined, embedded, interwoven with a great many other things besides the 'truth,' which is itself a representation" (p. 272).

Said shows rather effectively the limits of Massignon's intellectual world. The most important of these is the scholar's tendency to perceive present Middle Eastern realities with reference to traditionally defined cultural or spiritual values. Massignon saw the earthbound experiences of colonialism, economic oppression, love, death, and so on through the "dehumanized lens" of a quasi-metaphysical conception of Semitic essence. He perceived the Palestinian conflict, for example, in terms of the quarrel between Isaac and Ishmael. Here as elsewhere Said makes short work of appeals beyond a corrupt present to an authentic tradition. Such appeals, however·sympathetic, are always suspect in their disparagement of current processes of cultural and political invention. Ultimately Massignon could not avoid participation in a "will to knowledge over the Orient and on its behalf" (p. 272).

If even a "genius" such as Massignon can be so restricted, it becomes difficult to escape the bleak though rigorous conclusion that all human expression is ultimately determined by cultural "archives," and that global truth must be the result of a battle of "discursive formations" in which the strongest prevails. Said is uneasy with so Foucauldian a conclusion. He goes on to reassert a transcendent humanist standard, rescuing Massignon, who is after all "a very human being" from an institutional determination now qualified as only a "dimension" of his "productive capacity." Massignon does in the end rise above his culture into a "broader history and anthropology." Massignon's statement "nous sommes tous des Sémites" shows, according to Said, "the extent to which his ideas about the Orient could transcend the local anecdotal circumstances of a Frenchman and of French society" (p. 274). A very human being becomes a humanist. But the privilege of standing above cultural particularism, of aspiring to the universalist power that speaks for humanity, for the universal experiences of love, work, death, and so on, is a privilege invented by a totalizing Western liberalism. This benevolent comprehension of the visions produced by mere "local anecdotal circumstances" is an authority that escapes Said's criticism.

Said sometimes presents his critical posture as "oppositional" (p. 326), a stance of open attack on imperial power and knowledge (see Said 1976, 1979). More frequently, though, he qualifies himself positively as a humanist. This stance seems to presuppose a particularist, even individualist attitude combined with cosmopolitanism and a general valorization of creative process. For example T. E. Lawrence is taken to task for writing (in a rather admirably self-conscious passage) of "Arabs" rather than of "individual Arabs with narratable life histories" (p. 229). Such general statements, Said argues, "necessarily subordinate" an Arab's specific feeling of joy, of sadness, of injustice in the face of tyranny, and so on. Said castigates Orientalism for its construction of static images rather than historical or personal "narratives." The "human experience," whether that of the individual Orientalist or of his or her objects of study, is flattened into an asserted authority on one side and a generalization on the other. Said characterizes the human realities thus elided with quotations from Yeats—"'the uncontrollable mystery on the bestial floor,' in which all humans live," and "the foul rag and bone shop of the heart" (pp. 230, 110).

It is still an open question, of course, whether an African pastoralist shares the same existential "bestial floor" with an Irish poet and his readers. And it is a general feature of humanist common denominators that they are meaningless, since they bypass the local cultural codes that make personal experience articulate. Said's resort to such notions underlines the absence in his book of any developed theory of culture as a differentiating and expressive ensemble rather than as simply hegemonic and disciplinary. His basic values are cosmopolitan. He approves as an alternative to Orientalism the cultural hermeneutics of Erich Auerbach, Ernst Robert Curtius, and Clifford Geertz. He appears to endorse the anthropological commonplace that "the more one is able to leave one's cultural home, the more easily is one able to judge it, and the whole world as well, with the spiritual detachment *and* generosity necessary for true vision" (p. 259). The anthropologist as outsider and participant-observer (existential shorthand for the hermeneutical circle) is a familiar

modern *topos*. Its wisdom—and authority—is expressed with a disturbing beauty by Hugh of St. Victor (quoted by Said from Auerbach): "The
man who finds his homeland sweet is still a tender beginner; he to whom
every soil is as his native one is already strong; but he is perfect to whom
the entire world is as a foreign land" (p. 259).

Said's humanist perspectives do not harmonize with his use of methods
derived from Foucault, who is of course a radical critic of humanism. But
however wary and inconsistent its appeals, *Orientalism* is a pioneering
attempt to use Foucault systematically in an extended cultural analysis.
Its difficulties and successes should thus be of interest to historians, critics, and anthropologists.

We have already encountered the central notion of discourse. For
Said a discourse is the cultural-political configuration of "the textual attitude" (pp. 92–94). The most extreme example of this attitude is *Don
Quixote;* its condensed modern formulation is Flaubert's *Dictionnaire
des idées reçues*. People prefer order to disorder; they grasp at formulas
rather than actuality; they prefer the guidebook to the confusion before
them. "It seems a common human failing," Said writes, using the word
human with significant ambivalence, "to prefer the schematic authority
of a text to the disorientations of direct encounters with the human" (p.
93). In certain conditions this textual attitude hardens into a body of rigid
cultural definitions that determine what any individual can express about
a certain acutality. This "reality" coalesces as a field of representations
produced by the discourse. The conditions for discursive hardening are
not clearly defined by Said, but they appear to be related to an ongoing
imbalance of power that permits—perhaps obliges—a politically and
technologically stronger culture or group to define weaker groups. Thus
in Said's analysis occidental culture through the discourse of Orientalism
"suffused" the activity of orientals with "meaning, intelligibility, and reality." The Orientalist discourse, which, according to Said, did not significantly change after the late eighteenth century, generated a dumb
show of oriental images. "Actual human interchange between Oriental
and Westerner" (p. 95) was systematically repressed. Orientals had no
voice on the "Orientalist Stage."

Said's general attempt to extend Foucault's conception of a discourse
into the area of cultural constructions of the exotic is a promising one.
Foucault's overall undertaking has of course been scrupulously ethno-

centric. In attempting to isolat[e]   [Eu]ropean
thought he has avoided all com[   ] meaning. There are no evocations [   ] ~~sauvage~~, or Hopi linguistic
categories, and the like. Foucault probably believes such appeals to be
methodologically dubious, and he contrasts Western civilization only
whimsically to Borges' "Chinese encyclopedia" at the outset of *Les mots
et les choses*. Foucault is interested in the ways in which a given cultural
order constitutes itself by means of discursive definitions: sane-mad,
healthy-sick, legal-criminal, normal-perverse. The illicit categories for
Foucault exist not as areas of an outlaw freedom but as culturally produced, arranged experiences.

Said extends Foucault's analysis to include ways in which a cultural
order is defined externally, with respect to exotic "others." In an imperialist context definitions, representations, and textualizations of subject
peoples and places play the same constitutive role as "internal" representations (for example of the criminal classes in nineteenth-century Europe)
and have the same consequences—discipline and confinement, both
physical and ideological. Therefore "the Orient," in Said's analysis, exists
uniquely *for* the Occident. His task in *Orientalism* is to dismantle the
discourse, to expose its oppressive system, to "clear the archive" of its
received ideas and static images.

Foucault is not easily imitated. His writing has been a series of experiments and tactical interventions rather than a methodical program.
Said's appropriation of Foucault strikes a committed, moral note. Con-
trasting (and preferring) Foucault to Derrida, Said notes that the latter's
"endless worrying of representation" from "within" canonical Western
texts does not permit critical attention to move beyond the written (however "indecidable") to the social and political, to the *institutions* underlying an imperial and hegemonic "Western thought." Foucault's brand of
criticism, unlike Derrida's, "reads" a prison or a hospital, a legal system,
or—as Said does in *Orientalism*—a geopolitical artifact such as De Les-
seps' canal (seen as an Orientalist inscription). "By virtue of Foucault's
criticism we are able to understand culture as a body of disciplines having the effective force of knowledge linked systematically, but by no
means immediately, to power." Culture as Said conceives it is little more
than "a massive body of self-congratulating ideas" and of "disciplines"
that the critic must unmask and oppose without claiming—by virtue of a
system or sovereign method—to stand outside of "history, subjectivity, or
circumstance." "The critical consciousness . .). having initially detached

itself from the dominant culture" thereafter adopts "a situated and responsible adversary position" (Said 1978b:709, 690, 713).

It is rather difficult, however, to qualify Foucault's restless guerrilla activity on behalf of the excluded, against *all* totalizing, defining, essentializing alliances of knowledge and power as "situated and responsible." Said himself deploys a rather loose collection of "adversary theoretical models" derived from Foucault, Gramsci, Lukács, Fanon, and others (1979:16). A key political term for Said is *oppositional,* and it is fairly clear what this means in the limited context of a book such as *Orientalism,* which "writes back" at an imperial discourse from the position of an oriental whose actuality has been distorted and denied. More generally, however, it is apparent that a wide range of Western humanist assumptions escape Said's oppositional analysis, as do the discursive alliances of knowledge and power produced by anticolonial and particularly nationalist movements.

⅄

Beyond his overall stance as "oppositional" cultural critic Said makes use of other Foucauldian approaches that should be discussed briefly. Most significant is his adoption of the posture of critical retrospection that Nietzsche called genealogy. In this Said is true to Foucault's later evolution away from the methodology of layered "archaeological" discontinuity exemplified in *The Order of Things* and *The Archaeology of Knowledge* and towards a presentation of the lineages of the present, as exemplified in *Discipline and Punish* and especially *The History of Sexuality,* volume 1.

The field of Orientalism is genealogically distributed in two ways: synchronically (constituting in a unified system all Western textual versions of the Orient) and diachronically (plotting a single lineage of statements about the East, running from Aeschylus to Renan to modern political sociology and "area studies"). Like all genealogies Said's grows more specific as it approaches the present it has been constructed to explain and affect. Thus the bulk of his account describes the heyday of Orientalism in the nineteenth and early twentieth centuries. This is followed by an attempt to generate meanings in the current Middle East situation with reference to this classical tradition. The aim here is not, of course, the one most usual in genealogies—a new legitimation of the present— but rather, as in Foucault's *History of Sexuality* and *Madness and Civilization,* radical *de*-legitimation. A certain degree of anachronism is openly embraced.[1] Genealogy, like all historical description and analysis, is constructive. It makes sense in the present by making sense selectively *out of* the past. Its inclusions and exclusions, its narrative continuities, its judgments of core and periphery are finally legitimated either by convention or by the authority granted to or arrogated by the genealogist. Genealogy is perhaps the most political of historical modes; but to be effective it cannot appear too openly tendentious, and Said's genealogy suffers on this score. To his credit he makes no secret of the restrictive choices involved.

First, Said limits his attention almost exclusively to statements about the Arab Middle East—omitting, regretfully but firmly, the Far East, India, the Pacific, and North Africa. The omission of the Maghreb is crucial, for it ensures that Said will not have to discuss modern French Orientalist currents. In a French context the kinds of critical questions posed by Said have been familiar since the Algerian war and may be found strongly expressed well before 1950. It would simply not be possible to castigate recent French "Orientalism" in the way that he does the discourse of the modern American Middle East "experts," which is still shaped by Cold War patterns and by the polarized Arab-Israeli conflict.

Said's second genealogical limitation restricts the national traditions under consideration to the British and French strands, with the addition of a recent American offspring. He is obliged to rule out Italian, Spanish, Russian, and especially German Orientalisms. The highly developed nineteenth-century German tradition is cast as peripheral to French and English pioneers but, more important, as not constituted like these two in a close relationship with colonial occupation and domination of the Orient (pp. 16–19). In effect, German Orientalism is too disinterested and thus atypical of a genealogy that *defines* the discourse as essentially colonialist. If Said's primary aim were to write an intellectual history of Orientalism or a history of Western ideas of the Orient, his narrowing and rather obviously tendentious shaping of the field could be taken as a

---

1. In *Discipline and Punish* (1975:35) Foucault writes of his intention to produce a history of the prison: "Par un pur anachronisme? Non, si on entend par là faire l'histoire du passé dans les termes du présent. Oui, si on entend par là faire l'historie du présent" (p. 35). His fullest statement on genealogy is "Nietzsche, Genealogy, History" (1977). This chapter discusses only those works by Foucault that were available at the time of publication of *Orientalism*. I do not consider his refinements and transgressions of historical method following the first volume of *History of Sexuality*.

fatal flaw. But his undertaking is conceived otherwise and is openly an oppositional genealogy. If Said's genealogy sometimes appears clumsily rigged (the final all-too-predictable zeroing in on the Middle East and abrupt jump from Continental to American "Orientalism" is the least convincing of its "continuities"), one need not reject the entire critical paradigm.

Said is perfectly correct to identify retrospectively a "discourse" that dichotomizes and essentializes in its portrayal of others and that functions in a complex but systematic way as an element of colonial domination. It is important that this discourse be recognized wherever it exists; but the discourse should not be closely identified with the specific tradition of Orientalism. Its field of application has been far more general. The problem with the book, at least from a theoretical standpoint, is its title. In attempting to derive a "discourse" directly from a "tradition," Said abandons the level of cultural criticism proposed by Foucault and relapses into traditional intellectual history. Moreover, in portraying the discourse as based on essentially nineteenth-century modes of thought, Said gives himself too easy a target. He does not question anthropological orthodoxies based on a mythology of fieldwork encounter and a hermeneutically minded cultural theory—orthodoxies he often appears to share.

It is apparent that "discourse" analysis cannot safely be founded on redefined "traditions." Nor can it be derived from a study of "authors." The general tendency in modern textual studies has been to reduce the occasion of a text's creation by an individual subject to merely one of its generative or potentially meaningful contexts. While recognizing the importance of this separation of the text from the work (Barthes: "The work is held in the hand, the text in language"), Said has resisted radical structuralist attacks on phenomenology and on the essential (beginning and continuing) function of an authorial intention. *Beginnings* (1975), which preceded *Orientalism*, is a detailed and perspicuous meditation on this set of issues. It is concerned precisely with the problem, experienced by a wide range of modernist writers, of being an "author." Steering a complex course between individualist conceptions of creativity on the one hand and on the other reductions of "the moving force of life and behaviour, the *forma informans*, intention" (p. 319) to an external system, whether cultural or critical, Said suggests an intermediate analytical *topos* that he calls a "career." The modern author's intention is not so much to produce works as it is to begin (and to continue beginning) to write. A career is the ensemble of these complex historically and culturally situated intentions. It is always in process, always being begun in specific situations, and never possessing either a stable essence or a shaped biographical finality. The author is reconceived, and in the face of structuralist dissolution rescued.

It is not surprising, then, that Said, in discussing Orientalism as a discourse and a tradition, adopts what he calls a "hybrid perspective." "Foucault believes that in general the individual text or author counts for very little; empirically, in the case of Orientalism (and perhaps nowhere else) I find this not to be so" (1978a:23). This doggedly empirical and curiously qualified assertion separates Said sharply from Foucault. What is important theoretically is not that Foucault's author counts for very little but rather that a "discursive formation"—as opposed to ideas, citations, influences, references, conventions, and the like—is not produced by authorial subjects or even by a group of authors arranged as a "tradition." This methodological (not empirical) point is important for anyone involved in the kind of task Said is attempting. One cannot combine within the same analytic totality both personal statements and discursive statements, even though they may be lexically identical. Said's experiment seems to show that when the analysis of authors and traditions is intermixed with the analysis of discursive formations, the effect is a mutual weakening.

None of the authors discussed in *Orientalism* is accorded a "career" in the complex sense posited by *Beginnings,* but all are portrayed as instances of Orientalist discourse. Unlike Foucault, however, for whom authorial names function as mere labels for discursive statements, Said's authors may be accorded psychohistorical typicality and are often made through their texts to have representative Orientalist experiences. One example among many, chosen for the familiarity of its subject, is Said's reading of a passage from Marx—the end of his article "The British Rule in India" (Said 1978a:153–157).

Marx denounces an affront to "human feeling"—the spectacle of Indian social life brutally disrupted, "thrown into a sea of woes" by imperialism; but he quickly reminds his readers that "these idyllic village communities" have always been the foundation of "Oriental despotism." They have "restrained the human mind within the smallest possible compass, making it the unresisting tool of superstition, enslaving it beneath the traditional rules, depriving it of all its grandeur and historical energies." England, Marx goes on to say, is history's agent; its task is to "lay the material foundations of Western Society in Asia." Said scents Orientalism in the reference to despotism and in a later citation of Goethe's *Westöstlicher Diwan*. He identifies a "romantic redemptive project," which assumes the general Western privilege of putting the Orient—stagnant, dismembered, corrupt—back together. Marx is also convicted of subsuming "individuals" and "existential human identities" under "artificial entities" such as "Oriental," "Asiatic," "Semitic," or within collectives such as "race," "mentality," and "nation."

Here an effective reading begins to get out of hand. It is unclear why Said does not also convict Marx of subsuming individuals under the "artificial entities" "class" and "history." Furthermore, if Marx's participation in Orientalism derives from his inattention to existential, individual cases, one wonders how social or cultural theory is ever to be "humanly" built. In addition, it is well known that Marx heaped "Orientalist" scorn and condescension upon the "idiocy of rural life" wherever he found it, believing that such stagnant, repressive situations had to be violently transformed before they could improve. Here Said skirts "unfairness" to Marx. While legitimately isolating Orientalist aspects of the text, he too quickly skims over its rhetorical intentions. Moreover, Said soon abandons any discussion of Orientalist *statements* and goes on to uncover in the text a typical Orientalist *experience*. Marx, we are told, at first expressed "a natural human repugnance" toward the suffering of orientals; he felt a "human sympathy," a "fellow feeling." This "personal human experience" was then "censored" by a process of Orientalist labeling and abstraction, "a wash of sentiment" was repressed by "unshakable definitions." (Said writes in the past tense, as if this is what really happened in Marx's mind.) "The vocabulary of emotion dissipated as it submitted to the lexicographical police action of Orientalist science and even Orientalist art. An experience was dislodged by a dictionary definition" (p. 155). By now Said could not be farther from Foucault's austere pages, where all psychologizing is forbidden and where authors escape at least having to go through such instructive "experiences." Said's descriptions of Orientalist discourse are frequently sidetracked by humanist fables of suppressed authenticity.

Discourse analysis is always in a sense unfair to authors. It is not interested in what *they* have to say or feel as subjects but is concerned merely with statements as related to other statements in a field.[2] Escaping

---

2. On the initial definition of this field, which he calls a "discursive formation," see Foucault's strictures in *The Archaeology of Knowledge* (1969: chap.

an impression of unfairness and reductionism in this kind of analysis is a matter of methodological rigor and stylistic tact. Foucault, at least, does not appear unfair to authors because he seldom appeals to any individual intentionality or subjectivity. "Hybrid perspectives" such as Said's have considerably more difficulty escaping reductionism.[3]

Indeed Said's methodological catholicity repeatedly blurs his analysis. If he is advancing anthropological arguments, Orientalism appears as the cultural quest for order. When he adopts the stance of a literary critic, it emerges as the processes of writing, textualizing, and interpreting. As an intellectual historian Said portrays Orientalism as a specific series of influences and schools of thought. For the psychohistorian Orientalist discourse becomes a representative series of personal-historical experiences. For the Marxist critic of ideology and culture it is the expression of definite political and economic power interests. Orientalism is also at times conflated with Western positivism, with general definitions of the primitive, with evolutionism, with racism. One could continue the list. Said's discourse analysis does not itself escape the all-inclusive "Occidentalism" he specifically rejects as an alternative to Orientalism (p. 328).

✢

Though Said's work frequently relapses into the essentializing modes it attacks and is ambivalently enmeshed in the totalizing habits of Western humanism, it still succeeds in questioning a number of important anthropological categories, most important, perhaps, the concept of culture. In this final section I shall sketch out some of these issues, the most far-reaching questions raised by *Orientalism*.

The effect of Said's general argument is not so much to undermine

---

2). Foucault's method ignores "influences" and "traditions," demotes "authors," and holds in suspense any criteria of discursive unity based on the persistence or commonality of "objects," "styles," "concepts," or "themes." It may be noted that Said makes use of all these familiar elements from the history of ideas.

3. Said's critical approach can in fact be quite disturbing, especially when he is uncovering Orientalism in lesser-known figures than Marx, among whom the disjuncture between discursive statements and personal expressions is less immediately apparent. A particularly blatant example may be seen in his use of the great Sanskrit scholar and humanist Sylvain Lévi in order to show the connection of Orientalism with imperial politics (Said 1978:249–250). The misleading image of someone intensely concerned with European "interests" in the Orient (the word *interest* is inserted into Lévi's discourse) is nowhere qualified. For an affirmation that modern Orientalists have been far less reductive than Said portrays them to be see Hourani 1979.

the notion of a substantial Orient as it is to make problematic "the Occident." It is less common today than it once was to speak of "the East," but we still make casual reference to "the West," "Western culture," and so on. Even theorists of discontinuity and deconstruction such as Foucault and Derrida continue to set their analyses within and against a Western totality. Said shares their assumptions inasmuch as he portrays the Western culture of which Orientalism is an exemplar as a discrete entity capable of generating knowledge and institutional power *over* the rest of the planet. Western order, seen this way, is imperial, unreciprocal, aggressive, and potentially hegemonic. At times, though, Said permits us to see the functioning of a more complex dialectic by means of which a modern culture continuously constitutes itself through its ideological constructs of the exotic. Seen in this way "the West" itself becomes a play of projections, doublings, idealizations, and rejections of a complex, shifting otherness. "The Orient" always plays the role of origin or alter ego. For example Renan working in his "philological laboratory" does not simply concoct the scholarly *topos* of the Semitic Orient but in the same process produces a conception of what it means to be European and modern (pp. 132, 146).

Here Said's argument reinforces Stanley Diamond's (1974) contentions that Western culture can conceive of itself critically only with reference to fictions of the primitive. To this dialectical view we may usefully add the overall perspective of Marshall Hodgson's historical work, which portrays "Europe" as, until the late eighteenth century, merely "a fringe area of the Afro-Euroasian zone of agrarianate cultured life" (see particularly Hodgson 1974, 1963, and Burke 1979, an excellent survey of Hodgson's complex work). If we adopt along with these perspectives a generally structuralist suspicion of all quests for origins (the origins of the West in Greece or in Christianity), we are left with a totality in process, composed and recomposed in changing external relations.

When we speak today of the West, we are usually referring to a force—technological, economic, political—no longer radiating in any simple way from a discrete geographical or cultural center. This force, if it may be spoken of in the singular, is disseminated in a diversity of forms from multiple centers—now including Japan, Australia, the Soviet Union, and China—and is articulated in a variety of "micro-sociological" contexts (see Duvignaud 1973). It is too early to say whether these processes of change will result in global cultural homogenization or in a new order of diversity. The new may always look monolithic to the old. For the moment, in any event, all dichotomizing concepts should probably be held in suspicion, whether they be the West-rest ("Third World") split or developed-underdeveloped, modern-premodern, and so on. It is at this level that Said's critique of the discourse he calls Orientalism becomes most significant. Moreover, if all essentializing modes of thought must also be held in suspense, then we should attempt to think of cultures not as organically unified or traditionally continuous but rather as negotiated, present processes. From this standpoint Said's refusal to appeal to any authentic and especially traditional oriental realities against the false stereotypes of Orientalism is exemplary. His main concern is not with what was or even what is but with what is becoming. Although of this process he tells us very little, the fundamental question is posed: on what basis may human groups accurately (and we must also add morally) be distinguished?

The concept of culture used by anthropologists was, of course, invented by European theorists to account for the collective articulations of human diversity. Rejecting both evolutionism and the overly broad entities of race and civilization, the idea of culture posited the existence of local, functionally integrated units. For all its supposed relativism, though, the concept's model of totality, basically organic in structure, was not different from the nineteenth-century concepts it replaced. Only its plurality was new (see Chapter 10, section 2). Despite many subsequent redefinitions the notion's organicist assumptions have persisted. Cultural systems hold together; and they change more or less continuously, anchored primarily by language and place. Recent semiotic or symbolic models that conceive of culture as communication are also functionalist in this sense (see Leach 1976:1, Geertz 1973, Schneider 1968).[4]

A submerged but crucial emphasis of Said's study is his restless suspicion of totality. His critique of Orientalist procedures for enclosing and characterizing "the Orient" may be applied to the presumably more precise and even "natural" entity of culture. I have already noted with the example of Massignon Said's distaste for the most sympathetic appeals to

---

4. Geertz offers a striking and problematical image of cultural organization not as a spider or a pile of sand but as an octopus "whose tentacles are in a large part separately integrated, neurally quite poorly connected with one another and with what in the octopus passes for a brain, and yet who nonetheless manages to get around and to preserve himself, for a while anyway, as a viable, if somewhat ungainly entity" (1973:407–408). Culture remains, barely, an organism.

tradition. Having stressed so thoroughly that the Orient is a constituted entity, he goes on to suggest "that the notion that there are geographical spaces with indigenous, radically 'different' inhabitants who can be defined on the basis of some religion, culture or racial essence proper to that geographical space is equally a highly debatable idea" (1978a:332). In his final pages he asks the most important theoretical questions of his study. "How does one *represent* other cultures? Is the notion of a distinct culture (or race, or religion, or civilization) a useful one?" (p. 325).

Such questions need to be posed and need to be allowed to stand in sharp relief. Having asked them, one does well to avoid quick recourses to alternate totalities. (As we have seen, Said himself has recourse to humanist cosmopolitanism and conceptions of personal integrity as well as to a notion of authentic development alternately glossed as "narrative" or as a vaguely Marxist "history.") It is high time that cultural and social totalities are subjected to the kind of radical questioning that textual ensembles have undergone in recent critical practice (for example Derrida 1970; Barthes 1977; Said 1978b and 1975). Said's attack on essences and oppositional distinctions is here very much to the point; but collectively constituted *difference* is not necessarily static or positionally dichotomous in the manner of Orientalism as Said describes it. There is no need to discard theoretically all conceptions of "cultural" difference, especially once this is seen as not simply received from tradition, language, or environment but also as *made* in new political-cultural conditions of global relationality.

How are these new conditions to be conceived now that the "silence" of the Orient is broken; now that ethnography, as Leiris suggested, can be multidirectional; now that authenticity, both personal and cultural, is seen as something constructed vis-à-vis others? In these circumstances should our ideas of relationality be drawn from the metaphors of conversation, hospitality, and exchange, as humanists such as Massignon, Sylvain Lévi, and Mauss have urged? Or must we prefer the figures of military maneuver sometimes invoked by Foucault. It may be true that the culture concept has served its time. Perhaps, following Foucault, it should be replaced by a vision of powerful discursive formations globally and strategically deployed. Such entities would at least no longer be closely tied to notions of organic unity, traditional continuity, and the enduring grounds of language and locale. But however the culture concept is finally transcended, it should, I think, be replaced by some set of relations that preserves the concept's differential and relativist functions and that avoids the positing of cosmopolitan essences and human common denominators.

It should be pointed out that these prescriptions are in the nature of what Conrad urged in *Heart of Darkness*—a "deliberate belief." The planet's cultural future may indeed reside in the entropy Lévi-Strauss laments in *Tristes tropiques* or in the ideological hegemony Said portrays in his bleaker passages (1978a:323–325). Like Said's commitment to the human, any residual faith in culture—that is, in the continuing ability of groups to make a real difference—is essentially an idealistic choice, a political response to the present age in which, as Conrad wrote, "we are camped like bewildered travellers in a garish, unrestful hotel" (19:11:1). It is the virtue of *Orientalism* that it obliges its readers to confront such issues at once personally, theoretically, and politically. For its author, as for Conrad, there can be no natural solutions. Palestine is perhaps the twentieth century's Poland, a dismembered nation to be reinvented. Said, like the Polish-English writer whom he admires and frequently quotes, recognizes that personal and cultural identities are never given but must be negotiated. This is an important emphasis of Said's first book, a penetrating study of Conrad (1966). It would be wrong to dismiss this kind of situation as aberrant, as the condition of exiles. The unrestful predicament of *Orientalism,* its methodological ambivalences, are characteristic of an increasingly general global experience.

Its author's complex critical posture may in this sense be taken as representative. A Palestinian nationalist educated in Egypt and the United States, a scholar deeply imbued with the European humanities and now professor of English and comparative literature at Columbia, Said writes as an "oriental," but only to dissolve the cateogry. He writes as a Palestinian but takes no support from a specifically Palestinian culture or identity, turning to European poets for his expression of essential values and to French philosophy for his analytical tools. A radical critic of a major component of the Western cultural tradition, Said derives most of his standards from that tradition. The point in saying this is to suggest something of the situation within which books such as *Orientalism* must inevitably be written. It is a context that Said has elsewhere (in discussing George Eliot and the roots of Zionism) called "a generalized condition of homelessness" (1979:18). Such a situation generates difficult questions.

What does it mean, at the end of the twentieth century, to speak like Aimé Césaire of a "native land"? What processes rather than essences are involved in present experiences of cultural identity? What does it mean to write *as* a Palestinian? *As* an American? *As* a Papua–New Guinean? *As* a European? From what discrete sets of cultural resources does any modern writer construct his or her discourse? To what world audience (and in what language) are these discourses most generally addressed? Must the intellectual at least, in a literate global situation, construct a native land by writing like Césaire the notebook of a return?

Lo, a people dwelling alone, and not reckoning itself among the nations! —NUMBERS 23:9

12. Identity in Mashpee

IN AUGUST 1976 the Mashpee Wampanoag Tribal Council, Inc., sued in federal court for possession of about 16,000 acres of land constituting three-quarters of Mashpee, "Cape Cod's Indian Town." (The township of Mashpee extends inland from the Cape's southern shore, facing Martha's Vineyard, between Falmouth and Barnstable.) An unprecedented trial ensued whose purpose was not to settle the question of land ownership but rather to determine whether the group calling itself the Mashpee Tribe was in fact an Indian tribe, and the same tribe that in the mid-nineteenth century had lost its lands through a series of contested legislative acts.

The Mashpee suit was one of a group of land-claim actions filed in the late 1960s and 1970s, a relatively favorable period for redress of Native American grievances in the courts. Other claims were being initiated by the Gay Head Wampanoag Tribe on Martha's Vineyard; the Narragansets of Charlestown, Rhode Island; Western Pequots, Schaghticokes, and Mohegans in Connecticut; and Oneidas, St. Regis Mohawks, and Cayugas in New York. The Mashpee action was similar in conception to a much-publicized suit by the Passamaquoddy and Penobscot tribes laying claim to a large portion of the state of Maine. Their suit, after initial successes in Federal District Court, direct intervention from President Jimmy Carter, and five years of hard negotiation, resulted in a favorable out-of-court settlement. The tribes received $81.5 million and the authority to acquire 300,000 acres with Indian Country status.

The legal basis of the Penobscot-Passamaquoddy suit, as conceived by their attorney, Thomas Tureen, was the Non-Intercourse Act of 1790. This paternalist legislation, designed to protect tribal groups from spoliation by unscrupulous whites, declared that alienation of Indian lands could be legally accomplished only with permission of Congress. The act had never been rescinded, although throughout the nineteenth century it was often honored in the breach. When in the 1970s Indian groups appealed to the Non-Intercourse Act, they were attempting, in effect, to reverse more than a century of attacks on Indian lands. The alienations had been particularly severe for eastern groups, whose claim to collective land was often unclear. When court decisions confirmed that the Non-Intercourse Act applied to nonreservation Indians, the way was opened for suits, like those of the Maine tribes, claiming that nearly two centuries of Indian land transfers, even ordinary purchases, were invalid since they had been made without permission of Congress.

Although the Mashpee claim was similar to the Maine Indians', there were crucial differences. The Passamaquoddy and Penobscot were generally recognized Indian tribes with distinct communities and clear aboriginal roots in the area. The Mashpee plaintiffs represented most of the nonwhite inhabitants of what, for over three centuries, had been known as an "Indian town" on Cape Cod; but their institutions of tribal governance had long been elusive, especially during the century and a half preceeding the suit. Moreover, since about 1800 the Massachuset language had ceased to be commonly spoken in Mashpee. The town was at first largely Presbyterian then Baptist in its public religion. Over the centuries inhabitants had intermarried with other Indian groups, whites, blacks, Hessian deserters from the British Army during the Revolutionary War, Cape Verde islanders. The inhabitants of Mashpee were active in the economy and society of modern Massachusetts. They were businessmen, schoolteachers, fishermen, domestic workers, small contractors. Could these people of Indian ancestry file suit as the Mashpee Tribe that had, they claimed, been despoiled of collectively held lands during the mid-nineteenth century? This was the question a federal judge posed to a Boston jury. Only if they answered yes could the matter proceed to a land-claim trial.

The forty-one days of testimony that unfolded in Federal District Court during the late fall of 1977 bore the name *Mashpee Tribe v. New Seabury et al.*, shorthand for a complex, multipartied dispute. Mashpee Tribe referred to the plaintiffs, the Mashpee Wampanoag Tribal Council, Inc., described by its members as an arm of the Mashpee Tribe. A team of lawyers from the Native American Rights Fund, a nonprofit advocacy group, prepared their suit. Its chief architects were Thomas Tureen and Barry Margolin. In court the plaintiffs' case was argued by the trial lawyer Lawrence Shubow, with assistance from Tureen, Margolin, Ann Gilmore, and Moshe Genauer. New Seabury et al. referred to the New Seabury Corporation (a large development company), the Town of Mashpee (representing over a hundred individual landowners), and various other classes of defendant (insurance companies, businesses, property owners). The case for the defense was argued by James St. Clair (Richard Nixon's Watergate attorney) of the large Boston firm Hale and Dorr, and Allan Van Gestel of Goodwin, Proctor, and Hoar. They were assisted by a team of eight other lawyers.

The presence of the Town of Mashpee among the defendants requires explanation. It was not until 1869 that the community living in Mashpee was accorded formal township status. From 1869 until 1964 the town government was overwhelmingly in the hands of Indians. During this period every selectman but one was an Indian or married to an Indian. Genealogical evidence presented at the trial showed that the families of town officers were closely interrelated. No one contested the fact that before the 1960s Mashpee was governed by Indians. The disagreement was over whether they governed as an "Indian tribe."

This basic demographic and political situation, which had not altered drastically for over three centuries, was revolutionized during the early 1960s. Before then census figures showed a population in Mashpee fluctuating in the neighborhood of 350 Indians and "negroes," "coloreds," or "mulattoes" (the official categories shifted), and 100 or fewer whites. A reliable count of 1859, which served as a benchmark in the trial, listed only one white resident. After 1960 for the first time whites were recorded in the majority, and by 1970 whites outnumbered Indians and other people of color by 982 to 306. By 1968 two of the town's selectmen were whites, the third Indian. This proportion was in effect at the time of the lawsuit. Mashpee's white selectmen voted that the town should legally represent the non-Indian majority of property holders who were threatened by the land claim.

"Cape Cod's Indian Town" had finally been discovered. For centu-

ries a backwater and a curiosity, in the 1950s and 1960s Mashpee became desirable as a site for retirement, vacation homes, condominiums,
and luxury developments. Fast roads now made it accessible as a bedroom and weekend suburb of Boston. The new influx of money and jobs
was first welcomed by many of Mashpee's Indian residents, including
some of the leaders of the land-claim suit. They took advantage of the
new situation. The town government, still run by Indians, enjoyed a
surge in tax revenues. But when local government passed out of Indian
control, perhaps for good, and as the scale of development increased,
many Indians began to feel qualms. What they had taken for granted—
that this was their town—no longer held true. Large tracts of undeveloped land formerly open for hunting and fishing were suddenly ringed
with "No Trespassing" signs. The New Seabury development, on a
choice stretch of coastline, with its two golf courses and expansionist
plans, seemed particularly egregious. Tensions between traditional residents and newcomers increased, finally leading to the suit, filed with the
support of most, but not all, of the Indians in Mashpee. The land claim,
while focusing on a loss of property in the nineteenth century, was actually an attempt to regain control of a town that had slipped from Indian
hands very recently.

Earl Mills

*Earl Mills has taught high school in the Falmouth Public School sys-
tem for over twenty-five years.[1] Between 1952 and 1967 he lived in Falmouth, ten miles from Mashpee. Mills has taught physical education,
health, and social studies. He advises the student council and directs
various other extracurricular activities.*

*In Mashpee he shares ownership of the town's best restaurant with
his ex-wife, Shirley. He is its principal cook.*

*Since the mid-fifties Mills has held the title of Chief Flying Eagle of
the Mashpee Wampanoag Tribe.*

*On the witness stand he is earnest, engaging, very much the coach
or Boy Scout leader. Forty-eight years old, trim, athletic-looking, he
wears a striped necktie, blue blazer, loafers.*

Mills recalls his youth in Mashpee during the thirties and forties. He

---

1. The descriptions of persons and places date from the fall of 1977. Readers
should bear in mind that individuals' lives have changed since then, as have
aspects of the situation in Mashpee.

was never as good a hunter as his brother, Elwood, so he often skipped the frequent hunting trips. Early on he asked questions and read books. He questioned his grandmother, "the strong arm" behind his uncle (who had held the formal title of chief and was "a drifter"), and also his mother, the treasurer and tax collector of the town, "the strong arm behind me."

In the thirties, Mills recalls, some townspeople wore regalia occasionally, and a few spoke a little Indian dialect. He remembers the festive atmosphere of a close community—selling corn at town meetings, the yearly beach outings, the annual herring run.

As a child he was shown the location of "Indian taverns." These were not drinking places, according to Mills, but just places where paths crossed. You would pick up a stick, spit on it, and throw it on a heap to appease spirits in the area.

Mills says he can still identify two "Indian taverns," but most have long since been cleared away because the sticks, piled high, were a fire hazard.

This is the extent of the Indian rituals Mills reports. Raised a Baptist, he does not now consider himself a Christian; but he believes in a creator, "something greater than me."

Mills says that when he inquired after Indian artifacts, especially the traditional Mashpee plaited baskets, he was told by his father that "those fellows up around Cambridge must've taken them" (a reference probably to the Harvard Anthropology Department). His father showed him how to plait bark baskets, a skill he had acquired as a young man from Eben Queppish, a master basket maker in Mashpee.

Mills recalls that as a boy he made fun of the old-timers, including the medicine man of the period, William James.

In Falmouth High School Mills excelled in athletics. ("You had to be a scrapper to make it.") Sports were a road to confidence in a threatening environment. Outside of school, like his father and other Mashpee Indians, he served as a guide for hunting and fishing parties in the region.

Q.: "How was your youth different from that of any small-town youth?"

A.: "We were different. We knew we were different. We were told we were different."

Only in the late forties did Mills learn Indian dancing—in the army. On a lonely evening during basic training at Fort Dix two comrades, a Montana Chippewa and a New York Iroquois, performed their dances. Mills was chagrined to admit that he knew none himself.

Earl Mills tells about his five children—four by his first wife, who is part Navajo, and one by his second wife, who is Caucasian. The eldest, Roxanne, is married to a Choctaw. Earl Jr. (called "Chiefy") lives in Falmouth and in recent years has become a champion drummer at various Indian gatherings and powwows. Shelly, also a fine drummer, attends Native American festivals all over the Northeast. Robert lives on Commonwealth Avenue in Boston. "He's into quill work, leather work, skins." Nancy, the child of Mills's second marriage, is now six years old. She does Indian dances. Her parents agree that she is a Wampanoag.

Mills explains his duties as tribal chief. He teaches beadwork, leatherwork, and basketry in Mashpee. Overall his job is to be a mediator, to keep his people "on balance."

Under questioning he cannot or will not give any specific examples of his mediations. Mills tells how in the late fifties and early sixties he and three whites formed a committee to restore the Old Indian Meeting House in Mashpee. The meeting house, which had fallen into disrepair, had for many years been the most visible symbol of Indian life in the town.

During the fifties there had been a tribal constitution of some sort (the document is introduced into evidence), but Mills testifies that the tribe did not follow the constitution as written. Tribal meetings were held irregularly, with notice passed by word of mouth. (Where, St. Clair asks on cross-examination, are the minutes for these purported tribal meetings?)

In the early seventies, Mills says, he attended a grant-writing seminar at Dartmouth College, along with Amelia Bingham, a state employee (sister of John Peters, the tribal medicine man, and Russell Peters, chairman of the Tribal Council, Inc.). Mills says he had little originally to do with the land suit. As chief he simply approved the action of the incorporated body on behalf of the tribe. It was discussed in his restaurant kitchen.

Earl Mills testifies that he respects John Peters. The two of them represent the Mashpee traditionalist wing. The modernists, he says, people like Russell Peters, are the legal arm of the tribe and represent its interests in dealings with the government, the courts, and foundations.

St. Clair's questions portray Chief Flying Eagle as an opportunist following rather than leading his people. They reveal that Mills's traditional authority was recently challenged by Russell Peters and others who wanted to sell beer at the annual Mashpee powwow, a festival attended by a considerable number of tourists and other outsiders. Over the chief's *objections beer was sold. St. Clair harps on this evidence of lack of leadership. Rebuttals follow, concerning different tribal responsibilities and roles. There are references to President Carter's inability to control the (beer-related) behavior of his brother, Billy.*

On the stand Chief Flying Eagle often sounds like a social studies teacher; his speech is larded with pat anecdotes and homilies.

Only once, toward the end of his testimony, does he do something unexpected. Asked whether he often wears Indian regalia, Mills answers no, only at powwows. Then he suddenly tugs at his necktie, pulling two thin strings of beads from under his shirt. One, he says, is turquoise, from the Southwest. The other small strand was a gift from his father.

Many people in the courtroom are surprised by this apparently spontaneous revelation—surprised and, as Mills stuffs the beads back into his shirt and fumbles to readjust his tie, a little embarrassed.

Images

At the end of the trial Federal Judge Walter J. Skinner posed a number of specific questions to the jurors concerning tribal status at certain dates in Mashpee history; but throughout the proceedings broader questions of Indian identity and power permeated the courtroom. Although the land claim was formally not at issue, the lawyers for New Seabury et al. sometimes seemed to be playing on a new nightmare. At the door of your suburban house a stranger in a business suit appears. He says he is a Native American. Your land has been illegally acquired generations ago, and you must relinquish your home. The stranger refers you to his lawyer.

Such fears, the threat of a "giveaway" of private lands, were much exploited by politicians and the press in the Penobscot-Passamaquoddy negotiations. Actually small holdings by private citizens were never in danger; only large tracts of undeveloped land held by timber companies and the state were in question. In Mashpee the plaintiffs reduced their claim to eleven thousand acres, formally excluding all private homes and lots up to an acre in size. Large-scale development, not small ownership, was manifestly the target; but their opponents refused pretrial compromises and the kinds of negotiation that had led to settlement of the Maine dispute.

According to Thomas Tureen the sorts of land claims pursued in Maine, Mashpee, Gay Head, and Charlestown were always drastically circumscribed. At that historical moment the courts were relatively open to Native American claims, a situation unlikely to last. In a decision of 1985 permitting Oneida, Mohawk, and Cayuga Non-Intercourse Act suits the Supreme Court made it abundantly clear, in Tureen's words, "that Indians are dealing with the magnanimity of a rich and powerful nation, one that is not about to divest itself or its non-Indian citizens of large acreage in the name of its own laws. In short, the United States will permit Indians a measure of recompense through the law—indeed, it has done so to an extent far greater than any other nation in a comparable situation—but it ultimately makes the rules and arbitrates the game (Tureen 1985:147; also Barsh and Henderson 1980:289–293).

Seen in this light, the Mashpee trial was simply a clarification of the rules in an ongoing struggle between parties of greatly unequal power. But beneath the explicit fear of white citizens losing their homes because of an obscure past injustice, a troubling uncertainty was finding its way into the dominant image of Indians in America. The plaintiffs in the Non-Intercourse Act suits had power. In Maine politicians lost office over the issue, and the Mashpee case made national headlines for several months. Scandalously, it now paid to be Indian. Acting aggressively, tribal groups were doing sophisticated, "nontraditional" things. All over the country they were becoming involved in a variety of businesses, some claiming exemption from state regulation. To many whites it was comprehensible for Northwest Coast tribes to demand traditional salmon-fishing privileges; but for tribes to run high-stakes bingo games in violation of state laws was not.

Indians had long filled a pathetic imaginative space for the dominant culture; they were always survivors, noble or wretched. Their cultures had been steadily eroding, at best hanging on in museumlike reservations. Native American societies could not by defnition be dynamic, inventive, or expansive. Indians were lovingly remembered in Edward Curtis' sepia photographs as proud, beautiful, and "vanishing." But Curtis, we now know, carried props, costumes, and wigs, frequently dressing up his models. The image he recorded was carefully staged (Lyman 1982). In Boston Federal Court a jury of white citizens would be confronted by a collection of highly ambiguous images. Could a group of four women and eight men (no minorities) be made to believe in the persistent "Indian" existence of the Mashpee plaintiffs without costumes and props? This question surrounded and infused the trial's technical focus on whether a particular form of political-cultural organization called a tribe had existed continuously in Mashpee since the sixteenth century.

The image of Mashpee Indians, like that of several other eastern groups such as the Lumbee and the Ramapough, was complicated by issues of race (Blu 1980; Cohen 1974). Significant intermarriage with blacks had occurred since the mid-eighteenth century, and the Mashpee were, at times, widely identified as "colored." In court the defense occasionally suggested that they were really blacks rather than Native Americans. Like the Lumbee (and, less successfully, the Ramapough) the Mashpee plaintiffs had struggled to distinguish themselves from other minorities and ethnic groups, asserting tribal status based on a distinctive political-cultural history. In court they were not helped by the fact that few of them looked strongly "Indian." Some could pass for black, others for white.

Hazel Oakley, Hannah Averett

Mrs. Oakley is membership chairman of the tribe; Mrs. Averett, who is an active member of the Mashpee Baptist Church, works with Indian children in the public schools.

These women wear no Indian jewelry. They speak simply with New England accents about their childhood experiences, their values, their parents and grandparents.

They look like what they are: ordinary pillars of the community, churchwomen.

They describe their activities on behalf of the tribe. Mrs. Oakley has recently been establishing a membership list. It includes people living out of town as well as Indians who oppose the suit and who will testify for the defense in court.

Mrs. Averett looks to be in her fifties. She says that her earliest memories of community life in Mashpee were the powwows. She also recalls regular Sunday school picnics at a place called Daniel's Island, attended by Mashpee Wampanoags and their children. They played games and sang hymns. Her mother, grandfather, and relatives in the town told her Indian legends and stories—about Granny Squanett and Mausop and one about "some Indian maiden that swam in the lake with the trout."

English was spoken in the family, but Mrs. Averett recalls that some of her older relatives knew "Wampanoag language." The only time she heard her grandfather speak the old tongue was once when his mother was sick and he held a long conversation with her in her room. Mrs. Averett's mother said to him, "Dad, why didn't you tell me you could speak Indian?" When he made no reply, Hannah asked, "Grandpa, why

*didn't you tell us you could speak Indian? Why didn't you teach us?" He
said, "I just want my children to learn the English language and learn it
as well as they can."*

*Mrs. Averett recalls her mother's herbal remedies—teas and cough
medicines, skunk grease rubbed on for a chest cold—some of which she
still uses.*

*Mrs. Averett has done housework for a living since she was a girl.
During the war years, however, she went to New Bedford to do defense
work in a Goodyear plant, then to the Boston Naval Yard, where she was
a rope maker. From there she went to the Hood Rubber company, did a
few years in Boston shoe factories, and then went back to housework. In
1952 she married William Averett. He died in 1958, and she returned to
Mashpee. "I had two sons to bring up. I felt I could do it better down
there. I felt that if anything should happen to me, my people were there.
If I needed help, my people would be there to help me."*

*Three years ago Mrs. Averett joined the Mashpee Wampanoag Tribal
Council, Inc., and became active in federally funded Indian education
programs. She testifies that the immediate motivation for her involvement
came from her youngest son. He used to take walks in the woods after
school—she didn't know where. "One day he came in and he asked me,
he said, 'Why don't you do something about this?'" He explained that he
often went to a favorite spot where deer grazed. "He said, 'It was the
most beautiful sight you could ever see. Now they're putting up a golf
link, and I'll never see it again.'"*

*Since 1974 Mrs. Averett has been chairperson of the Indian Educa-
tion Parent Committee, a federally funded Indian education program to
help Mashpee Wampanoag children in the schools. The committee organizes tutoring, arts and crafts programs, local and general Indian history classes, sessions with Chief Mills and Medicine Man Peters, visits
from other native groups, field trips to the United Nations in New York,
to the Museum of the American Indian, to historic sites in Gay Head.
"This is to expand the culture of our people, to see how other tribes, other
people live."*

*Mrs. Averett is also chairperson of the board of trustees of the Mash-
pee Baptist Church.*

*On cross-examination she is asked about possible inconsistencies in
her claim to Indian identity: You don't eat much Indian food, do you?
Only sometimes. You use regular doctors, don't you? Yes, and herbs as
well.*

How do you know your ancestors? My mother, grandparents, word of mouth. Have you traced your ancestry? Did you use the 1859 census? (introduced as evidence at the trial). What about being a devout Baptist and an Indian?

Mrs. Averett testifies that she respects the medicine man, John Peters (calling him a "counselor"). She respects Indian beliefs: the Great Spirit, the land, "grandmother moon and the earth and all those things . . . They are very dear to me, and I respect them. But I also respect God through my Christian belief. And to me God and the Great Spirit are the same."

She has recently received an Indian name, Bright Star, from the medicine man. She isn't sure she is allowed to go into details about her naming ceremony: there is a prayer, a circle formed. "Everything is round, as our lives."

She likes to see drumming and dancing being taught to today's children. They do it the way other kids skip rope.

Outside the courtroom during a recess some of the Mashpee women talk fondly about their children's Indian activities. "But he's got to cut that hair!" "If only they took care of it, but, you know . . ." "He looks like a wild man!"

The Sea

Ramona Peters is a college-educated woman in her twenties. After participating in a training program at the Children's Museum in Boston, she has recently returned to Mashpee, where she teaches classes in Indian language and lore. During her testimony she relates a myth about a giant who swims over to the Wampanoag tribe at Gay Head on Martha's Vineyard. On his return the giant turns into Moby Dick, the great white whale.

(I suddenly realize that the Indians in this courtroom are descendants of Tashtego, the Gay Head harpooner of Melville's Pequod. This connection somehow gives everything a strange reality and depth grafted now onto my own literary mythology.)

A good deal of testimony at the trial concerns Cape Cod Indians' closeness to the sea—long traditions of shellfishing and work on whaling vessels in the nineteenth century. Vernon Pocknett, an activist and *nephew of Mabel Avant, the town's leading traditionalist and historian during the forties and fifties, tells of a federal CETA program Title 3 grant to encourage modern aqua-farming by Mashpee Indians.*

Would the jury see aqua-farming as a "traditional" activity?

Borderlines

Mashpee Indians suffered the fate of many small Native American groups who remained in the original thirteen states. They were not accorded the reservations and sovereign status (steadily eroded) of tribes west of the Mississippi. Certain of the eastern communities, such as the Seneca and the Seminoles, occupied generally recognized tribal lands. Others—the Lumbee, for example—possessed no collective lands but clustered in discrete regions, maintaining kinship ties, traditions, and sporadic tribal institutions. In all cases the boundaries of the community were permeable. There was intermarriage and routine migration in and out of the tribal center—sometimes seasonal, sometimes longer term. Aboriginal languages were much diminished, often entirely lost. Religious life was diverse—sometimes Christian (with a distinctive twist), sometimes a transformed tradition such as the Iroquois Longhouse Religion. Moral and spiritual values were often Native American amalgams compounded from both local traditions and pan-Indian sources. For example the ritual and regalia at New England powwows now reflect Sioux and other western tribal influences; in the 1920s the feathered "war bonnet" made its appearance among Wampanoag leaders. Eastern Indians generally lived in closer proximity to white (or black) society and in smaller groups than their western reservation counterparts. In the face of intense pressure some eastern communities have managed to acquire official federal recognition as tribes, others not. During the past two decades the rate of applications has risen dramatically.

Within this diversity of local histories and institutional arrangements the long-term residents of Mashpee occupied a gray area, at least in the eyes of the surrounding society and the law. The Indian identity of the Penobscot and Passamaquoddy was never seriously challenged, even though they had not been federally recognized and had lost or adapted many of their traditions. The Mashpee were more problematic. Partisans of their land claim, such as Paul Brodeur (1985), tend to accept without question the right of the tribal council, incorporated in 1974, to sue on behalf of a group that had lost its lands in the mid-nineteenth century.

They see the question of tribal status as a legal red herring, or worse, a calculated ploy to deny the tribe its birthright. However procrustian and colonial in origin the legal definition of tribe, there was nonetheless a real issue at stake in the trial. Although tribal status and Indian identity have long been vague and politically constituted, not just anyone with some native blood or claim to adoption or shared tradition can be an Indian; and not just any Native American group can decide to be a tribe and sue for lost collective lands.

Indians in Mashpee owned no tribal lands (other than fifty-five acres acquired just before the trial). They had no surviving language, no clearly distinct religion, no blatant political structure. Their kinship was much diluted. Yet they did have a place and a reputation. For centuries Mashpee had been recognized as an Indian town. Its boundaries had not changed since 1665, when the land was formally deeded to a group called the South Sea Indians by the neighboring leaders Tookonchasun and Weepquish. The Mashpee plaintiffs of 1977 could offer as evidence surviving pieces of Native American tradition and political structures that seemed to have come and gone. They could also point to a sporadic history of Indian revivals continuing into the present.

The Mashpee were a borderline case. In the course of their peculiar litigation certain underlying structures governing the recognition of identity and difference became visible. Looked at one way, they were Indian; seen another way, they were not. Powerful *ways of looking* thus became inescapably problematic. The trial was less a search for the facts of Mashpee Indian culture and history than it was an experiment in translation, part of a long historical conflict and negotiation of "Indian" and "American" identities.

⼂

(This is how I came to see the Mashpee case, and the account I give of it reflects my way of seeing. As a historian and critic of anthropology I tend to focus on the ways in which historical stories are told, on the alternate cultural models that have been applied to human groups. Who speaks for cultural authenticity? How is collective identity and difference represented? How do people define themselves with, over, and in spite of others? What are the changing local and world historical conditions determining these processes?

At the Mashpee trial these were the kinds of questions that interested me and that now organize my account. I am not fictionalizing or inventing anything, nor am I presenting the whole picture. The reality presented here is the reality of a specific interest and field of vision.

I attended most of the trial, and I've used my courtroom notes as a guiding thread. I've read what has been published about the history of Mashpee and the litigation, notably Francis Hutchins' *Mashpee: The Story of Cape Cod's Indian Town* (1979), Paul Brodeur's *Restitution: The Land Claims of the Mashpee, Passamaquoddy, and Penobscot Indians of New England* (1985), and William Simmons' *Spirit of the New England Tribes* (1986). I've had access to Rona Sue Mazur's Ph.D. thesis in anthropology at Columbia University, "Town and Tribe in Conflict: A Study of Local-Level Politics in Mashpee, Massachusetts" (1980). And I have consulted the trial record. But I haven't systematically interviewed participants or done firsthand research in the archives or in Mashpee.

It should be clear from what follows that I am portraying primarily the trial, not the complex lives of Indians and other ethnic groups in Mashpee. Still, in the process I make strong gestures toward truths missed by the dominant categories and stories in the courtroom. Thus I invoke as an absence the reality of Mashpee and particularly of its Indian lives. I do this to maintain the historical and ethnographic seriousness of the account, a seriousness I wish both to assert and to limit.

I accept the fact that my version of the trial, its witnesses, and its stories may offend people on several sides of the issue. Many individual positions are more complex than I have been able to show. My account may be objectionable to Native Americans for whom culture and tradition are continuities, not inventions, who feel stronger, less compromised ties to aboriginal sources than my analysis allows. For them this version of "identity in Mashpee" may be about rootless people like me, not them.

It is, and is not only, that.

When I report on witnesses at the trial, the impressions are mine. Others I spoke with saw things differently. The trial record—which stenographically preserves, by a precise but not infallible technique, the meaningful, spoken sounds of the trial—provides a check on my impressions. It does not, of course, provide much information on the *effect* of witnesses or events in the courtroom. It omits gestures, hesitations, clothing, tone of voice, laughter, irony . . . the sometimes devastating silences.

I offer vignettes of persons and events in the courtroom that are obviously composed and condensed. Testimony evoked in a page or two may run to hundreds of pages in the transcript. Some witnesses were on the stand for several days. Moreover, real testimony almost never ends the way my vignettes do; it trails off in the quibbles and corrections of redirect and recross-examination. While I have included for comparison a verbatim excerpt from the transcript, I have generally followed my courtroom notes, checked against the record, and have not hesitated to rearrange, select, and highlight. Where quotation marks appear, the statement is a fairly exact quotation; the rest is paraphrase.

Overall, if the witnesses seem flat and somewhat elusive, the effect is intentional. Using the usual rhetorical techniques, I could have given a more intimate sense of peoples' personalities or of what they were really trying to express; but I have preferred to keep my distance. A courtroom is more like a theater than a confessional.

Mistrustful of transparent accounts, I want mine to manifest some of its frames and angles, its wavelengths.)

John Peters

Peters is about fifty years old. He wears a sport jacket with a turtleneck sweater. He is graying, dignified, and appears somewhat taciturn. He speaks with broad New England vowels.

Peters is medicine man of the Mashpee Wampanoag Tribe.

He testifies that whereas he and Earl Mills, Chief Flying Eagle, are leaders of the tribe, they are not alone. All elders are leaders. Women are leaders: Mary Lopez, Hannah Averett ("in the education field"), Mrs. Mills (Earl Mills's mother), Hazel Oakley.

He describes a growing interest in Native American religion. Asked about traditional rituals in Mashpee, he recalls participating in the peace pipe ceremony, offerings to the Great Spirit, "for as long as I can remember."

Newpaper notices from 1936 are introduced as evidence. They report tribal meetings and "Indian Day" services at the Old Indian Meeting House. Peters remembers these services. He and his father were in the choir. Reverend Redfield (the Baptist minister) and William James (the medicine man) both participated. Christian hymns were sung. The peace pipe was smoked.

Peters tells of his youth and training as a medicine man. There were no specific ceremonies or rites of passage. An old man, Russell Mingo, talked at Saturday dinners about Indian matters. "We kids didn't under-

stand." In his late teens Peters approached William James with questions, and he learned "things about Mother Earth." Neither James nor his parents ever spelled much out. "A medicine man doesn't force things on you."

Peters is a strong, understated presence. Also a savvy witness. Under cross-examination he pauses for a long time after hostile or baited questions. Often he slowly repeats the question before answering, turning it over in public view.

Peters recalls his school days. The Mashpee were called "thieving Indians" or "Womps" (from Wampanoag). The latter was not always pejorative, he adds. The school basketball team was called the Womps, the cheerleaders the Wompettes.

On cross-examination Peters is reminded that the traditional ceremony "Indian Day" was proclaimed by the governor of Massachusetts, who was not an Indian. Reverend Redfield was not an Indian either. And smoking the peace pipe was not limited to Indians. The Mashpee parish and the Old Mashpee Meeting House Corporation all depended on non-Indian participants. How can he claim, as he does, that they are "arms of the Mashpee Tribe"?

Q.: What does it take to be a member of the Mashpee Tribe? A.: Tracing ancestry back to your great-grandfather or great-grandmother. How do you know? We know each other. Who was your great-grandmother? (Peters cannot recall her first name.) Was she an Indian? Yes. Have you traced this specifically? No. Who was your great-grandfather? Charles Peters. Wasn't he a preaching Indian from Martha's Vineyard? Yes. Not a Mashpee Wampanoag Indian? No.

Peters is asked about the years he has lived away from Mashpee while still serving as medicine man. In 1964 he worked for more than a year in Hawaii as a private detective. Between 1973 and 1976 he was based on Nantucket. He testifies that from the latter residence he was able to stay in touch. He employed Mashpee people in his various business ventures.

With a brother and nephew he is currently part owner of Peters Fuel Oil. The concern owns two trucks and does a moderate business. Q.: This is a private, not a communal tribal business? A.: Yes.

Peters testifies about a land-development plan proposed some years back by a company he founded with various family members, the Ashers Path Development Corporation. He is confronted with blueprints for the development that was submitted to the town but never carried through. The blueprints show an extensive subdivision into thirty-seven lots.

Peters is reminded of his years in business as a general contractor and of making bids on projects for the New Seabury Corporation (now a symbol to many Indians of excessive development). He is unclear about whether he has since left contracting and real estate.

When pressed on the conflict between business activities and his role as medicine man, he comments that the art of making money is probably inconsistent with being an Indian; but all Mashpee Indians make money. It depends on how you do it.

He is asked, Was what you were doing as a developer a destruction of the earth? Exactly what part of your business was consistent with Indian values? Peters offers no clear answers. But, he adds, "if I had developed that plan, I'd have been violating my principles."

Peters testfies that until recently he didn't spend enough time as medicine man counseling people. Early in his career he was much less conscientious than he is now. During the last five years he has changed "totally."

Peters is asked about current Indian religious practices in Mashpee. He can specify no customary rites at birth or at puberty. He has himself been married and divorced twice without any special Indian ceremony. He was married in a Baptist church by a white minister. Asked whether it was a typical Baptist ceremony, Peters replies that he can't say, since all Christian marriages seem the same to him.

How many "followers of traditional religion" are there now in Mashpee? Peters won't guess and questions the word followers. It's not a question of authority, he says, of leaders and followers. A person can be very religious without worshipping in a building or participating in a formal gathering.

Who are the "traditionalists" in Mashpee? It's hard to be sure. Maybe there are a hundred or so. His brother Russell (chairman of the Tribal Council, Inc.) is not a traditionalist. As for his other brothers and sisters, he hasn't formed an opinion.

Peters testifies that the Supreme Sachem, Elsworth Oakley, a Mashpee, has recently designated him Supreme Medicine Man of the Wampanoag Nation. He has passed his local duties to a young man, Skip Black. "He's been in my mind for some time."

Peters says that he and Oakley are currently helping groups of Wampanoags in New Bedford and Brockton to form tribal structures.

Q.: "Do the new tribes you're creating there have any plans to bring lawsuits?"

A.: "You mean, taking over New Bedford and Brockton?"

History I

The case against the plaintiffs was straightforward: there never had been an Indian tribe in Mashpee. The community was a creation of the colonial encounter, a collection of disparate Indians and other minorities who sought over the years to become full citizens of the Commonwealth of Massachusetts and of the Republic. Decimated by disease, converted to Christianity, desirous of freedom from paternalistic state tutelage, the people of mixed Indian descent in Mashpee were progressively assimilated into American society. Their Indian identity had been lost, over and over, since the mid-seventeenth century.[2]

The plague. When the English Pilgrims arrived at Plymouth in 1620, they found a region devastated by a disease brought by white seamen. The settlers walked into empty Indian villages and planted in already cleared fields. The region was seriously underpopulated. In the years that followed Puritan leaders like Myles Standish pressed steadily to limit Indian territories and to establish clear "properties" for the growing number of newcomers. Misunderstandings inevitably ensued: for example whites claimed to own unoccupied land that had been ceded to them for temporary use.

Richard Bourne of Sandwich, a farmer near what is now Mashpee Pond and a tenant on Indian lands, studied the language of his landlords and soon became an effective mediator between the societies. He was friendly to the area's inhabitants, remnants of earlier groups, who came to be called South Sea Indians by the settlers to the north. He believed that they needed protection; becoming their advocate, he negotiated formal title to a large tract adjoining his farm (which in the meantime he had managed to purchase). His ally in these transactions was Paupmunnuck, a leader of the nearby Cotachesset.

---

2. The two "histories" that follow represent the best brief interpretive accounts I could construct of the contending versions of Mashpee's past. They draw selectively on the expert testimony presented at the trial—testimony much too long, complex, and contested to summarize adequately. The overall shape of the two accounts reflects the summation provided at the end of the testimony by each side's principal attorney. "History I" owes a good deal to Francis Hutchins' book *Mashpee: The Story of Cape Cod's Indian Town* (1979). This book takes a somewhat more moderate position than the courtroom testimony on which it is based. "History II" owes something to the general approach of James Axtell's book *The European and the Indian* (1981). Axtell was witness for the plaintiffs.

Bourne's "South Sea Indian Plantation" was to become a refuge for Christian converts, for as white power increased, it became increasingly dangerous for Indians to live around Cape Cod unless they came together as a community of "praying Indians." Under Bourne's tutelage the Mashpee plantation was a center for the first Indian church on the Cape, organized in 1666.

Thus Mashpee was originally an artificial community, never a tribe. It was created from Indian survivors in an area between the traditional sachemdoms of Manomet and Nauset—the former centered on the present town of Bourne at the Cape's western edge, the latter near its tip.

Conversion to Christianity. Badly disorganized after the plague and confronted by a growing number of determined settlers, the Cape Cod Indians made accommodations. Live and let live was not the Puritan way, especially once their power had been consolidated. Tensions and conflicts grew, leading to war in 1675 with the forces of the Wampanoag Supreme Sachem Metacomet ("King Philip"). After Metacomet's defeat Indians who sympathized with him were expelled from their lands. Many, including some who had remained neutral, were sold into slavery.

The price for living on ancestral lands in eastern New England was cooperation with white society. The Mashpee, under Bourne's tutelage, became model Christians. By 1674 ninety Mashpee inhabitants were counted as baptized, and twenty-seven were admitted to full communion. The "praying Indians" were entering a new life. They stopped consulting "powwows" (medicine men, in seventeenth-century usage); they respected the Sabbath and other holy days, severed ties with "pagans," altered child-rearing practices, dressed in new ways, washed differently. The changes were gradual but telling. They reflected not only a tactical accommodation but also a new belief, born of defeat, that the powerful white ways must be superior. When Bourne died in 1682, his successor as Protestant minister was an Indian, Simon Popmonet, son of Bourne's old ally Paupmunnuck. This was a further sign that the Indians were willingly giving up their old ways for the new faith.

"Plantation" status. Once the South Sea Indian Plantation had been established, its inhabitants' claim to their land rested on a written deed and on English law rather than on any aboriginal sovereignty. Like other "plantations" in New England, the community at Mashpee was a joint-ownership arrangement by a group of "proprietors." Under English law proprietors were licensed to develop a vacant portion of land, reserving part for commons, part for the church, and part for individual holdings. All transfers of land were to be approved collectively. This plantation-proprietory form, as applied to early Cape Cod settlements such as Sandwich and Barnstable, was intended to evolve quickly into a township where freemen held individual private property and were represented in the General Court of the colony. The white plantations around Mashpee did evolve directly into towns. From the late seventeenth century on their common lands were converted into private individual holdings in fee simple. Mashpee followed the same course, but more slowly. As late as 1830 its lands were the joint property of proprietors.

For complex historical reasons Mashpee's progress toward full citizenship lagged almost two centuries behind that of its neighbors. An enduring prejudice against Indians and their supposed lack of "civility" certainly played a part, for during the early and mid-eighteenth century the Indian plantation was governed in humiliating ways by white "guardians." Nonetheless, development toward autonomy, while delayed, did occur. In 1763, after a direct appeal to King George III, Mashpee won the right to incorporation as a district, a step on the road to township status and a liberation from oppressive meddling by white outsiders. Then, beginning in 1834 and culminating in 1870, a series of acts of the Massachusetts legislature changed the Mashpee plantation into an incorporated town. Its inhabitants had overcome the prejudice and paternalism that had so long hemmed them in. They were now full-fledged citizens of Massachusetts.

Taking the colonists' side. From early on the Indian inhabitants of Mashpee gave signs of active identification with the new white society. During King Philip's War a certain Captain Amos, probably a Nauset from near Sandwich, led a group of Indians against Metacomet. Amos became a prominent inhabitant of Mashpee after the conflict ended. A century later the district of Mashpee sent a contingent to fight in the Revolutionary War against the British, a commitment of troops even greater than that of the surrounding white towns. Reliable accounts estimate that about half the adult male population died in the war. A Mashpee Indian, Joshua Pocknet, served at Valley Forge with George Washington. At these critical moments, therefore, the descendants of the South Sea Indians showed something more than simple acquiescence under colonial rule. Their enthusiastic patriotism strongly suggests that they had identified with white society, relinquishing any sense of a separate tribal political identity.

Intermarriage. Mashpee's population showed two significant periods of expansion. During the 1660s and 1670s there had been an influx of Indians from elsewhere on the Cape. Then after a century of relative equilibrium the population rose again in the 1760s and 1770s. Census figures are inexact and subject to interpretation, but it seems clear that before 1760 the principal newcomers were a steady trickle of New England Indians: Wampanoags from Gay Head and Herring Pond, Narragansets and Mohicans from Connecticut, Long Island Montauks. Immigration was restrained by the tutelage of outside "guardians," some of whom had an interest in keeping Mashpee small so that "unused" Indian lands could be made available for whites. After 1763, however, the newly incorporated district opened its borders to a variety of new settlers. A few whites entered by marriage but maintained a separate legal status. Their progeny, if one parent was Indian, could become proprietors. At least one white man "went native," living in a wigwam—just as the Indian residents of Mashpee were abandoning the last of theirs. Four Hessian mercenaries stayed on after the Revolutionary War and married Mashpee women. It is recorded that they accepted Indian manners.

The 1776 census counted fourteen "negroes" in a total population of 341. Significant intermarriage with freed black slaves occurred in this period, but it is difficult to say how much since common parlance, reflected in the census, sometimes mixed diverse peoples of brownish skin color in categories such as "Indian," "mulatto," or "negro." Intermarriage between blacks and Indians was encouraged by a common social marginality and by a relative shortage of men among the Indians and of women among the blacks. The local racial mix also included Cape Verde islanders and exotic imports resulting from the employment of Mashpee men in the far-flung sailing trades and women in domestic service: a Mexican and an Indian from Bombay are mentioned in the written sources.

By 1789 Mashpee's white minister, the Reverend Gideon Hawley, had become so concerned about Mashpee being overrun by blacks and foreigners that he engineered a return to plantation status, with himself as guardian of the town's threatened authenticity. This return to a restrictive paternalism was a setback for Mashpee's ability to grow and develop into a distinctive, independent nonwhite community. It was not until the 1840s, after a long conflict with Hawley's successor, the Reverend Phineas Fish, that local leaders finally rid themselves of outside tutelage. The struggle for citizenship had been slowed but not stopped. By the time of the final transition from plantation to township status in the four decades after 1830 the American citizens of Mashpee had become a complex mix—"colored" in contemporary parlance—that included several American Indian, black, and foreign ingredients.

Mashpee becomes a town. In 1834, following a popular rebellion against the outside authority of the Presbyterian minister Fish, district status was again accorded by the Massachusetts General Court. The Mashpee were no longer wards of the state and, like other towns, were governed by three elected selectmen. But full citizenship did not follow, largely because the proprietors of Mashpee wished to preserve traditional restraints on the sale of lands to outsiders. Leaders such as Daniel Amos argued that many inhabitants of Mashpee were not yet ready for the responsibilities of citizenship and unrestricted property rights. They might sell their lands irresponsibly or be maneuvered into debt; the community would be invaded and broken up. In practice the entailment on property did not seal off Mashpee from growth. To qualify as a landowner one had to trace ancestry to at least one Indian proprietor; and by the mid-nineteenth century quite a few individuals around the Cape could make this claim. In 1841–42, at the urging of Indian entrepreneurs such as Solomon Attaquin, who had returned to Mashpee with the end of state tutelage, most of the district's common lands were divided among its individual proprietors—men, women, and children. Lands could now be freely bought and sold, but still only among proprietors.

This progress did not go uncontested. Mashpee was divided among those who, like Attaquin—self-made men reflecting the era's dominant laissez-faire capitalist ethos—wanted to move quickly to remove all barriers to individual initiative and others who wanted to move more slowly or who saw in the old plantation entailments a guarantee of community integrity. In 1868 matters finally came to a head. A petition to the General Court from two of Mashpee's three selectmen and twenty-nine residents requested an end to all land-sale restrictions and the granting of full state and federal voting rights. This petition was promptly countered by a "remonstrance" signed by the third selectman and fifty-seven Mashpee residents urging that the district's status not be altered. A public hearing was called to air the differing views.

The hearing, which took place in early 1869, marks a crucial turning point in Mashpee history. Records of its disagreements offer a rare access to a diversity of local voices and opinions. Those who spoke in favor of the proposed changes evoked centuries of degrading state tutelage and second-class status. It was time, they said, for Mashpee inhabitants to be full citizens, to stand on their own. If this meant that some would fail or be displaced from their lands, so be it. They spoke also of the commercial advantages to the region of making portions of its land available for outside capital investment. Representatives of Mashpee's "colored non-proprietors" (a status that gave certain mulattoes and blacks all rights of proprietorship except title to land) also favored the changes in legal status. As valued members of the community they felt the restriction on landholding to be an insult and a reminder of an inferior condition they had in every other respect left behind.

Others opposed the changes. They argued that the influx of outside capital would be a very mixed blessing, and without the present protections many who were not wealthy and wise to the ways of business would soon be displaced. They would find themselves, in the words of one speaker, "ducking and dodging from one city to another, and gain no residence." Some proprietors did not think the right to vote in state and federal elections worth the risk; the present system, providing real control over Mashpee's government, seemed sufficient to local needs. The Reverend Joseph Amos ("Blind Joe " Amos), the community's most influential spiritual voice and leader of a successful Indian Baptist movement three decades earlier, opposed the changes. He said that another generation of preparation was needed before the proposed step could safely be taken. Solomon Attaquin, who owned the Hotel Attaquin, a renowned hunting lodge in Mashpee, spoke for abandoning the district's special status. He evoked a lifelong dream of full citizenship and equality, a dream shared with others in the community. Those who had worked long and hard for this day should not have to die without gaining the status of free men in the commonwealth and the nation.

A vote was taken. Eighteen favored participation in federal and state elections, eighteen were opposed. The removal of land restrictions was sharply rejected, twenty-six to fourteen. Despite this vote by a minority of the total population the recorded discussions clearly showed a consensus in favor of ultimately ending Mashpee's special status, with disagreements only on the timing. The Massachusetts General Court, recognizing this fact and more impressed by Mashpee's "progressive" voices, in 1870 formally abolished the status of "Mashpee proprietor." All lands were henceforth held in fee simple with no restrictions on alienation. All residents, whatever their ancestry, now enjoyed equal status before the law. The transfer of town lands to outsiders began immediately.

This turning point marked the end of Mashpee's distinctive institutional status stemming from its Indian past. Though the community was divided on the change, the most dynamic, forward-looking leaders favored it; whatever their hesitations on timing, community members willingly embraced their future as Massachusetts and United States citizens.

Assimilation. During the years between 1870 and the 1920s Indians throughout the nation were forced to abandon tribal organizations and to become individual citizen-farmers, workers, and businessmen. This was the period of the Dawes Act with its extensive land-allotment projects west of the Mississippi. Not until the twenties was there much evidence anywhere of tribal dynamism. Mashpee residents continued to live as before, working as hunting and fishing guides, servants, and laborers in various trades. The town remained a backwater. To find steady work people often had to move to nearby towns or even farther afield. The historical record contains little evidence of any distinctly Indian life in Mashpee before the Wampanoag revival movements of the twenties. The town apparently did not undergo any major demographic or social changes and remained a rather cohesive community of long-term residents, most of whom were of varying degrees of Indian descent. Significantly, between 1905 and 1960 the category "Indian" disappeared from Mashpee's federal census records. The more than two hundred individuals who had previously been so classified were now listed as either "colored" (distinct from "negro") or "other." Only in 1970 would they again be called Indian. In the eyes of the state the majority of Mashpee's inhabitants were simply Americans of color.

Some of these Americans participated in the founding of the Wampanoag Nation in the late twenties. At that time various more-or-less theatrical revivals of Indian institutions were under way. People in Mashpee showed interest, but the daily life and government of the town were not materially affected. The Wampanoags did not, like many other Indian groups in the thirties, take advantage of the turnaround in policy at John

Collier's Bureau of Indian Affairs (BIA) to reorganize themselves as a federally recognized "tribal" unit. The new sense of Indianness around Mashpee was a matter of county fairlike powwows, costumes, and folkloric dances.

The individuals of Indian ancestry from Mashpee who filed suit in 1976 were American citizens similar to Irish- or Italian-Americans with strong ethnic attachments. Individuals such as Earl Mills and John and Russell Peters had simply taken advantage of the latest wave of pan-Indian revivalism and the prospect of financial gain to constitute themselves as a Mashpee Tribe. Mashpee's distinctive history was in fact a story of Indian-Christian remnants who over the centuries had repeatedly given up their customs and sovereignty. Theirs had been a long, hard struggle for equality and respect in a multiethnic America.

Vicky M. Costa

Vicky Costa is seventeen years old; her father is Portuguese, her mother Indian. She considers herself an Indian. She looks like any American teenager.

Q.: How do you know you're an Indian? A.: My mother told me.

She speaks softly. Judge Skinner asks her to speak up so the court can hear. "Think of yourself shouting across a field to those people," indicating the jury, "over there." (The "field" is a courtroom cluttered with lawyers' tables, papers, documents, items of evidence.)

Vicky Costa does not shout, and everyone listens closely. She tells about the values she is currently learning in Mashpee: "To walk on Mother Earth in balance, and to respect every living thing."

Q.: How often do you dance? A.: All the time. Q.: When did you dance most recently? A.: Last night.

She describes her Indian dancing. She says she first learned at a powwow "a long time ago." Now she attends powwows regularly.

She names the dances: animal names, "blanket dance," "fancy dance." In the "round dance" they turn and dance to the good and bad spirit, moving in both directions so neither of the spirits will be offended. Is there music? Singing? Just the round-dance song. The purpose of the animal dances? To imitate the animals, mocking them. To thank the Creator for that animal.

(The mood in these questions and answers is conversational, quiet. Is it partly because this time Ann Gilmore of the plaintiffs' trial team is

conducting the examination? It is one of the rare moments in the trial when a woman speaks directly with another woman.. For whatever reasons the prevailing sense of contest and performance is gone.)

Costa testifies that she has been studying what she calls the "Wampanoag language" for one-and-a-half years. She says that as a girl she had to go to the Baptist church but now believes in Indian values.

On cross-examination she assents to hostile questions with the devastating American teenage shrug: "Yeah . . . yeah . . . yeah . . ."

History II

The case against the Mashpee plaintiffs was based on a reading of Cape Cod history. Documents were gathered, interpreted, and arranged in a coherent sequence. The story emerged of a small mixed community fighting for equality and citizenship while abandoning, by choice or coercion, most of its aboriginal heritage. But a different, also coherent, story was constructed by the plaintiffs, drawing on the same documentary record. In this account the residents of Mashpee had managed to keep alive a core of Indian identity over three centuries against enormous odds. They had done so in supple, sometimes surreptitious ways, always attempting to control, not reject, outside influences.

The plague. Aboriginally the concept of tribe has little meaning. The "political" institutions of Native American groups before contact with Europeans varied widely. Cape Cod Indian groupings seem to have been flexible, with significant movement across territories. Communities formed and reformed. In this context it is unclear whether the elders of local villages or sachems or supreme sachems should be identified as "tribal" leaders. These individuals had supreme power in some situations, limited authority in others. The plague was a disaster, but it did not decimate the Cape to the extent that it did the Plymouth area. In any event the response of the survivors at Mashpee, regrouping to form a cohesive unit, was a traditional political response, albeit to an unusual emergency. Written sources reflect only the views of whites, such as the evangelist Bourne, who saw his "praying Indians" paternalistically as passive remnants. The intentions of leaders such as Paupmunnuck and his kin are not recorded.

Thus it is anachronistic to say that the community gathered at what would later be called Mashpee was not a tribe. It is well known that the political institutions of many bona fide American Indian "tribes" actually emerged during the nineteenth and twentieth centuries in response to white expectations and power. Neat analytic categories such as "political organization," "kinship," "religion," and "economy" do not reflect Indian ways of seeing things. The simple fact remains that Bourne's South Sea Indian Plantation was a discrete community of Cape Cod Indians living on traditional Indian land—an arrangement that, through many modifications, survived until the mid-twentieth century.

Conversion to Christianity. Accounts of conversion as a process of "giving up old ways" or "choosing a new path" usually reflect a wishful evangelism rather than the more complex realities of cultural change, resistance, and translation. Recent ethnohistorical scholarship has tended to show that Native Americans' response to Christianity was syncretic over the long run, almost never a radical either-or choice. Moreover, in situations of drastically unequal power, as on Puritan Cape Cod, one should expect the familiar response of colonized persons: outward agreement and inner resistance.

The disruptions caused by disease, trade, and military conquest were extreme. All Indian societies had to adjust, and they developed varying strategies for doing so. Some passed through revitalization movements in the late eighteenth and early nineteenth centuries, led by messianic figures: the Delaware Prophet or Handsome Lake. These movements incorporated Christian features in a new "traditional" religion. Other groups renewed native culture by using Christianity for their own purposes. The white man's religion could be added on to traditional deities and rites. Beliefs that appeared contradictory to Puritan evangelists coexisted in daily life. Native American religions are generally more tolerant, pragmatic, and inclusive than Christianity, a strongly evangelical, exclusive faith.

This is not to say that groups such as the South Sea Indians did not embrace Christianity in good faith or find there a source of spiritual strength. It is only to caution against the either-or logic of conversion as seen by the outsiders whose accounts dominate the written record. The gain of Christian beliefs did not necessarily mean the loss of Indian spirituality. It is easy to be impressed by surface transformations of clothing and public behavior and to forget that continuous kin ties and life on a familiar piece of land also carry potent "religious" values.

Adopting Christianity in Mashpee was not merely a survival strategy in an intolerant, hostile environment. The faith of the "praying Indians" kept a distinctly indigenous cast. Beginning with Richard Bourne's successor, Simon Popmonet, Indian ministers in Mashpee preached in Massachusett, a practice that continued throughout the eighteenth century. When white missionaries were imposed from outside, they were forced to use some Massachusett or to compromise, like Gideon Hawley, who conducted bilingual services in tandem with a respected Indian pastor, Solomon Briant. Moreover, the historical record before 1850 is filled with conflict between authoritarian missionaries and Indian church members. Hawley, who served from 1757 to 1807, progressively alienated his parishioners, especially after Solomon Briant's death in 1775. His successor, Phineas Fish, lost virtually all local support and in 1840, after a protracted struggle, was physically ejected from the Old Indian Meeting House by irate Indian Christians.

Baptist revivalism had already won over most of the congregation, a change tied to a political assertion of Indian power. As in many nativist revitalization movements, an Indian outsider took a leading role—in this case William Apes, a young Pequot Baptist preacher. Blind Joe Amos had already acquired a larger following for his all-Indian Baptist meetings than the Congregationalist minister, Fish.

The situation was volatile. Apes, a firebrand with a vision of united action by "colored" peoples against white oppressors, stimulated a Masphee "Declaration of Independence" in 1833 on behalf of a sovereign Mashpee Tribe. (This was one of the few times before the twentieth century that the word *tribe* appears in the historical record.) The effect of the declaration and of the political maneuvers that ensued was to wrest control of the town's religion from the outsider Fish, reclaiming the Meeting House and funds from Harvard University supporting Indian Christianity for the majority faith, which was now Baptist. Mashpee returned to district status, free of outside governors.

Over the centuries Indians in Mashpee fought to keep control first of their Presbyterian and then their Baptist institutions. Religion was a political as well as a spiritual issue. Well into the 1950s the New England Baptist Convention habitually referred to Mashpee as "our Indian church." The exact nature of Mashpee Christian belief and practice over the centuries is obscure. The historical record does not inform us, for example, of exactly what took place in Blind Joe Amos' insurgent Baptist services during the 1830s; but even the partial written record makes it clear that Christianity in Mashpee, symbolized by the Old Indian Meeting House, was a site of local power and of resistance to outsiders. At recurring intervals it was a focus of openly Indian, or "tribal," power.

"Plantation" status. Leaders of the South Sea Indians probably recognized, with Bourne, that title to land under white law was needed if it was not to be despoiled by an aggressive colonization; but seventeenth-century English proprietory forms did not unduly restrict their ability to function as an Indian community. Collective ownership of land, with individual use rights, could be maintained. The legal status that to some appeared an impediment to progress in fact protected the traditional life ways of Indian proprietors.

Although eastern Indians were not accorded reservation lands, Mashpee's plantation status created a de facto reservation. Unlike all its neighbors Mashpee did not quickly become a town but had the status forced on it in 1869. The plantation was widely considered to be Indian land held collectively in a distinctive manner. The reasons for keeping Mashpee "backward," a pupil of the state, were often racist and paternalist; but from the viewpoint of a small group struggling to maintain its collective identity, the proprietorship arrangement was an effective way of having legal status while also maintaining a difference. While there was internal disagreement at times, the majority of Mashpee proprietors consistently favored keeping the plantation land system. This was changed only by legislative fiat in 1969, against their expressed wishes. Until then an "archaic" status had been effectively used to preserve Indian lands in a collective form through rapidly changing times. The land-claim suit aimed to restore a situation illegally altered by the Massachusetts legislature.

Taking the colonists' side. The fact that some South Sea Indians fought against Metacomet in King Philip's War does not prove that they were abandoning their Indian sovereignty or independence. More did not fight, and the motivations of those who did are a matter of speculation. There was nothing new about Indians making war on other Indians. Moreover they may have had little choice. Puritan authorities were on the warpath, and even "loyal" Indians were punished during and after the war by loss of lands and slavery.

As for the war against England, again we should be wary of imputing motives. The Mashpee Indians who served in the Revolutionary Army may not have done so primarily as "American" patriots. They were, among other things, rebelling against the authority of their missionary Hawley, an ardent Tory. Moreover, as Indian status has evolved in the United States, it has been legally recognized that the privileges of citizenship (including the decision to unite in war against a common enemy) do not contradict other arrangements establishing special group identity and status. One can be fully a citizen and fully an Indian.

To expect Cape Cod Indians to hold themselves apart from the historical currents and conflicts of the dominant society would be to ask them to commit suicide. Survival in changing circumstances meant participation, wherever possible on their own terms. Staying separate or uninvolved would be to yield to the dangerous fantasies of protectors, like Hawley, who worked to keep the Mashpee pure—and under his tutelage. The inhabitants of Mashpee again and again resisted this restrictive "authenticity." The record confirms that they wanted integrity but never isolation.

Intermarriage. There was a good deal of racial mixing in Mashpee, but the exact extent is hard to determine, given the shifting categories of different censuses and doubts about how race was actually measured. Mashpee was a refuge for misfits, refugees, and marginal groups. At certain times a natural alliance against dominant white society formed between the town's Indian "survivors" and newly freed blacks. The crucial issue is whether the core Indian community absorbed the outsiders or were themselves absorbed in the American melting pot.

Historical evidence supports the former conclusion. Since whites and people of color who settled in Mashpee during the eighteenth and most of the nineteenth centuries could not become proprietors, this limited the influx; non-Indians remained a significant but small minority. Children with one Indian parent could become full community members. Intermarriage frequently occurred, and thus the purity of Indian blood was much diluted; but the legal and social structure consistently favored Indian identification. With land entailment and the maintenance of close kin ties among property holders a core was maintained. In any event blood is a debatable measure of identity, and to arrive at quotas for determining "tribal" status is always a problematic exercise. There are federally recognized tribes as mixed as the Mashpee, and organized Indian groups vary widely in the amount of traceable ancestry they actually require for membership.

Ethnohistorical studies show that in New England the mixing of different communities was common well before the Pilgrims' arrival. Adoption was frequent, and it was customary to capture and incorporate opponents in war. Indians were in this respect color blind. In colonial times a large number of white captives stayed with their captors, adopting Indian ways, some even becoming chiefs. Mashpee's later openness to outsiders—as long as the newcomers intermarried and conformed to Indian ways—was a continuation of an aboriginal tradition, not a loss of distinct identity.

In 1859, after more than a century of intermarriage and sporadic population growth (the dilution of Indian stock lamented by the missionary Hawley), a detailed report by the commissioner for Indian affairs, John Earle, offered a census of the "Marshpee Tribe" that included 371 "natives" and 32 "foreigners." The latter were people living on the land without proprietary rights and not lineal descendants of Indians. They were described as "Africans" and "colored." Only one "white" was listed. The names of "natives" listed on the 1859 census served in the trial as a benchmark of continuous "tribal" kinship ties.

Mashpee becomes a town. There is strong documentary evidence that most of the proprietors between 1834 and 1869 wanted to hold on to Mashpee's special land restrictions. Commissioner Earle asserts this in his report. "Progressives" such as Attaquin were more vocal, and their testimony thus receives more weight in the record than the less articulate majority who in 1869 voted decisively against township status. Spokesmen (note how few female voices are "heard" by history, although the role of women at the center of community life was undoubtedly crucial) such as Blind Joe Amos and his brother Daniel urged postponing the transition. They argued that most people in Mashpee were too "immature," not "ready" to dispose of their land individually. Give us just one more generation, Daniel Amos asked in the 1830s. His brother asked the same thing in the late 1860s. What do these arguments signify?

For those who see Mashpee's "development" and assimilation as inevitable, such statements require no interpretation: they simply show that even the traditionalists in Mashpee were ready eventually to give up their special status. But this is to assume the historical outcome. The Indian proprietors of Mashpee valued community integrity and possessed effective public and informal leadership. They had shown much strength and initiative in dealing with their various "protectors." The early historical record reveals a steady stream of petitions—1748, 1753, 1760—on behalf of the "poor Indians of Marshpee called the South Sea Indians" protesting abuses by the agents appointed to watch over them. More recently they had successfully asserted their autonomy against the missionaries Hawley and Fish. They were hardly "immature." Yet throughout the mid-nineteenth century Mashpee proprietors temporized, hesitated in the face of an "inevitable" progress. Their ability to protect their community from the coercions and enticements of white society was evidently precious to them.

The modified plantation status they had secured in 1834 gave them a way of keeping collective control over land and immigration while not isolating the community from interaction with the surrounding society. Even the "allotment" of lands sanctioned at that time reproduced an aboriginal land arrangement. Parcels were traditionally given to families for exclusive use while ultimate collective ownership was maintained. (In 1834, moreover, three thousand acres were formally kept as common land.) Continuing entailments on land sales outside the community guaranteed a flexible nineteenth-century tribalism. In this context public arguments about Mashpee's "immaturity" should be seen as ways of addressing an outside audience, the Massachusetts General Court, which still thought of the plantation as a ward of the state and which had already decided and again would arbitrarily decide its fate. It would be impolitic in addressing this body to say that Mashpee rejected full township status in the name of a distinctive vision of Indian community and citizenship. An argument for delay couched in paternalist rhetoric was more likely to succeed.

This interpretation of the debates in 1869 is at least as plausible as a literal reading of the recorded public utterances. Mashpee, like Indian communities throughout their recent history, was split between modernists and traditionalists. The traditionalists prevailed in the vote, but the modernists swayed the authorities. In changing Mashpee's land entailment the legislature violated both simple democracy and the Federal Non-Intercourse Act of 1790. But even the forced change—although it ultimately brought much land into non-Indian hands—was not fatal. The Mashpee Indians used their new imposed status as they had their former one. For almost a century local government was kept firmly in the hands of a closely interrelated group of town officers. Mashpee remained "Cape Cod's Indian Town."

Assimilation. The Mashpee Indians did not "assimilate." The term's linear, either-or connotations cannot account for revivalism and for changes in the cultural and political climate between 1869 and 1960. There have been better and worse times in the United States to be publicly Indian. The late nineteenth and early twentieth centuries were among the worst. Government policy strongly favored tribal termination and the dispersal of collective lands. It was not until the late 1920s that the failure of allotment schemes was recognized and a "New Indian Policy" instituted at the BIA that favored tribal reorganization. If there is little evidence in the historical record of "tribal" life in Mashpee between 1869 and 1920, it is no surprise. Many groups all over the nation that would emerge later as tribes kept a low profile during these years. Mashpee seemed to be simply a sleepy town run by Indians, known for its good hunting and fishing. There was no political need or any wider context for them to display their Indianness in spectacular ways. Everyone knew who they were. A few attended the Carlisle Indian School in Pennsylvania during this period. Traditional myths and stories were told around kitchen tables; the piles of sticks at Mashpee's "Indian taverns" or "sacrifice heaps" grew into enormous mounds; life close to the land went on.

The history of Indian tribes in the United States has been punctuated by revival movements. The 1920s saw the organization of the Wampanoag Nation, with various explicit tribal institutions including a supreme sachem and a renewed interest in more public Indian displays: dances, regalia, powwows, and the like. As in all revitalization movements "outside" influences from other Indian groups played a major role. Eben Queppish, who had once ridden with Buffalo Bill's Wild West Show, taught traditional basket making and on demand donned his Sioux war bonnet. Individuals from Mashpee participated in nationally known groups such as the Thunderbird Indian Dancers. The effects of these revivals were largely cultural. There was little need for political reorganization in Mashpee, for the town was still governed by an unchallenged Indian majority. Political reorganization of a more explicit "tribal" structure would occur during a later revivalist period, the ferment spurred by the loss of town control after 1968.

Like other tribal groups the Mashpee have been opportunists, taking advantage of propitious historical contexts and undergoing external influences. They have survived as Indians because they have *not* conformed to white stereotypes. They have lived since aboriginal times in a traditional locale. They have maintained their own hybrid faith. Over the centuries they have controlled the rate of intermarriage and have fought for the political autonomy of their community. Explicitly tribal political structures have sometimes been visible to the outside world, as in 1833, the 1920s, and the 1970s, but for the most part these structures have been informal. Often the "tribe" in Mashpee was simply people deciding things by consensus, in kitchens or at larger ad hoc gatherings where no records were kept. The chief in Mashpee, when there was one, shared authority with a variety of respected leaders, women and men. Politics was not hierarchical and did not need much in the way of institutional forms. The "tribe" in Mashpee was simply shared Indian kinship, place, history, and a long struggle for integrity without isolation. Sometimes the Baptist parish served as an arm of the tribe; so did the town government. When the Mashpee Wampanoag Tribal Council, Inc. filed suit in 1976, it did so as a new legal arm of the tribe.

Russell Peters

Dressed in a blue three-piece business suit, Russell Peters is indistinguishable from a half-dozen lawyers in the courtroom. He is clean-cut, and his speech is sprinkled with technocratic jargon: he says "utilize" instead of "use," he "provides input." Brother of the tribal medicine man, John Peters, the witness is president of the Mashpee Wampanoag Tribal Council, Inc.

After graduating from college, Peters did military service in Korea and Europe. He then held jobs in Philadelphia and Boston, living away from Mashpee for a total of eighteen years. In 1974 he left a job at Honeywell Laboratories and returned to Mashpee to work for the coalition for Eastern Native Americans (CENA), a private organization heavily dependent on federal funds. At CENA he earned $14,000, a $9,000 cut in salary from his former employment. The project soon ended, and he and others were out of work. In 1974 he participated in the founding of the Tribal Council, Inc., becoming its first president.

Currently Peters is project director of a television series on eastern Native Americans. As president of the Tribal Council, Inc., he receives no salary.

He testifies that the council is "the business arm of the tribe." It does what the tribe should not do: "No self-respecting tribe would become incorporated."

He says that before bringing suit on behalf of the Mashpee Indians the council was primarily concerned with securing grants from the federal government, usually through CENA, such as the 1976 grant for aquafarming. Various employment programs have also been funded. Peters mentions a CENA Title 3 Indian project in which his input led to a distinction between Mashpee Wampanoag and Gay Head Wampanoag groups.

The Tribal Council, Inc., has helped with funds for clearing fifty-five acres acquired for tribal use. It has helped organize powwows and a clambake to dedicate this first acquisition of tribal land. Peters testifies that two unity conferences have been held there in the last year and a half. At these events the council participates, but the leaders are the chief and the medicine man.

Currently the council is operating on a $30,000 federal grant. Its headquarters is the parsonage. Peters says that he is serving a term as one of three members of the parish committee. The council pays $50 or $60 a month rent for its headquarters.

Peters admits that there have been conflicts with the chief, Earl Mills, problems of defining roles; but these are being worked out. Naturally, he says, we consulted with our chief in preparing the land-claim suit.

Since 1968 Peters has been licensed as a real estate broker, but he has sold only a couple of houses. His wife, also a broker, has sold six and a few parcels of land. Peters Enterprises, comprising Russell and three siblings, developed a fifteen-acre subdivision. Of the five houses built two are now occupied by Peters and his brother John, the other three by non-Indians. Peters Enterprises no longer functions.

The witness adds that, with his son, he is involved in the early experimental stages of developing a new product called "Reflecto-Shield."

Russell Peters testifies that he has several times run for public office—the planning board, the board of assessors—but without success.

Peters is asked about his percentage of Indian ancestry. He cannot say. He thinks that his father, Stephen Amos Peters, came to Mashpee sometime before he was born. His father had formerly lived in Boston and New Bedford and was involved in real estate. Some of his father's forebears may have lived on Martha's Vineyard. He cannot trace exactly the genealogy he claims goes back to 1859 in Mashpee. His mother, born in Georgia and raised in Boston, is not a member of the tribe. He knows very little about Blind Joe Amos, a possible relation through his father.

Q.: Had he been substantially involved with the plaintiff group before formation of the Tribal Council? A.: No, he had been absent for
almost twenty years. Had he participated in powwows? Yes, by attending.
Like hundreds of others? No. A Mashpee Indian participates differently. Is
he a religious person? No. A traditionalist? Well, traditional values, yes.
But not exhibited too much.

The witness is asked about a sworn deposition taken before the trial
in which he had joked about having to wear a "$200 hippie suit."

Peters says he is not comfortable wearing Indian regalia.

History III

The following excerpt from the cross-examination of Ramona Peters
by James St. Clair is quoted directly from the trial record.

Q.: All right. Now, you've told us that when you've been here,
within the last year or two, as I understand it, you have organized a
singing society comprised roughly of about eight people, is that right?

A.: I didn't say that I organized it.

Q.: Well, did you?

A.: Jointly with another singer.

Q.: Who is the other singer?

A.: Well, two other singers.

Q.: Who were the other singers?

A.: Tony Pollard and Earl Mills, Jr.

Q.: Tony Pollard is the same one that comes from New Bedford?

A.: Yes.

Q.: He is not a Mashpee, member of the Mashpee group, is he?

A.: He is now.

Q.: He is now?

A.: The Mashpee group, he lives there.

Q.: I'm sorry, I can't hear you.

A.: He lives there now, yes.

Q.: He lives there now. He lives in Mashpee, is that right?

A.: Yes.

Q.: Therefore, you say he's a member of the Mashpee group because
he lives in Mashpee?

A.: Because you say Mashpee group.

Q.: All right. You understand that I'm referring to the plaintiffs in this
case when I say the Mashpee group?

A.: No, I'm sorry.

The Court: There is a little bit of a problem here. Mr. St. Clair refuses to say "tribe," so he says "group," and we worked this out with Mr. Pocknett yesterday. What he refers to as a group is what you refer to as a tribe. Now, the question is, is the gentleman from New Bedford part of what you refer to as a tribe?

The Witness: No.

Q. (By Mr. St. Clair): Now, since you've been in Mashpee—let's see, you returned from Boston about when?

A.: I commuted to Boston.

Q.: But you spent your time in Boston, as I understrand it.

A.: I worked it so I could work at home as practical experience, my latter part of the training program.

Q.: When you say this singing society that you, Mr. Pollard, and another person organized, when was that done, 1976?

A.: Yeah, thereabouts.

Q.: When you say you've been teaching young people, that is under thirty, how to make things such as totems, regalia, traditional clothing and giveaways, over what period of time have you been doing this?

A.: Oh, probably since I was 15, there in Mashpee.

Q.: No, but I understand you are now engaged in some sort of informal classes.

A.: Yes, I'm doing that now.

Q.: Is that right?

A.: Yes.

Q.: Teaching people to do these things, is that right?

A.: Yes.

Q.: You say about half of the members of the group that you would call a tribe have participated?

A.: In making things with me?

Q.: Yes.

A.: No, I don't believe I said half.

Q.: How many people attended these informal classes?

A.: If I include the making of a canoe, that would encompass nearly the entire tribe. They all participated in it.

Q.: Well, you testified that you were engaged in teaching people how to make drums, totems, regalia, traditional clothing, and giveaways?

A.: I don't think I said I teach them, I said we do this together.

Q.: I see. You also conduct a language class?

A.: Tony conducts the class, I attend.

Q.: You are learning, you are trying to learn the language, right?

A.: Yes.

Q.: That's been within the last year, is that so?

A.: That's true.

Q.: And then you have been conducting informal history classes?

A.: Yes.

Q.: In this last year?

A.: Yes, during this last year and other years as well.

Q.: Well, you told us, did you not, that you've been conducting history classes, and about half of the people have shown up?

A.: They are informal classes and not all done in one place. There is no formal thing about it, no students, I don't call them students, they are my people. We talk to each other, therefore, educational teaching happens.

Q.: You are in the role of a teacher, are you not?

A.: No. Sometimes—what do you mean "role of a teacher?"

Q.: Haven't you done a lot of study of history?

A.: I've done a lot of studying, and I've been taught, yes.

Q.: Didn't you study when you were in Boston, history?

A.: I studied museum training, museum—

Q.: Didn't you tell us you studied history?

A.: I told you I did research when I was here, yes.

Q.: All right. You studied history when you were in college as well, didn't you, too?

A.: Sometimes.

Q.: And you've done a lot of studying about the people in Mashpee recently, haven't you?

A.: Not recently, no.

Q.: Well, in any event, you were in effect telling others about what you had learned, isn't that right?

A.: That is correct.

Q.: That's because they hadn't known about it, isn't that right?

A.: Not in all cases, no.

Q.: Well, if they had already known about it, there would be no point in you telling them about it, would there?

A.: We like to talk about ourselves.

Q.: No, please. If you were telling them about it, it would be because they didn't know about it, isn't that right?

A.: Not at all times, no.

Q.: Well, most of the time, isn't that so? Can't you answer that question?

A.: For the young people, yes.

Q.: Sure. And if it hadn't been for you, they wouldn't have known anything about it, isn't that right?

A.: No.

Q.: I see. You were telling them something they already knew? Is that your testimony, Miss Peters?

A.: No.

Q.: And when you organized the singing society, there wasn't anything there before that, either, was there, of that nature?

A.: Not the same group, not the same songs.

Q.: And you had to teach the people how to make drums and totems and regalia because they didn't know how to make them, isn't that right?

A.: No.

Q.: Is it your testimony that they taught you?

A.: Some of them did, yes.

Q.: I see. You had gone taking courses out West in a program called the teepee program, right?

A.: Yes, sir.

Q.: And then you had gone upstate New York and spent how many months?

A.: Nine or ten.

Q.: Traveling around with groups up there, how long?

A.: Well, 10 months, 9 months.

Q.: Would it be unfair for me to suggest, Miss Peters, that you are an activist in the Indian movement?

A.: What kind of movement?

Q.: You are not aware of an Indian movement?

A.: There is an organization that has a name Indian Movement.

Q.: Is it unfair of me to ask you whether or not you are an activist in that group?

A.: Unfair?

Q.: Yes.

> Mr. Tureen: Counsel has not made clear what group he is asking about.
>
> The Court: You are objecting to the question?

Mr. Tureen: I am, your Honor.

The Court: The objection is sustained to the question in that form.

Q.: *You have been very active in Indian affairs, have you not?*

A.: *Yes, I have.*

Q.: *Principally in the Far West?*

A.: *Well, I was there, but—*

Q.: *And in upstate New York?*

A.: *Indian affairs of what nature, any particular nature?*

Q.: *Didn't you tell us you traveled around with a number of Iroquois groups?*

A.: *I traveled around in a spiritual caravan.*

Q.: *And you have been personally in Mashpee then for about a year now, right?*

A.: *Yes.*

Q.: *Now, where you went to school out West in Oklahoma, I assume you told people there, the students there, where you came from?*

A.: *Yes.*

Q.: *And what group you said you were affiliated with?*

A.: *Yes.*

Q.: *And their knowledge of that group you said you were affiliated with was based on what you told them, wasn't it?*

A.: *And alumni.*

Q.: *Well, let's see, your mother went there?*

A.: *Yes, and Eleanor Sturgis went there.*

Q.: *How many people from Mashpee went to Bacone College to your knowledge, Junior College?*

A.: *I think five or six.*

Q.: *You, your mother, and who?*

A.: *Eleanor Sturgis.*

Q.: *Is she a relative of yours?*

A.: *No.*

Q.: *And who are the others, if you know?*

A.: *Robert Alan Maxim, Gail Marcellino Andras, Errol Hicks, and myself.*

Q.: *And now, before you went away to school—Incidentally, is that a private institution, if you know?*

A.: *Private?*

Q.: *Is it owned and operated by the state or federal government or is it owned and operated on a private basis, if you know?*

A.: Private.

Q.: Do you know or are you guessing?

A.: I am not sure what they call themselves, Daughters of American Revolution, and some Christian organizations involved in it.

Q.: Let's see, the Daughters of the American Revolution is not an organization that you would associate with Indians, is it?

A.: In our history, yes.

Q.: Pardon?

A.: I said in our history, yes, Wampanoag history—Mashpee Wampanoag history.

Q.: Daughters of the American Revolution, in your understanding of what you say is your history, have an Indian origin?

A.: It is not our history, but we were involved with that revolution and 149 of our Mashpee people died in that fighting for your independence.

Q.: Fighting for what?

A.: Independence.

Q.: But it is your understanding that the Daughters of the American Revolution have an Indian origin or are in some way related to persons of Indian descent?

A.: They embrace me as a member.

Q.: Pardon?

A.: I said the women that I met that were involved with the Daughters of American Revolution felt a kinship with me because of the Mashpee Wampanoags that had died in the war.

Q.: All right. Now when you attended schools on Cape Cod . . .

The Experts

Expert testimony by professional anthropologists and historians played a major role in the Mashpee trial. The defense rested much of its case on the historical testimony of a single scholar, while the plaintiffs depended more on anthropologists. Indeed the trial can be seen as a struggle between history and anthropology.

The principal expert witnesses were, for the plaintiffs, James Axtell, a well-known ethno-historian, and Jack Campisi, an anthropologist who had written on the Oneida of New York State. They were seconded by William Sturtevant of the Smithsonian Institution and the Sioux scholar-activist Vine Deloria. Ann Borden Harding, a professional genealogist, traced at least one ancestor from the 1859 "Marshpee Tribe" census to nearly all the currently claimed tribal members. The defense relied on a sociologist, Jean Guillemin, who had written an ethnography of Micmac Indians in Boston (Guillemin 1975), and Francis Hutchins, a historian. Trained in political science and the author of respected works on India, Hutchins had recently shifted his research to Native American history.

All of the experts gave detailed testimony whose fine points I cannot represent here. On the stand, as might be expected, many subtleties and qualifications were lost: lawyers pressed the scholars for sharp, unambiguous opinions. As in all long trials the sequence of testimony mattered. Axtell's testimony from early in the proceedings was only dimly remembered by the time Hutchins wrapped up the case for the defense.

I have already summarized a good deal of Axtell's testimony in the History II section and that of Hutchins in History I. Both experts based their testimony on essentially the same corpus of historical documents unearthed by research teams from both camps. The defense, advised by Hutchins, devoted major resources to historical research, building its positive case largely around the presentation of a "complete" documented record of Mashpee history.

The plaintiffs placed more reliance on the oral testimony of living Mashpee Indians and on anthropological accounts of Native American life in Mashpee and other comparable cultures. Campisi did a stint of ethnographic "fieldwork" on the Cape, but because of professional and budgetary constraints he was restricted to short periods of participant observation and interviewing. (His fieldwork was repeatedly parodied by St. Clair as "twenty-four days and nights in Mashpee." There was occasional talk of issuing a subpoena for his field notes.) Campisi made no claims for the professional adequacy of his research; but as a result of what he had seen, heard, and read, as a professional anthropologist he felt able to assert that elements of an Indian way of life and a real if minimal tribal organization did exist in Mashpee.

人

Over strenuous defense objections the crucial question is posed:
Campisi: I believe they are a tribe.
Judge: Your belief is one thing. Is it your professional opinion as an anthropologist that they are a tribe?
Campisi: Yes.
What does a professional anthropologist mean by tribe? Campisi lists

five criteria: (1) a group of Indians, members by ascription—that is, by birth, (2) a kinship network, (3) a clear consciousness of kind—"we" versus "they," (4) a territory or homeland, and (5) a political leadership.

Campisi testifies that he asked Indians in Mashpee about their relatives and found evidence of "a very close interrelated network of kinsmen." He found "a lot of people who did not live in Mashpee but who retained a contact." Relatives from Falmouth, Marston Mills, Yarmouth, Hyannis, even from California regularly return to Mashpee for the powwow or other community events.

Campisi testifies that the Mashpee Baptist church is a force neither for nor against cohesion and a sense of Indian identity. The Indian community currently contains Christians and "traditionalists." While the latter probably form a numerical majority, the picture is complicated by syncretic relationships between the two belief systems. Asked to define the term syncretic *he answers with a story about an old Oneida man, a devout Baptist, shaking the pumpkin at a water cure and explaining: "Didn't Jesus cure? Didn't he give us the power to cure?"*

He explains that events such as the powwows or summer "homecoming" are ways of identifying Mashpees as a distinct group. Although the powwow caters to outsiders and tourists, it also operates on other more exclusive levels. Gatherings of this sort have a social function, drawing together the dispersed community, and also a spiritual, educational function (their pageants and ceremonies are concerned with moral subjects and Indian history; they teach reverence for the earth). Parts of the unity conferences are sacred and closed to outsiders. During his visits in Mashpee Campisi found evidence of a naming ceremony and planting and harvesting ceremonies (informal, at the family level). He testifies that the yearly herring run (which he has never observed personally) has traditional significance. It is an ecological, social, economic, calendrical event. In cross-examination it emerges that there are more than fifty herring runs in Massachusetts, with the taking of fish regulated in ways similar to those in Mashpee.

Campisi explains the division of labor between traditionalists (the chief and medicine man) and modernists (the Tribal Council, Inc.). He tells of other recognized tribes that do not speak an Indian language. He distinguishes "acculturation" from "assimilation." In the latter process a sense of separate identity is lost; but there are different levels of assimilation. Behavioral assimilation might include American Indians adopting Western clothing: in this domain Mashpee have adopted many traits.

"There is also the level of cultural assimilation. That is where you alter your value systems, your attitudes, where you adopt fully the belief system of an outside society. To an extent I don't think that has happened."

Judge: "I don't understand the phrase, 'To an extent it hasn't happened.' Does that mean to an extent it has happened?"

Campisi: "Well, I think in certain kinds of values it has happened. The value about a market economy: the Mashpees are involved in a market economy. They go to work, they buy, and they sell, and they own and disown, and that is not a cultural value we usually attach to aboriginal Indian tribes. So that is a value that has changed."

Judge: "What about the Baptist affiliation?"

Campisi: "In some ways religion has changed, they have affiliated religiously. But then the problem comes that they have colored the Baptist with value systems from the past, too, in certain aspects."

Judge: "What are you referring to when you say that?"

Campisi: "When you get individuals who are devoted Baptists who also give you viewpoints and value systems which are identifiable as Mashpee Indian or generically as Indian—"

Judge: "I haven't got that clear, yet. What are those value systems which you identify as being characteristically Indian which you say are retained even among those Mashpees who are Baptist?"

Campisi: "Well, the attitude with respect to the reverence for the earth, which is a large concept that Indian people deal with, that you use the earth and you return to the earth, that you don't waste, that you are put on the earth not to sustain yourself, and you owe an obligation to sustain the earth you are put on."

Judge: "I don't mean to be facetious about this, I'm trying to get it defined. Do you see a distinction between a Mashpee Baptist who holds these things, and, say, a Sierra Club Baptist who feels the same way; is there some difference in the attitude?"

Campisi: "From what I know about the Sierra Club, they are probably very similar."

Judge: "It's not unique?"

Campisi: "It might have been a borrowing from the Indian by the Sierra Club."

Judge: "Or vice versa."

Campisi: "Well, since they were here before the Sierra Club—"

Like all the experts at the trial Campisi is pressed to distinguish a tribe clearly from an ethnic group. How is it like and unlike the Amish, for example? First, a tribe has a traceable heritage to aboriginal ancestors. And second, it is strongly connected to land, to the fact of being indigenous.

(Here as elsewhere the trial's most conspicuous double bind surfaces. To sue for land the Mashpee must be a tribe; to be a tribe they must have land.)

Various questions successfully blur the distinction between tribe and ethnic group. Is Mashpee volunteer leadership different from that of an ethnic group? No.

Is anthropology a social science, Mr. Campisi? Why does Morton Fried, a respected authority, write that the concept of tribe is a myth invented in the late eighteenth century? What about the categories proposed by Elman Service in his book Profiles in Anthropology: *band, tribe, chiefdom, state? Aren't the Mashpee more like a band? Don't some anthropological sources describe them as a band? Isn't Elman Service a respected anthropologist? What is your framework? Aren't you making up your definitions as you go along?*

And aren't the Indian ceremonies you describe in Mashpee little more than casual gestures?

"What I think I'm trying to say, Mr. St. Clair, is that your gesture may be my rite."

Anthropological categories ricochet strangely around the courtroom. For example kinship: I suddenly notice that lawyers call their opposing colleagues "brother." And totemism: Judge Skinner gets caught up in a description of clan structure among the Oneida and its absence in Mashpee. Curious, he asks Campisi how the clan is related to the totem. A technical discussion ensues about totemic symbols and emblems in Iroquois and Algonquian societies. Suddenly some of us notice, just above Skinner's head on the wall of the federal courtroom, a large eagle.

An adversary system of justice, the need to make a clear case to counterbalance an opposing one, discourages opinions of a "yes, but," "it depends on how you look at it" kind. Experts on the stand were required to answer the question: Is there a tribe in Mashpee? Yes or no? On cross-examination, confronted with evidence that their disciplines had no rigorous, commonly accepted definitions of key categories such as tribe, culture, and acculturation, the experts could only smile or wince and stick to their guns.[3]

Anthropologists speaking as scientific experts could not explain to the court that theirs was a historically limited and politically enmeshed discipline. They could not admit that many fieldworkers were now testifying in court on behalf of resurgent indigenous cultures as part of a postcolonial context governing how researchers from one society could represent or "speak for" another group. (There was a time when an anthropologist could casually refer to "my people"; now indigenous groups can speak of "our anthropologist"!) On the stand it was difficult to explain that the word *tribe* could mean different things to a scholar discussing a range of aboriginal systems, reservation Indians of the nineteenth century, and legally reorganized groups of the 1930s, or that the term was unlikely to mean the same thing for an author of evolutionist theories writing in the 1950s and an expert evaluating the aspirations of eastern Indian communities in the 1970s.

William Sturtevant's testimony compared various Native American tribes. Rather than asserting a sharp definition of the institution, he portrayed a field of family resemblances and local histories. He suggested that it would be simplistic and unjust to establish a list of essential "tribal" attributes against which individual cases could then be checked.[4] On cross-examination this flexibility was made to appear as fuzziness or as an opportunistic, sliding set of criteria. Vine Deloria also testified to the variety of Native American institutions. Pressed to define *tribe* he answered: "As I use it and as I understand other Indian people using it, it

---

3. Lawrence Rosen provides a good overview of the anthropologist as expert witness (1977), discussing the constraints of the adversary system, ethical dilemmas, persistent problems of defining terms such as *tribe, band, nation,* and *chief.* Rosen suggests that the role of anthropologists in legal proceedings will probably increase, and he offers advice for scholars preparing themselves to enter a dangerous but necessary arena.

4. See Sturtevant 1983 for his reflections on the contestation of the concept of tribe at the trial. He suggests the need for a concrete, "polythetic" definition flexible enough to accommodate considerable local variation. This is supported by the legal scholar L. R. Weatherhead in his useful survey of the issue of tribal status in the courts (1980). Weatherhead refers to "'tribe' in the ethnohistorical sense . . . not to a stock anthropological definition of 'tribe' but rather to the peculiar history of each Indian group. Thus, in speaking of reconciling the legal and ethnohistorical meanings of 'tribe,' we are talking about deriving a legal standard flexible enough to include the different social, political, and cultural arrangements of each American Indian group" (p. 5).

means a group of people living pretty much in the same place who know who their relatives are. I think that's the basic way we look at things."

Q.: *"Can a group be a tribe without a political organization?"*

A.: *"This is getting increasingly difficult to respond to, because we don't make the distinctions that you do in the Anglo world: religious, political, and everything else. What you are talking about is a group of people who know where they are. They may have to respond to outside pressures and adopt political structures, religious structures, or economic structures to deal with the outside society. There's no question I can answer if I have to begin to divide that community up and say we have these identifiable structures, the same way you do in the white man's world, because it's not the way I look at it."* (A defense motion to strike the answer as nonresponsive is denied.)

The anthropologists on the stand were clearly more comfortable with a polymorphous notion of culture than with the political category of tribe. And given the court's unwillingness to establish a rigid initial definition, much, if not most, of the testimony at the trial concerned the status of Indian "culture," broadly conceived, in Mashpee. This cornerstone of the anthropological discipline proved to be vulnerable under cross-examination. Culture appeared to have no essential features. Neither language, religion, land, economics, nor any other key institution or custom was its sine qua non. It seemed to be a contingent mix of elements. At times the concept was purely differential: cultural integrity involved recognized boundaries; it required merely an acceptance by the group and its neighbors of a meaningful difference, a we-they distinction. But what if the difference were accepted at certain times and denied at others? And what if every element in the cultural melange were combined with or borrowed from external sources?

At times the experts seemed to suggest that culture was always acculturating. But then how much historical mix-and-match would be permissible before a certain organic unity were lost? Was the criterion a quantitative one? Or was there a reliable qualitative method for judging a culture's identity? Was it necessary to frequent the people in question? In anthropology coherent representations of a way of life are expected to be based on fieldwork. But would a year's fieldwork in Mashpee have produced a professional account significantly better than Campisi's "twenty-four days and nights"? Doubtless yes; but would a year be enough to gain the trust of all factions in the area, Indian and white?

Campisi's limited familiarity with life in Mashpee was far greater than that of the opposing anthropological expert. Jean Guillemin, a sociologist by training, did no credible fieldwork in Mashpee at all. She had little choice: only a few Indian people would speak with her. The bulk of her testimony was thus based on sworn depositions taken by order of the court before the trial from a random sample of fifty Mashpee residents. On this basis, along with the evidence of written documents, she had no hesitation in affirming that Mashpee Indians never had a distinct culture and never were a tribe. The Mashpee clearly differed from the Micmacs she had written about and knew firsthand. Micmacs had maintained continuous ties of kinship and political authority over the years; their language had survived; and they possessed a land base in the Canadian Maritime Provinces to which they regularly returned. In cross-examination Guillemin's research practice of "anthropology by deposition" was effectively attacked, while her definition of *tribe* was shown to be heavily weighted toward formal leadership and sovereignty, exactly the elements most lacking in Mashpee.

Guillemin defended the adversarial questions and answers of the pretrial depositions as a source of social scientific data. This led to rebuttals by experts on social science methodology, covering sampling techniques, investigator bias, the value of telephone surveys, and so on. She derived statistical tables based on the depositions showing a low level of familiarity with Indian myths and legends in the randomly sampled cross-section of Mashpee Indians. The plaintiffs challenged these as misleading pseudoscience. Judge Skinner finally allowed the tables to be shown to the jury, explaining to the lawyers at the side bar that he personally found them unconvincing but that he could not find a cogent reason for excluding these subjective conclusions while admitting Campisi's equally selective and subjective opinions. Interpretive and quantitative approaches to the study of society did battle in the courtroom, and neither came out looking rigorous.

Guillemin's inability to talk with Indians in Mashpee seriously undermined her credibility as an anthropological expert; but the difficulties and resistance she encountered raised a general doubt. How could a balanced, neutral cultural account ever be produced in a politically divided situation? Could any expert speak without bias in such a situation? Campisi was very clearly "positioned" in Mashpee, primarily associated with one segment of the population. Unlike a historian, an anthropologist drawing on fieldwork cannot—even in theory—control all the available evidence. A community reckoning itself among possible futures is not a finite archive. Unlike a psychiatric expert, moreover, an anthropologist cannot claim to have met alone with his or her subject—a "culture."

William Sturtevant

William Sturtevant is curator of North American ethnology at the Smithsonian, editor of a detailed multivolume reference work on North American Indians. His comparative knowledge of the field is extensive. Sturtevant's most prolonged professional fieldwork was with the Florida Seminoles. He has not done research in Mashpee but since 1936 has known that there were Indians there because his parents had a summer house nearby in Woods Hole. On the stand he provides general concepts and comparative expertise on eastern Indian groups.

Sturtevant distinguishes ethnic neighborhoods from tribes. Beyond the fact that they are not Indian, ethnic neighborhoods are more permeable, he says. A Chicago Irishman can come to South Boston and be accepted as a community member. This may not apply with Native Americans—a Gay Head in Mashpee for example.

Sturtevant distinguishes acculturation from assimilation. The former involves the adoption of cultural traits, the borrowing of customs; it is a matter of degree. The latter refers to a relation between societies, the incorporation of one society into another. A completely assimilated society no longer exists. Acculturation, he says, has taken place among all Indian tribes.

The Mashpee powwow is an example of acculturation. The word and custom are old, but the rituals, pageants, dances, and so on are influenced by white and other Indian institutions.

Sturtevant testifies that acculturation is relatively unimportant in the determination of tribal status. There are other universally recognized tribes as acculturated as the Mashpee.

It is characteristic of life in many Indian tribes for members to stay away for extended periods while keeping up ties and returning to the center to retire.

Sturtevant introduces the concept of an "emerging tribe." The Seminoles, for example, split off from the Creeks, moved into Spanish Florida, and became a new tribe. Tribes are not always aboriginal but can be created in changing historical circumstances. This seems to have occurred with the South Sea Indians in Mashpee.

In cross-examination the Mashpee-Seminole comparison is attacked.

Q.: The Seminoles fought three wars against the colonists and United States, the Mashpee didn't. So the two aren't really comparable, are they? A.: Well there are similarities, also many differences.

Sturtevant is confronted with an article he had written in 1968 surveying Indian communities of the eastern United States, including the Mashpee. He is asked, If they are a tribe now, why didn't you call them one then? Why did you use the word community throughout the article and not tribe? What is the difference? Haven't you changed your mind for the purposes of this case? Portions of the text are debated.

In his article Sturtevant claims that "a restrictive definition of Indian identity" has caused much suffering. Can he give an example? Yes: insisting that you can't be an Indian unless you are a member of a federally recognized tribe. Or saying you can't be an Indian if you have black ancestry. Or defining Indianness by "some fairly high degree of blood quantum."

On the question of how much Indian ancestry it is appropriate to require of a tribe Sturtevant cites the difficulty of determining exact genealogies earlier than the mid-nineteenth century. Degree of ancestry varies enormously among tribes. It is not a crucial determinant of identity. What counts is some descent from aboriginal Indians, a bounded (though permeable) social group, recognition of this group by self and others, and some autonomous political organization.

Judge Skinner imagines a lineage traced seven generations back yielding only one aboriginal Indian among hundreds of ancestors in that generation. If there are now about three thousand progeny traceable to this single Indian ancestor living together in a community, and if all of Sturtevant's other criteria are met, would that community be an Indian tribe? The expert ponders. "Yes." He smiles. "It would be an extremely interesting one."

Q. (St. Clair): "The South Sea Indians, where did they come from?
A.: "Across the Bering Straits."
Q.: "Across the Bering Straits. Now that would be about—"
A.: "Twenty-five thousand B.C."
Q.: "And you consider that a helpful answer, do you, Doctor?"

A.: "Yes."

Q.: "Is it your view that the Mashpee constituted a tribe at the time of contact?"

A.: "I think it's unknowable."

Q.: "You don't know whether they were a tribe at the time of contact?"

A.: "I don't."

Courtroom Notes

Remember not to take what happens here as normal. Notice the abstractness of the rules and rituals, the way life in Mashpee appears in court through an odd refracting and enlarging lens.

Mashpee on the stand: nervous, tight, secretive, eager. In the audience: car pools of the faithful, selectmen in three-piece suits and stylish haircuts, young Indians in jewelry, headbands. Mashpee scattered on the courtroom benches, nodding to or looking coolly past one another, sharing private jokes. None of it is admissible evidence.

Earl Mills pulls his necklaces out from under his tie, but too eagerly. The act uncomfortably expresses what the trial is about: *proving,* making visible and theatrical something subtle, near the skin.

人

By late December the town of Mashpee alone is out $350,000 in trial costs.

人

Indianness. The court clings to its saving abstraction—tribe—an Indian institution that never authentically existed, though not in the way the defense is arguing. "Tribe" is attached to Indians, a way of differentiating them, giving them both an identity and a political structure—things that can be dealt with.

In the courtroom: seeing and not seeing this tribe, guessing at life in Mashpee.

人

Theater of the courtroom. Dramatic poses struck by the attorneys: mock incredulity, anger, bathos. "Secret" conferences at the side bar. The actors' makeup is too blatant, their gestures too crude. St. Clair harps too long on a point, but his audience is a more distant one than that currently watching. He plays to the jury members a month hence as they try to remember key points from the accumulated jumble of facts.

Before the session Judge Skinner, looking thin in shirtsleeves, sets out his books and papers on the bench. Then he leaves to make his robed "entrance."

Characters in the drama develop. The judge: benevolent, testy, distracted, curious. The different personalities on the attorneys' teams. The mysterious jury takes shape. By half time they have relaxed, chatting during consultations at the side bar, nudging one another when Skinner seems for an instant to be nodding off. In the elevator they joke about passing around colds.

Lawyers and spectators guess at the meaning of the jury's reactions, but there is little sign of consistent sympathy for either side. As the trial nears its end, these curiously passive actors become the center of attention.

⅄

There is a second privileged audience. Certain things are addressed to the jury, others to the record.

The jury looks on as oral testimony is made into a text. They are not themselves allowed to write, but court stenographers capture every word for the trial record. This document is used both to refresh the jurors' memories and as a basis for later appeals and judgments. While the court is a theater of dramatic gestures, it is also a machine for producing a permanent document.

Notice those small virtuoso performances, the quiet comings and goings of the stenographers (trained to hear not separate words but articulated sequences of sound).

⅄

An oral ("tribal"?) way of settling a dispute—by consensus. Everyone concerned talks, listens, argues for as long as necessary until a solution acceptable to all is found. Everyone's view of the "facts" shifts; some wear down others, compromise, cajole, berate, make trade-offs. If no consensus can be reached on a crucial matter, the group splits.

This process is preserved in an enclave of orality within the vast writing machine of the law: the jury room.

The jury's consensual procedure is used to settle either-or choices:

guilty or not guilty, tribe or no tribe, sane or insane. The jury cannot propose concrete solutions. They decide that one side has won, the other lost. The adversary system is designed not to produce a judgment that will satisfy everyone or that may be renegotiated next year if the situation changes. It determines winners and losers, a decision on the permanent truth of the case.

In this sense the law reflects a logic of literacy, of the historical archive rather than of changing collective memory. To be successful the trial's result must endure the way a written text endures.

But doesn't the adversary system for producing recordable facts and durable judgments assume a mediating culture surrounding its theatrical confrontations? After all, the abstractly opposed viewpoints are resolved by the common sense of a jury of "peers." And what if this shared culture and its common sense assumptions are precisely what is at issue in the proceedings?

Indian life in Mashpee—something that was largely a set of "oral" relations, formed and reformed, remembered in new circumstances— had to be cast in permanent, "textual" form. The Indians on the stand had to convince a white Boston jury of their difference without conversation or—as happens in practice—living nearby, struggling to work out who is who. The plaintiffs had to represent themselves through scripted exchanges with attorneys, statements for the record, proceedings witnessed, passively and objectively, by jury members with no right to enter, to ask, or to venture an opinion.

⅄

Vignette: Judge Skinner telling Vicky Costa to think of herself "shouting across a field . . . to those people over there."

Richardson Jonas

Richardson Jonas is a Mashpee Indian, raised in town and now living and owning property there. He is fifty years old, powerfully built, dignified, opinionated, stubborn. In appearance Jonas is one of the more "Indian-looking" witnesses to take the stand. He was subpoenaed by the defense.

Jonas' wife is of Portuguese ancestry. They have four children. He believes that the majority of his forebears on his father's side were Indian.

On his mother's side (she came from North Carolina) he doesn't know.
He can't specify percentages.

Jonas says he went to grade school in Mashpee and graduated from
high school in Falmouth. He grew up with Russell Peters and Earl Mills,
was active as a youth in the Baptist church but is not now a churchgoer.

From 1952 to 1954 he served in the U.S. Army Eighty-second Air-
borne Division and has been a leader of the local American Legion chapter. Jonas is a union construction worker for a New Bedford company. He
has also served for more than ten years on the Mashpee Planning Board.

He recalls powwows in the early 1940s. They were held on private
land, always with drumming and songs (none of them purely Mashpee
in origin). There was a model Indian village, knicknacks for sale. He
manned an American Legion food concession at the powwow.

He does not know of any specific Indian ceremonies for marriage,
puberty, birth, or healing; but at the powwow, he recalls, "they had what
appeared to be some sort of religious practices."

Jonas is not a member of the Tribal Council, Inc. He says that he was
never invited to any tribal meetings before the incorporated body was
formed. Although he is a friend of Earl Mills', he cannot say what Mills
does as chief or how and when he was chosen by his predecessor, Elsworth Oakley. In Jonas' view the work of Mills and medicine man Russell
Peters is "ceremonial."

He testifies that he has never heard the word tribe used as much as
in recent years.

He is asked about his work on the town planning board. Jonas insists
that although he has developed a piece of property, he is "not a developer." Currently he holds a few parcels of land, "possibly six." (The cross-
examination shows that he has an interest in as many as twenty-one properties.) He vehemently denies feeling any resentment toward the lawsuit
or the Tribal Council because of these land interests.

Jonas says that when he calls himself a Wampanoag Indian, he is
referring to his Indian ancestry and not to any tribal affiliation. He does
not know what a tribe is. When pressed he hazards a definition: "I would
think that a tribe would be where you have a chief, and he's the governmental factor over those who serve under him."

On cross-examination the witness is confronted with conflicting
statements from his deposition collected before the trial. At that time he
defined tribe differently, largely in terms of Indian ancestry. He described
the Baptist church as "the traditional religion of the Mashpee Wampanoags."

Jonas admits that the American Legion Post, which serves a wider area than Mashpee proper, is the only community organization he has been active in. He is proud of his Indian heritage and cares about the Wampanoag future. He has never participated in Indian education projects or in the Meeting House restoration or in the museum or in "Blind Joe Amos Day" or in any of the Tribal Council activities. He wasn't asked to help and didn't volunteer.

Are his children Indians? He won't say. Don't they participate in powwows? Yes. Does one of his daughters wear regalia? Yes.

Does he hold himself apart from the Indian community? (Vehemently) No.

Having been to more than twenty powwows, can he say who organized them? He does not know.

In 1975 at the meeting where fifty-five acres were transferred to the Mashpee "tribe" for "tribal purposes," did he vote for the article? Yes. The use of the term tribe *made perfect sense to him then, didn't it? Why didn't he protest its use? Jonas says he really didn't give the matter much thought.*

Q. (Shubow): "You have lived in Mashpee all your life, right?"

A.: "Yes, I have."

Q.: "Do you like being part of the community?"

A.: "Yes."

Q.: "Is it because you want to live as part of a Mashpee Wampanoag Indian community where your ancestors have lived?"

A.: "I don't think I, as you say that question, I don't think of it like that. I want to live there because my roots are here, and my ancestry is here. And I have property here and whatnot here that belonged to my ancestors way back in the 1800s."

The Record

The defense's crucial positive testimony was that of its historian, Francis Hutchins, who stayed on the stand for nearly five full days. His long, meticulous recitation of historical particulars summed up the case against the Tribal Council. Hutchins' manner on the stand was unhurried and thorough. He moved from document to document: deeds, petitions, laws, missionary correspondence, town records, state papers. He led the court again through the plague, the arrival of the Pilgrims, Richard Bourne's plantation scheme for the South Sea Indian remnant. He explained English proprietary law, described the early deeds drafted by

Bourne, recounted the transformation of the Mashpee Indians into Christian patriots. He documented their long struggle against second-class status, culminating in the community's final emergence as a township in 1869.

Hutchins' recitation was exhaustive, frequently tedious. He avoided dramatic gestures. For long periods he seemed little more than a conduit for the historical record. Unlike James Axtell, who was occasionally ironic about his own expertise and who openly raised the question of scholarly bias, Hutchins stuck to the facts. After so many clashing oral testimonies one had the sense of being on solid documentary ground. Everything rested on specific written evidence.

It was easy to forget that this historical narration was not a matter of walking on continuous solid ground but was more like jumping from one stone to the next. The documents relevant to life in Mashpee were often few and far between, biased in complex ways. The stones Hutchins landed on were slippery. One had to balance on them in a certain way. For example a missionary's "factual" record of how Indians had fallen from their proud ancestral past could reflect primarily his own discomfort at recent community changes that he was unable to control. A deed might record white more than Indian notions of ownership.

Hutchins' testimony—and his book (1979) based on it—leave no room for deep ambiguity. In his discourse the facts simply tell a story; they are not *made* to speak. Nor does the historian weigh the massive silences of the archives—Mashpee life as seen and lived by the vast majority of participants who did not write.

(Recall again that the presentation you are now reading is very different from the one in the courtroom. This is not a description. Unlike the two "histories" provided earlier, the defense's complete account of Mashpee's past was not followed immediately by a contradictory full account. Coming as it did at the end of the long trial, the weight and coherence of Hutchins' long history lesson could not be adequately countered.)

Hutchins moves ahead. The Wampanoag revivals of the 1920s appear in newspaper accounts and printed memoirs. Eben Queppish dons a Sioux war bonnet; Indian road shows are described; Nelson Simons, who attended the Carlisle Indian School, teaches basketry in Mashpee, falsely claiming descent from a Pequot chief who fought against the whites. The Wampanoag nation is created with its offices of chief and medicine man.

Hutchins is asked if a Mashpee tribe might have used the town government after 1869 for its own purposes:

You reviewed the governmental structure of the town in the twenties and thirties? Yes. And there was no office in town called chief? That is correct.

The Verdict

When Hutchins finished, the defense rested its case. The two principal attorneys, St. Clair and Shubow, then delivered their summations. Each was a review of the trial's evidence in the form of a compelling story. Life in Mashpee over the centuries was given two heroic shapes and outcomes. Shubow recounted "an epic of survival and continuity." St. Clair celebrated a "slow but steady progress" toward "full participation" in American society.

Judge Skinner then gave his instructions. He reviewed the course of the trial, mentioning briefly each witness. He reminded the jurors that the burden of proof was with the plaintiffs; they must prove by preponderance of the evidence (but not, as in a criminal case, beyond a reasonable doubt) the existence of a tribe in Mashpee. In its decision the jury was free to rely on inference and circumstantial evidence. They should not be unduly swayed by the authority of experts but must trust their own common sense judgment of the witnesses' credibility, weighing how well their conclusions matched the evidence presented, observing their way of speaking, even their "body English."

The jurors would be asked to decide whether the proprietors of Mashpee were an Indian tribe on six dates pertinent to the land-claim suit: (1) July 22, 1790, the date of the first Federal Non-Intercourse Act; (2) March 31, 1834, when Mashpee achieved district status; (3) March 3, 1842, when land was partitioned to individuals; (4) June 23, 1869, the end of all alienation restraints; (5) May 28, 1870, incorporation of the Town of Mashpee; and (6) August 26, 1976, commencement of the present suit.

Skinner told the jurors that they would also be required to decide on a seventh question: Did a tribe in Mashpee exist *continuously* during the relevant historical period? If not, the plaintiffs would fail. Moreover the judge instructed the jurors that if at any time they found tribal status in

Mashpee to have been voluntarily abandoned, then it could not be revived. Once lost, it was lost for good.

The judge specified the legal definition of *tribe* that would apply, a matter about which there had been considerable suspense. Skinner opted for a relatively loose formula preferred by the plaintiffs and drawn from the case of *Montoya v. United States,* 1901: "*A body of Indians of the same or similar race united in a community under one leadership or government and inhabiting a particular, though sometimes ill defined, territory.*" For the plaintiffs to win, all the key factors of race, territory, community, and leadership had to be continuously present.

Skinner reviewed the testimony related to key factors of the definition.

Race. Exogamy and an influx of outsiders into a tribe is normal and necessary. The crucial question was whether the outsiders had been incorporated. If the jurors found that the group had Indian ancestry and had opted to focus on that ancestry rather than others, this could satisfy the racial requirement.

Territory. By holding land legally under an English proprietorship, Indians did not thereby become English. Without a reservation system there was no other way to secure land in New England. The jury had to decide whether the Mashpee proprietors used the English arrangement to preserve their tribal form or whether they preferred the English way, and thus abandoned the old form. Skinner warned against the "Catch-22" of requiring a formal land base in this case, since that was precisely what the suit was about.

Community. An "Indian community," Skinner cautioned, is not just "a community of Indians." Boundaries are crucial and can be maintained in various ways. The jury had to decide on the basis of incomplete historical evidence whether Mashpee constituted a discrete community with a definite boundary. A community for the purposes of *Montoya* is something more than a neighborhood.

Leadership. At this small scale leadership can be informal. Sovereignty, a requirement raised by the defense, is inappropriate; but tribal leadership should have roots in a once-sovereign Indian political community. The jury was to rely on its common sense about participation and leadership, the balance of core enthusiasts and people peripheral to the group. There must be more than a coterie claiming to speak for an Indian community. There is no inherent contradiction between serving as a tribal leader and functioning in the wider society, for example as a businessman. Skinner pointed to the gaps in the historical record. Evidence of tribal leadership in Mashpee between 1870 and 1920 is particularly scarce.

The issue of tribal existence is complex, the judge concluded, but it is not more so than issues of sanity or criminal intent, which are routinely decided by juries. Skinner expressed confidence in this jury's ability to weigh the evidence, argue freely, persuade, and finally reach unanimity on the seven yes-or-no questions.

⋏

The jurors were sequestered, accompanied by a large pile of documents. After twenty-one hours of deliberation they emerged with a verdict:

Did the proprietors of Mashpee, together with their spouses and children, constitute an Indian tribe on any of the following dates:

July 22, 1790? No.	June 23, 1869? No.
March 31, 1834? Yes.	May 28, 1870? No.
March 3, 1842? Yes.	

Did the plaintiff groups, as identified by the plaintiff's witnesses, constitute an Indian tribe as of August 26, 1976? No.

If the people living in Mashpee constituted an Indian tribe or nation on any of the dates prior to August 26, 1976, did they continuously exist as a tribe or nation from such date or dates up to and including August 26, 1976? No.

⋏

The verdict was a clear setback for the Indians' suit. But as a statement about their tribal history it was far from clear. Judge Skinner, after hearing arguments, finally decided that despite its ambiguity—the apparent emergence of a tribe in 1834—the jury's reply was a denial of the required tribal continuity. His dismissal of the suit has since been upheld on appeal.

The verdict remains, however, a curious and problematic outcome. We can only speculate on what happened in the jury room—the obscure chemistry of unanimity. What was done with the pile of historical documents during the twenty-one hours of discussion? Did the jurors search for a false precision? Asked to consider specific dates, did they conscientiously search the record for evidence of tribal institutions, for mention of the word *tribe?* If so, their literalism was nonetheless different from that encouraged by the particularist history of the defense, for the jury found that Mashpee Indians were inconsistently a tribe. Violating the judge's instructions, they found that a tribe first did not, then did, then did not again exist in Mashpee. Historical particularism does not by itself yield coherent developments or stories. Entities appear and disappear in the record.

The jurors' response contained an element of subversion. In effect it suggested that the trial's questions had been wrongly posed. Asked to apply consistent criteria of tribal existence over three centuries of intense change and disruption, the jury did so and came up with an inconsistent verdict.

Afterthoughts

The court behaved like a philosopher who wanted to know positively whether a cat was on the mat in Mashpee. I found myself seeing a Cheshire cat—now a head, now a tail, eyes, ears, nothing at all, in various combinations. The Mashpee "tribe" had a way of going and coming; but something was persistently, if not continuously, there.

The testimony I heard convinced me that organized Indian life had been going on in Mashpee for the past 350 years. Moreover a significant revival and reinvention of tribal identity was clearly in process. I concluded that since the ability to act collectively as Indians is currently bound up with tribal status, the Indians living in Mashpee and those who return regularly should be recognized as a "tribe."

Whether land improperly alienated after 1869 should be transferred to them, how much, and by what means was a separate issue. I was, and am, less clear on this matter. A wholesale transfer of property would in any case be politically unthinkable. Some negotiation and repurchase arrangement—such as that in Maine involving local, state, and federal governments—could eventually establish a tribal land base in some portion of Mashpee. But that, for the moment, is speculation. In the short run the outcome of the trial was a setback for Wampanoag tribal dynamism.

In Boston Federal Court, Cape Cod Indians could not be seen for what they were and are. Modern Indian lives—lived within and against the dominant culture and state—are not captured by categories like tribe or identity. The plaintiffs could not prevail in court because their discourse and that of their attorneys and experts was inevitably compromised. It was constrained not simply by the law, with its peculiar rules, but by powerful assumptions and categories underlying the common sense that supported the law.

Among the underlying assumptions and categories compromising the Indians' case three stand out: (1) the idea of cultural wholeness and structure, (2) the hierarchical distinction between oral and literate forms of knowledge, and (3) the narrative continuity of history and identity.

The idea of cultural wholeness and structure. Although the trial was formally about "tribal" status, its scope was significantly wider. The *Montoya* definition of tribe, featuring race, territory, community, and government, did not specifically mention "cultural" identity. The culture concept in its broad anthropological definition was still new in 1901; but the relatively loose *Montoya* definiton reflected this emerging notion of a multifaceted, whole way of life, determined neither by biology nor politics. By 1978 the modern notion of culture was part of the trial's common sense.

In the courtroom an enormous amount of testimony from both sides debated the authenticity of Indian culture in Mashpee. Often this seemed to have become the crucial point of contention. Had the Mashpee lost their distinct way of life? Had they assimilated? In his summation for the plaintiffs Lawrence Shubow took time to define the term *culture* anthropologically, distinguishing it from the "ballet and top hat" conception. Closely paraphrasing E. B. Tylor's classic formula of 1871, he presented culture as a group's total body of behavior. He said that it included how people eat as well as how they think. Using the anthropological definition, he argued that ecology, the special feeling for hunting and fishing in Mashpee, the herring eaten every year, spitting on a stick at an "Indian tavern," these and many other unremarkable daily elements were integral parts of a whole, ongoing way of life.

It is easy to see why the plaintiffs focused on Indian culture in Mashpee. Culture, since it includes so much, was less easily disproven than tribal status. But even so broadly defined, the culture concept posed problems for the plaintiffs. It was too closely tied to assumptions of organic form and development. In the eighteenth century culture meant simply "a tending to natural growth." By the end of the nineteenth century the word could be applied not only to gardens and well-developed individuals but to whole societies. Whether it was the elitist singular version of a Matthew Arnold or the plural, lower-case concept of an emerging ethnography, the term retained its bias toward wholeness, continuity, and growth. Indian culture in Mashpee might be made up of unexpected everyday elements, but it had in the last analysis to cohere, its elements fitting together like parts of a body. The culture concept accommodates internal diversity and an "organic" division of roles but not sharp contradictions, mutations, or emergences. It has difficulty with a medicine man who at one time feels a deep respect for Mother Earth and at another plans a radical real estate subdivision. It sees tribal "traditionalists" and "moderns" as representing aspects of a linear development, one looking back, the other forward. It cannot see them as contending or alternating futures.

Groups negotiating their identity in contexts of domination and exchange persist, patch themselves together in ways different from a living organism. A community, unlike a body, can lose a central "organ" and not die. All the critical elements of identity are in specific conditions replaceable: language, land, blood, leadership, religion. Recognized, viable tribes exist in which any one or even most of these elements are missing, replaced, or largely transformed.

The idea of culture carries with it an expectation of roots, of a stable, territorialized existence. Weatherhead (1980:10–11) shows how the *Montoya* definition of tribe was designed to distinguish settled, peaceful Indian groups from mobile, marauding "bands." This political and military distinction of 1901 between tribe and band was debated again, in technical, anthropological terms, during the Mashpee trial. How rooted or settled should one expect "tribal" Native Americans to be—aboriginally, in specific contact periods, and now in highly mobile twentieth-century America? Common notions of culture persistently bias the answer toward rooting rather than travel.

Moreover the culture idea, tied as it is to assumptions about natural growth and life, does not tolerate radical breaks in historical continuity. Cultures, we often hear, "die." But how many cultures pronounced dead or dying by anthropologists and other authorities have, like Curtis' "vanishing race" or Africa's diverse Christians, found new ways to be different? Metaphors of continuity and "survival" do not account for complex historical processes of appropriation, compromise, subversion, masking, invention, and revival. These processes inform the activity of a people not living alone but "reckoning itself among the nations." The Indians at Mashpee made and remade themselves through specific alliances, negotiations, and struggles. It is just as problematic to say that their way of life "survived" as to say that it "died" and was "reborn."

The related institutions of culture and tribe are historical inventions, tendentious and changing. They do not designate stable realities that exist aboriginally "prior to" the colonial clash of societies and powerful representations. The history of Mashpee is not one of unbroken tribal institutions or cultural traditions. It is a long, relational struggle to maintain and recreate identities that began when an English-speaking Indian traveler, Squanto, greeted the Pilgrims at Plymouth. The struggle was still going on three-and-a-half centuries later in Boston Federal Court, and it continues as the "Mashpee Tribe" prepares a new petition, this time for recognition from the Department of the Interior.[5]

The hierarchical distinction between oral and literate. The Mashpee trial was a contest between oral and literate forms of knowledge. In the end the written archive had more value than the evidence of oral tradition, the memories of witnesses, and the intersubjective practice of fieldwork. In the courtroom how could one give value to an undocumented "tribal" life largely invisible (or unheard) in the surviving record?

As the trial progressed the disjuncture of oral and literate modes sharpened. The proceedings had been theatrical, full of contending voices and personalities, but they ended with a historian's methodical recitation of particulars. In the early portions of the trial the jurors had been asked to piece together and imagine a tribal life that showed recurring vitality but no unimpeachable essence or institutional core. Indianness in Mashpee often seemed improvised, ad hoc. The jury heard many wishful, incomplete memories of childhood events and debatable versions of recent happenings. In what may be called the "oral-ethnographic" parts of the trial many—too many—voices contended, in

---

5. In the preceding discussion I am not suggesting that the ethnographic categories of culture and tribe, however compromised, should be subsumed in the recent and more mobile discourse of ethnicity. Ethnicity, as usually conceived, is a weak conception of culture suitable for organizing diversity within the pluralist state. The institution of *tribe*, still trailing clouds of aboriginal sovereignty and reminiscent of its eighteenth-century synonym *nation*, is less easily integrated into the modern multiethnic, multiracial state. The resurgent cultural-political identity asserted by Indian tribes is more subversive than that of Irish-Americans or Italian-Americans: Native Americans claim to be both full citizens of the United States *and* radically outside it.

its "documentary" ending too few. A historian's seamless monologue was followed by attorneys' highly composed summations, two fully documented stories. There was no way to give voice to the silences in these histories, to choose the unrecorded.

The court imposed a literalist epistemology. Both sides searched the historical records for the presence or absence of the word and institution *tribe*. In this epistemology Indian identity could not be a real yet essentially contested phenomenon. It had to exist or not exist as an objective documentary fact persisting through time. Yet oral societies—or more accurately oral domains within a dominant literacy—leave only sporadic and misleading traces. Most of what is central to their existence is never written. Thus until recently nearly everything most characteristically Indian in Mashpee would have gone unrecorded. The surviving facts are largely the records of missionaries, government agents, outsiders. In the rare instances when Indians wrote—petitions, deeds, letters of complaint—it was to address white authorities and legal structures. Their voices were adapted to an imposed context. The same is true even in the rare cases in which a range of local *voices* was recorded, for example the public debates of 1869 on township status.

History feeds on what finds its way into a limited textual record. A historian needs constant skepticism and a willingness to read imaginatively, "against" the sources, to divine what is not represented in the accumulated selection of the archive. Ultimately, however, even the most imaginative history is tied to standards of textual proof. Anthropology, although it is also deeply formed and empowered by writing, remains closer to orality. Fieldwork—interested people talking with and being interpreted by an interested observer—cannot claim to be "documentary" in the way history can. For even though the origin of evidence in an archive may be just as circumstantial and subjective as that in a field journal, it enjoys a different value: archival data has been found, not produced, by a scholar using it "after the fact."

The distinction between historical and ethnographic practices depends on that between literate and oral modes of knowledge. History is thought to rest on past—documentary, archival—selections of texts. Ethnography is based on present—oral, experiential, observational—evidence. Although many historians and ethnographers are currently working to attenuate, even erase this opposition, it runs deeper than a mere disciplinary division of labor, for it resonates with the established (some would say metaphysical) dichotomy of oral and literate worlds as well as with the pervasive habit in the West of sharply distinguishing synchronic from diachronic, structure from change. As Marshall Sahlins (1985) has argued, these assumptions keep us from seeing how collective structures, tribal or cultural, reproduce themselves historically by risking themselves in novel conditions. Their wholeness is as much a matter of reinvention and encounter as it is of continuity and survival.

The narrative continuity of history and identity. Judge Skinner instructed the jury to decide whether the Indians of Mashpee had *continuously* constituted a tribe prior to filing suit in 1976. For the land claim to go forward the same tribal group had to have existed, without radical interruption, from at least the eighteenth century. The court's common sense was that the plaintiffs' identity must be demonstrated as an unbroken narrative, whether of survival or change. Both attorneys in their summations duly complied.

St. Clair's story of a long struggle for participation in plural American society and Shubow's "epic of survival and continuity" had in common a linear teleology. Both ruled out the possiblity of a group existing discontinuously, keeping open multiple paths, being *both* Indian *and* American.

An either-or logic applied. St. Clair argued that there had never been a tribe in Mashpee, only individual Indian Americans who had repeatedly opted for white society. His story of progress toward citizenship assumed a steady movement away from native tradition. Identity as an American meant giving up a strong claim to tribal political integrity in favor of ethnic status within a national whole. Life as an American meant death as an Indian. Conversely Shubow's Mashpee had "survived" as a living tribe and culture from aboriginal times; but the historical record often contradicted his claim, and he sometimes strained to assert continuity. The plaintiffs could not admit that Indians in Mashpee had lost, even voluntarily abandoned, crucial aspects of their tradition while at the same time pointing to evidence over the centuries of reinvented "Indianness." They could not show tribal institutions as relational and political, coming and going in response to changing federal and state policies and the surrounding ideological climate. An identity could not die and come back to life. To recreate a culture that had been lost was, by definition of the court, inauthentic.

But is any part of a tradition "lost" if it can be remembered, even generations later, caught up in a present dynamism and made to symbolize a possible future?

The Mashpee were trapped by the stories that could be told about them. In this trial "the facts" did not speak for themselves. Tribal life had to be emplotted, told as a coherent narrative. In fact only a few basic stories are told, over and over, about Native Americans and other "tribal" peoples. These societies are always either dying or surviving, assimilating or resisting. Caught between a local past and a global future, they either hold on to their separateness or "enter the modern world." The latter entry—tragic or triumphant—is always a step toward a global future defined by technological progress, national and international cultural relations. Are there other possible stories?

Until recently the "history" accorded to tribal peoples has always been a Western history. They may refuse it, embrace it, be devastated by it, changed by it. But the familiar paths of tribal death, survival, assimilation, or resistance do not catch the specific ambivalences of life in places like Mashpee over four centuries of defeat, renewal, political negotiation, and cultural innovation. Moreover most societies that suddenly "enter the modern world" have already been in touch with it for centuries.

The Mashpee trial seemed to reveal people who were sometimes separate and "Indian," sometimes assimilated and "American." Their history was a series of cultural and political transactions, not all-or-nothing conversions or resistances.[6] Indians in Mashpee lived and acted *between* cultures in a series of ad hoc engagements. No one in Boston Federal Court, expert or layperson, stood at the end point of this historical series, even though the stories of continuity and change they told implied that they did. These stories and the trial itself were episodes, turns in the ongoing engagement. Seen from a standpoint not of finality (survival or assimilation) but of emergence, Indian life in Mashpee would not flow in a single current.

---

6. William Simmons' collection and analysis of New England Indian folklore, *Spirit of the New England Tribes* (1986), not available at the time of the trial, provides much evidence for the productive interpenetration of Christian and Native American sources. It shows how Indian "tradition" was maintained through appropriation and interaction, transmitted both orally and in writing. Simmons provides background on the Mashpee Wampanoag culture hero, the giant Maushop, who, in Ramona Peters' testimony, unexpectedly turned into Moby Dick. The plaintiffs' lawyers and experts made little appeal to continuing Indian folklore, perhaps because of its evident implication in the religious traditions and fairytales of surrounding ethnic groups.

Interpreting the direction or meaning of the historical "record" always depends on present possibilities. When the future is open, so is the meaning of the past. Did Indian religion or tribal institutions disappear in the late nineteenth century? Or did they go underground? In a present context of serious revival they went underground; otherwise they disappeared. No continuous narrative or clear outcome accounts for Mashpee's deeply contested identity and direction. Nor can a single development weave together the branching paths of its past, the dead ends and hesitations that, with a newly conceived future, suddenly become prefigurations.

人

(Hesitations. In 1869 Blind Joe Amos and the majority of Mashpee proprietors agreed that they were not yet ready to become citizens of Massachusetts, separate entrepreneurs with individual control over their lands. They held back, declining a "progressive" step imposed by the legislature. Was it from backwardness? Confusion? Fear? Or something else: an alternate vision? A different voice?

What Susan Howe (1985) has written about a woman—Emily Dickinson, working during the same decade from another place of New England "isolation"—echoes strangely the Indian predicament: the problem of finding a different way through capitalist America.

> HESITATE from the Latin, meaning to stick. Stammer. To hold back in doubt, have difficulty speaking. "*He* may pause but *he* must not hesitate"—Ruskin. Hesitation circled back and surrounded everyone in that confident age of aggressive industrial expansion and brutal Empire building. Hesitation and Separation. The Civil War had split America in two. *He* might pause, *She* hesitated. Sexual, racial, and geographical separation are at the heart of Definition. Tragic and eternal dichotomy—if we concern ourselves with the deepest Reality, is this world of the imagination the same for men and women? What voice when we hesitate and are silent is moving to meet us? (p. 22)

In 1869 Joe Amos and the others did not go on record as resisting full citizenship. Separation and dichotomy were not their agenda: they were already more than half-caught up in a new America. It is important to distinguish hesitation from resistance, for hesitation need not oppose *or* acquiesce in the dominant course. It can be an alert waiting, thinking, anticipating of historical possibilities. Along with the history of resistances we need a history of hesitations.)

Stories of cultural contact and change have been structured by a pervasive dichotomy: absorption by the other *or* resistance to the other. A fear of lost identity, a Puritan taboo on mixing beliefs and bodies, hangs over the process. Yet what if identity is conceived not as a boundary to be maintained but as a nexus of relations and transactions actively engaging a subject? The story or stories of interaction must then be more complex, less linear and teleological. What changes when the subject of "history" is no longer Western? How do stories of contact, resistance, and assimilation appear from the standpoint of groups in which exchange rather than identity is the fundamental value to be sustained? Events are always mediated by local cultural structures. By focusing on the peripheral places, the neglected "islands of history," in Sahlins' words, "we . . . multiply our conceptions of history by the diversity of structures. Suddenly there are all kinds of new things to consider" (1985:72).

In the diversity of local histories—like that of Mashpee—we find distinctive processes and directions. The channeled, inevitable flow of events begins to loop, waver, and fork. In 1830, for example, was the proprietary status of the Mashpee Indians an eroded "survival" from archaic English law, a social form destined to disappear? Or by the nineteenth century had it become a specific invention, a novel way to live on Indian land in modern America, a possible future? Neither story is false; both can be amply documented from the historical record. To say that the strange "tribal" integrity of the Mashpee Plantation was destined to disappear is to accept the history of the victors. But the suit filed a century later was an attempt to reopen this foregone conclusion. Mashpee's semiautonomous plantation, a specific mix of individual citizenship and collective entailment, now appeared not as a historical dead end but as a precursor of reinvented tribalism. No return to a pure Wampanoag tradition was at issue, but rather a reinterpretation of Mashpee's contested history in order to act—with other Indian groups—powerfully, in an impure present-becoming-future.

Whatever the trial's outcome "tribal" life had once again become powerful in Mashpee. Only a literal, backward-looking sense of authenticity (one no group would willingly apply to itself, only to others) could deny this emergent reality. The Wampanoag Supreme Sachem, Elsworth Oakley, commented after the verdict: "How can a white majority decide on whether we are a tribe? We know who we are."

The future of Native American life on Cape Cod after the setback in court is uncertain.

入

The years immediately following the verdict were marked by disarray in Mashpee. An anticipated petition to the Department of the Interior for tribal status was slow to emerge. During this period the Bureau of Indian Affairs standardized its procedure for recognition claims, following criteria similar to those required by the court in *Mashpee* v. *New Seabury et al.* (Weatherhead 1980:17). The Indians in Mashpee watched with misgivings the progress of a petition by their fellow Wampanoags at Gay Head. In 1986 the petition was turned down in a preliminary finding. Government experts cited an insufficient degree of community specificity over the years and a loss of tribal political authority after Gay Head became a township in 1870. Gay Head's history was similar to Mashpee's.

Appealing the preliminary finding, the Native American Rights Fund presented additional evidence, compiled by Jack Campisi, of continuing social networks among Gay Head Indians and of a line of tribal authority after 1870. On February 8, 1987, for the first time ever the Bureau of Indian Affairs reversed a negative preliminary finding. The Gay Head Wampanoags were given full tribal recognition.

Quotations from a Native American Rights Fund press release:

Henry Sockbeson, the Penobscot attorney representing the tribe: "This decision means that the Gay Head will be able to settle their land claim within a few months. Under the terms of the settlement the Tribe will receive approximately 250 acres of land that can be developed. We anticipate that they will use it for housing and economic development."

Gladys Widdiss, chairperson of the Wampanoag Tribal Council of Gay Head, Inc.: "I am delighted. This now means that the Tribe can function in a formally recognized manner. Our status as a tribe can no longer be in doubt. Recognition means that our survival as a tribe for generations to come is assured."

Jack Campisi and Native American Rights Fund attorneys are working on Mashpee's petition.

Two Snapshots

Mrs. Pells is an Indian born in Mashpee. She is seventy-one years old, now living eighteen miles away near the Bourne Bridge, and is an active member of the Tribal Council, Inc. She is dignified, slow-speaking.

She shows an enlarged photograph of her grandmother, Rebecca Hammond, Blind Joe Amos' daughter.

She has been a member of the Mashpee Wampanoag tribe "since birth."

She testifies that she lived in New York between 1928 and 1972, where she was active in a number of Native American organizations. During the 1940s she was secretary of the "American Indian Thunderbird Dancers." Most of the dancers did not originate in Massachusetts, and only one of the dancers was from Cape Cod.

入

"Chiefy" Mills is Earl Mills's teenage son. He says he knows he is an Indian because his father told him. He likes to hunt and hang around with his cousins in Mashpee. A champion drummer, he participates often in Native American gatherings around New England. Recently he was among the young people arrested at a camping retreat held to promote Indian consciousness on the fifty-five acres of tribal land in Mashpee.

Chiefy Mills is bushy-haired, dressed like an ordinary teenager. He wears some jewelry.

Q. (St. Clair): "I notice you have a headband and some regalia?"

A.: "Yes."

Q.: "How long have you been wearing such clothing?"

A.: "Oh, I have been wearing a headband as long as needed, when my hair was long enough."

Q.: "How long has that been?"

Judge: "That which you have on there, is that an Indian headband?"

A.: "It is a headband."

Judge: "It has some resemblance to an ordinary red bandanna?"

A.: "Right, that's what the material is, yes."

Judge: "A bandanna you buy in the store and fold up in that manner?"

A.: "Yes."

References ⍓ Sources ⍓ Index

REFERENCES

Abdel-Malek, Anouar. 1963. "L'orientalisme en crise." *Diogène* 24:109–142.

Achebe, Chinua. 1984. "Foreword." *Igbo Arts: Community and Cosmos,* ed. H. M. Cole and C. C. Aniakor, pp. vii–xi. Los Angeles: Museum of Cultural History, UCLA.

Adotevi, Stanislaus. 1972–73. "Le musée inversion de la vie." *L'art vivant* (special issue, "Le musée en question") 36:10–11.

Alexander, Edward. 1979. *Museums in Motion: An Introduction to the History and Functions of Museums.* Nashville, Ky.: American Association for State and Local History.

Alexandre, Pierre. 1971. "De l'ignorance de l'Afrique et de son bon usage: Notule autobiocritique." *Cahiers d'études africaines* 43:448–454.

————, ed. 1973. *French Perspective in African Studies.* London: Oxford University Press for the International African Institute.

Alloula, Malek. 1981. *Le harem colonial: Images d'un sous-érotisme.* Trans. Myrna and Wlad Godzich as *The Colonial Harem.* Minneapolis: University of Minnesota Press, 1986.

Ames, Michael. 1986. *Museums, the Public, and Anthropology: A Study in the Anthropology of Anthropology.* Vancouver: University of British Columbia Press.

Apollinaire, Guillaume. 1918. *Calligrammes,* trans. Anne Hyde Greet. Berkeley: University of California Press, 1980.

Artaud, Antonin. 1976. *The Peyote Dance.* New York: Farrar, Straus, and Giroux.

Asad, Talal. 1986. "The Concept of Cultural Translation in British Social Anthropology." In *Writing Culture: The Poetics and Politics of Ethnography,* ed. James Clifford and George Marcus, pp. 141–164. Berkeley: University of California Press.

———, ed. 1973. *Anthropology and the Colonial Encounter.* London: Ithaca Press.

Axtell, James. 1981. *The European and the Indian: Essays in the Ethnohistory of Colonial America.* Oxford: Oxford University Press.

Babcock, Barbara, Guy Monthan, and Doris Monthan. 1986. *The Pueblo Storyteller: Development of a Figurative Ceramic Tradition.* Tucson: University of Arizona Press.

Bahr, D., J. Gregorio, D. Lopez, and A. Alvarez. 1974. *Piman Shamanism and Staying Sickness (Ka:cim Mumkidag).* Tucson: University of Arizona Press.

Baines, Jocelyn. 1960. *Joseph Conrad: A Critical Biography.* New York: McGraw-Hill.

Bakhtin, Mikhail. 1937. "Forms of Time and the Chronotope in the Novel." In *The Dialogic Imagination,* ed. Michael Holquist, pp. 84–258. Austin: University of Texas Press, 1981.

——— 1953. "Discourse in the Novel." In *The Dialogic Imagination,* ed. Michael Holquist, pp. 259–442. Austin: University of Texas Press, 1981.

Balandier, Georges. 1960. "Tendances de l'ethnologie française." *Cahiers internationaux de sociologie* 27:11–22.

Banham, Reyner. 1986. *A Concrete Atlantis: U.S. Industrial Building and European Modern Architecture.* Cambridge, Mass.: MIT Press.

Barsh, Russel, and James Youngblood Henderson. 1980. *The Road: Indian Tribes and Political Liberty.* Berkeley: University of California Press.

Barthes, Roland. 1957. *Mythologies.* Paris: Editions du Seuil.

——— 1968. "L'effet de réel." Reprinted in R. Barthes. *Le bruissement de la langue,* pp. 167–174. Paris: Editions du Seuil, 1984.

——— 1970. *L'empire des signes.* Trans. Richard Howard as *Empire of Signs.* New York: Hill and Wang, 1982.

——— 1977. *Image Music Text.* New York: Hill and Wang.

——— 1979. "African Grammar." In R. Barthes, *The Eiffel Tower and Other Mythologies,* pp. 103–109. New York: Hill and Wang.

——— 1980. *La chambre claire.* Trans. Richard Howard as *Camera Lucida.* New York: Hill and Wang, 1981.

Bataille, Georges. 1930. "L'Amerique disparue." In Jean Babelon et al., *L'art précolombien,* pp. 5–14. Paris: Les Beaux Arts.

——— 1949. *La part maudite.* Reprint. Paris: Editions de Minuit, 1967.

——— 1957. *L'erotisme.* Paris: Editions de Minuit.

Baudrillard, Jean. 1968. *Le système des objects.* Paris: Gallimard.

Baumgarten, Murray. 1982. *City Scriptures: Modern Jewish Writing*. Cambridge, Mass.: Harvard University Press.

Beaucage, Pierre, Jacques Gomila, and Lionel Vallée. *L'experience anthropologique*, pp. 71–133. Montreal: Presses de l'Université de Montréal.

Becker, Howard. 1982. *Art Worlds*. Berkeley: University of California Press.

Benjamin, Walter. 1969. *Illuminations*, ed. Hannah Arendt. New York: Schocken Books.

———— 1977. *The Origin of German Tragic Drama*. London: New Left Books.

Benveniste, Emile. 1971. *Problems in General Linguistics*. Coral Gables, Fla.: University of Miami Press.

Berger, John, and Jean Mohr. 1981. *Another Way of Telling*. New York: Pantheon.

Berreman, Gerald. 1972. "Behind Many Masks: Impression Management in a Himalayan Village." In *Hindus of the Himalayas*, pp. xvii–lvii. Berkeley: University of California Press.

Bick, Mario. 1967. "An Index of Native Terms." In Bronislaw Malinowski, *A Diary in the Strict Sense of the Term*, pp. 299–315. New York: Harcourt, Brace, and World.

Bing, Fernande. 1964. "Entretiens avec Alfred Métraux." *L'homme* 4(2):20–23.

Blachère, Jean-Claude. 1981. *Le modèle nègre: Aspects littéraires du mythe primitiviste au XXe siècle chez Apollinaire, Cendrars, Tsara*. Dakar: Nouvelles Editions Africaines.

Blu, Karen. 1980. *The Lumbee Problem: The Making of an American Indian People*. Cambridge: Cambridge University Press.

Blumenson, Martin. 1977. *The Vildé Affair: Beginnings of the French Resistance*. Boston: Houghton Mifflin.

Boon, James. 1972. *From Symbolism to Structuralism*. Oxford: Blackwell.

———— 1982. *Other Tribes, Other Scribes: Symbolic Anthropology in the Comparative Study of Cultures, Histories, Religions and Texts*. Cambridge: Cambridge University Press.

Bouiller, Henry. 1961. *Victor Segalen*. Paris: Mercure de France.

Bourdieu, Pierre. 1977. *Outline of a Theory of Practice*. Cambridge: Cambridge University Press.

Breton, André, et al. 1980. "Ne visitez pas l'Exposition coloniale." In *Tracts surréalistes et déclarations collectives*, ed. J. Pierre. Paris: Terrain Vague.

Brodeur, Paul. 1985. *Restitution: The Land Claims of the Mashpee, Passamaquoddy, and Penobscot Indians of New England*. Boston: Northeastern University Press.

Brooks, Peter. 1984. *Reading for the Plot: Design and Intention in Narrative*. New York: Knopf.

Bulmer, Ralph, and Ian Majnep. 1977. *Birds of My Kalam Country*. Auckland: University of Auckland Press.

Bunn, James. 1980. "The Aesthetics of British Mercantilism." *New Literary History* 11:303–321.

Burke, Edmund III. 1979. "Islamic History as World History: Marshall Hodgson,

'The Venture of Islam.'" *International Journal of Middle East Studies* 10:87–101.

Burridge, K. O. L. 1973. *Encountering Aborigines*. New York: Pergamon.

Caillois, Roger. 1939. *L'homme et le sacré*. Paris: Libraire E. Leroux.

Calame-Griaule, Geneviève. 1965. *Ethnologie et langage: La parole chez les Dogon*. Paris: Gallimard.

Cantwell, Robert. 1984. *Bluegrass Breakdown: The Making of the Old Southern Sound*. Urbana: University of Illinois Press.

Carpenter, Edmund. 1975. "Collecting Northwest Coast Art." In Bill Holm and Bill Reid, *Indian Art of the Northwest Coast*, pp. 9–49. Seattle: University of Washington Press.

Casagrande, Joseph, ed. 1960. *In the Company of Man: Twenty Portraits of Anthropological Informants*. New York: Harper and Row.

Centilivres, Pierre. 1982. "Des 'instructions' aux collections: La production ethnographique de l'image de l'orient." In *Collections passion*, ed. J. Hainard and R. Kaehr, pp. 33–61. Neuchâtel: Musée d'Ethnographie.

Césaire, Aimé. 1983. *Aimé Césaire: The Collected Poetry*, trans. Clayton Eshleman and Annette Smith. Berkeley: University of California Press.

Chaney, David, and Michael Pickering. 1968a. "Democracy and Communication: Mass Observation 1937–1943." *Journal of Communication*, Winter: 41–56.

――― 1968b. "Authorship in Documentary: Sociology as an Art Form in Mass Observation." In *Documentary and the Mass Media*, ed. John Corner, pp. 29–46. London: Edward Arnold.

Chapman, William. 1985. "Arranging Ethnology: A. H. L. F. Pitt Rivers and the Typological Tradition." In *History of Anthropology*. Vol. 3, *Objects and Others*, ed. George Stocking, pp. 15–48. Madison: University of Wisconsin Press.

Clifford, James. 1979. "Naming Names." *Canto: Review of the Arts* 3(1):142–153.

――― 1980. "Fieldwork, Reciprocity, and the Making of Ethnographic Texts." *Man* 15:518–532.

――― 1982a. *Person and Myth: Maurice Leenhardt in the Melanesian World*. Berkeley: University of California Press.

――― 1982b. Review of *Nisa*, by Marjorie Shostak. *London Times Literary Supplement*. Sept. 17:994–995.

――― 1986a. "Partial Truths." In *Writing Culture*, ed. James Clifford and George Marcus, pp. 1–26. Berkeley: University of California Press.

――― 1986b. "On Ethnograhic Allegory." In *Writing Culture*, ed. James Clifford and George Marcus, pp. 98–121. Berkeley: University of California Press.

――― 1986c. "The Tropological Realism of Michel Leiris." Introduction to *Sulfur* 15 (special issue of Leiris translations), ed. James Clifford, pp. 4–20.

References that have been incorporated into this book are listed by chapter number in Sources following this section.

————, and George Marcus, eds. 1986. *Writing Culture: The Poetics and Politics of Ethnography.* Berkeley: University of California Press.

Codrington, R. H. 1891. *The Melanesians.* Reprint. New York: Dover, 1972.

Coe, Ralph. 1986. *Lost and Found Traditions: Native American Art: 1965–1985.* Seattle: University of Washington Press.

Cohen, David. 1974. *The Ramapo Mountain People.* New Brunswick, N.J.: Rutgers University Press.

Cohen, Marcel. 1962. "Sur l'ethnologie en France." *La pensée* 105:85–96.

Cole, Douglas. 1985. *Captured Heritage: The Scramble for Northwest Coast Artifacts.* Seattle: University of Washington Press.

Cole, Herbert, and Chike Aniakor, eds. 1984. *Igbo Arts: Community and Cosmos.* Los Angeles: Museum of Cultural History, UCLA.

Comaroff, Jean. 1985. *Body of Power, Spirit of Resistance: The Culture and History of a South African People.* Chicago: University of Chicago Press.

Condominas, Georges. 1972a. "Marcel Mauss et l'homme de terrain." *L'arc* 48:3–7.

———— 1972b. "Marcel Mauss, père de l'ethnographie française." *Critique* 279:118–139.

Conrad, Joseph. 1899. *Heart of Darkness.* New York: Norton Critical Editions, 1971.

———— 1911. *Victory.* London: Methuen.

Copans, Jean. 1973. "Comment lire Marcel Griaule? A propos de l'interprétation de Dirk Lettens." *Cahiers d'études africaines* 49:165–157.

———— 1974. *Critiques et politiques de l'anthropologie.* Paris: Maspéro.

———— 1975. *Anthropologie et impérialisme.* Paris: Maspéro.

Crapanzano, Vincent. 1977. "The Writing of Ethnography." *Dialectical Anthropology* 2(1):69–73.

———— 1980. *Tuhami: Portrait of a Moroccan.* Chicago: University of Chicago Press.

Davenport, Guy. 1979. "Au tombeau de Charles Fourier." In *Da Vinci's Bicycle.* Baltimore: Johns Hopkins University Press.

De Certeau, Michel. 1980. "Writing vs. Time: History and Anthropology in the Works of Lafitau." *Yale French Studies* 59:37–64.

———— 1984. *The Practice of Everyday Life.* Berkeley: University of California Press.

Defert, Daniel. 1982. "The Collection of the World: Accounts of Voyages from the Sixteenth to the Eighteenth Centuries." *Dialectical Anthropology* 7: 11–20.

De Ganay, Solange. 1941. *Les devises des Dogon.* Paris: Institut d'Ethnologie.

Delafosse, Louise. 1976. *Maurice Delafosse: Le berrichon conquis par l'Afrique.* Paris: Societé Française d'Histoire d'Outre-Mer.

Delafosse, Maurice. 1909. *Broussard: Les états d'âme d'un colonial.* Paris: Hermann.

Demarle, M., ed. 1957. *Marcel Griaule, conseiller de l'Union française.* Paris: Nouvelles Editions Latines.

Depestre, René. 1980. *Bonjour et adieu à la négritude.* Paris: Robert Lafont.

Derrida, Jacques. 1970. "Structure, Sign, and Play in the Discourse of the Human Sciences." In *The Languages of Criticism and the Sciences of Man,* ed. R. Macksey and E. Donato, pp. 246–272. Baltimore: Johns Hopkins University Press.

Deschamps, Hubert. 1975. *Roi de la brousse: Mémoires d'autres mondes.* Paris: Berger-Levrault.

Desnos, Robert. 1929. "Rossignol." *Documents* 1(2):117; 1(4):215.

Devereux, Georges. 1967. *From Anxiety to Method in the Behavioral Sciences.* The Hague: Mouton.

Diamond, Stanley. 1974. *In Search of the Primitive: A Critique of Civilization.* New Brunswick, N.J.: Dutton.

Dias, Nelia. 1985. "La fondation du Musée d'Ethnographie du Trocadéro (1879–1900): Un aspect de l'histoire institutionelle de l'anthropologie française." Thesis, troisième cycle, Ecole des Hautes Etudes en Sciences Sociales, Paris.

Dieterlen, Germaine. 1941. *Les âmes des Dogon.* Paris: Institut d'Ethnologie.

——— 1951. *Essai sur la religion Bambara.* Paris: Presses Universitaires de France.

——— 1955. "Mythe et organisation sociale en Soudan français." *Journal de la Société des Africanistes* 25:119–138.

——— 1957. "Les resultats des missions Griaule au Soudan français (1931–1956)." *Archives de sociologie des religions* Jan.–June:137–142.

Dilthey, Wilhelm. 1914. "The Construction of the Historical World in the Human Sciences." In *W. Dilthey: Selected Writings,* ed. H. P. Rickman, pp. 168–245. Cambridge: Cambridge University Press, 1976.

Dominguez, Virginia. 1986. "The Marketing of Heritage." *American Ethnologist* 13(3):546–555.

Douglas, Mary. 1967. "If the Dogon." *Cahiers d'études africaines* 28:659–672.

Drummond, Lee. 1981. "The Cultural Continuum: A Theory of Intersystems." *Man* 15:352–374.

Duchet, Michèle. 1971. *Anthropologie et histoire au siècle des lumières.* Paris: Maspéro.

Dumont, Jean-Paul. 1978. *The Headman and I.* Austin: University of Texas Press.

Dumont, Louis. 1972. "Une science en devenir." *L'arc* 48:8–21.

Duvignaud, Jean. 1973. *Le langage perdu: Essai sur la différence anthropologique.* Paris: Presses Universitaires de France.

——— 1979. "Roger Caillois et l'imaginaire." *Cahiers internationaux de sociologie* 66:91–97.

Dwyer, Kevin. 1977. "On the Dialogic of Fieldwork." *Dialectical Anthropology* 2(2):143–151.

——— 1979. "The Dialogic of Ethnology." *Dialectical Anthropology* 4(3):205–224.

———— 1982. *Moroccan Dialogues*. Baltimore: Johns Hopkins University Press.

Ehrmann, Henry W. 1976. *Comparative Legal Cultures*. Englewood Cliffs, N.J.: Prentice-Hall.

Einstein, Carl. 1915. *Negerplastik*. Trans. T. and R. Burgard as *La sculpture africaine*. Paris: Crès, 1922.
———— 1929. "André Masson, étude ethnologique." *Documents* 1(2):93–104.

Evans-Pritchard, E. E. 1969. *The Nuer*. Oxford: Oxford University Press.
———— 1974. *Man and Woman among the Azande*. London: Faber and Faber.

Fabian, Johannes. 1983. *Time and the Other: How Anthropology Makes Its Object*. New York: Columbia University Press.

Fahim, Hussein, ed. 1982. *Indigenous Anthropology in Non-Western Countries*. Durham: University of North Carolina Press.

Favret-Saada, Jeanne. 1977. *Les mots, la mort, les sorts*. Paris: Gallimard. Trans. Catherine Cullen as *Deadly Words*. Cambridge: Cambridge University Press, 1981.
———, and Contreras, Josée. 1981. *Corps pour corps: Enquête sur la sorcellerie dans le Bocage*. Paris: Gallimard.

Feest, Christian. 1984. "From North America." In *"Primitivism" in Twentieth Century Art*, ed. William Rubin, pp. 85–95. New York: Museum of Modern Art.

Fenton, James. 1984. *Children in Exile: Poems 1968–1984*. New York: Random House.

Fernandez, James. 1978. "African Religious Movements." *Annual Review of Anthropology* 7:195–234.
———— 1985. *Bwiti: An Ethnography of the Religious Imagination in Africa*. Princeton: Princeton University Press.

Firth, Raymond, et al. 1957. *Man and Culture: An Evaluation of the Work of Bronislaw Malinowski*. London: Routledge and Kegan Paul.
———— 1977. "Anthropological Research in British Colonies: Some Personal Accounts." *Anthropological Forum* 4 (special issue).

Fischer, Michael. 1986. "Ethnicity and the Post-Modern Arts of Memory." In *Writing Culture: The Poetics and Politics of Ethnography*, ed. James Clifford and George Marcus, pp. 194–233. Berkeley: University of California Press.

Fisher, Philip. 1975. "The Future's Past." *New Literary History* 6(3):587–606.

Fontana, Bernard. 1975. Introduction. In Frank Russell, *The Pima Indians*. Tucson: University of Arizona Press.

Fortes, Meyer. 1973. "On the Concept of the Person among the Tallensi." In *La notion de personne en Afrique noire*. Paris: C.N.R.S.

Foster, George, et al., eds. 1979. *Long-Term Field Research in Social Anthropology*. New York: Academic Press.

Foster, Hal. 1985. *Recodings: Art, Spectacle, Cultural Politics*. Port Townsend, Wash.: Bay Press.

Foucault, Michel. 1966. *Les mots et les choses*. Trans. as *The Order of Things*. New York: Random House, 1970.

———— 1969. *L'archaeologie du savoir*. Trans. A. M. Sheridan Smith as *The Archaeology of Knowledge*. London: Harper Colophon, 1972.

———— 1975. *Surveiller et punir*. Trans. Alan Sheridan as *Discipline and Punish*. New York: Vintage, 1979.

———— 1976. *La volonté de savoir*. Trans. Robert Hurley as *The History of Sexuality*. Vol. 1. New York: Pantheon, 1978.

———— 1977. "Nietzsche, Genealogy, History." In *Language, Counter-Memory, Practice*, pp. 139–164. Ithaca, N.Y.: Cornell University Press.

———— 1980. *Power/Knowledge*. New York: Pantheon.

Freeman, Derek. 1983. *Margaret Mead and Samoa: The Making and Unmaking of an Anthropological Myth*. Cambridge, Mass.: Harvard University Press.

Fried, Morton. 1975. *The Notion of Tribe*. Menlo Park, Calif.: Cummings.

Fussell, Paul. 1975. *The Great War and Modern Memory*. Oxford: Oxford University Press.

Geertz, Clifford. 1968. "Thinking as a Moral Act: Ethical Dimensions of Anthropological Fieldwork in the New States." *Antioch Review* 28:139–158.

———— 1973. *The Interpretation of Cultures*. New York: Basic Books.

———— 1976. "From the Native's Point of View: On the Nature of Anthropological Understanding." In *Meaning in Anthropology*, ed. Keith Basso and Henry Selby, pp. 221–238. Albuquerque: University of New Mexico Press.

———— 1983. "Works and Lives: The Anthropologist as Author." Lectures delivered at Stanford University, March 1983. In press. Stanford, Calif.: Stanford University Press, 1988.

Giddens, Anthony. 1979. *Central Problems in Social Theory: Action, Structure and Contradiction in Social Analysis*. Berkeley: University of California Press.

Gide, André. 1927. *Voyage au Congo*. Paris: Gallimard.

———— 1928. *Le retour du Tchad*. Paris: Gallimard.

Gilot, Françoise. 1964. *Life with Picasso*. New York: McGraw-Hill.

Gilsenan, Michael. 1986. *Imagined Cities of the East: An Inaugural Lecture*. Oxford: Clarendon Press.

Ginzburg, Carlo. 1980. "Morelli, Freud and Sherlock Holmes: Clues and Scientific Method." *History Workshop* 9 (Spring):5–36.

Goffman, Erving. 1959. *The Presentation of Self in Everyday Life*. Garden City, N.Y.: Doubleday.

Goldman, Irving. 1980. "Boas on the Kwakiutl: The Ethnographic Tradition." In *Theory and Practice: Essays Presented to Gene Weltfish*, ed. Stanley Diamond, pp. 334–336. The Hague: Mouton.

Gomila, Jacques. 1976. "Objectif, objectal, objecteur, objecte." In Pierre Beaucage, Jacques Gomila, and Lionel Vallée, *L'experience anthropologique*, pp. 71–133. Montreal: Presses de l'Université de Montréal.

Goody, Jack. 1967. Review of *Conversations with Ogotemmêli*, by M. Griaule. *American Anthropologist* 69:239–241.

Graburn, Nelson, ed. 1976. *Ethnic and Tourist Arts*. Berkeley: University of California Press.

Greenblatt, Stephen. 1980. *Renaissance Self-Fashioning: From More to Shakespeare*. Chicago: University of Chicago Press.

Greimas, A. J., and François Rastier. 1968. "The Interaction of Semiotic Constraints." *Yale French Studies* no. 41:86–105.

Griaule, Marcel. 1929. "Crachat." *Documents* 1(7):381.

——— 1930. *Documents* 2(1):46–47.

——— 1933. "Introduction méthodologique." *Minotaure* 2:7–12.

——— 1934a. *Les flambeurs d'hommes*. Paris: Calmann-Lévy.

——— 1934b. "Mission Dakar-Djibouti." *Minotaure* 2 (special issue).

——— 1937. "L'emploi de la photographie aérienne et la recherche scientifique." *L'anthropologie* 47:469–471.

——— 1938. *Masques Dogons*. Paris: Institut d'Ethnologie.

——— 1943. *Les Saô légendaires*. Paris: Gallimard.

——— 1946. "Notes de terrain, Dogon, Ogotemmêli" (11 microfiches). Paris: Musée de l'Homme, 1974.

——— 1948a. *Dieu d'eau: Entretiens avec Ogotemmêli*. Paris: Editions du Chêne. Trans. R. Butler and A. Richards as *Conversations with Ogotemmêli*. London: Oxford University Press for the International African Institute, 1965.

——— 1948b. "L'action sociologique en Afrique noire." *Présence africaine*, March-April:388–391.

——— 1948c. *Les grandes explorateurs*. Paris: Presses Universitaires de France.

——— 1951. "Préface." In G. Dieterlen, *Essai sur la religion Bambara*, pp. vii–x. Paris: Presses Universitaires de France.

——— 1952a. "Le savoir des Dogon." *Journal de la Société des Africanistes* 22:27–42.

——— 1952b. "Connaissance de l'homme noir." In *La connaissance de l'homme au XXe siècle*, pp. 11–24, 147–166. Neufchâtel: Musée d'Ethnographie.

——— 1952c. "L'enquête orale en ethnologie." *Revue philosophique*, Oct.-Dec.:537–553.

——— 1953. "The Problem of Negro Culture." In *Interrelations of Cultures*, pp. 352–378. UNESCO. Reprint. Westport, Conn.: Greenwood Press, 1971.

——— 1957. *Méthode de l'ethnographie*. Paris: Presses Universitaires de France.

———, and Germaine Dieterlen. 1965. *Le renard pâle*. Vol. 1. Paris: Institut d'Ethnologie.

Guidieri, Rémo, and Francesco Pellizzi. 1981. Editorial. *Res* 1:3–6.

Guillemin, Jean. 1975. *Urban Renegades: The Cultural Strategy of American Indians.* New York: Columbia University Press.

Guss, David. 1986. "Keeping It Oral: A Yekuana Ethnology." *American Ethnologist* 13(3):413–429.

Haacke, Hans. 1975. *Framing and Being Framed.* Halifax: The Press of the Nova Scotia College of Art and Design.

Hainard, Jacques, and Rolland Kaehr, eds. 1982. *Collections passion.* Neuchâtel: Musée d'Ethnographie.

———— 1985. *Temps perdu, temps retrouvé: Voir les choses du passé au présent.* Neuchâtel: Musée d'Ethnographie.

———— 1986. "Temps perdu, temps retrouvé. Du coté de l'ethno . . ." *Gradhiva* 1 (Autumn):33–37.

Handler, Richard. 1985. "On Having a Culture: Nationalism and the Preservation of Quebec's *Patrimoine.*" In *History of Anthropology.* Vol. 3, *Objects and Others,* ed. George Stocking, pp. 192–217. Madison: University of Wisconsin Press.

Handler, Richard, and Jocelyn Linnekin. 1984. "Tradition, Genuine or Spurious." *Journal of American Folklore* 97:273–290.

Hannerz, Ulf. n.d. "The World System of Culture: The International Flow of Meaning and its Local Management." Manuscript.

Haraway, Donna. 1985. "Teddy Bear Patriarchy: Taxidermy in the Garden of Eden, New York City, 1908–1936." *Social Text,* Winter:20–63.

Harris, Wilson. 1973. *The Whole Armour* and *The Secret Ladder.* London: Faber and Faber.

Hartog, François. 1971. *Le miroir d'Hérodote: Essai sur la représentation de l'autre.* Paris: Gallimard.

Heller, Thomas, Morton Sosna, and David Wellbery, eds. 1986. *Reconstructing Individualism: Autonomy, Individuality, and the Self in Western Thought.* Stanford: Stanford University Press.

Hiller, Susan. 1979. Review of "Sacred Circles: 2,000 Years of North American Art." *Studio International,* Dec.:8–15.

Hinsley, Curtis. 1983. "Ethnographic Charisma and Scientific Routine: Cushing and Fewkes in the American Southwest, 1879–1893." In *History of Anthropology.* Vol. 1, *Observers Observed,* ed. George Stocking, pp. 53–69. Madison: University of Wisconsin Press.

Hobsbawm, Eric, and Terence Ranger. 1983. *The Invention of Tradition.* Cambridge: Cambridge University Press.

Hodgson, Marshall. 1963. "The Interrelatedness of Societies in History." *Comparative Studies in Society and History* 5:227–250.

———— 1974. *The Venture of Islam.* Vol. 1. Chicago: University of Chicago Press.

Hollier, Denis, ed. 1979. *Le Collège de Sociologie.* Paris: Gallimard.

Honour, Hugh. 1975. *The New Golden Land.* New York: Pantheon.

Houghton, Walter. 1957. *The Victorian Frame of Mind.* New Haven: Yale University Press.

Hountondji, Paulin. 1977. *Sur la "philosophie" africaine.* Trans. Henri Evans as *African Philosophy: Myth and Reality.* Bloomington: Indiana University Press, 1983.

Hourani, Albert. 1967. "Islam and the Philosophers of History." *Middle Eastern Studies* 3:204–268.

———— 1979. "Orientalism." *New York Review of Books,* March 8:29–30.

Howe, Susan. 1985. *My Emily Dickinson.* Berkeley: North Atlantic Books.

Hutchins, Francis. 1979. *Mashpee: The Story of Cape Cod's Indian Town.* West Franklin, N.H.: Amarta Press.

Hymes, Dell, ed. 1969. *Reinventing Anthropology.* New York: Pantheon.

Imperato, Pascal. 1978. *Dogon Cliff Dwellers: The Art of Mali's Mountain People.* New York: L. Kahan Gallery.

Jackson, Anthony, ed. 1987. *Anthropology at Home.* London: Tavistock.

Jakobson, Roman. 1959. "Boas' View of Grammatical Meaning." In *The Anthropology of Franz Boas,* ed. Walter Goldschmidt, pp. 139–145. San Francisco: American Anthropological Association.

Jameson, Fredric. 1981. *The Political Unconscious: Narrative as a Socially Symbolic Act.* Ithaca: Cornell University Press.

———— 1979. "Marxism and Historicism." *New Literary History* 11(1): 41–73.

Jamin, Jean. 1977. *Les lois du silence: Essai sur la fonction sociale du secret.* Paris: Maspéro.

———— 1979. "Une initiation au réel: A propos de Segalen." *Cahiers internationaux de sociologie* 66:125–139.

———— 1980. "Un sacré collège ou les apprentis sorciers de la sociologie." *Cahiers internationaux de sociologie* 68:5–30.

———— 1982a. "Objets trouvés des paradis perdus: A propos de la Mission Dakar-Djibouti." In *Collections passion,* ed. J. Hainard and R. Kaehr, pp. 69–100. Neuchâtel: Musée d'Ethnographie.

———— 1982b. "Les métamorphoses de *L'Afrique fantôme.*" *Critique* 418:200–212.

———— 1985. "Les objets ethnographiques sont-ils des choses perdues?" In *Temps perdu, temps retrouvé: Voir les choses du passé au présent,* ed. J. Hainard and R. Kaehr, pp. 51–74. Neuchâtel: Musée d'Ethnographie.

———— 1986. "L'ethnographie mode d'inemploi: De quelques rapports de l'ethnologie avec le malaise dans la civilisation." In *Le mal et la douleur,* ed. J. Hainard and R. Kaehr, pp. 45–79. Neuchâtel: Musée d'Ethnographie.

Jencks, Charles. 1973. *Le Corbusier and the Tragic View of Architecture.* London: Penguin.

Jones, Nicholas Burton, and Melvin Konner. 1976. "!Kung Knowledge of Animal Behavior." *Kalahari Hunter-Gatherers,* ed. R. Lee and I. De Vore, pp. 325–348. Cambridge, Mass.: Harvard University Press.

Jules-Rosette, Benetta. 1984. *The Messages of Tourist Art.* New York: Plenum.

Karady, Victor. 1981. "French Ethnology and the Durkheimian Breakthrough."
     Journal of the Anthropological Society of Oxford 12:165–176.
——— 1982. "Le problème de la légitimité dans l'organisation historique
     de l'ethnologie française." *Revue française de sociologie* 32(1):17–36.
Karl, Frederick. 1979. *Joseph Conrad: The Three Lives.* New York: Farrar, Straus,
     and Giroux.
Kaufman, Walter, ed. 1954. *The Portable Nietzsche.* New York: Vintage.
Keesing, Roger. 1974. "Theories of Culture." *American Anthropologist* 2:73–97.
Kermode, Frank. 1980. *The Genesis of Secrecy: The Interpretation of Narrative.*
     Cambridge, Mass.: Harvard University Press.
Khatibi, Abdelkebir. 1976. "Jacques Berque ou le saveur orientale." *Les temps
     modernes* 359:2159–2181.
Kroeber, A. L. 1931. Review of *Growing Up in New Guinea,* by Margaret Mead.
     American Anthropologist 36:248.
———, and Clyde Kluckhohn. 1952. *Culture: A Critical Review of Con-
     cepts and Definitions.* New York: Vintage.

Lacoste-Dujardin, Camille. 1977. *Dialogue des femmes en ethnologie.* Paris:
     Maspéro.
Lafitau, Joseph-François. 1724. *Moeurs des sauvages ameriquains comparées
     aux moeurs des premiers temps.* Paris: Saugrain l'ainé et Charles Etienne
     Hochereau.
Langham, Ian. 1981. *The Building of British Social Anthropology.* New York:
     Dover.
Laude, Jean. 1968. *La peinture française (1905–1914) et "l'art nègre."* Paris: Edi-
     tions Klincksieck.
Leach, Edmund. 1976. *Culture and Communication.* Cambridge: Cambridge
     University Press.
Lebeuf, Jean-Paul. 1975. Review of *Mystagogie et mystification,* by D. A. Let-
     tens. *Journal de la Société des Africanistes* 45:230–232.
Leclerc, Gérard. 1972. *Anthropologie et colonialisme.* Paris: Fayard.
Leenhardt, Maurice. 1932. *Documents néo-calédoniens.* Paris: Institut d'Ethno-
     logie.
——— 1937. *Do Kamo: La personne et le mythe dans le monde mélané-
     sien.* Paris: Gallimard. Trans. Basia Gulati as *Do Kamo: Person and Myth
     in the Melanesian World.* Chicago: University of Chicago Press, 1979.
——— 1950. "Marcel Mauss." *Annuaire de l'Ecole Pratique des Hautes
     Etudes, Section des Sciences Religieuses,* pp. 19–23.
Lienhardt, Godfrey. 1961. *Divinity and Experience: The Religion of the Dinka.*
     Oxford: Oxford University Press.
Leiris, Michel. 1929a. "Alberto Giacometti." *Documents* 1(4):209–211. Trans. J.
     Clifford in *Sulfur* 15(1986):38–41.
——— 1929b. "L'eau à la bouche." *Documents* 1(7):381–382. Trans. L.
     Davis in *Sulfur* 15(1986):41–42.
——— 1929c. "Compte rendu de *L'ile magique* de William Seabrook."
     Documents 1(6):334.

———— 1930. "L'oeil de l'ethnographie: A propos de la Mission Dakar-Djibouti. *Documents* 2(7):405–414.

———— 1934. *L'Afrique fantôme.* Reprinted with new introduction. Paris: Gallimard, 1950.

———— 1935. "L'Abyssinie intime." *Mer et Outre-mer,* June:43–47.

———— 1938a. "Du musée d'ethnographie au Musée de l'Homme." *Nouvelle revue française* 299:344–345.

———— 1938b. "Le sacré dans la vie quotidienne." In *Le Collège de Sociologie,* ed. Denis Hollier, pp. 60–74. Paris: Gallimard, 1979.

———— 1946. *L'age d'homme.* Paris: Gallimard. Trans. Richard Howard as *Manhood.* Berkeley: North Point Press, 1985.

———— 1948. "Avant propos." *La langue secrète des Dogons de Sanga,* pp. ix–xxv. Paris: Institut d'Ethnologie.

———— 1948–1976. *La règle du jeu.* Vols. 1–4, *Biffures, Fourbis, Fibrilles, Frêle bruit.* Paris: Gallimard.

———— 1950. "L'ethnographe devant le colonialisme." In *Les temps modernes* 58. Reprinted in *Brisées,* pp. 125–145. Paris: Mercure de France, 1966.

———— 1953. "The African Negroes and the Arts of Carving and Sculpture." In *Interrelations of Cultures,* pp. 316–351. Westport, Conn.: UNESCO.

———— 1958. *La possession et ses aspects théâtraux chez les Ethiopiens de Gondar.* Reprint. Paris: Le Sycomore, 1980.

———— 1963. "De Bataille l'impossible à l'impossible *Documents*." *Critique* 195–196. Reprinted in *Brisées,* pp. 256–266. Paris: Mercure de France, 1966.

———— 1966a. *Brisées.* Paris: Mercure de France.

———— 1966b. "The Musée de l'Homme: Where Art and Anthropology Meet." *Realities* 182:57–63.

———— 1968. "The Discovery of African Art in the West." In M. Leiris and J. Delange, *African Art.* New York: Golden Press.

———— 1981. *Le ruban au cou d'Olympia.* Paris: Gallimard.

Leroi-Gourhan, André. 1982. *Les racines du monde.* Paris: Pierre Belford.

Lettens, D. A. 1971. *Mystagogie et mystification: Evaluation de l'oeuvre de Marcel Griaule.* Bujumbura, Burundi: Presses Lavigerie.

Lévi-Strauss, Claude. 1943. "The Art of the Northwest Coast at the American Museum of Natural History." *Gazette des beaux arts,* Sept.:175–182. Partially reprinted in *La voie des masques,* pp. 9–14. Paris: Plon, 1979.

———— 1945. "French Sociology." In *Twentieth Century Sociology,* ed. Georges Gurvitch and Wilbert Moore, pp. 503–537. New York: Philosophical Library.

———— 1950. "Introduction à l'oeuvre de Marcel Mauss." In M. Mauss, *Sociologie et anthropologie,* pp. ix–lii. Paris: Presses Universitaires de France.

———— 1952. *Race and History.* Paris: UNESCO.

———— 1955. *Tristes tropiques,* trans. John and Doreen Weightman. New York: Athenaeum, 1975.

————— 1960. "Leçon inaugurale." Trans. M. Layton as "The Scope of Anthropology." In *Structural Anthropology*. Vol. 2, pp. 3–32. New York: Basic Books, 1976.

————— 1976. "The Work of the Bureau of American Ethnology." In *Structural Anthropology*. Vol. 2. New York: Basic Books.

————— 1978. "Preface." In Roman Jakobson, *Six Lectures on Sound and Meaning*, pp. xi–xxvi. Cambridge, Mass.: MIT Press.

————— 1983. "New York post-et préfiguratif." In *Le regard éloigné*, pp. 345–356. Paris: Plon.

————— 1985. "New York in 1941." In *The View from Afar*, pp. 258–267. New York: Basic Books.

Levin, Gail. 1984. "'Primitivism' in American Art: Some Literary Parallels of the 1910s and 1920s." *Arts*, Nov.:101–105.

Lewis, I. M. 1973. *The Anthropologist's Muse*. London: London School of Economics and Political Science.

Lourau, R. 1974. *Le gai savoir des sociologues*. Paris: Union Générale des Editions.

Lowie, Robert. 1940. "Native Languages as Ethnographic Tools." *American Anthropologist* 42(1):81–89.

Lukács, Georg. 1964. *Studies in European Realism*. New York: Grosset and Dunlap.

Lyman, Christopher. 1982. *The Vanishing Race and Other Illusions: Photographs of Indians by Edward Curtis*. New York: Pantheon.

Macnair, Peter, Alan Hoover, and Kevin Neary. 1984. *The Legacy: Tradition and Innovation in Northwest Coast Indian Art*. Vancouver: Douglas and McIntyre.

Macpherson, C. B. 1962. *The Political Theory of Possessive Individualism*. Oxford: Oxford University Press.

Makreel, Rudolf. 1975. *Dilthey: Philosopher of the Human Sciences*. Princeton: Princeton University Press.

Malinowski, Bronislaw. 1915. "The Natives of Mailu." *Transactions of the Royal Society of Southern Australia*. 39:49–706.

————— 1916. "Baloma: Spirits of the Dead in the Trobriand Islands." In *Magic, Science and Religion*. Garden City, N.Y.: Natural History Press.

————— 1922. *Argonauts of the Western Pacific*. London: Routledge.

————— 1932. "Pigs, Papuans and Police Court Perspective." *Man* 32:33–38.

————— 1935. *Coral Gardens and Their Magic*. Bloomington: University of Indiana Press.

————— 1967. *A Diary in the Strict Sense of the Term*. New York: Harcourt, Brace, and World.

Malroux, Paule. 1957. "Marcel Griaule." In *Marcel Griaule, counseiller de l'Union français*, ed. M. Demarle, pp. 13–16. Paris: Nouvelles Editions Latines.

Maquet, Jacques. 1964. "Objectivity in Anthropology." *Current Anthropology* 5:47–55.

Marcus, George. 1980. "Rhetoric and the Ethnographic Genre in Anthropological Research." *Current Anthropology* 21:507–510.

———— 1985. "A Timely Rereading of *Naven:* Gregory Bateson as Oracular Essayist." *Representations* 12:66–82.

———— 1986. "Contemporary Problems of Ethnography in the Modern World System." In *Writing Culture,* ed. James Clifford and George Marcus, pp. 165–193. Berkeley: University of California Press.

————, and Dick Cushman. 1982. "Ethnographies as Texts." *Annual Review of Anthropology* 11:25–69.

————, and Michael Fischer. 1986. *Anthropology as Cultural Critique: An Experimental Moment in the Human Sciences.* Chicago: University of Chicago Press.

Matthews, J. H. 1977. *The Imagery of Surrealism.* Syracuse: Syracuse University Press.

Mauss, Marcel. 1902. *Esquisse d'une théorie générale de la magie.* Trans. Robert Brain as *A General Theory of Magic.* New York: Norton, 1972.

———— 1913. "L'Ethnographie en France et à l'étranger." In *Oeuvres.* Vol. 3:395–434. Paris: Editions de Minuit, 1969.

———— 1923. "Essai sur le don." In *Sociologie et anthropologie,* pp. 145–279. Paris: Presses Universitaires de France, 1950. Trans. Ian Cunnison as *The Gift.* New York: Norton, 1967.

———— 1924. "Rapports réels et pratiques de la psychologie et de la sociologie." In *Sociologie et anthropologie,* pp. 283–310. Paris: Presses Universitaires de France, 1950. Trans. Ben Brewster as "Real and Practical Relations between Psychology and Sociology." In *Sociology and Psychology,* pp. 1–32. London: Routledge and Kegan Paul, 1979.

———— 1930. *Documents* 2(3):177.

———— 1931. "Instructions sommaires pour les collecteurs d'objets ethnographiques." Musée d'Ethnographie du Trocadéro. Pamphlet prepared with the assistance of M. Leiris and M. Griaule.

———— 1934. "Les techniques du corps." In *Sociologie et anthropologie,* pp. 363–386. Paris: Presses Universitaires de France, 1950. Trans. Ben Brewster as "Body techniques." In *Sociology and Psychology,* pp. 95–123. London: Routledge and Kegan Paul, 1979.

———— 1938. "Une catégorie de l'esprit humain: La notion de personne, celle de 'moi.'" In *Sociologie et anthropologie* pp. 333–362. Paris: Presses Universitaires de la France, 1950.

———— 1947. *Manuel d'ethnographie.* Paris: Payot, 1967.

———— 1950. *Sociologie et anthropologie.* Paris: Presses Universitaires de France.

———— 1968–69. *Oeuvres.* Vols. 1–3, ed. Victor Karady. Paris: Editions de Minuit.

Mazur, Rona Sue. 1980. "Town and Tribe in Conflict: A Study of Local-Level Politics in Mashpee, Massachusetts." Ph.D. diss., Columbia University.

Mead, Margaret. 1939. "Native Languages as Field-Work Tools." *American Anthropologist* 42(20):189–205.

——— 1971. *The Mountain Arapesh.* Vol. 3. Garden City, N.Y.: Natural History Press.

——— 1977. *Letters from the Field: 1925–1975.* New York: Harper and Row.

Mead, Sidney Moka, ed. 1984. *Te Maori: Maori Art from New Zealand Collections.* New York: Harry Abrams.

Ménil, René. 1981. *Tracées: Identité, nègritude, esthétique aux Antilles.* Paris: Robert Lafont.

Merleau-Ponty, Maurice. 1947. *Humanisme et terreur.* Paris: Gallimard.

Métraux, Alfred. 1963. "Rencontre avec les ethnologues." *Critique* 195–196: 677–684.

Michel-Jones, Françoise. 1978. *Retour au Dogon: Figure du double et ambivalence.* Paris: Le Sycomore.

Miller, J. Hillis. 1965. "Conrad's Darkness." In *Poets of Reality,* chap. 1. Cambridge, Mass.: Harvard University Press.

Mintz, Sidney. 1972. "Introduction to the Second English Edition." In Alfred Métraux, *Voodoo in Haiti.* New York: Schocken.

Mitchell, Juliet. 1984. *Women: The Longest Revolution.* London: Virago.

Monroe, Dan. 1986. "Northwest Coast Native American Art Reinstallation Planning Grant." Application for NEH funding on behalf of the Oregon Art Institute, Portland, Oregon.

Mullaney, Steven. 1983. "Strange Things, Gross Terms, Curious Customs: The Rehearsal of Cultures in the Late Renaissance. *Representations* 3:40–67.

Nadeau, Maurice. 1965. *The History of Surrealism.* New York: Macmillan.

Najder, Zdzislaw. 1964. *Conrad's Polish Background: Letters to and from Polish Friends.* Oxford: Oxford University Press.

——— 1983. *Joseph Conrad: A Chronicle.* New Brunswick, N.J.: Rutgers University Press.

Nash, June. 1975. "Nationalism and Fieldwork." *Annual Review of Anthropology* 4:225–245.

——— 1979. *We Eat the Mines, the Mines Eat Us: Dependency and Exploitation in Bolivian Tin Mines.* New York: Columbia University Press.

Ogono d'Arou. 1956. "Allocution prononcée au cours des funérailles du Marcel Griaule à Sanga." *Journal de la Société des Africanistes* 26:8–10.

Ortner, Sherry. 1984. "Theory in Anthropology since the Sixties." *Comparative Studies in Society and History* 26:126–166.

Pala, S. 1931. *Exposition coloniale internationale de Paris, 1931.* Paris: Bibliothèque de la Ville de Paris.

Paulme, Denise. 1977. "Sanga 1935." *Cahiers d'études africaines* 65:7–12.

Payne, Harry. 1981. "Malinowski's Style." *Proceedings of the American Philosophical Society* 125:416–440.

Pietz, William. 1985. "The Problem of the Fetish, 1." *Res* 9 (Spring):5–17.
Pomian, Krzysztof. 1978. "Entre l'invisible et le visible: La collection." *Libre* 78(3):3–56.
Pratt, Mary Louise. 1977. "Nationalizing Exoticism: Spanish America after Independence." *Inscriptions* 2:29–35.
Price, Richard. 1973. Introduction. In *Maroon Societies*. New York: Anchor.
——— 1983. *First Time: The Historical Vision of an Afro-American People*. Baltimore: Johns Hopkins University Press.
Price, Sally. 1986. "L'esthetique et le temps: Commentaire sur l'histoire orale de l'art." *L'ethnographie* 82:215–225.
———, and Richard Price. 1980. *Afro-American Arts of the Suriname Rain Forest*. Berkeley: University of California Press.
Pye, Michael. 1987. "Whose Art Is It Anyway?" *Connoisseur*, March:78–85.

Queneau, Raymond. 1981. *Contes et propos*. Paris: Gallimard.

Rabassa, José. 1985. "Fantasy, Errancy, and Symbolism in New World Motifs: An Essay on Sixteenth-Century Spanish Historiography." Ph.D. diss., University of California, Santa Cruz.
Rabinow, Paul. 1977. *Reflections on Fieldwork in Morocco*. Berkeley: University of California Press.
——— 1986. "Representations Are Social Facts: Modernity and Post-Modernity in Anthropology." In *Writing Culture: The Poetics and Politics of Ethnography*, ed. J. Clifford and G. Marcus, pp. 234–261. Berkeley: University of California Press.
———, and William Sullivan, eds. 1979. *Interpretive Social Science*. Berkeley: University of California Press.
Radcliffe-Brown, A. R. 1922. *The Andaman Islanders*. Reprint. New York: The Free Press, 1948.
Rama, Angel. 1982. *Transculturación narrativa y novela latinoamericana*. Mexico City: Siglo XXI.
Rentoul, Alex. 1931a. "Physiological Paternity and the Trobrianders." *Man* 31:153–154.
——— 1931b. "Papuans, Professors and Platitudes." *Man* 31:274–276.
Reynolds, B. 1983. "The Relevance of Material Culture to Anthropology." *Journal of the Anthropological Society of Oxford* 2:63–75.
Richards, A. I. 1967. "African Systems of Thought: An Anglo-French Dialogue." *Man* 2:286–298.
Rickman, H. P., ed. 1976. *Wilhelm Dilthey: Selected Writings*. Cambridge: Cambridge University Press.
Ricoeur, Paul. 1971. "The Model of the Text: Meaningful Action Considered as a Text." *Social Research* 38:529–562.
Rivet, Paul. 1929. Untitled article. *Documents* 1(3):130–134.
——— 1948. "Organization of an Ethnological Museum." *Museum* 1:110–118.

————, and Georges-Henri Rivière. 1933. "Mission ethnographique et lin-
   guistique Dakar-Djibouti." *Minotaure* 2:3–5.
Rivière, Georges-Henri. 1968. "My Experience at the Musée d'Ethnologie," *Pro-
   ceedings of the Royal Anthropological Institute,* pp. 117–122.
   ———— 1979. "Un rencontre avec Georges-Henri Rivière." *Le monde.* July
   8–9, p.15.
Robbins, Bruce. 1986. *The Servant's Hand: English Fiction from Below.* New
   York: Columbia University Press.
Rosaldo, Renato. 1980. *Ilongot Headhunting 1883–1974: A Study in Society and
   History.* Stanford: Stanford University Press.
Rosen, Lawrence. 1977. "The Anthropologist as Expert Witness." *American An-
   thropologist* 79:555–578.
Rouch, Jean. 1978a. "Ciné transe." *Film Quarterly* 2:2–11.
   ———— 1978b. "Le renard fou et le maître pâle." In *Système des signes:
   Textes réunis en hommage à Germaine Dieterlen,* pp. 3–24. Paris:
   Presses Universitaires de France.
Rubin, William, ed. 1984. *"Primitivism" in Modern Art: Affinity of the Tribal and
   the Modern.* 2 vols. New York: Museum of Modern Art.
Rupp-Eisenreich, Britta, ed. 1984. *Histoires de l'anthropologie.* Paris: Klinck-
   sieck Editions.

Sahlins, Marshall. 1985. *Islands of History.* Chicago: University of Chicago Press.
Said, Edward. 1966. *Joseph Conrad and the Fiction of Autobiography.* Cambridge, Mass.: Harvard University Press.
   ———— 1975. *Beginnings: Intention and Method.* New York: Basic Books.
   ———— 1976. Interview. *Diacritics* 3:30–47.
   ———— 1978a. *Orientalism.* New York: Pantheon Books.
   ———— 1978b. "The Problem of Textuality: Two Exemplary Positions." *Critical Inquiry,* Summer:706–725.
   ———— 1979. "Zionism from the Standpoint of its Victims." *Social Text* 1:7–
   58.
   ———— 1986a. *After the Last Sky: Palestinian Lives.* New York: Pantheon.
   ———— 1986b. "On Palestinian Identity: A Conversation with Salman Rushdie." *New Left Review* 160:63–80.
Saisselin, Rémy. 1984. *The Bourgeois and the Bibelot.* New Brunswick, N.J.:
   Rutgers University Press.
Sarevskaja, B. I. 1963. "La *Méthode de l'ethnographie* de Marcel Griaule et les
   questions de méthodologie dans l'ethnographie française contemporaine."
   Cahiers d'études africaines 4(16):590–602.
Schaeffner, André. 1929. "Les instruments de musique dans un musée d'ethnog-
   raphie." *Documents* 1(5):248.
Schneider, David. 1968. *American Kinship: A Cultural Account.* Englewood
   Cliffs, N.J.: Prentice-Hall.
Schwab, Raymond. 1950. *La renaissance orientale.* Paris: Payot.
Seabrook, William. 1929. *L'ile magique.* Paris: Firmin-Didot.
   ———— 1931. *Les secrets de la jungle.* Paris: J. Haumont.

Segalen, Victor. 1907a. *Les immémoriaux*. Paris: Editions du Seuil.

——— 1907b. "Dans un monde sonore." *Mercure de France* 16(8):648–668.

——— 1912. *Stèles*. Peking (private edition). Critical edition. Paris: Plon, 1963. Trans. Nathaniel Tarn as *Stelae*. London: Unicorn Press, 1969.

——— 1916. *Peintures*. Paris: Crès. Reprint. Paris: Gallimard, 1983.

——— 1922. *René Leys*. Paris: Gallimard, 1971.

——— 1929. *Equipée: Voyage au pays du réel*. Paris: Gallimard, 1983.

——— 1975. *Briques et tuiles*. Montepellier: Editions Fata Morgana.

——— 1978. *Essai sur l'exotisme*. Montepellier: Fata Morgana.

——— 1979. *Thibet*. Paris: Mercure de France.

———, and Henry Manceron. 1985. *Trahison fidèle: Correspondance 1907–1918*. Paris: Editions du Seuil.

Shostak, Marjorie. 1981. *Nisa: The Life and Words of a !Kung Woman*. Cambridge, Mass.: Harvard University Press.

Sieber, Roy. 1971. "The Aesthetics of Traditional African Art." In *Art and Aesthetics in Primitive Societies*, ed. Carol F. Jopling, pp. 127–145. New York: Dutton.

Simmons, William. 1986. *Spirit of the New England Tribes: Indian History and Folklore, 1620–1984*. Hanover, N.H.: University Press of New England.

Slagle, Logan. 1986. Tribal Recognition and the Tolowa. Lecture presented at conference on the Nature and Function of Minority Literature, University of California, Berkeley, May 25.

Sontag, Susan. 1977. *On Photography*. New York: Farrar, Straus, and Giroux.

Soupault, Philippe. 1927. *Le nègre*. Reprint. Paris: Seghers, 1975.

Sperber, Dan. 1975. *Rethinking Symbolism*. Cambridge: Cambridge University Press.

——— 1981. "L'interprétation en anthropologie." *L'Homme* 21(1):69–92. Trans. in *On Anthropological Knowledge*, pp. 9–34. Cambridge: Cambridge University Press, 1985.

Spivak, Gayatri Chakravorty. 1987. *In Other Worlds: Essays in Cultural Politics*. New York: Methuen.

Steinbright, Jan, ed. 1986. *Alaskameut '86: An Exhibit of Contemporary Alaska Native Masks*. Fairbanks: Institute of Alaska Native Arts.

Stewart, Susan. 1984. *On Longing: Narratives of the Miniature, the Gigantic, the Souvenir, the Collection*. Baltimore: Johns Hopkins University Press.

Stocking, George. 1968. "Arnold, Tylor and the Uses of Invention." In *Race, Culture and Evolution*, pp. 69–90. New York: The Free Press.

——— 1974. "Empathy and Antipathy in *Heart of Darkness*." In *Readings in the History of Anthropology*, ed. Regna Darnell, pp. 85–98. New York: Harper and Row.

——— 1987. *Victorian Anthropology*. New York: The Free Press.

———, ed. 1983. *History of Anthropology*. Vol. 1, *Observers Observed: Essays on Ethnographic Fieldwork*, esp. "The Ethnographer's Magic: Fieldwork in British Anthropology from Tylor to Malinowski," pp. 70–119. Madison: University of Wisconsin Press.

Stott, William, 1973. *Documentary Expression and Thirties America*. New York: Oxford University Press.

Sturtevant, William. 1969. "Does Anthropology Need Museums?" *Proceedings of the Biological Society of Washington* 82:619–650.

———— 1973. "Museums as Anthropological Data Banks." In *Anthropology beyond the University,* ed. A. Redfield. *Proceedings of the Social Anthropological Society* 7:40–55.

———— 1983. "Tribe and State in the Sixteenth and Twentieth Centuries." In *The Development of Political Organization in Native North America,* ed. Elizabeth Tooker, pp. 3–15. Washington: The American Ethnological Society.

Talbot, Steven. 1985. "Desecration and American Indian Religious Freedom." *Journal of Ethnic Studies* 12(4):1–18.

Taussig, Michael. 1980. *The Devil and Commodity Fetishism in South America*. Chapel Hill: University of North Carolina Press.

———— 1987. *Shamanism, Colonialism, and the Wild Man: A Study in Terror and Healing*. Chicago: University of Chicago Press.

Tedlock, Barbara. 1984. "The Beautiful and the Dangerous: Zuñi Ritual and Cosmology as an Aesthetic System." *Conjunctions* 6:246–265.

————, and Dennis Tedlock. 1985. "Text and Textile: Language and Technology in the Arts of the Quiche Maya. *Journal of Anthropological Research* 41(2):121–146.

Tedlock, Dennis. 1979. "The Analogical Tradition and the Emergence of a Dialogical Anthropology." *Journal of Anthropological Research* 35(4):387–400. Reprint. In D. Tedlock, *The Spoken Word and the Work of Interpretation,* pp. 321–338. Philadelphia: University of Pennsylvania Press, 1983.

Thornton, Robert. 1983. "Narrative Ethnography in Africa, 1850–1920." *Man* 18:502–520.

Tibawi, A. L. 1963. "English Speaking Orientalists: A Critique of Their Approach to Islam and to Arab Nationalism." *Muslim World* 53(3–4):185–204, 298–313.

Tiryakian, E. A. 1979. "L'école durkheimienne et la recherche de la société perdue: La sociologie naissante et son milieu culturel." *Cahiers internationaux de sociologie* 66:97–114.

Todorov, Tzvetan. 1981. *Mikhail Bakhtine: Le principe dialogique*. Paris: Editions du Seuil.

Trinh T. Minh-ha. 1986. "Difference: 'A Special Third World Women Issue.'" *Discourse* 8:11–37.

Tureen, Thomas. 1985. "Afterword." In Paul Brodeur, *Restitution,* pp. 143–148. Boston: Northeastern University Press.

Turnbull, Colin. 1962. *The Forest People*. New York: Simon and Schuster.

Turner, Victor. 1967. *The Forest of Symbols: Aspects of Ndembu Ritual*. Ithaca, N.Y.: Cornell University Press.

———— 1975. *Revelation and Divination in Ndembu Ritual*. Ithaca: Cornell University Press.

Tyler, Stephen. 1981. "Words for Deeds and the Doctrine of the Secret World." In *Papers from the Parassession on Language and Behavior,* pp. 34–57. *Proceedings of the Chicago Linguistic Society.* Chicago: Chicago University Press.

Vitart-Fardoulis, Anne. 1986. "L'objet interrogé: Ou comment faire parler une collection d'ethnographie." *Gradhiva* 1 (Autumn):9–12.

Vogel, Susan. 1985. Introduction. In *African Masterpieces from the Musée de l'Homme,* pp. 10–11. New York: Harry Abrams.

———, and Francine N'Diaye, eds. 1985. *African Masterpieces from the Musée de l'Homme.* New York: Harry Abrams.

Volosinov, V. N. (M. Bakhtin?). 1973. *Marxism and the Philosophy of Language.* New York: Seminar Press.

Wagner, Roy. 1980. *The Invention of Culture.* Rev. ed. Chicago: University of Chicago Press.

Walker, James. 1917. *The Sun Dance and Other Ceremonies of the Oglala Division of the Teton Dakotas.* Anthropological Papers. Vol. 16. New York: American Museum of Natural History.

——— 1982a. *Lakota Belief and Ritual,* ed. Raymond de Mallie and Elaine Jahner. Lincoln: University of Nebraska Press.

——— 1982b. *Lakota Society,* ed. Raymond J. DeMallie. Lincoln: University of Nebraska Press.

——— 1983. *Lakota Myth,* ed. Elaine Jahner. Lincoln: University of Nebraska Press.

Watt, Ian. 1979. *Conrad in the Nineteenth Century.* Berkeley: University of California Press.

Weatherhead, L. R. 1980. "What Is an 'Indian Tribe'?—The Question of Tribal Existence." *American Indian Law Review* 8(1):1–48.

Webster, Steven. 1982. "Dialogue and Fiction in Ethnography." *Dialectical Anthropology* 7(2):91–114.

Weiner, Annette. 1976. *Women of Value, Men of Renown.* Austin: University of Texas Press.

Whisnant, David. 1983. *All That Is Native and Fine: The Politics of Culture in an American Region.* Chapel Hill: University of North Carolina Press.

Willett, Frank, et al. 1976. "Authenticity in African Art." *African Arts* 9(3):6–74 (special section).

Williams, Elizabeth. 1985. "Art and Artifact at the Trocadéro." In *History of Anthropology.* Vol. 3, *Objects and Others,* ed. George Stocking, pp. 145–166. Madison: University of Wisconsin Press.

Williams, Raymond. 1966. *Culture and Society, 1780–1950.* New York: Harper and Row.

——— 1973. *The Country and the City.* New York: Oxford University Press.

——— 1976. *Keywords.* New York: Harper and Row.

Williams, William Carlos. 1923. *Spring & All.* Paris: Contact Publishing Company. Reprint. New York: Frontier Press, 1970.

———— 1963. *Paterson*. New York: New Directions.

———— 1967. *The Collected Later Poems*. New York: New Directions.

Winner, Thomas. 1976. "The Semiotics of Cultural Texts." *Semiotica* 18(2):101–156.

Yannopoulos, T., and D. Martin. 1978. "De la question au dialogue: A propos des enquêtes en Afrique noire." *Cahiers d'études africaines* 71:421–442.

SOURCES

These are the original titles of previously published sections of this book. They are reprinted here by permission of the publishers. All have been edited, and major revisions are indicated.

Chapter 1. "On Ethnographic Authority." *Representations* 1(1983):118–146.
Chapter 2. "Power and Dialogue in Ethnography: Marcel Griaule's Initiation." In *History of Anthropology.* Vol. 1, *Observers Observed: Essays on Ethnographic Fieldwork,* ed. George Stocking, pp. 121–156. Madison: University of Wisconsin Press, 1983.
Chapter 3. "On Ethnographic Self-Fashioning: Conrad and Malinowski." In *Reconstructing Individualism: Autonomy, Individuality, and the Self in Western Thought,* ed. Thomas C. Heller, Morton Sosna, and David Wellbery, pp. 140–162. Stanford: Stanford University Press, 1985.
Chapter 4. "On Ethnographic Surrealism." *Comparative Studies in Society and History* 23(1981):539–564. Revised.
Chapter 5. "Encounters with the Exotic." *Times Literary Supplement,* June 22, 1984, pp. 683–684. Revised.
Chapter 6. "Interrupting the Whole." *Conjunctions* 6(1984):282–296. Revised.
Chapter 7. "A Politics of Neologism." *Hambone* 4(1984):193–198.

Chapter 8. "The Jardin des Plantes (Postcards)." *Sulfur: A Literary Tri-Quarterly of the Whole Art* 12(1985):153–156.

Chapter 9. "Histories of the Tribal and the Modern." *Art in America* (April 1985):164–177.

Chapter 10. Sections 1 and 2. "Objects and Selves: An Afterword." In *History of Anthropology.* Vol. 3, *Objects and Others: Essays on Museums and Material Culture,* ed. George Stocking, pp. 236–247. Madison: University of Wisconsin Press, 1985. Revised.

Chapter 11. Review. "Edward Said, *Orientalism.*" *History and Theory* 19(1980): 204–223.

Index